The Millennial Map to Millions in Real Estate

Small changes that create life-changing wealth and freedom

Scott Schindelar

ISBN: 979-8-9865435-0-5

Acknowledgements

I need to first thank my family, Cassidy, Atlas, and Isle. Thank you for the constant love and patience! I love you, and I'm excited for what's to come. Thank you to my parents and all of the authors whom I learned from and motivated change in my own life; my best friend, strategist, and mentor, Matt; my rockstar lender, Megan; the first private lender turned friend who believed in my projects, Becky; and my friends who helped me review this text prior to publishing, Mark, Steven, and David. Lastly, thank YOU (every reader of this text) for investing in yourself!

I hope this book changes your life and the lives of the people you care about.

Table of Contents

Forward

You might not acknowledge it, but every decision you make today will impact your future. Why not make decisions today that will positively impact your finances? You can become successful and financially comfortable in a short time by taking action on the following advice. Everything worth doing is worth doing, even if it isn't done perfectly! Don't get caught up in perfection—get caught up in analysis, action, and problem solve as needed.

Whether people are asking or not, I typically push financial advice towards everyone I like; I don't work to educate people whom I don't like. I trust that you'll use your powers for good! Now that that's off my chest, here we go!

Whose opinions matter? Whom do you trust? How often do we ask for the opinions of others, though their opinions have no more merit than our own? Consider each person's perspective and track record before accepting advice. Even though their opinion may have no credibility, once you hear it, how much will it impact your decision? Even with the professionals whom you rely on for sound advice, consider their track record and motivations. Would you trust health advice from an unhealthy doctor? Spanish lessons from a non-fluent Spanish speaker? How about financial advice from someone who isn't a self-made money-making machine? I once read a book that stated something along the lines of, Wall Street is the only place people fly their personal jets to take financial advice from people riding subways. Employees and business owners often earn titles that establish their credibility as an expert, but book work doesn't translate to real life mastery,

1

experience does! Make sure the advice you're taking is coming from a source of real-life mastery and expertise! Not simply book knowledge.

For instance, your attorney will keep you out of legal trouble, but their appetite for risk and professional liability will affect their advice. My attorney once told me, "I'll make $150,000 every year with no risk; I know you'll make a lot more money than me, but you'll be taking risks along the way." Prior to structuring a deal, I ask my attorney and/or CPA how to accomplish my desired outcome. However, I never begin my question with "Can I …," but rather with "How do I …." Take this strategy to heart, apply the "How do I" thinking to every problem, starting today.

This book was not written for the person that needs to be convinced of the amazing benefits and opportunities that real estate investing can provide. I hope you've already determined it's a proven path to financial success. This book is being written for the early investor who needs help creating a plan and wants to start taking action. It's also for the experienced investor that wants to learn a few modern tricks. The goal is to provide an efficient map to your financial freedom using the tools we all have at hand, without syndicating deals. Syndicating requires you to take on partners. The strategies in this book allow you to be the sole owner! Your brain needs to adopt a "How do I" mentality when it comes to every problem. I'll give concrete examples and introduce math to solidify the ideas presented in this book. Please know that the numbers are rounded, and the processes are slightly simplified, but the outcomes are real, the processes are sound, and if you stick to the map, you'll make a big impact on your long-term financial success.

I want to leave an impact. I want you to realize that a financially successful future can be accomplished quickly and safely if you focus your energy, change your beliefs about money, and commit to simple, yet strategic actions. We're talking about taking calculated risks, and I'm suggesting that you bet on yourself after doing the appropriate research. I love educating people about the opportunities of real estate investing and truly believe anybody can be successful if they act and make the necessary changes. Be accountable! It's easy to say I need to lose 10 pounds, but you can say that for years without taking action until something motivates you to act … like being single. Decide that now is the time for you to be financially "single," and act, starting today!

What's the common thread I've seen in successful young real estate investors? A willingness to make life changes based on financial intelligence, not emotional, and a willingness to be patient enough for the delayed gratification of success! Simply put, you need the desire and ability to plan, set goals, work towards those goals, and be patient! Without patience, small successes don't have the opportunity to compound into large successes! Set high goals and figure out how to accomplish them in your personal life, financial life, and overall well-being. Sacrifice, sacrifice, and sacrifice some more, and be willing to work your ass off until the plan works for you. Take calculated risks! You will learn and possibly benefit from every deal, the great ones, the mediocre ones, and especially the mistakes. After enough practice playing the game and analyzing deals, you will be more confident and proficient at assessing investment opportunities, minimizing those mistakes. Analyze the numbers on other people's deals, attend a seminar or two, read books, pick a growing market to narrow your search, and, the most inconvenient part, move if you have to.

None of these actions will make you a penny, they'll actually cost you money and time. The only chance you have to make money is by taking action. After it starts working and you've closed a few deals, keep sacrificing and feeding your bank account with the plan of funneling all capital towards asset acquisition and renovations. The interest you're earning from your bank is much lower than the current inflation rate. Don't plan to keep your money in the bank. As soon as you have enough money to buy a cash flowing asset, buy it! This sounds easy, but it's stressful and hard to continually use your reserves for investments! You need to understand the power of compounding investments. Don't change your living expenses to absorb the newly acquired cash flow after realizing small successes unless you want to keep making small successes.

I've met many investors who buy two, three, or four properties then destroy their momentum by quitting their job or buying a huge liability such as a nicer home or toys. This is a choice you'll be faced with in the near future but maintaining your momentum by understanding how liabilities affect your purchasing power is critical to gaining great wealth. Purchasing excess liabilities just 1 or 2 years too early could set you back many years from accomplishing life-changing wealth. If you want to make waves of money, then stay the course and make financial decisions, not emotional decisions.

I want you to read this book, commit to 5 years of living below your means, work towards qualifying for all the good low-interest debt you can secure, and make waves of cash for the rest of your life. People ask me for real estate advice often, and I repeat the same big picture ideas. The road map I've followed and continually advertise, leverages cheap debt and high leverage positions while acquiring cash flowing assets. If banks are issuing highly leveraged, cheap debt, then we all have the correct tools at hand for this wealth building strategy. For years, I've hyper-focused myself in multifamily real estate investing; you need to decide if this is the path for you. If you've already decided that, this book will be a great tool for years to come.

I want this book to be influential to all age groups, but especially to the millennial community. I hear excuse after excuse from my peers whenever I talk investing with them. It's hard to listen to. I want my friends and peers to enjoy the same level of success and freedom that my family has experienced. It's great to be successful, but incredibly disappointing to not share the experiences with our friends and family. Anybody can take control of their time and finances by getting educated and starting to take simple strategic actions today.

It's hard to make life changes—it's more comfortable hitting cruise control on daily life because you know what to expect. Are you comfortable hitting cruise control on life until 65+? If you're not satisfied with the outcome, then why are you not changing the inputs? To follow the wise words of Warren Buffett, "If you can't find a way to make money while you sleep, you are going to work until you die." Seek financial education and follow a path to financial freedom, not the illusion of working and saving to retirement. Stop wasting your time on social media, stop wasting your money on avocado toast, and stop wasting your trust on advice from unqualified sources. The illusion that our working force is chasing, collecting an hourly paycheck to retire at 65, helps the wealthy grow their wealth and keeps the working class doing what they do best, clocking in and clocking out for the majority of their lives.

With that said, I'm excited for you to start taking action and making moves towards financial independence. Once you get there, do good with your money. Always work toward the goal of creating a more perfect world. Help others by being a bright light of success and motivation. Be HUNGRY for improvement and change. Decide today that you will start taking simple, yet strategic, actions to impact your future!

Chapter 1: My Story

After graduating college in 2012, I went into the oil field making $65,000 to $70,000 per year and leveraged that income to purchase my first 26 units by 2016. This took 4 years of aggressive deal hunting, a couple of personal residence moves, high-interest hard money loans, and long-term strategizing to continue leveraging employment income to qualify for profitable debt. I strategized and took every opportunity available to invest in cash flow, and now I'm excited to share a map to that cash flow. I've continued down this path and, as of 2021, at the age of 32, I have a triple-digit residential rental portfolio—all 100% owned by myself, as well as owning commercial assets, and having gained a vast amount of experience.

Using this road map, I've been able to accomplish and gain experience flipping single-family properties, flipping multifamily properties, reposition underutilized office space into multifamily housing, owning and leasing a sports bar, subdivision land development, repositioning hospitality buildings into long-term residential units for individuals and for the state of Colorado as sober living, repositioning a foreclosed bank into Class A coworking space, owning and managing my town's local real estate investment group, owning and growing a property management company, along with holding a position on a local nonprofit's board, volunteering my time, donating dollars, and giving free advice to everybody who's asked along the way.

In the first 5 to 6 years of my investment career, I made every sacrifice possible to save money and qualify for loans. That commitment has allowed me to accomplish my greatest feat, growing a family, providing them advantages of the wealthy, all while having the ability to spend quality time with them each day. I have two young sons and a fantastic, loving partner. We've been able to travel ... a lot, live in our dream home, participate in every activity they'd like, all while committing time to the community, playing racquetball regularly, getting 8 hours of sleep a night, and having freedom of time. My goal was to be rich, happy, and well rested, not to own real estate, not to learn finance or to own businesses, but to be rich and always have a smile on my face. Work backwards from your goals to establish a path to the destination. You won't fall to the top of a mountain; you need to choose a path and start taking steps to get there. Starting today will get you there faster than tomorrow! What are your goals and your motivations?

As a kid, I had two standout middle school teachers: Mr. Ruising for Science and Mrs. Steelman for Algebra 1. The impact they left on me led to future degrees in multiple science disciplines. The goal of those degrees was to earn a high-paying job and amass wealth. Among other reasons, I believed that if I were wealthy, I could afford to become a teacher. Funny, right? I picked a path to financial freedom so I could work a job because I wanted the job, not because I wanted the money the job provides. First things first, I never wanted to worry about supporting my family, and financial freedom was a necessity. On top of being financially free, I wanted to ensure I was in control of my time. Financial education is a funny thing; very few people have it!

My father taught me to work hard, nothing was free, pay your dues, avoid debts, and save. He would often say, "there's no free lunch" regarding working hard for anything—fitness, a good grade, fielding a ground ball, or ironically, actually buying lunch. I never argued with him ... but I also never questioned where he was eating this imaginary lunch. What if we picked a buffet? Or, better yet, could we buy a fruit tree that returned food for the rest of its life? Due to his financial education, my father also worked NONSTOP for most of my childhood. With my only financial guidance coming from somebody who's career I DIDN'T want to emulate, how much value should I give his financial advice? Funny enough, in my head, I gave it merit and structured many years of education around it. I was taught to work hard, aim for a six-figure job, and save my way to retirement.

I chased that idea and chased the mirage of saving to success. After 4 years of college, I got a well-paying job, lived frugally, and was saving about $3,200 per month. With the application of simple math, it would take me 26 years to save $1 million. I remember rounding down to 20 years with speculative raises and bonuses. I wasn't going to wait another 20 years to gain wealth, but, at the end of the day, is $1 million wealth? Going back to my engrained "financial education," I "knew" the answer was to take on two to four more years of schooling and any of the associated debt. If I could earn an advantaged degree, I could reach a higher level of income and save my way to wealth. That makes sense, right? If I could only make $150,000 per year and live the same frugal lifestyle, I would attain $1 million in approximately 7 years. After accomplishing the education, getting the job, and saving my way to a million dollars, I would only be about 34 years old. That didn't seem too far away, but, again, is $1 million wealth?

Along comes the 2012 presidential election. What did I do? Talked with my circle of friends about the expected outcomes, trusted the opinion of somebody equally as uneducated as myself, and gambled ALL of my savings on a stock. I believed my overly confident friend who was clearly educated by the best political science scholars while working through his engineering degree *Cough, Cough, sarcasm*. He was sure that the Republican party was going to win the election and a particular group of stocks would take off. The election went the other way and that uneducated investment cost me over 50% of my savings, in one night. That felt awful, but it's a lesson that I'm happy to have learned when I only had $10,000 of savings.

Fortunately, a few months later, that stock bounced back, and I learned another great lesson. Be patient with your investments, you only lose money if and when you sell. While patiently waiting for the stock to bounce back, I had continued saving and had taken the initiative to find my own avenue of investment. Why was I willing to make huge financial decisions and give credibility to others' financial advice? I literally grew up seeing my father's guidance in action. Did he accomplish the goals I had set for myself concerning financial and time freedom? We weren't wealthy, and he had no freedom of time.

I needed to reconsider and change my trajectory. I needed to be seeking advice from somebody who had accomplished the goals I was setting for myself. This was a pivotal time in my life. I realized that MY opinion was the most valuable, and I needed to stop looking for direction from the people around me. Unlike my college coursework in science and math, finance was something that required debate, was opinionated, and there wasn't a simple "right answer." Would I take exercise advise from somebody who's never been in a gym? Why would I take financial advice from somebody who hadn't accrued great wealth?

I was going to seek financial education from the financially successful. Long story short, I found multifamily real estate investing. I'm embarrassed to say it, but I'll come clean. I don't remember the first real estate book that led me down the path to multifamily investing. That book did a good job of explaining the leverage one could create with real estate and helped me establish a new trajectory on my path to financial freedom. It was such a great book, that I quickly gifted it to a friend and sought additional education in my newfound niche of multifamily investing. That book was never returned, and I hope it's still being passed around today!

I listened to podcasts, read books, participated in forums, and worked though other people's deals. I wanted to know what people were looking at, how to analyze a purchase, and how to manage the investment to ensure safety and success. I ran deal after deal, built spreadsheet after spreadsheet, and asked lots of questions along the way I focused on information from success stories. The same formulas were used repeatedly, and there seemed to be a simple road map to building a portfolio of cash flow. I knew math, I understood the idea of leverage, and I had a job that could qualify me for the debt I wanted, so I needed to start taking action!

Again, I talked to my trusted inner circle about my planned path to real estate cash flow. Everybody said NO. The people I previously trusted about finance disagreed with my plan ... but I wanted to accomplish more than they had; why should I listen to them? I used their naysaying as motivation and acted quickly. I purchased the initial 26 units by qualifying for debt! I leveraged my W-2 income, my accumulated rental income, and the knowledge of local property managers, maintenance people, lenders, and brokers to maintain as many working hours as possible while acquiring these assets.

I rode this financial strategy to a point of cash flow that will provide income for the rest of my life, my kids' lives, and with good financial education, future generations' lives. If I can remove the financial burden from my future generations, how much can they give back? What will they be able to focus on accomplishing if money isn't their goal? This simple road map allowed me to extend my reach and touch bigger projects, while also having the freedom to spend time with my family. With this freedom, I've been able to make memories with my family that I'll cherish for the rest of my life.

It's easy to get caught up in the day's stresses when you're starting the journey and constantly making sacrifices. Most people will make excuses and tell themselves that "making sacrifices causes too much discomfort and it isn't worth it." I tell those people to suck it up or work for the rest of their lives. Those 5 to 6 years of sacrifice, if structured correctly, will lead to priceless freedoms for the rest of your life.

Chapter 2: Invest NOW
Why NOW and Why Real Estate

Please take a second to analyze your current path. Ask yourself what your goals are? Ten rentals? Two million dollars in performing real estate? Maybe $5,000 per month in excess passive income? Personally, $5,000 per month passively was my first goal. Based on your track record, how long will it take to reach your goals? What are you currently prioritizing in your daily life?

In 5 years, will you look back favorably on those prioritizations, or will you even remember spending that unrenewable resource, your time? For example, how many of us in 5 years would say, "I'm so happy to have read that social media post or the ever so positive news"? Even more controversial, will you look favorably on your weekly routine of visiting your favorite coffee shop or restaurant? How many decisions can you actively change NOW that will shorten your trip to tomorrow's success? How many of your daily routines will positively influence your life 5 years down the road? Take a minute to imagine yourself in 5 years and look backwards. How much are the decisions you're making today limiting your ability to make influential changes to your financial future? This is a difficult exercise but it's important.

The point is not to dwell in yesterday's decisions, but rather to identify what those decisions were and what you can do to cut that "financial fat"— those wasted dollars and time. What can you change to give yourself every advantage tomorrow? A friend once told me that poor people have poor habits. A homeless person without poor habits would not remain homeless.

Don't get caught in this cycle by being unwilling to change your imprudent habits. If you're already making those smart financial decisions by sacrificing today's comforts for tomorrow's spoils, what are you doing to maximize the financial velocity of those decisions? Are you prepared to take some risks? Look at a historic graph of interest rates. Are rates at an all-time low? YES! Your purchasing power will decrease by around 10% for every 1% that interest rates increase on a 30-year loan. Take advantage of the interest rates available today!

If you haven't said it already, one day you'll come to the realization that the best time to buy was yesterday and the second-best time is today. Worried that home values will be lower tomorrow? Or are you anticipating interest rates to drop soon? Remember, you're buying for cash flow, and you can only lose money if you sell the real estate, but you're not selling. Did you miss the "perfect" property and now you're waiting for another "perfect" proper-ty? Many properties will fit into the box if you've defined reasonable metrics and you spend enough time analyzing deals. You ran the numbers, and you're buying cash flow. Now is the right time to start because in 5 years, you'll be able to look back and say, "I did" instead of "I wish I did." If you start now, you'll start your exponential trajectory today. If the average person lives ~29,000 days, starting tomorrow means you'll miss out on one more day of your earned freedoms. Time is the most precious resource, and, fortunately, financial freedom helps you take control of your time.

Another way to look at the risk of not starting now is by understanding how you're losing money when saving. Since 2000, the US dollar has experienced an average annual inflation of over 3%, and it's projected to be much higher post-COVID-19. What is inflation? Simply put, inflation is the decreased purchasing power of each dollar. How much can your $1 purchase today vs. yesterday vs. 20 years ago? The ability to purchase real estate, lumber, a cheeseburger, anything. As the world inflates, the cost-of-living increases and so should wages. The cost to produce a home, often referred to by appraisers as "replacement cost," is going up. This replacement cost is going up due to the increased cost of materials needed, increased cost of the dirt to build on, and increased cost for every labor hour required. In the long term, that's a great hedge against home values going down and staying down. I say that now, but let's see how quickly 3D printing disturbs production costs in the future.

How much interest is your savings account creating? Interest earned from bank accounts has averaged under 1% for a long time. If you compare your earned interest to the rate of inflation, your money is decreasing its purchasing power by 2% annually. Additionally, if your mortgage has a lower interest rate than current inflation, then your equity is growing while your payments are static and the VALUE of the debt decreases. Do not pay off your mortgage early if your interest rate is below the market's inflation and don't store excess money in the bank if your bank is paying less interest then the current markets inflation. These are both scenarios that result in a financial loss. Get your money working for you, not working for the bank.

Real Estate investing will make you rich, it's not a get-rich-quick proposition, but it does work and it's physically collateralized. If your stock drops to $0, you lose all of your money. If your real estate values decrease, what happens? You only lose money if you sell, and luckily the value of the home has nothing to do with people's need for a roof over their head. Hopefully, you're renting for a healthy profit and, worst-case scenario, you could move in. Most of the world's self-made millionaires created their wealth by investing in real estate. For all of history, the owners of assets have been the wealthiest group, and you can create huge positions of leverage acquiring real estate using today's available tools.

Today, you need to make decisions and act upon them. I know it's hard to make life-changing moves but stop telling yourself the "time isn't right." If the time isn't right today, what makes you think it will be right tomorrow? You can make excuses. Most people I try to educate on real estate have an endless list of "why they can'ts." Start asking yourself "How can I?" If your worst-case scenario happens, wouldn't you rather that happen today, so you can rebuild, instead of tomorrow when you have less time to recover? I, like you, was very concerned of the worst-case scenario when I started, but I invested early with the mentality that if I went bankrupt, I'd want it to happen early in life.

This mentality motivated me to act quickly! Hopefully, right now you're not saying, "I don't have enough savings, the real estate values are too high, interest rates are on the rise, there are no suitable properties available, I will only purchase in a specific neighborhood, etc." These are excuses! You need to be seeking solutions! Rephrase the limiting belief. How can I qualify for this loan? How do I find the right property? Where can I afford to invest? What acquisition strategies should I use when interest rates are on the rise? What I want to convince you of is that today's the day to start, it's better than tomorrow, and if you start problem solving, you can reach your destination. Keep taking steps in the correct direction and don't make excuses on your path. If you do, your arrival time will only be delayed.

Leveraging Your Dollar

I've used the word "leverage" a few times now. I want to explore this word in a financial context. When you hear the word "leverage," do you think of a crowbar? The idea of using a tool to maximize your output is a concrete idea when applied to physics, but how do you create leverage with your money? Please follow this simplified example to express my idea of financial leverage.

Say that you have $10,000 in the bank and want to buy gold or cryptocurrencies or stocks; the story is the same for all. For this example, you buy $10,000 of a chosen cryptocurrency, and in the first year, it quadruples in value. That's an amazing 300% increase! Your $10,000 is now worth $40,000—you made $30,000!

First, assess the likelihood of this asset continuing to quadruple in value each year. Next, assess how easy it will be to access that capital and how much you can actually liquidate after the taxes and fees. If you made the money but can't access it due to staking, fees, taxes, etc., how much money did you really create? Even though it's worth 4x your invested capital, do you own an asset or a liability? Is this reproducible year over year or did you take a gamble and the stars happened to align in your favor? Ultimately, you invested $10,000, purchased $10,000 worth of something and that something increased in value, there was no leverage in your acquisition since $10,000 purchased $10,000 worth of something.

Now, let's apply leverage to the same amount of capital. You have $10,000 which will be used as a down payment on a home loan. There are a lot of loan options, which require a range of down payments. The lower the down payment, the higher your leverage. For this analysis, we'll run numbers utilizing a Federal Housing Administration (FHA) Loan. This is a widely available product that you'll probably qualify for. FHA loans work on one- to four-unit properties and require 3.5% down payment. Based on $10,000 of investment capital, you have the necessary down payment for a $285,714 home ($10,000/.035 = X, where X is the total purchase price). You can buy $285,714 worth of something instead of $10,000 worth of something.

Now, let's say housing values increases by 10% in year one. How much equity was gained? Ten percent of $285,714 is $28,714, we'll say $28,500 for ease; your asset appreciated $28,500 on a $10,000 investment. Additionally, these funds are accessible by refinancing or qualifying for a home equity line of credit (HELOC). This allows you to keep your position of leverage optimized, and you're not subject to pay taxes on the funds. This real estate investment example provided a similar return to the previous example, but the market only had to appreciate 10% instead of 400%. What is the likelihood of real estate values going up 10% in year 1 vs. year 2 or 3? Is 10%

growth sustainable? Or, more importantly, is 400% growth sustainable? This is a simple way to understand leverage and utilizing this type of owner-occupied loan allowed you to create 96.5% leverage since your $10,000 purchased $285,714 worth of something.

Understanding Assets

The next word I'd like to discuss is "asset." An asset is something that has value and allows you to meet debts. Allows you to meet debts is a big deal and an easy metric to gauge. Please think about what this means. If it's not actively paying bills with cash flow, then it's not an asset. With that in mind, I don't consider my single-family house an asset. Thank you, Robert Kiyosaki, for opening my eyes with your books and game. It isn't an asset because it cost money each month; it does not provide money to meet debts. There are ways to make a single-family house an asset, and I'll discuss that later. Were the cryptocurrencies purchased in the first examples an asset? Only after you sell them and provide capital to meet debts. Pretty simple concept. What are the financial consequences of selling cryptocurrencies? How much of the total sales value will you keep as working capital, AKA how much actually hits your bank account? Those are questions you need to answer for yourself when analyzing any investment.

The goal in my eyes, and hopefully yours as well, is to keep as much gains as possible. The shelters provided by real estate are almost magical. I'll discuss it below, but first, you need to find a good CPA to discuss the advantages and disadvantages of your prospective investment strategies. From my research, I've determined that the depreciation and write-offs available to real estate investing allows me to keep a higher percent of my gains and is the avenue I've pursued.

As the example demonstrates, you can create an immense amount of leverage with owner-occupied loans. Maximizing your leverage means spending the smallest percentage of the total asset's purchase price at time of acquisition. If you buy $10,000 of something using $10,000, there is no leverage. If you use $10,000 to acquire a $285,714 asset, you've utilized 96.5% leverage on your dollars' purchasing power.

After gaining some experience and learning the right financing avenues, you can expect to create over 100% leverage positions! Yes, that means you borrowed more than the asset's purchase price when making the purchase! Additionally, I try to qualify and close on larger assets with more square footage and multiple units. If I can qualify for a $400,000 asset vs. a $300,000 asset and the market improves 10%, the $400,000 asset earned an additional

13

$10,000 in equity. In an apples-to-apples comparison with a 3.5% down payment, my out-of-pocket expense is a difference of $3,500 at time of acquisition for a $10,000 equity gain in year one.

There are loan products that most people don't know exist unless you're in the industry. You need to have these conversations with a rockstar lender! I'll talk about building your team later in this book but know that you NEED a team. When describing leverage in the previous example, I ran the numbers utilizing an FHA 3.5% down payment loan. That's one of the many options available to purchase a primary residence, and you'll need to explain to your lender what you're seeking. Some other examples are, $1,000 down USDA loans, $0 down VA loans, and based on your employment, possibly "Good Neighbor Next Door" loans (only public servants such as teachers, police officers, firefighters, and emergency medical tech qualify for these).

When talking to that rockstar lender, ask how you can create as much leverage as possible. If they ask why or try to talk you out of that decision (many people in your circle will likely do this), explain that you're staying as liquid as possible for renovations and following down payments. What is liquidity in terms of finances? Liquidity refers to your easily accessible cash. Typically, these funds are being stored in checking, savings, or money market accounts. We'll talk about interest vs. inflation later, but your liquidity is losing money while it sits, and you need to mitigate your losses by investing! NOW is the time to start because owner-occupied loans can't be purchased every 2, 4, or 12 months … but you can amass 10 owner-occupied loans with 30-year terms and 30-year amortization schedules!

Owner-occupied loans are not only easy to qualify for but also allow you to create a lot of leverage while establishing lower interest rates and long loan term locks on the financing. The lower your interest and the longer your loan term, the lower your monthly payments will be. Why not choose 15-year terms to decrease interest rates and pay off the asset? Does paying more money each month on your mortgage result in less money in the bank? YES! Even if the interest is slightly lower, compare the total monthly cost to service a 15-year vs. a 30-year loan. Your goal is to keep today's money available! You need money TODAY to buy more assets and improve the assets you've acquired. Also, what's the likelihood that you will keep that debt in place for the full term of your loan?

I typically start considering a cash-out refinance on investment properties when the debt-to-equity ratio drops below 3. Debt-to-equity ratio is calculated by dividing the mortgage balance by the property's equity. This ratio fluctuates as you make improvements, pay down the principal balance, and as the market appreciates/depreciates. This ratio simply shows that you have equity available to be tapped when doing a cash-out refinance. A property with a debt-to-equity ratio of 4 means the asset's position of leverage is 75% or that 25% of the asset is paid off, and a ratio of 3 means the asset's position of leverage has dropped to below 66.75% and 33.25% of the asset is paid off.

Like I said, you can't qualify for owner-occupied loans every 2, 4, or 12 months ... but there are circumstances that allow you to expedite the process of amassing owner-occupied loans. For example, have you made the excuse, "I'm not purchasing a home right now because I can't afford the property that will suit my growing family down the road?" Great! Buy that unsuitable house NOW with an owner-occupied loan and move in. That girlfriend, or pet, or job opportunity that is now negatively affected by the purchase of the house may provide your needed justification for an underwriter to approve you for another owner-occupied loan.

Let's explore this idea with an example. You purchase a house with an own-er-occupied loan in an affordable neighborhood, but there's no grass yard. Four months later, you adopt a pet and need a yard. Your current house is now not optimal for your pet, and you'd like a more suitable residence. It sounds like your life circumstances have changed and the owner-occupied home you recently purchased is no longer adequate. Life circumstances are often out of our control, and you can't be denied for a loan due to your circumstances changing.

Here's another great example: are you single right now? Buy a bachelor/bachelorette pad. A few months pass and now you're engaged. Does the home you just purchased with an owner-occupied loan suit you and your growing family? Does your partner look unfavorably at the property due to its history or is there a lack of available space, or is the neighborhood creating an issue, or ...? The list goes on. I think you get the point. Again, your life circumstances just changed, and because of that, you should be able to qualify for a new owner-occupied loan. Qualifying for that second owner-occupied loan may require you to pre-lease your existing home to manipulate your debt-to-income ratio (DTI Ratio), but this is strictly based on your income needs at the time of loan qualifications.

One last example. You have a friend who wants to rent a room from you; you execute a lease then provide this lease to your lender as additional income, the income improves your debt-to-income ratio, and helps you qualify for a higher loan amount. First, being able to qualify for a nicer home or a home in a nicer area is a life decision that may be acceptable by the underwriter to qualify you for a new owner-occupied property. Secondly, after your friend moved in, you established a one-year lease, and you're now committed to living with them for a whole year! Living with a roommate can be difficult, maybe there is an issue and you're no longer comfortable living with that roommate, maybe it's impacting your friends and family, or maybe there's a separate struggle that it's causing, whatever life brings, consider how it impacts your loan qualifications! That struggle may be an opportunity. In the end, the ultimate argument here is that you want to move to a primary home without roommates. This is reason enough to work toward qualifying for a new owner-occupied loan.

Again, when your life changes, see if you can create an opportunity to qualify for another owner-occupied loan. This way of thinking allows you to maximize the financial opportunities of owner-occupied loans by understanding the rules. Here's a quick personal example that I'll explain in detail at the end of this book. I purchased a 4-plex with an owner-occupied FHA 3.5% down payment loan and the sellers told the tenants I was the buyer. After purchasing the property and occupying it, the residents hounded me about their rent, lease requirements, improvements, etc. When you're uncomfortable going outside due to your neighbors, I argue that the home is no longer suitable for occupancy. This was the underlying justification I needed to have my lender qualify me for a new owner-occupied loan. I just needed to deal with the hassle of moving, again.

Chapter 3: The First Steps
Small Changes and Proactive Homework to Prepare for Success

Decide it's time to start taking control. Make a plan. Do you look at your finances often? Where are you wasting money, and how can you cut expenses? What's your guilty pleasure? Be disciplined and save—every dollar available to you is a dollar you can leverage if you KEEP it. I read a great piece of advice from Tim Ferris in his book Tribe of Mentors that's stuck with me. One of these mentors stated that discipline is the answer to everything you need. Are you short on time? Be disciplined with your schedule. Are you short on money? Be disciplined with your spending. Are you out of shape? Be disciplined about fitness and eating habits. Pay attention to the things you want and make the necessary changes to accomplish those desires. If you make a plan and are disciplined about the actions needed to accomplish your goal, you'll be actively working toward those goals every day.

The most important hurdle for you to overcome is your doubt. Maybe you're debt averse and will justify inaction with this mindset. Maybe you have no savings and will justify this as your barrier to entry. Maybe you'll come up with an off-the-wall reason to remain on the side lines. You need to decide that it's worth taking some calculated risk and bet on yourself. You also need to overcome the idea that you can't afford it. Do you really think you can't save money or are you not able to save money with your current habits? How many things are sitting around your house gathering dust and being ignored that others would find valuable? Start with the goal of putting $1,000 in the bank and keep those saving habits after it's been accomplished. Have you talked to your family about your goals of owning a home? Get educated about the process and your options! Maybe there's an owner carry purchase option right in front of your eyes or a family member that would be excited help you get started. You'll never know unless you decide to be actionable and start taking steps.

Are you learning? You're reading this book, so I hope so. Other than this, what else are you learning and when do you allot time for learning? If you want to build financial wealth through real estate, learn everything you can and target in on your niche. Look up data on your current county or a market of interest. You need to understand the community and determine what's needed in that community. Speculating on a trailer park? There's a book for you. Don't have time to learn? Do you listen to music when sitting in traffic, going to the gym, gardening, or cooking? Substitute audiobooks or podcasts when you're completing mindless tasks!

Personally, I love audiobooks and use them as a tool whenever my brain isn't working on a different problem. It's hard to maximize your learning time while multitasking, so you need to pay close attention and be prepared to revisit later. I suggest listening to books during monotonous tasks starting today, now, right now. Is audible on your home screen? I listen to a couple of books at a time, and whenever I get to content that I should be taking notes on, I listen, rewind, listen again, then go to a different book until I can sit down and really take it in. When I can devote 100% of my attention, I listen to that content a final time and take notes.

Always consider how you can apply the information being given to you. Some books will seem trivial, but it only takes one or two powerful insights to change your life. Pay attention and be ready! Don't learn and ignore. Don't listen and then forget. Don't just go through the motions of learning and taking notes, only to put those notes in a place to be forgotten. If the information was valuable enough to take notes on, keep those notes handy. The best way to solidify the information and expand on the newly learned content is by discussing it! Bring up what you're learning in conversation at every opportunity. Not only does teaching help cement the idea in your brain, but it also makes you more actionable.

Control your circle of influence. If you hang out with rafters, you'll probably learn how to row a boat; if you hang out with vegetarians, you may eat less meat; if you hang out with drug addicts …. It may be fun for a while but look out. The following story is not about real estate, but I think it's a powerful analogy that can be applied to many of life's challenges. This example was outlined in a great book, *How Not to Die* by Dr. Michael Greger.

Read it, and you'll likely become a healthier person.

The example went like this: Have you, your mom, and your grandmother all had esophagus surgery related to the same general issue? Do you believe the cause of that issue to be a genetic problem that was unavoidable? What if the cause of that esophagus issue was actually due to habits your grandmother lived by and taught to your mother who, in turn, taught to you? If you take personal accountability and think of what could cause the problem instead of pointing your finger at genetics, maybe you could take control of the problem that you thought was uncontrollable. Better yet, maybe you'll make long term changes in your life that will impact your children and grandchildren's habits. If you're accountable to this extent, then you may keep following generations of your family from having the same "genetic" issue—which has just been an "excuse"—which leads to "unavoidable esophagus surgery."

What if you apply this same way of thinking to your non-biological life habits? I believe we all have more control than we give ourselves credit for. Take your life off cruise control and make changes even if they are uncomfortable. Look at the whole picture and make a plan to improve your life instead of chalking your life's difficulties up to "unavoidable" and "out-of-my-control" scenarios.

Let's apply the above esophagus analogy to real estate investing. Are your parents successful real estate investors? Are your friends successful real estate investors? The way we typically pick our friends is by finding people with shared interests. We enjoy these people because they know about the things we're interested in and getting a second opinion only helps broaden our own knowledge. Are those shared interests like esophagus-surgery-causing habits that dominate your personal time, resources, and conversations? Are they pursuits that will lead you to a successful future? Or are they just enjoyable? Are you making the excuse that these interests are worth the time and monetary expense because they provide immediate gratification? If you were to put those hobbies on the backburner and start focusing your attention on investing, how much time would be available?

Let's take that to the next level. You become so committed to learning about real estate investing that you start attending local meetings and meet people with similar interests or goals. Those relationships and conversations will not only help you stay committed to your goals but also bring powerful "aha" moments. Celebrate success and follow them! Talk about your local market, talk about money, and talk about strategies to accomplish your goals. Rich people talk about money; it's not taboo. After you start talking about money, you'll gain insights and learn about others' financial strategies.

The US dollar hasn't been backed by gold since 1971 when $35 US dollars could buy an ounce of gold. For an understanding of how much the dollar's purchasing power has decreased, today it takes almost $1,700 to purchase the same ounce of gold! In reality, today's dollar is backed by debt because every dollar created by the FED (Central bank) requires a borrower to establish a loan (debt) to account for that created dollar. Money is fiat and should be looked at as a number. This number is a puzzle piece or variable in an algorithm that can return many outcomes. The output you're seeking is the most efficient path to grow that number. What is an algorithm? It's a sequence of steps. An easy-to-understand analogy would be a recipe. Let's say there are seven different ingredients and a specific order to follow when introducing those ingredients. If you follow the steps and quantities, you'll get the expected result. But if you change the order and quantities, your finished product will be different than expected.

You'll be giving yourself a great advantage by talking money and real estate with people who are interested and educated on those topics. Those conversations are often immediately applicable and will help you grow as an investor. I was lucky enough to make a best friend who turned into a mentor and later into a business partner. We still talk real estate constantly and really enjoy each other's insights! Things are always changing so you need to always be learning. To this day, we still enjoy mountain biking, playing racquetball, lifting weights, and impromptu trips all while discussing real estate, renovation strategies, tech integrations, deal structures, capital solutions, tax concerns, management fees, and more—all real estate and all manipulatable factors.

This time and energy discussing specific topics was as valuable to my learning as the books, podcasts, and blogs. On top of being educationally valuable, discussing the topic with someone close to you makes you accountable and motivated. Take action. Without action, you only have knowledge. I know a very educated financially savvy PhD in economics. This man can out-graph and over-analyze the heck out of a deal, but he can't close one. Action! Make it a priority. Ask yourself, "How Do I Close?" And hold yourself accountable.

I said it above, and I'll say it again. STOP WASTING MONEY. Every dollar you save is a dollar you can leverage. Think about inflation and the decreased purchasing power of each of your dollars. Maybe a dollar feels insignificant in your pocket, but every dollar you spend today is like losing $5 of purchasing power a few years down the road. The power of leverage is so old and so strong, Archimedes said, "Give me a place to stand and a lever long enough, and I will move the world." A long crowbar gives more prying power than a short crowbar; this is called mechanical advantage. Following this train of thought, every dollar you save is adding to the length of your figurative crowbar. Maximize your potential by not being wasteful. Those dollars were already earned, don't waste them on one-time satisfactions when they could be leveraged. Increase the length of your financial crowbar to improve your quality of life … for the rest of your life. If you play your cards correctly, the use of that leverage could give your children and grandchildren an advantage otherwise squandered.

Quick math for the leverage argument regarding adding $10,000 of savings. If you already have a decent savings, congratulations, add to the pile! If you don't have $10,000, you need to make a plan to figure out where that money will come from. If you were motivated to save money, could you eliminate expenses every day that add up to $5, $10, or $25? Retaining $25 per day for 400 days saves you $10,000. Utilizing the FHA loan's 3.5% down payment requirement, your $10,000 is all that's needed for a $285,000 4-plex. If you already used your FHA loan … and so did your partner, then maybe you can qualify for an FHA loan together, or you may be required to put 5-25% down using a different loan product. Alternative loan products could be conventional owner-occupied loans, VA loans, USDA loans, and the list goes on and on!

A 5-10% down payment will drop your purchasing power substantially, so try to use the lowest down payment option available every time. Obviously, 0% is better than a $1,000 down option, and 3.5% down is better than 5% or 10%. The big picture idea is that even at 10% down, you have 90% leverage on your money! I'll explain about how to analyze the deal to ensure safety later, but your newly acquired $200,0000+ asset is a tool to create cash flow, decrease your taxable burden by providing expenses and deductions, acts as a store of wealth that buoys with the market, and, best of all, provides a home! I believe my early frugality was an important part of my efficient path to 100+ rental units.

There are a lot of ways to get to your goals and countless ways to build a portfolio, but I believe taking these initial steps is the safest way to acquire massive assets quickly. Being intentional and aware of my habits for 5 to 6 years allowed me to purchase assets that created enough cash flow to feel comfortable borrowing higher interest, riskier money for acquiring additional assets. I could have decided at unit 26 that it was time to buy my dream home, but instead, I leveraged the cash flow from those 26 units to borrow more money and grow faster. Building a mindset of continued investment and growth instead of spending will grow your portfolio exponentially and could change the lives of your great great grandchildren if managed correctly.

While saving money is good, don't save too much. It's funny to say, but don't! There's a huge opportunity cost to keeping all your money liquid. What does keeping your money liquid mean? Liquid or liquidity refers to the money you can access quickly! Typically, these funds are in checking, savings, or money market accounts. It's important to have easily accessible money for emergencies but having too much money hurts you. If it's sitting in a savings account, historically, you're losing around 2% of it each year to inflation. That is an approximation related to pre-COVID inflation data.

My simple savings rule is to keep 6 months' worth of debt servicing in the bank at all times. When a bank underwrites your liquidity, they typically want to see 6 months' worth of debt servicing or up to 7.5% of your global debt in liquidity. On top of the 6 months' liquidity in the bank, it's nice to have lines of credit or other sources of capital readily available for emergency repairs or a good deal that unexpectedly pops up. That toilet will clog, and it's worth paying somebody else to deal with it so you can focus on deal hunting.

Chapter 4: Build Your Team

Meet a great real estate agent, or better yet, a couple of them! Don't sign a blanket agreement giving your exclusive right to purchase with a single agent and don't push to solely work with friends or family. You need a real estate agent(s) with a lot of experience, long term knowledge of the local multifamily market, and preferably is an investor or services a lot of investors. You will be making a lot of offers, getting a lot of no's, and terminating on the contracts that stop making sense during your due diligence period.

You don't want to feel pressured to close on a deal that doesn't make sense because you're afraid of souring a close relationship. The agent you're working with can be a friend, family member, or someone you don't know. They just need to earn your business by brining deals and knowledge! Every agent will say they can fill your needs and wants you to sign an exclusivity agreement; don't do it! You don't want a typical agent because you don't want to be a typical buyer! You're building a team to make you a successful and exceptional investor.

With that in mind, your agent should be exceptional. Years of deeply engrained knowledge is only going to help you make better decisions. That agent should have connections with investors and have referrals for property managers, lenders, and handymen. Additionally, that agent should have knowledge about neighborhoods constructed by corner-cutting contractors, localized environmental concerns, your community's future development plans, the list goes on and on. If your agent is exceptional, they will have more information than you'd expect. Ask for their opinions and take notes. That broker should also be a source of off-market deals. Treat agents well, respect their time and opinions, but, at the end of the day, they get paid a percentage of what you spend. The standard rate is 3% of the purchase price to the buyer's agent and 3% of the purchase price to the seller's agent. This 6% is pulled from the seller's proceeds at the closing table and paid to each agent. When buying a house, an agent's incentive is for you to buy quickly. The more time they spend with you before getting an offer accepted, the less money they make on their time. Don't forget, you can compensate the broker in other ways than buying a property. If they're doing a great job for you, then send them referrals and take them to lunch. Never feel pressured to close on a deal because of the time an agent has put into your offer. You should be making a lot of offers and only closing on the offers that make financial sense after the inspection objection period has lapsed.

When making an offer, there are 3 possible outcomes: Either the offer is accepted, it's countered, or it's not responded to. An accepted offer sparks excitement and worry. You will be excited that the seller is motivated to close but worried that you're paying too much. You'll also be worried that the seller knows something about the property that you don't. When an offer is immediately accepted, I plan to work the price down during the inspection objection term. In the event that an offer is countered, you have to revisit your numbers and see if the terms are tolerable. While making sure the countered price makes sense, you can feel relieved that the sellers want to work towards a mutually beneficial sale. I typically don't accept a counter proposal, but instead, follow up with a counter that splits the difference between my initial offer and their countered price. Again, during the inspection objection term, you have the opportunity to shed light on maintenance issues that the seller can repair or address with a decrease in purchase price. Lastly, your offer may not be responded to at all. If this happens, you know that the offer is way below the seller's expectations in some regard. The seller might not be willing to negotiate because they believe the original price is fair, because they either have an offer behind the scenes, no urgent need to close, or because you included terms that they won't accept. It may not be because of the price you offered conflicts with the dates or loan type might be the issue for them. Ask your real estate agent if the seller's agent can shed any light on the terms that the seller wants to see in your offer.

Real estate agents are motivated to reach a closing and collect their check and should be eager to help. Many sellers have unrealistic expectations when they first list a property, and those expectations are lowered every day a property sits on the market. If you can't find common ground with verbal communication, then step away temporarily and resubmit your offer in 30-45 days. It costs nothing to offer, and you can terminate an accepted contract without losing any money. When an offer is accepted, you've bought yourself time to complete the necessary due diligence, and you've eliminated competition from other prospective buyers.

Also, after an offer is accepted, it's human nature to start spending that money internally. Many sellers see a closing date on a contract and know they are profiting X dollars on X date, so they start building a shopping cart in their head. When you need to address inspection items and ask for repairs or a decrease in purchase price, the seller feels that the money and, thus, the items in their mental shopping cart are being taken away.

Submit lots of offers. After they're accepted, research and renegotiate as needed. When submitting inspection objection items, push for the seller to repair items instead of adjusting the price. If the seller is willing to fix the needed items, then you are effectively wrapping your renovation costs into your loan instead of pulling those funds from your bank account and wasting time completing repairs after closing. If the sellers will not adjust their price or repair items to meet your financial needs, terminate the contract and get your earnest money back. Your agent won't be excited to have you terminate but explain that the numbers don't work without them doing X, Y, and Z. Hopefully that earnest money can immediately be resubmitted with a different contract on a back-up property.

There are lots of properties out there. Be dynamic and buy for cash flow. Explain to your agent what requirements are needed for a property to be a possibility and let them work! Make offers and close a deal with them. Don't waste their time with showings that you have no interest in buying or making an offer on. If your agent closes a deal for you and gets paid efficiently for their time, then they'll keep you in mind on future deals.

I said it above and I'll say it again, an agent is typically compensated for their work by earning a percentage of the total sales price. Read *Freakonomics* by Steven Levitt and Stephen J. Dubner. This duo will open your eyes to a lot of statistical anomalies. One of the anomalies brought to light pertains to real estate agents' earned commissions in relation to days on market and sales price. The difference in an agent's commission is less than $300 when buying or selling a house for an extra $10,000! Obviously, you, the seller or buyer, will always be motivated by a $10,000 difference. The question is, if it takes an extra 2 weeks of work for that $10,000 price difference which results in an additional $300 commission to the agent, is there enough financial incentive to keep your agent motivated? What is the punchline for their research?

When an agent was selling their own house, they were more patient which resulted in more days on market to achieve a higher sales price.

Make sure you get a lending referral from somebody with local market knowledge who's done a lot of deals. You aren't asking for a referral with the best terms, you're asking for the lender that closes the more difficult loans. This lender should have a minimum of 5 years in the industry, underwriting experience, a track record of working with multifamily investors, and is hopefully an investor themselves. You want to work with like-minded individuals so try to find a lender that invests. It's very difficult to qualify a lender; take referrals from experienced investors and test the water.

Interest rates are important, but most lenders will be within .25% of each other. If you get a quote from a different lender that has better terms, ask your preferred lender to match those terms. Sometimes they can match the terms and sometimes they can't, but don't hold it against them. Every lender will guarantee they can close your loan as good as the next lender, but that's a lie. Take it from somebody who's been denied for a LOT of loans. I can't tell you how many hours I've wasted trying to lower my interest rate by .25% only to get denied and return to my rockstar lender. Personally, I've learned this lesson many times and now go directly to my rockstar lender without a second thought. The most important factor for me is the lender's ability to close the loan! Even if interest rates are .25% higher, having a rockstar lender on your team will save you a lot of time and thus a lot of money.

I don't expect you to take this advice because it initially won't make sense to sign off on a loan when you're being offered better terms down the street. My advice here is to learn your lesson after the first denial. If you get a great referral that closes your loans, then keep going back! You may think that you'll be locking in 30-year terms and not revising this lender regularly but that's not true. Assets appreciate, your renters pay down the principal balance, and you'll be able to capture that equity with cash-out refinances every 3-5 years (if you want to). Pay a few extra dollars and gain the peace of mind that comes with knowing you're not wasting your time working towards a loan denial. Hopefully, you're a creditworthy borrower and your first loan is easy to close, but as your portfolio grows over the next 12-48 months it will be more difficult to acquire this debt. There will be a time when the lender needs to be highly competent to help you reach the closing table.

I will always remember hunting for a lender to close my first loan. I first attempted to use a friend who was working at Wells Fargo, and I was denied after completing hours of paperwork. Next, I was referred by a local builder to his lender of choice, his referral denied me about two weeks later. After these two denials, I thought I was un-lendable and needed to wait a few months to restructure my debt-to-income ratio. That was until a local investor advised otherwise. This local investor referred me to her lender. That lending referral closed my first deal in about 30 days and has since been invaluable to my growth. That lender was able to underwrite a deal in-house and nearly guaranteed a closing within 30 days after a simple round of due diligence questions. To this day, I'm still committed to using this lender whenever possible.

The ability to quickly exit a project and recuperate your invested capital is vital for rapid growth. The weight lifted off your shoulders after a final touch-up paint job or placing a tenant is a mirage of success. After completing renovations on a project, your job isn't complete until you have refinanced the asset. When you refinance, you will be securing low interest, long-term, highly leveraged debt and hopefully will be recapturing all of your investment capital! The following are some questions I'd suggest asking a lender during the vetting process: How long have they been in the industry? Do they have multifamily clients that are repeat customers? Ask if their underwriter is down the hall, in another building, or in another state. Modern underwriting is completed by automated systems, entering bad data will return bad data. A good lender with close proximity to the underwriter and knowledge of the systems will clear up misunderstandings. Does their company impose overlays and what are their overlays? Overlays are requirements imposed by a company to ensure loans can be resold on the secondary market. Words of wisdom, inexperienced lenders may be ignorant of their company's overlays. A good example of an overlay would be minimum credit score requirements. There is not a minimum credit score requirement imposed by the Federal Housing Administration (FHA). Minimum credit score requirement to qualify for an FHA loan are imposed by your lending entity, not the fair housing association.

Next question: how much rental income seasoning is needed before it's acknowledged as income? Some lenders only need an executed lease to qualify rental income, some need 3 months' history, and some want 12 months. Additionally, you need to know what percentage of the rental income on your leases can be applied toward your calculated debt-to-income ratio (DTI Ratio). A debt-to-income ratio is a required calculation by every lender and is a simple math problem. Your debt is calculated by adding up all your required monthly payments, and your income is your gross monthly income before taxes and deductions. When qualifying a borrower and calculating income for an acquisition, you need to make sure the lender is accounting for the leases you're purchasing with the property. Some lenders will only qualify 30% of the leases' rental amount toward your income, while others can use 80% or 90%! The more rental income the lender can count toward your "I" in the DTI calculation, the more debt you can qualify for.

A knowledgeable lender that can qualify most of your leases' rental income will increase your loan approvals and likely get you to closing faster. The faster you get to closing on a purchase, the sooner you get to take advantage of being a property owner. The faster you get to closing on a refinance, the sooner your invested capital will be available for you to re-invest. It may take some time to find the right lender but look for referrals and don't be afraid of staying local. My rockstar lender happens to be a local lender whose rates are usually a little higher, but I'm loyal to her services. Even though the rates are slightly higher, I use her repeatedly because she gets the job done and gives sound advice to accomplish my goals! I speak with this lender whenever buying or refinancing 1-4-unit properties. I speak with her to ensure acquisitions are structured in a way that doesn't compromise my anticipated exit strategy. She saves me time and helps structure deals on the front side so I can work within her box of products when refinancing at the end of the process. Yes, the higher interest rates slightly decrease my cash flow, but I save so much time through the process that I don't consider it a loss. That saved time and headache is invaluable! If I find one deal during any of that saved time, then I've probably made up for .25% interest rate increase on all of the loans she's closed combined.

You don't need to be ready to purchase to find a lender. Visit a few referrals, explain what you're trying to accomplish, and hopefully you'll learn a few things. If they check the needed boxes, let them pull your credit, get a pre-approval to establish your borrowing limit, and start working on their suggested credit repair items. This lender should openly make suggestions about credit repair. If they don't, ask them what you should focus on. You want to increase your pre-approved amount and open the funnel to as many properties as possible. Even if you don't want a $600,000 investment, it's nice to know what you can qualify for. Alternatively, say you find a $600,000 investment property but only qualify for $525,000. Can you find a part time W-2 job to provide the necessary pay stubs to increase your DTI? How much additional work income or rental income will you need to qualify for the increased loan amount? Find out what you can qualify for and how long you'll have to wait before starting the process over again. Sounds risky, but you will have already done the math to ensure your rent covers your monthly payments you need to focus on qualifying and closing. I will go into more detail about how to protect yourself and run the numbers to establish securities in a later chapter of this book.

Gather property management (PM) referrals and interview them. Ask for property management referrals from multifamily investors, networking groups, local agents, lenders, and online resources. Give the most weight to long standing clients, not referral partners or renters. Use seasoned professionals' referrals to find this invaluable team member. This partner is vital to your long-term success and in a best-case scenario, you are establishing a multiyear relationship. Yes, you can switch property managers if you don't like them, but there is a huge cost and time expense to doing so. Discuss your acquisition plan and your preapproval information when meeting property managers. Ask them if they know of any property owners who are considering selling. Sometimes, the property manager will have a great lead. If the property manager knows they'll retain the ongoing property management services and collect monthly management fees on top of making a sales commission, that's a nice incentive for them to help you close a deal. Alternatively, you don't want a property manager that turns over their management portfolio annually with sales. Some property managers make the bulk of their money by selling off units for angry landlords after they've done a poor job managing the units. Do not sign an exclusive listing agreement with your property manager! Keep your goals aligned by making sure everyone makes money when they've worked for it.

The PM is a key person on your team, and you need to vet them. Hopefully, you find a great one and stick with them for a long time. But heads up, there's a good chance you'll dislike your property manager. Property management is a very difficult job, and you shouldn't give too much weight to their companies' overall star ratings. Angry residents often review their property managers, but happy residents don't. If you're reading through the reviews, look for reviews submitted by property owners. With a little effort, you can probably track down the owner that left that review, and you should ask them specific questions. You should also go to the property manager and request referrals to long-standing client and a directory of properties they manage. Drive by their units to inspect exterior maintenance and/or knock on a door to ask the residents how their experience has been.

In my opinion, the most important operational questions when vetting a property manager are in relation to maintenance and fee structures. I'd suggest asking the following questions during an interview. What fees are charged to the owner, and what fees are charged directly to an incoming applicant? What monthly fees are charged to their residents? What is their eviction process, and how is it billed? Who does your maintenance, and how is it coordinated and billed? This question should lead to a lengthy discussion. Some follow-up questions to ask when discussing maintenance should look like: What's the property manager's mark-up on completed work orders? Will the property manager forward all work orders to your designated vendor(s)? Do they have an in-house handyman, and if so, what's their hourly rate? What's the rate billed to the property owner for that handyman's work? What tasks can that handyman handle and is he available to renovate properties on top of his maintenance duties? Do they have a 24-hour hotline that receives calls and sends a third-party tech immediately? Or does that third-party hotline troubleshoot the issue before assigning the work to a designated vendor? If they do not have a 24-hour answering service, how do they address after hours emergencies?

While a 24-hour hotline that sends a tech sounds like the best process, I would argue that it's a huge problem. Often, urgent maintenance calls that result in large bills are actually simple inconveniences that were handled incorrectly. Quick example: Your tenant has no hot water at 11pm and reports an emergency work order. Your property manager has a hotline that answers the call or responds to the digital submission and sends a third-party vendor, a plumber, to fix the problem. That plumber is going to likely bill you for an after-hours service trip charge, an increased hourly rate due to it being after-hours, and will most likely require a 1-hour minimum, even if it's a 10-minute fix. The plumber arrives and finds out the pilot light is out, pushes the igniter button, waits a few minutes to ensure it stays lit, and leaves. From his arrival at the resident's door until his departure, maybe only a total of 15 minutes elapsed. However, you get a $250-500 bill and lose your month's cash flow with one service request. What if similar events take place two to three times a month?

Now let's say the emergency work-order is fielded by an in-house tech or a 24-hour answering service that helps troubleshoot the problem. While troubleshooting the problem over the phone, the tenant is asked if the light on the front of the water heater is blinking. If it's not, they instruct the resident to push the igniter button and resolve the problem themselves. Best case scenario, the resident learns how to resolve this issue and addresses it without making a phone call next time. Worst case scenario, the resident can't figure it out, but the issue is identified, and the in-house handyman is capable of resolving the issue instead of a plumber. You, the property owner, are now assessed a much smaller bill for this service request by eliminating the plumber and keeping most of your month's cash flow intact. At the end of the year, this cash flow will help you qualify for more loans. It's a beautiful and compounding cycle. You'll be adding cash flow, qualifying for loans, renovating, leasing the property, refinancing to get your invested money back, and going right back to your lender for another pre-approval.

Next question for your Property Manager (PM): how does your company generate leads and convert those leads into residents? What are the property managers average days vacant between residents, AKA turnover time? Turnover time is the time it takes to move out current tenants, renovate the space, get the space clean and ready for renting again, market the property, show the property, screen applicants, and execute a new lease. For a rental priced at $1,500 per month, each day the building is vacant costs the property owner over $50 in lost rent plus the cost of their mortgage plus the utilities plus the risks that come with units sitting vacant. Do the math so you know what the total daily cost is when your unit is vacant. Simply add up your costs and divide it by the number of days in a month. Knowing this daily cost will help motivate you to ask more questions and create an efficient turnover process. Often, that process is expedited by buying the right materials and being willing to spend extra money for labor.

On top of the lost rent, a vacant property is a maintenance headache. A vacant property has a much higher chance of being vandalized, pipes freezing, small leaks creating major damage, etc., all while you're responsible for paying the bills. When your PM leases a property, do they charge a lease-up fee? This incentivizes your PM to perform! For example, suggest aligning interests by giving them a lease-up fee of 50-100% of your first month's rent if the property is rented within 20-30 days after a move out.

Make sure to set expectations. If the property isn't leased in 30 days, the PM would forfeit that lease up fee. I love utilizing tech whenever and wherever possible due to the chance of human error. I market my vacancies on as many websites as possible, pay for leads each month, and utilize artificial intelligence (AI) to guarantee that every lead receives a text message offering a showing immediately. The sooner an interested party is contacted after showing interest in your unit, the more likely you are to convert the lead into a showing, a showing into an application, and an applicant into a resident. It doesn't matter if it's 1 pm or 1 am, after a lead clicks on a picture of my property on any website and adds contact information, my property management software's artificial intelligence sends them a text message and pushes to set up an in-person showing.

The likelihood of converting that lead into an applicant decreases by the minute. If you contact them within a few minutes of gaining their online attention with a showing invitation, then you have a much greater chance of monetizing that lead. Yes, even at 2 am. Make sure there is quick action, every lost lead could cost you a great resident and extend your turnover time. Also, if you're paying for leads, every missed lead is an unnecessary expense on your income statement! Once that prospect has been converted to an in-person showing, it's your PM's job to convert them into a resident, but, hopefully, the AI communication has already impressed and motivated the resident to move in. I love when 5, 10, or even 20+ people are booked for in-person showings by our AI to view one vacancy during a one-hour time slot. Your chances of finding a great applicant are higher, and the competition is a great motivator. Mass showings will help maximize your rental rates by creating competition and help you negotiate quickened move-in times. For example, "If you can execute a lease starting this Friday, then you will get priority."

Next questions to ask: What actions are taken by the PM when a resident is late on rent? How quickly and how often are they called? What does that conversation sound like? There are two approaches, the humane approach and the rigid approach. The humane approach requires discussing the issue, validating it, setting up a payment plan, then ongoing monitoring. The rigid approach is less time consuming. The staff would immediately begin applying fines and working toward an eviction if they don't cure the issue in a set number of days. The latter of these options is best for the property manager because it saves time, and most PMs will make a profit on the eviction process. The humane approach is time intensive for the PM but often benefits the property owner. My team utilizes the humane approach but makes sure to hold residents to the agreed terms. In my opinion, after all expenses are paid and time is spent qualifying a resident, that resident should be given an opportunity to prove themselves even if they've hit unexpected struggles. If the resident doesn't follow through on their side of the agreement and/or stops communicating with the office, we promptly start the eviction process.

The next question will result in a long conversation and is dependent on the type of property and area of your investment. What qualifying factors does the PM suggest when screening applicants for your investment property? The qualifications for an applicant to lease a $4,000 per month house vs. a $1,000 per month apartment are different. The more expensive the property, the more qualified the applicant should be.

Due to the increased risk, expensive properties need to have additional safeties put in place. For a $1,000 per month apartment, I require a minimum of 2.5x the monthly rent in verifiable income, credit score of 580 or higher, $0 in collections to previous landlords, no evictions in the past 7 years, along with a list of automatic disqualifying factors. These automatic disqualifiers are only partially stipulated by the property owner; your PM is required to follow fair-housing laws. A few of the additional disqualifying factors that I implement are no sex offenders and no felony offenses in the past 7 years for violent crimes or for the manufacturing or distribution of narcotics. Do I care about smokers or pets? No, but I want to know about these factors prior to the resident taking occupancy. If you know the circumstances, then those factors can be considered in your qualification process.

Also, you want to know about pets, so they are monetized during your leasing process. Your PM should ask questions in a way that promotes an honest response and attempt to verify some of the information. Instead of asking, do you have a pet? Ask, how many pets do you have and what breed are they? This will more likely receive an honest answer. This answer can be verified when talking with previous landlords or by doing an online search. Should you accept pets or not? That's your choice, but I happily accept them and add a monthly pet rent to their lease. People love their pets, and many responsible people own pets. I want to keep the funnel open to as many good applicants as possible while also avoiding a resident sneaking a pet into my property because they thought it was a disqualifying factor. Any pet that's sneaked onto the property is a lease violation that could result in eviction expenses along with a missed monetization opportunity. Along with accepting pets, make sure your PM will inspect the property and establish a fixed limit on cats and dogs allowed in each unit.

Next PM question is if there are additional tenants on the lease, does the PM charge an additional fee for each person? I think they should, as extra tenants result in additional wear and tear along with higher utility costs. Additional residents in a unit have the potential of creating additional cash flow but definitely creates higher operating expenses. Does your property manager push for cosigners when qualifying a borderline applicant or ask if they're willing to prepay rent? What software do they use, and can they set you up for automated reports each month?

Ask a few property managers these questions and take notes on their answers. After interviewing your referrals, you'll have a good grasp of what each PM's process looks like and, hopefully, have the information needed to make a good decision. Even though you will only choose one PM to employ, all these PMs can be deal sources. Make sure they know what YOU are looking for and that you're able to close on those types of properties quickly. Before signing any contracts, remember that you're the employer, and make sure you know what your employee, the PM, is responsible for. Hopefully that PM is willing to be transparent because you want to have a way to monitor their performance without constantly calling them. Their software should have view-only access options that allow you to keep an eye on the metrics. If they aren't using good software, definitely consider using a different PM. Property management is a difficult job that takes a lot of communication and time for a small monthly margin so it's helpful to remove any unnecessary hurdles. Review but don't hound your PM over every detail. If you create a toxic relationship by nit picking, it won't improve service.

The last pre-investment team member to locate during your due diligence seems simple and obvious but is very consequential and will be critical to your success. You need to locate an honest handyman who is a jack of all trades, shows up on time, works hard, and can buy their own materials. They should have a basic understanding of plumbing, electrical, and HVAC, but ideally, they're very familiar with all. Ask for referrals and call lots of handymen. After you get a referral, test them on different jobs before deciding you found the right person. Having somebody that can do all trades means they can evaluate a job from beginning to end. Either build material lists online or review the material lists your vendor builds for each job. I suggest you require the vendor to pick out their own materials and deliver those materials to the job site. It's nice to have suggestions on material alternatives and an eye for efficiencies, but don't take their advice blindly. Always question their suggestions—they're not investors for a reason. Did they suggest installing granite countertops in your $1,000 per month rental? Or high-end cabinets? Only you can determine the right material choices to reach your desired finished product, but always be value conscious. Don't forget, you're renovating a rental! Your future renters don't care about how much you spent on the countertops, and they probably won't respect them any more than they would formica, tile, or concrete. When you see a chip in your new countertop because a renter opened a beer bottle on the edge, it will hurt your feelings. Ultimately, they're just a renter, and it was your decision to over-improve the property. If you overspend on repairs, it's only going to hurt YOU, the property owner. Make a plan and stick to it. Invest and repair with a financial plan, not an emotional plan.

Aside from value-conscious material suggestions, verify your handyman's work from beginning to the end of a job, and point out flaws so they know you're paying attention. If you can do the entire project with one person or one team, that efficiency will save time and lead to fewer phone calls. Ask their rate and don't waste their time. After you find a good one that shows up on time, provides good service, and is appreciative of your prompt payments, LOCK THEM IN! Finding and keeping a good handyman is critical to protecting cash flow and maintaining the condition of the asset. Offer steady work without wasting their time on bids, tell them you'll pay regularly, and preferably with bank transfers, give them the freedom to make suggestions and support them if they want to bring on a helper. This additional helper should improve their efficiency, make them extra money, and hopefully save the property owner some money. That helper would be charged at a lower rate than the lead, but the lead would still get a portion of their helper's hourly rate. The owner's bigger savings will come in the form of time - the time it took to complete renovations. When discussing work with potential new handymen, I emphasize that they won't waste their time bidding work. I want them to show up and start working on day one, I'll pay them for their work immediately after completion, and I'll be qualifying them for future work based on their output. If they want steady work and steady pay from me, they need to perform.

All handymen will tell you they're quick, capable, hard workers, but you need to continue reviewing and verifying this on every job. Additionally, expect most of them to overpromise, overbook their schedule, accomplish less than they advertised, and possibly contact you for payment daily. I know and agree that it's an annoyance to be constantly contacted for payment, but that inability to save money leads to a very dedicated employee. I like to set a weekly pay schedule for the first one or two payments then a bimonthly pay schedule once we have an established relationship. Handymen who live paycheck to paycheck are typically very consistent because they need to be. At the same time, if they're completely broke and calling you for payment constantly, keep an eye out for theft via extra hours and over ordering materials to use on a different owner's project. Having a handyman who can afford to buy their own materials creates valuable efficiencies, but you need to know how much material a job should require and verify orders.

My handyman uses a text to confirm the business credit line for the bulk of purchases and if my manager isn't available to approve the order, I encourage everyone to buy the materials themselves and charge back to me on their invoices. A job that sits unfinished for any amount of extra days because the handyman couldn't afford $50 worth of materials costs you a revisit to the job and days of additional vacancy time! Days of vacancy is likely a couple hundred dollars in lost rental income alone. You want to earn preferred scheduling and prioritization from this vendor, pay them promptly—don't low-ball their services—respect their opinions, keep track of your excess materials, and be friendly but not friends. You may need to fire this person in 3-6 months. Why do you want them to be friendly? You want them to be friendly because they will be talking to your other tenants and possibly be present when applicants show up to view the unit.

After gaining experience repositioning assets acquired with low-interest, highly leveraged, owner-occupied loans, you'll hit a barrier in your investment career. You'll run out of owner-occupied loan eligibility or down payment capital. When you reach this investment wall, creative financing terms or utilizing a private or hard-money lender will be essential for your growth.

Don't expect to start your investing career by utilizing high-interest private or hard-money. This debt is dangerous and should be utilized with caution. Don't get me wrong, this type of funding is integral to your long-term growth, but you shouldn't seek these funds until gaining experience. While gaining experience, ask other investors for private and hard-money referrals. Private money lenders and hard-money lenders are not the same thing. Hard-money lenders are typically the liaisons between private money and you, the borrower. If you are able to find private lending sources, you'll likely save money on monthly interest, origination points, and prepayment costs, along with gaining flexibility on loan terms and loan-to-value ratios. Generally speaking, hard-money lenders access funds from external private sources, while private lenders are lending their own funds. Since hard-money lenders are handling other people's money, they need to be licensed and follow certain guidelines. It's pretty easy to locate hard-money lenders because they advertise, while private lenders are found via referrals.

There are a couple advantages to using hard-money lenders, but the biggest advantage is their lending limits. Typically, they have access to more funds than private lenders because of the pooled funding sources. While private money and hard-money lenders will likely lend at similar interest rates, hard-money lenders have less room to negotiate and are subject to rules etched in stone. For example, you'll probably be required to pay for an appraisal when using hard-money lenders, but, in my experience, private lender usually don't require one. You'll also see a list of additional fees imposed by hard-money lenders on your settlement statement like underwriting fees, loan origination fees, and payoff fees. You need to get a list of these expenses when starting communications with your lenders so you can factor in the expense. Since private lenders are lending their own funds, they can be flexible with all lending criteria and, hopefully, waive a few expenses that hard-money lenders cannot. You can establish a high position of leverage utilizing either of these funding sources, but, in both cases, the high-interest payments will absorb your cash flow and hurt your borrowing ability. The monthly interest payments on these loans add up quickly, so they need to be added into your expense column when building a plan. Time isn't your friend when utilizing hard-money, and so it's worthwhile to make a plan before borrowing the money or you could get stuck in a bad position.

As mentioned above, private lenders are more difficult to locate than hard-money lenders. Tap into your team and investment network to ask for private money referrals. I love getting personal referrals to private money lenders because of the credibility it establishes. Title companies and real estate attorneys are great referral sources for private money. Title companies know who's lending money because they sit through so many closings, the question is if they'll provide the referral to you. Real Estate oriented attorneys also work with private lenders regularly. To get a private money referral from an attorney will take persistence and patience. Build an investment resume and identify a prospective project that the attorney can advertise on your behalf. Offer to take people to lunch and offer a referral fee for anybody helping you source this team member.

On one occasion I had financing fall through four days before a deal was closing, and I didn't have a backup in place. In response, I called as many private money referrals as I could think of and offered a $5,000 referral fee if they located a lender that could close the deal. Three days before closing, I was connected to an investor outside of my market that had funds available and heard great things about me. That $5,000 incentive motivated a real estate agent that I'd never done a real estate transaction with to speak on my behalf, vouch for my track record, and essentially prequalifying me to work with this lender. Amazingly enough, we were able to put contracts in place and get the deal funded within that three-day window. Initially it was hectic, but the deal got done, the project went as planned, and that private lender has since funded multiple deals for me.

If you are asking the right people and still not gaining private money referrals, then you need new team members or you need to build a stronger relationship with your team members! Make the most out of every referral! Be concise when you communicate, make your payments on time, communicate with your lender as the project progresses, and make sure you give 30 days' notice before paying them off! If you follow those steps when working with a private lender, then that lender will likely be disappointed when you're paying them off and ask you to keep the money working. Do good business, and you will establish a consistent, reliable, long term lending source.

Typically, private lenders require a proforma that helps the lender determine the assets' future value. You will also need to produce a capital expenditure (CapX) spreadsheet showing anticipated timelines and costs. When utilizing these high-interest funding sources, I've borrowed anywhere from 90% to 120% of the asset's purchase price. When borrowing over 100% of the asset's purchase price, you will need to collateralize their funds with additional assets. This is easy to accomplish if you took the previous chapter's advice and acquired a few owner-occupied multifamily properties.

Be sure to know how much equity you have in those assets and the monthly cash flow of each building. You want to instill confidence in the lender by having multiple exit strategies available. Lenders need to know their funds are secure and having a seasoned-performing renovated multifamily building is a great piece of collateral to offer.

I typically offer additional collateral in the form of a second position on one or multiple buildings, depending on the available equity. This is called cross collateralization. By adding additional collateral and over-borrowing on projects, you can accomplish an acquisition and renovation without spending any of your own money. You'll be subject to paying additional interest on the borrowed funds, but if you can add a substantial amount of equity to the property, then you may still get cash out when refinancing. This is the goal. When you're able to start accomplishing cash-out refinances on cash flowing buildings that were repositioned with $0 of your own money, then you've learned how to play the game. Re-read the last sentence if you didn't understand it! Once you can accomplish these results, you are making infinite returns. Again, this is a high-risk game, and you need to move quickly. You've leveraged your other assets as collateral to accomplish this outcome. Have multiple exit strategies in mind to avoid losing hard-earned assets.

Chapter 5: How to Spend Your Time

Time is your most valuable resource, spend it wisely, and leverage it! The same mentality you apply to leveraging your financial resources should be applied to your time. What do I mean by this? How much money do you make at work? If you can earn more money per hour than your handyman, then you shouldn't be doing handyman work. Work more to afford more professional labor instead of doing the labor yourself. Hopefully, you can afford a few hours of professional handyman labor for every hour of your earned wage. If not, it still likely makes sense to spend your time at work due to the vendor's speed and experience. Do your job, make more money to help qualify for loans, and pay good laborers to do their job.

Are you trying to save money on materials by using secondhand products? If they require customization to fit your application, then I suggest not buying them. The idea of spending hours fixing materials instead of hours installing materials means there's vacancy loss to be calculated on top of labor hours. Yes, you may save 50% or more of the materials cost and get better quality materials (example: solid wood cabinets vs. entry level materials) but the hours spent modifying those materials quickly outweighs the savings. You want to streamline the process by giving your handyman the tools to finish jobs quickly and move on. This will save you time, money, and headaches along with decreasing turnover time stresses. It's easy to quantify this loss after going through the process a few times, but you should just take my advice. Don't create more headaches—streamline the process. Just buy cabinets that fit and get them installed immediately so you can get the job done and market that rental!

Can you dedicate a week saving $20-30 per hour by painting? Probably! I want to convince you that it's worth hiring two professionals to finish in a fraction of the time. Those professionals will likely do a better job than you in less time, and you want the expense (on your taxes)! By not hiring out the work you are eliminating a claimable item on your tax return. Having bills to claim against your income producing property on your tax return is an asset that will help decrease your taxable burden. Hiring professionals will also decrease your turnover time and allow you to earn rent sooner! On top of that, how much stress did those professionals eliminate? With the saved time, were you able to hunt for more income-producing deals? Were you able to rest so you put more hours in at your job? Generating additional income at work and in your rental property will only aid next year's loan qualifications. Don't do the handyman job! You're working to become an investor. Are you using your time to save yourself money or are you focusing your time on making money? Save money by improving efficiencies, continually asking your vendor for input, buying the right materials, and by establishing deadlines with financial punishments. Work to save time completing projects in ways that don't monopolize hours of your day because your time comes with huge opportunity costs. If you're focusing your time looking for deals and making offers, that time will pay off ... but who knows how much? If you're focusing your time on saving money, you know exactly what you are saving—$20 to $50 per hour. How much does this "savings" cost? It will likely cost weeks or months of lost rent, added stress, lost income hours at your job, and possibly a missed acquisition opportunity. Spend the money on a handyman to get it done!

I discussed being frugal to save money for down payments earlier in this book, and I stand behind that! This isn't the place to be frugal. Stick to your 5-year plan and be intentional with your spending—don't consider the money spent finishing a job as wasteful spending. You're investing money, improving your asset, and working toward generating cash flow. It will be bothersome reviewing line items for work you could have personally accomplished, such as painting or removing trash, but spend the money to get it done quickly and spend your time at work to focus on investing in cash flow. Even if it takes your bank account to an uncomfortable place, when you finish the project, you'll be reimbursed with cash flow monthly and hopefully a cash-out refinance in the near future. Get it done right now. Worry about getting it done perfectly after you're already successful and can afford to lose rental income nit-picking.

Did you read the last paragraph and tell yourself, "I can't afford another property so I should be spending my time renovating"? I don't know your situation, but I'd be willing to bet you're wrong. Looking at the situation from a 10,000-foot view. For every hour you spend working on the project, you're saving the hourly rate of a handyman. Is that handyman getting rich from his hourly rate? First, stop justifying saving money by wasting time, that money deserves to be pumped into your asset. Saving money to slow down the project is the opposite of what you want to accomplish. It's easy to grasp the cost of one hour of labor but very hard to grasp the value of one hour creating more money. There's an incredibly high opportunity cost to spending your time texturing walls and inhaling drywall dust. Increase your reach to find deals, go to networking events, call every for-sale-by-owner sign you pass, knock on the door, or leave a note on distressed properties. If nobody answers, talk to their neighbors, locate your county's pre-foreclosure list, and leave a note on the property owners' door before they're foreclosed on! On the note, I offer to cash them out or explain the steps that would lead to a wrap of their existing mortgage.

In wrapping a mortgage, it would require me to stop the foreclosure process by paying off all delinquencies, inherit their mortgage, improve their credit by establishing regular payments, and help relocate them since they likely don't have the funds to do it themselves. If the note turns into a phone conversation, then I need to explain the advantages and disadvantages of both options. Communicating that the seller has a couple options and that you're working to help them is very important. This strategy can allow the buyer to inherit low-interest debt and equity while providing the delinquent mortgagee a safety net from destroying their credit, recording a foreclosure, and accruing more debt. With interest rates being historically low in the recent past, we, as investors, should be attempting to secure that amazing low-interest long-term debt. Creatively financed acquisitions can allow you to retain that low-interest debt and avoid dealing with bankers or todays rates all together.

A great use of your time is talking to other investors about projects, explaining what you're looking for, and learning who's on their teams. Help and offer to give back wherever you can. In the long run, those people will help you if you've helped them. Look at as many properties as possible and run the numbers. Pass that info along if you can't purchase it yourself! Find a great property but the price isn't right? Determine what price makes sense, get it under contract at a middle ground price and work the price down with inspection objection items. It costs nothing to make an offer, and you can get your earnest money back for most of your contract term. There's no risk to the buyer when an offer is accepted! During your inspection objection period, you could claim your pet hates the house and get all of your earnest money back—the goal is to get it under contract! Once it's under contract and you identify items that need repair, the seller will be much more willing to negotiate. Continue negotiating and close if the terms make sense or terminate the contract, get your earnest money back, and get more offers out.

I hope we're past this but I'm going to keep pushing on it. If you still think you should be doing the daily manual labor, you're ignoring the opportunity costs of missing a deal and you're missing the point of maximizing skilled workers' time. If you're not networking or learning, you should be earning! Every dollar earned will help qualify for that following investment. Benjamin Franklin once said, "Every penny saved is a penny earned." But those pennies' value decreases every year sitting in the bank, so do you want to save it for long? I like to think that every penny earned is a penny I can leverage into a nickel, a nickel into a quarter and quarter into a dollar.

There are more options for accessing working capital than spending hours at work. Using your time to earn goes deeper than clocking in at work. That time can also be earned by sourcing other ways of generating working capital. Consider sourcing working capital from lines of credit, equity in a house, or friends and family. A great example of an alternative way to generate working capital is utilizing 0% interest lines of credit, or more specifically, 0% interest on business lines of credit. Why business lines of credit? Each business you establish should have a separate tax identification number issued by the IRS. This tax identification number is different from your Social Security number. When applying for a loan, you will need to provide your Social Security number but not the tax identification numbers for your entities. None of the business debt will reflect against your Social Security number unless you are missing payments and a negative inquiry is recorded on your personal credit report. What does this mean? Pay off all credit cards in your personal name, get your debt onto business lines of credit, and set up autopay to guarantee you never miss a payment! As long as you never miss a payment these business lines of credit will not reflect when pulling a credit report against your Social Security number. This is an available tool to keep your debt-to-income ratio as healthy as possible. If this is confusing, then I hope you understand after watching my YouTube explanation. Go to YouTube and search the following phrase, "Fund and Grow +Real estate investor Scott Schindelar."

I have personally used the company Fund&Grow to leverage 60 minutes of my time and a few thousand dollars into over $200,000 of working capital. Fund&Grow is a company that employs ex-bank employees to issue business lines of credit such as Chase, US Bank, Citi Bank, and Flagstar Bank. These ex-bank employees worked in the credit departments and intimately understand the process of qualifying for business lines of credit. It feels uncomfortable giving permission for somebody else to speak on your behalf but now somebody else's time and expertise is being utilized to provide YOUR project 0% working capital. This example leverages money, time, and your hard-earned credit score. Every hour the service spends qualifying you for 0% interest lines is an hour you get to spend earning, learning, or hunting for a good deal.

Let's continue extrapolating on the previous example's numbers utilizing 0% lines of credit. A 4-plex is purchased utilizing a 3.5% down payment FHA loan, this works out to a $10,000 down payment. Let's assume you lock in a 3% interest rate on this debt over 30 years with both taxes and insurance costing around $1,000 per year. The payment on this debt is approximately $1,300 per month. You purchased the property, knowing it needs $15,000 worth of renovations. You have reserve funds that could go toward these repairs, but you've learned to stay liquid for emergencies and will need this liquidity for following down payments. To complete the $15,000 of renovations, you utilize 0% lines of credit. You renovate the property by utilizing $15,000 of credit card debt and rent out the property. You have three rental units at $900 per month and the unit you're living in with one roommate generates $500 per month. You are cash flowing $3,200 per month in rent before paying expenses. Your principal, interest, taxes, and insurance payment (PITI payment) is $1,300 per month, utilities are $400 per month, and your credit card payments equal $300 per month. In a month with 100% economic occupancy (fully occupied with paying residents), you will collect an excess of $1,200 per month after paying these bills. Minimum payments are made on the business lines of credit for 11 months while you save $1,200 per month excess to pay off the card right before month 12. By month 11 of making minimum payments, you paid down the card with rental cash flow by $3,300 and you put the excess cash flow of over $13,200 in the bank ($1,200 monthly cash flow * 11 months = $13,200). Yes, before month 12 hits you need to pay off the remainder of that card's balance to avoid interest charges, but the card is paid off with the collected cash flow, not with the $15,000 savings you had on closing day.

On top of pushing off the $15,000 expense, you maintained security by staying liquid, generated a year's worth of rental cash flow for your tax return and maintained capital in the bank to help qualify for a following loan. Additionally, you earned an increased monthly wage by spending your time at work instead of renovating or hunting for capital sources, and you have a renovated property. You did all this while maintaining your $15,000 in the bank. The golden goose is the cash flow you just purchased with that initial $10,000 down payment. The cash flow you purchased with a $10,000 down payment effectively renovated your property because you structured it to do so. After month 6, when you've added $1,200 per month in savings to your $15,000 nest egg, you go back to your rockstar lender, lay out the numbers, and figure out how to qualify for another cash flowing loan! Fingers crossed, you qualify for another loan and close another deal all while continuing to make minimum monthly payments. Don't forget, you need to pay off the remaining debt the day before your 0% promotion ends and big interest starts accruing. Act fast to fully optimize this debt.

I know, it's stressful, but soon you'll be moving money around like puzzle pieces to navigate your way to financial security. Once you learn the rules of the game, creative finance will allow you to play real life monopoly. The stress of these projects will decrease with experience, and I suggest gaining some quick experience without the stress by running through other people's deals. Another tool to help build your financial knowledge base and hopefully decrease your stress load when making real life offers is Robert Kiyosaki's "Rich Dad's CASHFLOW 101" board game. CASHFLOW 101 is a fun, no risk way to change your perspective on debt (there is also a phone-based application you can download).

Spend time playing with an investment calculator or pro forma spreadsheet (Send me an email to maptomillionsinrealestate@gmail.com, and I'll send you mine!). In the four unit and under residential world of real estate, property value is determined by an appraiser who has to identify recent comparable sales. Recent comparable sales, or comps are verifiable sales that took place within a few miles of your subject property in the last 6 months. When entering a project, you'll be a few months away from finishing and seeking an appraisal, so it's difficult or impossible to forecast what comps will be available. Even though it's difficult, comps need to be considered to determine your After-Renovation Value, ARV for short. When valuing real estate with over four residential units, comps aren't as important, and you can determine the ARV with a simple calculation. Properties with five or more residential units are considered commercial and an appraiser will use a different approach when determining value.

When determining the value of a commercial asset appraisers will give more weight to the income approach and the replacement cost approach than the comparative sales approach. The replacement cost approach is self-explanatory; this approach requires the appraiser to estimate how much it would cost to rebuild a structure of the same quality. The income approach typically holds the most weight when appraising a commercial multifamily residential property. Why? Because these assets typically sell to investors and an investor analyzes these metrics when offering on a property.

Determining the value of a building using the income approach requires applying a Capitalization Rate (Cap Rate) to the buildings Annual Net Operating Income (NOI). This is where playing with an investment calculator or pro forma spreadsheet will be invaluable. After becoming familiar with one of these spreadsheets, you'll be able to approximate equity potential within a property on the spot. On the surface, the few hundred or thousand dollars per year of gained cash flow looks minimal, but when applied to the assets Capitalization Rate, there are large equity impacts. Sometimes, acting quickly and being the first to submit an offer is the only edge you need to get the deal. Understanding how property values change with small net operating income increases could be the only signal you need to make that early offer.

Here's an example utilizing Capitalization Rates. Again, Capitalization rates are most applicable when assessing values on commercial multifamily properties. A commercial multifamily property is a building with 5 or more residential units. The Capitalization Rate or Cap Rate for short is a simple ratio that quantifies the rate of return an asset provides. The closer that ratio is to one, the closer the Annual Net Operating Income (profit) is to the property's value. An asset with a Capitalization Rate of one can pay itself off in one year, and an asset with a Capitalization Rate of 10% can pay itself off in ten years.

The Capitalization Rate equation is Cap Rate = Net Operating Income divided by Value (Cap Rate = NOI/Value).

NOI is the Annual Net Operating Income, which is the numerator of this equation, and it's divided by the property's market value in the denominator. This simple math problem returns your Cap Rate as a decimal, multiply that decimal by 100 to return a percentage. Cap rates don't fluctuate daily and are based on the market conditions in your area along with the property type and condition. To determine an applicable Cap Rate, ask an agent or open an application like LoopNet to see what Cap Rates are being applied to similar properties in the area. LoopNet is free; download the app to explore commercial listings. After you determine the Cap Rate local agents are using on similar nearby real estate, you can apply this factor in your own evaluations. Now that you know the Capitalization Rate you can apply this variable to determine a property's value or determine its Net Operating

Income.

Algebraic manipulation of the Cap Rate formula:
Cap Rate = NOI / Value
NOI = Cap Rate x Value
Value = NOI / Cap Rate

This is powerful! A quick example follows to solidify this idea:

You're analyzing the purchase of a five-unit building. All units are renting for $1,000 per month and the property has $15,000 per year in expenses. You view the property with your PM and determine the rents are $100 per month under value. Before making an offer, you need to determine if there's enough value-add potential to jump into the deal. How much equity is gained by adding $100 per month per unit? Increasing rent by $100 per month x 5 units x 12 months equals $6,000 of additional income per year. If your property is assessed on a Capitalization Rate of 7%, you can calculate your added value using the formula: VALUE = NOI / Cap Rate. After filling in the blanks, VALUE = $6,000 / .07; punch those numbers into a calculator, and your Value equals $85,714! Making the single change, increasing rent by $100 per month per unit adds over $85,000 to the value of the asset. How much does it cost to increase rents? Sometimes, it takes a full renovation to accomplish this, sometimes it requires paint, new floors, and a new tenant but very often it only requires a conversation. Often, the inherited resident knows they've been renting at below market rates for years and do not want to move. After all, moving is expensive, time consuming, and stressful. If they determine it's not worth moving, the existing resident will sign your updated lease and accept the rent increase with little or no renovation work. If this is the situation, keep them happy by listening to their needs and address work orders promptly. This resident will be comparing you to their previous landlord so plan to be better than their previous landlord. You want to retain this resident as long as possible if they're willing to pay market rates and eliminate your need to make capital expenditures. Moving is expensive and a hassle. Nobody likes doing it, and you should always consider this when increasing rents annually; it's leverage in your negotiations. If you're short on funds and can't renovate the unit post purchase, work with the resident and do smaller rent increases to retain their occupancy. Additionally, you are increasing rents to market rates, not above them. If they want to move, they need to deal with the headache of moving and will likely be paying market rent at their new home anyways. Provide a nice home, repair it promptly, respect their space, and you'll likely retain the resident even after increasing the rent.

Automation, automation, automation! Use technology to your advantage. What can you set up and forget about? You should be able to set up auto pay for all of your bills and any bill not on autopay should go directly to your PM for payment. If your bank doesn't have the functionality to set up auto pay, change banks. If you're writing checks each month, then you're spending your time on maintenance. Maintenance doesn't make you money and is a bad use of time. On top of saving you time, the other beautiful advantage of setting up automated payments is that they're never missed. Computers don't make mistakes, and payments always go out on time. This is great for your credit, clears up brain space, and frees up your schedule on bill pay day. If you miss a payment, that means you, the human data enterer, did something wrong. Fix it once and it will be fixed for good. You're leveraging your time by spending a few minutes setting up autopay schedules! This one-time task will eliminate you spending a few minutes every month paying bills and eliminate the worry of a missed payment. To save even more time, I suggest establishing autopay settings that only notify you when a payment fails. I do not need the email clutter or brain space dedicated to additional notifications telling me payments were successful. The things that I want to catch my attention and earn my time are problems that need to be fixed, opportunities to analyze, or things that make me smile.

Occasionally, after onboarding new properties, payments may fall through the cracks. When that happens, somebody will be in touch to notify you! Call the bank to walk through your autopay settings and that problem should be resolved forever. For easier review and organization, I set up a bank account tied to each of my properties. When I need to audit a property's expenses or sell a property, it's easy to review and cancel all autopays by looking in one place. The worst-case scenario when setting up autopay is forgetting to delete the scheduled payments after selling a property. This is a hassle, but, at the end of the day, it's easy to account for and correct because the payments are digitally logged.

Pick standard materials. For goodness sake, stop spending entire days at Home Depot practicing interior design. HGTV is a lot of fun to watch, but they're TV shows. Those investors have different streams of income than real estate. Pick a neutral paint for every wall, a white for all ceilings and trim, a go-to flooring product, a standard tile for your bathrooms, along with a backsplash material and shower layout that your tile setter can duplicate. Take pictures to provide your vendors a reference and have your store of preference save your paint colors and flooring information for all future purchases. It's a real shame when your handyman gets touchup paint that is a few shades different from the original color. When this happens, you're forced to repaint an entire unit. Buy paint in 5-gallon buckets, you'll have a time savings by eliminating extra Home Depot days and have a stockpile to pull from when touch ups are needed. Also, you'll be leveraging your time and eliminate needing clarification from your handyman. I say you're leveraging your time because the decisions you spent time and energy making once, like tile, shower layout, your paint color, etc., can now be applied repeatedly. On top of the time and cost savings you get by using the same materials, your handyman will become more proficient and take control of their jobs. My tile guys know what tile to use, where to add an accent band, that they should be tiling all the way to the ceiling, and that they're expected to install two corner shelves at chest level. My other handymen know what color to paint walls vs. trim, to paint before laying floors, what flooring gets installed in living spaces vs. bathrooms, what direction to lay the flooring, where to find the scraps from the last job and the list goes on. Each of these established standards eliminate questions when ordering and installing materials.

A mistake I made that you could learn from: I verbally instructed a handyman about my paint color instead of telling them to request the paint mixer pull up my file. Instead of ordering up my standard "Light French Grey" for the walls, "French Grey" was requested and mixed up. The handyman was new and eager to impress, so he quickly got back to work and touched up walls throughout the unit. It was obvious that the colors were slightly different during touch ups, but he expected the colors to match once the wet paint dried. Obviously, it didn't match after drying, and this cost me, the owner, a full repaint. This equates to wasted labor hours, wasted materials, and two lost days of rent. Create standards, don't deviate, put those standards on file to eliminate human error, and you should be on your way to establishing a very efficient renovation process.

Picking standard materials eliminates many headaches, but you'll still be ordering project-specific materials. Compiling material lists and locating all of the needed items takes more time than you'd think. I suggest setting up an account with your big box stores pro area and routinely sending your shopping cart to your sales representative. The sales rep can then coordinate for their employees to locate materials and have them pulled and waiting for your handyman to pick up. Either you or your handyman can build this digital shopping cart, but email this list to the pro area and take advantage of their staff's hours when possible. Once it's in a nice pile, your vendors can schedule an early morning pick up and efficiently get the needed materials without losing a full day walking aisle after aisle shopping. Additionally, the user portals at the big box stores make it easy to review past material purchases; they even have a nice little image next to purchased items. Correctly using your user portal will save you time when looking back to locate materials and help ensure you don't miss expenses when it comes to tax preparation.

I've lost many days inside of Home Depot trying to save my handyman's time by picking up materials. More than 50% of the time, my efforts backfire. I typically return to the job site and find out that I got the wrong materials, or something was missing. Every time this happens, I look back frustrated at the losses that I caused. Trying to expedite my handyman's work has now cost me hours of my day, wasted time on the phone with the handyman asking questions, along with damage and/or a mess in my vehicle. All of this might be worth it if it saves my handyman time, but unfortunately, he typically has to go back to the store anyway for an exchange. Save yourself the time and do it digitally. Unless you have a high-level understanding of what's needed on the job site try to avoid shopping for your building materials. Compile digital shopping carts or have your handyman do this, send those lists to the store for the items to be pulled, and have your handyman pick up, review, and deliver the piles to your job site.

After setting expectations, give your PM and handyman the freedom to make some of their own decisions and address repairs without your permission. If you have already vetted a good handyman, instructed your PM to send that handyman to your repair calls, and educated that handyman on your standards and materials, why slow them down with another layer of communication? If it smells like cigarettes or there is damage needing touch ups, then get it painted immediately. Setting standards will help the handyman and PM make decisions on your behalf. They don't need permission to remove stained or urine-filled carpet in a bedroom. They know you want hard floors throughout, they know the flooring you use, and they should get it swapped today, not tomorrow.

Set standards, make it clear that you're making the units nicer. Avoid managing necessary repairs. Set expectations then give your PM permission to schedule the handyman and start working toward a rent-ready unit. To help set a benchmark, I require a call from my handyman on any repairs that will exceed $1,000. If the anticipated repair costs are under $1,000, then I do not want a phone call, I want to review pictures at the end of the job. Similarly, I suggest giving a benchmark for your PM to honor. For example, the PM should know that any repair under $1,000 doesn't require my approval and should be assigned to an available vendor immediately. I never want an inexpensive repair to sit unaddressed in an occupied or unoccupied unit, the sooner the repair is completed, the better. A minor repair that sits unfixed will hurt your showings, be forgotten about, sometimes turn into a larger issue, and if it's in an occupied unit, create a point of tension or an excuse for them to avoid paying rent. Alternatively, if the repair cost is over $1,000 then it needs to be completed by my preferred vendor, and I want to be involved in the discussion. If the unit is occupied, then I want to bring in extra hands to further expedite the repair. Set up these communication benchmarks but reevaluate and change them as needed. There are pros and cons to establishing these rules.

Example:
Pro: Eliminating the requirement of owner permission on minor repairs should save time and improve the resident's experience. Happy residents can be expected to take better care of the property, display better payment history, and reside for longer terms.
Con: Knowing that you will not be contacted for minor repairs makes it even more important to audit invoices each month. You need to pay attention to costs and occasionally request supporting documents to justify those costs.

Hopefully, this course of action makes your resident exceedingly happy and frees up time for the property owner to deal-hunt. At the end of the day, you approved the PM to spend the resident's rental payments on repairing your asset! Requiring owner permission on minor repairs slows down the process and adds an additional cost, your personal time. There will be times when you're frustrated with the outcomes and consider changing your course of action but run the numbers before implementing. There is a cost for your attention, that cost shouldn't be overlooked in the equation.

A helpful way to confidently audit work that didn't require your approval is by establishing a digital invoicing system that requires before and after pictures. Instruct your PM that the vendor cannot collect payment unless their invoice includes before and after pictures. Personally, I have a hard time stepping back and not micromanaging projects, but I've learned there is a detriment to working this way. You'll cause tension between you and your vendors, cost yourself valuable time, and, worst of all, set a precedent of being responsible for fielding simple questions repeatedly. You should be hiring a professional handyman with much more experience than you. Ask your PM for suggestions, tell your handyman what you would like to accomplish by the end of the project, and seriously consider their suggestions. If you listen and truly consider their suggestions, then you will have gained knowledge to apply to future projects. Simple example: instead of saying, "I want to add a second bathroom here" *points to ground*, ask "Where's the most cost-effective place for me to add a second bathroom?" and "Why here?"

Spend your time wisely. All the above information is to push you to spend your time working ON your businesses instead of IN your business. Establish systems and processes but review often and be cautiously optimistic. When you separate yourself completely, you'll be taken advantage of. You'll see it over and over, people do what you inspect, not expect. I add smart locks to my projects doors that time stamp every unlock and lock. I can always revisit that door to pull a log and see when and by whom the door was accessed. I suggest requiring pictures to document the days completed tasks from vendors. If you're hiring professionals, then take full advantage of their knowledge and skills. Let them build a digital cart for the project's materials and review their order before paying. Ask their opinions, pay them regularly to do their job, and audit their work. Keep everyone honest by making occasional site visits when handymen say they're arriving and ask what will be completed by the end of the day. Also, orient your bigger projects with incentives. For example, ask your vendor how long it will take them to paint, set cabinets, and replace floors. After they give you a timeframe, hold them to it by offering financial incentives. If you offer an extra $100 per day that they finish early, what would be incentivized? They would be motivated to give your job priority, show up early, stay late, and to use their time efficiently when on site. Your agreement should also outline a penalty imposed for each day the project goes past their deadline. The sooner they finish, the sooner you can start collecting rent to report on a tax return and leverage into loans. This is how you'll turn pennies into nickels, nickels into quarters, and quarters into dollars.

In recent years, I've been asked a lot of questions about short-term rentals. I'd like to discuss this regarding how you spend your time because of the time commitment each short-term rental requires. Short-term rentals make a lot of financial sense on paper but there are more moving parts then a standard rental property. Many investors are dabbling in this market to increase properties' income potential. If you can generate more income from the same property then there should be a positive impact on your debt-to-income ratio and in turn, increased loan qualifications, right?

The only ways to improve your debt-to-income ratio are by creating more reportable, taxable incomes that your lender can factor into the equation or by decreasing your fixed expenses. Let's quickly dive into what makes up your incomes and debts. Your "income" is calculated by totaling the gross monthly income before taxes from all sources deemed consistent. The caveat here is that those funds need to be deemed consistent for the underwriter to include them. The fixed expenses that make up your "debt" in the debt-to-income ratio are your mortgage payments (or rent), credit card payments, all loan payments (student, personal, auto, etc.) along with child support and alimony. The debt in your debt-to-income ratio has nothing to do with how often you eat out … unless you are actively adding that debt to your credit card bills. Saving money on optional expenses is important but those optional expenses are probably hurting your reserves, not your global debt. If you're buying avocado toast on credit and paying the interest each month on that expense, you need to change your habits quickly. Alternatively, lowering, AKA improving, your debt-to-income ratio by creatively increasing your "income," the denominator of the debt-to-income ratio, is where people try to make an impact with short-term rentals.

Advertising a bedroom in your home as a short-term rental is a creative way to generate additional income without establishing a long-term lease. Monetizing available space in your home via short-term rental or with a long-term lease is referred to as house hacking. Depending on the circumstances of your location, available space, and community needs, providing a room in your house as a short-term rental could be a lucrative option. When a short-term rental is in your home, there's no travel time to turn over the unit, and the day-to-day maintenance is easy to address. If there's a leak, you'll know. If the room hasn't been occupied in a few days, it costs very little time and effort to clean. Do they need an extra towel? You can knock on the door and deliver it to secure a 5-star review. Also, if the resident sneaks an extra occupant in for the night, you'll know and be able to monetize the guest.

To understand the opportunity and economics of short-term rentals, my partner and I hosted about 10 short-term rentals around our town in houses and apartment buildings. Some were downtown, within walking distance to the big-name hotels; some were up in the hills with views and access to trails. To open the funnel even bigger, there was a range from studios to 3 bedrooms added to the platform. We brought on a Superhost and gave her the responsibility of buying furnishings (with the owner's money), staging the property, marketing the property, and handling all ongoing communications. The Superhost was compensated on a profit-sharing model with the expectation that this would motivate her to perform. We justified partnering with a Superhost because they statistically command increased nightly rates and decreased vacancy.

Overall, we found that the income was greatly increased but the expenses and day-to-day responsibilities outweighed the financial gains. Our units maintained moderate occupancy but didn't maintain 5-star ratings; we averaged 4.5 stars. Additionally, the income wasn't stable. In summer months, the units did great, but in winter months, the income dropped off. Of the 10 Airbnbs, 9 were discontinued by month 12. The only unit that made financial sense to continue running was the unit attached to our personal house. At the time, we lived in a up/down duplex downtown and occupied the ground floor unit. The upstairs unit of our home was 600-square-foot, 1-bedroom, 1-bathroom with a full kitchen and access to a shared fenced-in backyard. This unit was easy to maintain; the management expense was an additional 30-45 minutes per day and more than doubled the unit's revenue. On a long-term lease, this unit rented for about $800 per month while the Airbnb income ranged from $1,200-$2,400 per month depending on the season.

Download a few applications and research short-term rentals in your area. Units may be commanding enough money during good-weather months to quadruple a long-term renter's revenue potential. Does that sound too good to be true? Well, it is! What are the shortcomings of short-term rentals aside from the increased time commitment and financial expenses? The income generated may exceed the expectations of a long-term lease, but is the income being recognized by your mortgage lender? Short-term rental income may not factor into your debt-to-income equation without two years of tax return history. When qualifying for a loan, the underwriter for your mortgage lender needs to determine if incomes are reliable sources of repayment. Unfortunately, the instability of short-term rentals requires additional historical data just like 1099 income. Alternatively, income generated by a long-term lease is viewed as stable income. One hundred percent of your long-term leases' rental income won't be added to your "income" in the equation, but, depending on the lender, 30-80% of the rent should be acknowledged immediately after the lease is signed. This little detail has huge financial consequences on the velocity of your money.

Short-term rentals also require additional day-to-day commitments and expenses. Yes, you need to fully furnish the unit and replace things as they break, but you're also making a mental commitment. Texting and answering questions for your residents doesn't take much time but dynamic pricing takes work. Dynamic pricing will allow you to maximize the nightly revenue from your short-term rental but requires attention. During times of vacancy, dynamic pricing requires you to monitor local competition whenever vacant, sometimes hourly, to make price adjustments. Maybe it's 6 pm and you have no reservation for the night, you'll want to drop your price below your closest competitor to get the bed filled! You may not get the price you wanted, but any dollars are more than $0. Dynamic pricing is now automated on many applications, but you'll have to vet the results.

Also, when you go on a trip, you'll find out how good your cleaner did, how well your stove is working, and you'll see what kind of havoc was wreaked by your residents' Thanksgiving celebration or New Year's party. Outside of the monetary benefits of short-term rentals, when you invite travelers to your home, you take the good with the bad. Sometimes, the room is left spotless, and you never see the guest; other times, the unit is left smelling like a tantric massage session and the sheets inherit the smell of essential oils—true story. Occasionally, you meet like-minded people who turn into friends. I even had a few short-term residents who were visiting town to look for a place to rent long term. It was a great way to transition short-term residents to long-term residents in other properties.

Short-term rentals require attention daily, and one bad review matters. One bad review or host-imposed cancellation will ruin your Superhost status and hurt your future income potential. Keep short-term rentals close to your primary residence or find a very dedicated person who can pay attention to the unit. Cleaners get sick, things break, and handymen sometimes take hours to arrive. When your short-term rental is only steps away, you'll save yourself from 1-star reviews and save money. Example: If a resident requests a fan at bedtime due to the unit being hot, a cleaning lady is sent at 9 pm to deliver this replacement fan across town and charges the property owner $35 for the afterhours delivery. The unit's nightly rate was $70. In the course of one request, you've lost 50% of your nightly rate instead of walking over and delivering it yourself. Some visitors will be easy to please and others won't, but that does not change the fact that each of their reviews matters.

Before committing to a short-term rental strategy, do your research and talk to your mortgage lender. Confirm with the lender that the income generated from your short-term rental will factor into your debt-to-income ratio and have them confirm with their underwriter that short-term rental income will not be a hindrance to your loan or refinance qualifications. This information is vital for a long-term loan qualification plan, you need your investment money to remain active! If the income requires a two-year stabilization period before being acknowledged as income, then this strategy will greatly slow down the velocity of your money. If the income is acknowledged and you attempt to do this on a large scale, consider leasing to a long-standing host and allowing them to sublet or host short-term rentals.

Allowing your lessee to run a short-term rental out of the unit commands an additional 15-25% on your rent rates, guarantees stable monthly income, and that income is in the form of a lease, exactly what your lender wants to see! Make sure your contract states which party is responsible for repairs, appliances, cleaning, and exterior maintenance. Secondly, I believe long-standing hosts with positive reviews have established credibility and can be great residents. A host with long-standing positive reviews is a committed business owner that needs to make regular payments and keep the unit in good shape to continue earning their living. Why charge a short-term rental host an extra 15-20% if they have a proven track record with great reviews? Because you are taking the risk and ultimately liable for your property. What happens if there is a global pandemic and people stop going on vacations for a few months? Does that short-term rental host have any other means to fulfill their financial obligations to your lease? Lastly, you are allowing unscreened strangers to occupy your residence on a regular basis, and it only takes one resident to create a financial burden?

Chapter 6: How to Analyze Deals and Limit Your Risk When Buying

Most people talk about avoiding debt because they don't know the difference between good debt and bad debt. Until I sought financial education, I was only told to steer clear of debt and save. With no education, "steer clear of debt" sounded pretty obvious. After gaining additional financial education, you'll realize the opportunity cost of saving. After telling my father I was buying a 4-plex and using most of my savings to do so, he advised against it. He was a saver and didn't understand the value of good debt. I understood his hesitation but needed to question the advice. My dad had never acquired cash flow by purchasing debt and was lacking the knowledge I needed. I could qualify for debt serviced at 3.5% interest and create 96.5% leverage. To simplify the numbers, for every $3.50, I could buy $96.50 worth of an asset that cash flowed, provided tax benefits, paid itself off, and appreciated over time! If this were reproducible, and every asset were cash flowing, how many assets would you want? If you don't understand the question, let me rephrase it even more simply. If you could qualify for debt and pay 3.5% interest but generate over 15% interest in profit, how much debt would you like to qualify for? Hopefully, you're saying, "I WANT ALL OF IT!" Good! Now you need to learn how to limit your risk, how to run the numbers, and how to position the debt so you can qualify for more.

Maximize your money's potential while limiting your risk by staying liquid. You'll be setting the stage for using other people's money (OPM) for most of your assets-acquisition cost and all of your monthly liabilities. Even though you're utilizing OPM for these costs, you need reserves. You need to keep savings or credit lines available for emergencies and underwriters' liquidity requirements. A banker will want to see at least 6 months' worth of monthly bills as available funds when qualifying you for a loan. Saving is safe and makes you sleep comfortably, but don't keep too much in the bank!

Again, every dollar in the bank is losing value. It's a balance you'll have to maintain, but you always need to have some liquidity. In an emergency, your equity probably won't save you, but your savings and lines of credit will. Think about this and plan ahead when considering paying 5% vs. 20% down payments. If you're analyzing a deal to have OPM pay your monthly liability, does it matter if OPM pays for mortgage insurance? I know it's counterintuitive because of decreased cash flow, but you need money in the bank to acquire more debt! Rent is paying the mortgage and mortgage insurance, so stay liquid for renovations and additional down payments. On a $200,000 house, 5% down payment is $10,000, a 20% down payment is $40,000. Paying 20% instead of 5% or an extra $30,000 to save a couple hundred dollars of cash flow each month by eliminating mortgage insurance is the wrong choice in my eyes. Let's say it's a $200 per month savings to put down an extra $30,000, the return on this investment is $30,000 divided by $200 = 150. That means it will take 150 months or 12.5 years to recuperate that $30,000 that you elected to pay. You're not putting less money down in order to keep money in the bank, you're putting less money down so you're a little closer to your following down payments. I'm going to provide a dramatic example to make my point. Assume these duplexes are identical; I'm simplifying the income and expenses line items to explain this point.

You have $200,000 and want to buy a duplex free and clear. You still have to pay taxes and insurance which amount to $135 per month. You occupy both units, and your residents pay $2,400 per month in rent. On a fully occupied building, you made $2,265 per month * 12 months = $27,180 in year one. How long will it take you to get your money back? It will take you $200,000 divided by $27,180 which equals 7.36 years. The time it would take to return all of your invested capital, AKA your 100% cash-on-cash return is 7.36 years! Yes, this example has been simplified by ignoring repairs, vacancy, rent increases, etc., but the numbers aren't far off. Why do I care about a 100% cash-on-cash return? Once all of your invested capital has been recuperated via rent collections or refi and the asset is cash flowing on a monthly basis, you've moved from making good returns to making infinite returns! Once you cross this threshold, you should be earning an infinite return on your investment for the rest of the time you own it!

What would the numbers look like if you made minimum down payments and used your $200,000 to close four investment loans? For comparison purposes, we'll assume you're buying 4 duplexes identical to the previous examples. Investment loans will require 25% down payments on each $200,000 duplex which is $50,000 per property. The investment loans are locked at 3.5% interest rates with 30-year terms. These loans result in monthly PITI payments (PITI payments are Principal, Interest, Taxes, and Insurance) of approximately $810 per month. $810 per month * 4 buildings * 12 months = $38,880 per year in total PITI payment expense. You rent all eight units in the four duplexes and generate $2,400 per month per building. $2,400 rent * 12 months equals $28,800 per year of rental collections on each building. $28,800 per year * 4 buildings = $115,200 per year in rental collections!

That was a lot of numbers in the previous paragraphs but it's simple math. Work through this example on paper if the numbers get jumbled in your head. For those of you listening to an audiobook, you can focus on the following summary and revisit the numbers whenever convenient. If you purchased four duplexes instead of one with that same $200,000 investment money, you would have collected $115,200 of rent in year one and been liable for $38,880 in PITI payments. After paying the PITI payments, you've generated $76,320 ($115,200 - $38,880) in excess rental collections in year one. What is your term for a full cash-on-cash return? For you to recuperate your $200,000 of invested capital and move to the land of infinite returns, it will take 2.62 years ($200,000 / $76,320 = 2.62 years)! In 2.62 years, you'll have a full return of your capital using this strategy vs. 7.36 years if you had bought one duplex free and clear.

There are additional advantages to using loans when purchasing cash flowing assets, but I want to focus on one advantage, maximizing your leverage. Using leverage to your advantage allowed your $200,000 of capital to purchase $800,000 worth of duplexes instead of $200,000 worth or duplexes. If real estate values increase by 10% during your first year of ownership while earning monthly cash flow, how much equity was generated due to market appreciation? $800,000 worth of duplexes appreciated 10%, this is $80,000 in added equity due to market appreciation alone. If one $200,000 duplex was purchased in that same year, there would have been less monthly cash flow and only $20,000 worth of equity was gained due to market appreciation. You won't be able to access this equity without refinancing or selling the building, but by year 5, if the market keeps improving, there is a great opportunity to refinance and access capital for additional investments. Alternatively, if real estate values go down by 10%

each year, your asset is still cash flowing, and you'll make money each year while waiting for the property values to bounce back! You've lost nothing unless you decide to sell the building.

Quick recap of the above idea:

Instead of collecting $28,800 in rental income in year one using $200,000 and no leverage, you collected $115,200 by utilizing 75% leverage on low-interest debt. Total collections after making PITI payments went from $27,180 to $76,320. Without utilizing leverage, you were able to generate exponential returns after 7.36 years, and after utilizing leverage, you were able to generate infinite returns after only 2.62 years. Not that you want to, but the cash flow generated in this example can pay off all four duplexes with rental collections in 7.86 years, without increasing rent. How was 7.86 years to pay off the buildings calculated? The calculation isn't completely accurate because there are missing variables to consider; however, it's close. I determined this 7.86-year principal pay down with the following math problem. $150,000 principal balance per building * 4 buildings = $600,000 in principal mortgage balance across all four duplex loans. $600,000 principal balance divided by the $76,320 annual cash flow = 7.86 years to pay off the principal. This exercise hopefully shows you that you can lose years by not being efficient with your decisions!

Above, I suggested that you don't want to pay off buildings. Why wouldn't you want to pay off buildings? If you don't want to pay them off, do you want to pay them down? After some education, you'll realize a few reasons to leave low-interest debt in place. First, with low-interest, highly leveraged debt available, if you have equity in a building, you should be tapping into the usable capital to grow your asset base. When you do this, you will put a large check in the bank and continue making monthly PITI payments with OPM. The OPM, in this case, is your resident's rent collection. If your debt is fixed at 3, 4, or 5%, how confident are you that you can make a margin on that debt? In other words, do you feel confident that you can generate more than 3, 4 or 5% returns from your investments each month? I hope so! Secondly, you can't write off an interest expense on your taxes to shelter income if you aren't paying interest. Lastly, not only is there an opportunity cost to leaving equity untapped, but buildings with a lot of equity are targets in the event of a lawsuit.

Stay leveraged; you're cash flowing over your payments, and you don't want to be a deep-pocket defendant if somebody falls down the stairs. It's not your choice whether you pay down your principal balance or not; you need to be making your monthly PITI payments so you're paying down your principal. Over the years I've asked many lenders if they have an interest only loan option. I have not found an advantageous product that would allow my PITI payment to be reduced to an ITI payment (interest, taxes, and insurance) but if I found an interest only option with low rates, I would be excited to explore the opportunity. With that said, since you're paying the principal down but don't want to pay it off, I suggest refinancing or selling using a tax deferred strategy (example: 1031 exchange) once there is excess equity available to you. To help determine at what point excess equity should be tapped, please refer to the exit strategies section of this book.

I am not an attorney, and laws are different state by state, but I strongly suggest holding title to your real estate assets in LLCs on top of staying leveraged to protect those assets. Hire a local real estate attorney and learn how to structure your ownership correctly. You should be shielding yourself from any lawsuits coming from within your rental property, and you want to shield any incidents that may happen outside of the asset from being able to go backwards and touch your buildings. By utilizing LLCs, you can accomplish these two forms of protection and provide yourself anonymity. My assets are all held by individual entities and each of those entities has a parent entity. It isn't expensive or time consuming to accomplish this, but you do need to learn and act! If you did not purchase your asset in the name of an LLC, it's okay and not too late. You can transfer title to your assets into an LLC with minimal paperwork or effort. In Colorado, this is an easy and inexpensive process. It requires filing a notarized quitclaim deed with the county's clerk and recorder. A quitclaim deed is a simple document that allows owners to change the legal ownership names on property.

Once the title has been transferred, do not forget to notify your insurance company. In the event of an insurance claim, if the insurance policy does not match the title holder's name, the claim likely won't be covered. Ask if you can name the LLC holding title as "additionally insured" to avoid any unnecessary communication with the mortgage holder. Your mortgage company may see this and require you transfer title back into your name, if this happens, file another quitclaim deed as needed and play the game. Seek counsel and file the correct paperwork before an incident occurs! Be preemptive, not reactionary or you will regret it.

Run the numbers—you need to qualify your debt as good debt. To analyze properties and determine their potential, you need to establish qualifying factors. The qualifying factors that a property must meet won't be the same for every market and is partially dependent on the investor's goals. Secondly, determine baseline qualifying factors that help you weed out low potential properties quickly. After a property passes your basic assessment, deep dive into the numbers!

Quick background on my market: I'm investing in a county of approximately 150,000 people, with a rapidly growing university. Our university is the fifth largest employer in the county. We're in a top-10 retirement state, and my county happens to be the warmest county in the state. As of 2021, the average wage is $47,400, average home price is $245,000, and our vacancy rate has been under 4% for years. Our top employers are in education, healthcare, and government.

You need to first pick your market by using available resources and establishing metrics. There are lots of online resources such as www.census.gov's "Access Local Data" tab and great books such as Long-Distance Real Estate Investing by David M Greene. There are entire books dedicated to helping early investors pick their market; leverage this information for your benefit. I was lucky enough to attend college in a community that was ripe with opportunity. Rents were high relative to home prices (price-to-rent ratio), the retirement and education sectors were growing, vacancy was near nonexistent, we had the only VA hospital within a four-hour drive, and the top employers were in three different sectors, healthcare, education, and government. I had personally seen a lot of growth during my years at college and anticipated growth to continue. Additionally, I found the community to be beautiful, friendly, and full of potential. At the end of the day, I was excited to live there and thought others would be too. There is not one right market, there are lots of markets and lots of opportunities. You'll find innumerable opportunities in many markets, but your niche may change.

I suggest sticking with your market after making an initial investment and growing your portfolio locally. It's a lot of work to build a team; save time by doing this once. Also, once you've grown a healthy portfolio, you'll gain negotiating power to mitigate expenses. Once the market is picked, you need to be analyzing deals. When analyzing a property, you should run the numbers and feel confident that all payments and repairs will be covered by rental income.

The initial questions you should analyze when qualifying a property are:
- Can I establish $300 per month per door in profit when occupied?
- Can I pay all expenses while maintaining 50% occupancy?
- Can you build enough equity to cover your total out of pocket expense?
- Can I get all my invested capital back in 18 months?

First, can you establish $300 per month per door in profit? Your pro forma calculator will be invaluable when doing this exercise. You are working to establish long-term cash flow, so you need to understand your long-term expenses and income. Expect your income and expenses to fluctuate but minimize this variability wherever possible. An example of this would be disqualifying properties subject to a homeowner's association (HOA). HOA dues are not fixed; they can change annually. Only lock in long-term debt that you can make profit off of! You're analyzing the numbers with as many certainties as possible. If an HOA can affect your profitability annually, then you've just added an unknown annual expense into the long-term analysis. You can use a property manager or online resources to first estimate your rental rates, then use those rates to calculate a gross income when occupied. Once you have income, decrease it by your local vacancy rate and move onto expenses. There are a lot of expenses to be totaled but you're looking for a ballpark number, not an exact number. I total the following expenses: approximated PITI payment, management fees at 10% of collections, depending on the properties condition, I estimate 5-8% of collections for maintenance, and lastly, I include an estimation of utility expenses. You do not need to be exact at this stage, you want to be close. After you go under contract on a property, you can request exact numbers from the seller to refine calculations.

Second, can you pay all expenses while maintaining 50% occupancy? This is not based on the rents that the current landlord is generating; this is based on the rents the asset SHOULD be generating. Buying properties with under market rents means you're buying a property with potential or you're buying a property with a lot of deferred maintenance. It might be a winner, or it might be a loser; you'll complete your due diligence after it's under contract. My county's vacancy rate has been under 4% for years. What are the odds of maintaining a 50% vacancy rate within a property for an extended period? This is unlikely with prompt renovations and good property management. Being capable of sustaining monthly payments on an asset in the unlikely event that you have 50% vacancy provides a lot of confidence! With this gained confidence and some experience, you will feel more comfortable stretching your purchasing power and leveraging up into more assets. You can quickly run the numbers on this by revisiting your pro forma calculator from the last exercise.

Third, can you build enough equity to cover the out-of-pocket expense to acquire and occupy the asset? Depending on your loan type and the properties condition, this could range from $1,000 of equity to over 50% of the purchase price. Adding equity is usually accomplished by inheriting under market rents, purchasing for under market value, and by adding sweat equity.

You will likely add equity to your asset with each of these variables. Do not plan on market appreciation to add equity! You need to play an active role building equity if you want control over the outcome. Market appreciation is the cherry on top; again, do not acquire a property and expect market appreciation to generate equity. Buying a property at under market value will probably take a lot of offers. You never know when an offer will be accepted, so don't be shy about submitting them.

Set realistic expectations for the after-renovation value, ARV, by having your real estate agent locate high value comparative sales. Once you have an anticipated max ARV, you can work backwards. Will your long-term financing loan require a $1,000 down payment or a 20% down payment? If your long-term loan requires a 20% down payment, then you need to generate at least 20% equity. In this scenario subtract a minimum of 20% from the anticipated ARV. Secondly, subtract your anticipated renovation costs to occupy the asset from your ARV. By subtracting these two expenses, you have determined your top of budget purchase price. When buying a property with major maintenance issues, your acquisition may require private or hard-money lenders prior to establishing a long-term loan.

When you utilize a private or hard-money lender, the interest is high, and you need to move fast. Do not forget to include the carrying costs of your high-interest loan into the total project cost. If there is a lot of deferred maintenance and you're required to borrow high-interest money for acquisition, then there needs to be large equity potential. Sellers love cash offers that close quickly so factor that appeal into the equation when making your offer. After closing with high-interest funds. your goal is to quickly refinance and pay off the high interest debt. In a best-case scenario. you can generate much more than 20% equity and get cash out when refinancing. Don't forget, all funds cashed out on a refinance are tax free since the funds are issued as debt. What does it mean for the funds to be issued as debt? "It" meaning you're paying that money back to your lender over the term of your loan.

And last but not least, can you recapture all of your invested capital in 18 months? This metric is highly dependent on your acquisition financing, how much equity you can generate during your project, and the amount of time it takes to complete renovations. To determine your total out-of-pocket expense, add your down payment, closing costs, carrying costs, and an estimation of the renovations required to reach 100% occupancy. Your renovation number will be inaccurate because of your limited information at this stage. You can roughly estimate this number by looking at pictures and reading the property description. If the building is being purchased with full occupancy, it makes this estimation easier, but either way, don't overestimate at this stage. Once you're under contract you will be refining this number.

Your total out-of-pocket expense will also fluctuate greatly based on your loan type and down payment requirement. For example: If you're purchasing a property without deferred maintenance using a low down payment, owner occupied option, then you may recuperate all of your invested capital with cash flow alone within 18 month. If your acquisition strategy requires a large down payment. then you will likely need to renovate and refinance the asset to return your capital in 18 months. There are lots of ways to buy a property, but you are working to build a portfolio in the fastest way possible. To ensure that the velocity of your money is maximized, always consider how long it will take to return your invested capital. If it takes over 18 months to get your initial investment back, consider passing on the deal or look for a different acquisition strategy. If you eagerly purchase a property without an exit strategy that returns 100% of your capital, then you have taken a wrong turn on your journey to financial freedom and probably cost yourself years.

If your property passed the initial round of qualifying factors, then it's time to deep dive into the numbers.

First, your expenses. If you haven't done this already, download or search for a PITI payment calculator. There are countless free options to choose from online, they all work the same. Make sure your calculator includes mortgage amount, loan term, interest rate, annual taxes, and annual insurance. You want these numbers to be as accurate as possible. Plug in the numbers to determine your monthly PITI payment based on current interest rates, loan terms, taxes from the county's assessor, and an insurance quote from your insurance representative. Side note, lock in 30-year terms to improve cash flow and pay with tomorrow's money. I want to keep today's dollars, as they're more valuable than tomorrow's. Again, PITI stands for Principal, Interest, Taxes, and Insurance.

There are lots of free web-based versions of these calculators. They're simple to use; gathering the information is the hard part. Don't guess when filling in the blanks, look up the data and use real numbers. Call an insurance agent to get a quote; it will cost you only a few minutes on the phone. Lastly, text your rockstar lender to request current interest rates. When texting the lender, say, "I'm running the numbers on a 4-plex. I need interest rates for owner-occupied and investment loans with the lowest possible down payment option, my credit score is X, and the building's address is X. Have you locked rates on something like this recently?"

After you collect the numbers, it's time to plug them in. Write down your monthly PITI payment liability and open your deal analysis spreadsheet. Your PITI payment cost goes at the top of your sheet right next to the address. Insurance and property taxes will fluctuate a little annually, but I disregard the variability when analyzing a purchase. After determining your PITI payment, use your deal analysis spreadsheet to calculate your potential income and additional expenses.

The income portion of your spreadsheet is simple but critical. It should require the number of units, the monthly rent on each of those units, and other potential income sources that you can charge a fee or premium for including. These are additional income-producing sources on top of your rent. Don't miss these line items! Some of the additional income-producing items are comfort items that residents appreciate having while others are fees imposed on a resident. Comfort items would include things like, access to coin-operated laundry on site, storage units, gym access, high-speed internet, etc. Imposed fees are additional income producing items imposed on residents to mitigate the property owner's risk. A few examples of these income producing sources would be additional resident rent, pet rents, credit risk mitigation fees, utility reimbursements, etc.

This spreadsheet will also have inputs for your expenses. Principle, interest, taxes, and insurance are already taken into account, so you'll need to input economic vacancy—use your local vacancy rate, utility costs, anticipated maintenance, property management costs, etc. Based on the properties location and condition, there could be additional expense line items to include. Examples are snow removal, state required property inspections, pool maintenance. I'll go through many of these line items below, but this isn't where the list ends, your property may have unique circumstances to account for.

Let's take a closer look at some additional income items we should consider:

- PETS: Let's start with something every landlord should know: You can NOT charge for service or emotional support animals. Require each pet's documentation to eliminate the mandatory monthly charge. With that being said, if you do not allow pets, residents will often sneak them in. I strongly suggest allowing pets and charging for them. I also want to encourage honesty about pet ownership. To encourage this, don't ask if your applicants have pets; ask how many pets they have. Have a pet policy that is known and make sure all parties sign it. You should be setting a limit and unlinking what behaviors are considered lease violations and grounds for fines or an eviction. You can charge a flat monthly rate for each pet, like $50 per month per pet, or a range of prices based on the animal and size, like $50 per month per pet or a range of prices based on the animal and size, like $50 per month per cat and small dogs under 25 pounds and $70 per month per dog over 25 pounds. You can also charge a variable rate for other pets, like birds, fish, or turtles. It sounds odd charging for pet fish, but a broken fish tank can cause a lot of damage!

Pet rents will add to your cash flow, and more cash flow helps your appraisals and future loan qualifications. Two pets at $50 per month is $1,200 per year in additional income. Remember, in properties with five units or more, Value = NOI / Cap Rate. When evaluating on a 7% Cap Rate; VALUE = $1,200 / .07; Value = $17,142.86. Charging for two pets will improve your properties value by $17,142.86 if it's being appraised using the income approach on a 7% Capitalization Rate. This is powerful! How much equity would be generated if the property was being appraised at a 5% or 6% Capitalization Rate?

- Additional Resident Rent: Again, encourage honesty in your application process by asking how many residents will need a key and monetize each resident. You can monitor this by purchasing a smart key system with programmable keys. By issuing smart keys, the residents will need to rent additional keys or leave their unit unlocked if additional residents are occupying the space. Much like pets, you should be performing periodic property inspections. When conducting inspections, it's typically easy to determine if additional residents are occupying the unit. In a one-bedroom unit, one key is provided to the lessee. If additional keys are needed, those keys are rented for a monthly fee. This imposed fee should vary based on the space and amenities being utilized by the additional resident.

In rentals priced at under $1,000 per month, a key rental of $25 per month is affordable. The imposed cost per month for an additional key rental should increase with a more expensive property but set an affordable limit. Why charge less for an additional resident key than a pet? Because people are smart, and you do not want to encourage deception. You want the resident to identify and be accountable for their additional resident as opposed to leaving the door unlocked or hiding a key. $25 per month doesn't sound like a lot, but this is an easy way to add $300 to your annual income. Each additional resident causes wear and tear along with additional utility usage. You should be monetizing additional residents because they're creating additional expenses for the property owner. Verify that local locksmiths cannot duplicate your smart keys. This is an important detail.

- Coin Operated Laundry: Consider outsourcing this to a third-party company that will maintain the machines on a profit-sharing model. This eliminates all your work on-site in laundry rooms. The machines are consistently maintained, digital payments eliminate stealing, and you're keeping most of the collections after the rental fee without dedicating your staff for upkeep. The company I utilize collects the first $30 per machine per month and 30% of all additional collections. I receive 70% of all funds collected over their initial $30 per machine requirement which is electronically transferred into my account each month. This is a Win-Win-Win scenario for everyone involved. You have an additional income-producing source that tenants need, the tenant has access to laundry services on site, and a third-party is providing the maintenance for the laundry services being used by the tenants. Maintaining the machines and collecting coins is not the most efficient use of your time! Please don't do it. Alternatively, if your units has laundry hookups, think about increasing your rent but do not include machines. If you include a washing machine that leaks, the damage was caused by your machine, and it's your expense. If the resident's washing machine leaks, it's the resident's machine and the resident's cost to repair. If the economics and space don't allow you to provide laundry, analyze the shortcoming before letting it terminate your deal. There's likely a laundromat nearby; don't make it an automatic disqualifier.

- Utility Reimbursement: Utility costs increase annually, especially Gas and Electric. Plan for your annual year-over-year costs to increase by 3-13%, depending on the service. Start charging a flat utility reimbursement for each of your renters to reimburse you, the owner, for paying electricity, gas, water, sewer, and trash. We will discuss internet separately. Once all units are paying a utility reimbursement, then you can eliminate the variable electric costs by installing solar and utilizing a low-interest solar loan. Once you have a fixed electrical cost you can establish a flat reimbursement amount that is profitable. I've even seen models where a usage meter is installed on each unit and the residents are billed back at current market rates based on how many kWh were consumed. Your solar payment is fixed, as the cost of electricity increases annually, your profit margin will now increase as well. Additionally, if you need a new roof prior to getting solar installed, you can roll the roof-replacement cost into your total tax credit for installing solar. At current time in the USA, there's a 26% tax credit available on that total cost! Still not worth the headache to consider adding solar debt? Look up your local services to determine the rate of increase in your area. In my area, gas increased by almost 14% in the last year, electric by around 4%, and next year, electricity costs will be increasing by over 12%. Those numbers are really motivating.

- Internet Reimbursement: There are a couple of ways to do this, but every resident wants internet and will purchase the utility to maintain access. For personal residences, finding monthly internet service for under $35 per month is very unlikely. If you can get fast service to the building for $99 per month and broadcast the services, it only takes three residents at $35 per month to make a profit. You can utilize local service providers and a networking company to broadcast internet to the entire building and recuperate that cost with an internet reimbursement line item in your leases. Advertise this as a savings to the resident and create an additional income stream on your cash flow statement. Another way to approach this income producing strategy would be to have high speed internet service connected to one building and broadcast that connection via radios between buildings. To accomplish this, you need a networking company and a line of sight between buildings. This is a great strategy if you have nearby assets with high rooflines. Accomplishing this is an expensive one-time cost but, long term, it helps consolidate bills for easy audit, maximizes your high-speed connection, and minimizes monthly expenses to increase cash flow.

- Storage: If you have unused space in your building, on your property, or a storage shed, clean it out, figure out how to secure it, and monetize the space! Do you have a yard that requires maintenance or active landscaping? Eliminate the expense by putting some form of storage in its place or fence it off and rent it back to a resident for their own private use. Your lease needs to define where belongings can be on the property and what items are allowed. If residents think they can collect belongings outside for free, then trash will accumulate. Make sure you or your PM perform drive-bys and post lease violations quickly. If a nonfunctioning car has been sitting, then ensure the resident has been posted with a notice to cure. If ignored, get it towed before another broken car shows up. Many people are addicted to collecting things. How many storage unit facilities do you drive by on a daily basis? Monetize your resident's need to collect by offering a local storage solution for a monthly fee. For dedicated storage access, $40-60 per month added as a line item on their lease is a great value add. Make a few phone calls and determine local prices for storage units. Your prices are likely much more affordable than the competition. It's not all income; you have maintenance expenses for these storage units as well. They often get damaged and vandalized, which requires some paint and siding repair, but residents appreciate the extra space and your properties' eye appeal will improve once belongings are housed in a closed storage.

- Credit Risk Mitigation Fees: This isn't a standard income, but I'd like to touch on it. After your PM screens a resident, you'll find out the good, bad, and sometimes ugly truth about their financial and criminal history. Some screening reports come back positive but have horrible credit. When that happens, ask for more information before denying them. If my applicant has bad or no credit but maintains good savings, has long-term employment, and has no criminal or eviction history, I like to approve them and apply a credit risk mitigation fee. This fee is an additional monthly charge on top of rent and typically coincides with a larger "security deposit" insurance plan. This additional monthly credit risk mitigation fee is waived upon lease renewal if the resident pays on time and in full during their initial lease term. The offered decrease in monthly charges after the lease term expires needs to be communicated. This savings for the resident is an incentive for good payment history and for multiyear tenancy.

And now for expenses:

- Economic Vacancy: You may say, "I'll never have a vacant unit because the need in my town is so high" or "I have friends who want to rent it immediately, and I'll generate income on day one." That may be true, but it's also very short sighted. The vacancy or, most importantly, the economic vacancy is any time you're not generating rental income. Before a resident moves into a property, it takes time to prepare the unit. You need to factor time for changing the locks, completing repairs, cleaning, possibly taking new marketing photos, marketing the unit, showing the unit to prospects, screening applicants, and, finally, executing a lease. That's a lot of steps and rarely takes under two weeks to complete. That time is your economic vacancy. Depending on your lease terms and the quality of your residents, you may be lucky enough to do this every two to three years, but there will be years when residents turn over quickly. Don't rush through your screening process. Do not expedite the process and move in a resident due to a sob story or urgent move in need. Collect all the data, meet the pets, research additionally after your PM sends you their findings, but don't pick based on emotions; pick based on data. Minimize your economic vacancy by minimizing bad residents. The average US tenancy is approximately two and a half years, good luck!

- Utility Costs: Water and sewer are costs imposed by your local municipality. If these utilities go unpaid, they'll create a lien against your property. Don't be caught holding this bill down the road with a lien on your property. Property owners should pay these bills and charge them back to the residents inside of the rent or with a ratio utility billing system. A ratio utility billing system or R.U.B.S. for short, divides your monthly cost between all units equally and charges the applicable costs back to the resident. Organizing this is automated if your PM is using good management software, discuss it with them. R.U.B.S. eliminates the variable utility expense with a zero sum. Alternatively, flat chargebacks inside of the rent could create a profit or loss depending on usage. As the property owner, you should keep trash service in your name as well. Call multiple providers, negotiate your costs, leverage signing a long-term contract with your service provider and keep the trash service active. You do not want a resident collecting trash in anticipation of making a dump run down the road. Keep the trash off your property, the broken window theory plays out. If one unit turns into a trash collecting nightmare, the trend will spread. Internet, electricity, and gas are utilities you'll need to address case by case. Think about including internet to multifamily buildings with over four units. Buildings with four units or less, leave as a resident responsibility. On over-four-unit properties, establish a high-speed connection and blanket the property with Wi-Fi. It's a value add to your residents and requires a minimal fee inside of rent to compensate for the service.

Gas and Electric are less clear cut. When a static utility rate is applied monthly, it can lead to abuse. If a resident knows they pay $150 per month for utilities, no matter how much they use, what will keep them from wasting power or water? I haven't seen it happen yet, but I've been concerned about cryptocurrency miners moving in. This would be a problem because of the massive amount of energy those machines require, making the resident money every hour and costing the owner. You can combat this fear in a few ways, adding a utility reimbursement lease addendum that addresses excess usage is one approach. This has minimized the concern of flat rate chargebacks being leveraged against the property owner, but it requires all units be sub-metered and monitored. If flat utility reimbursements are included, then work with your PM or attorney to draft an addendum that defines what usage is deemed abuse and defines a penalty for the lease addendum violation.

- Expected Maintenance: This is a hard number to lock down and is dependent on lots of variables. A few examples of these variables include when your structure was built, labor costs in your area, existing HVAC setup, age of wiring, quality of the previously completed renovations, along with pickiness of the resident and owner. I factor 7-9% of gross collections going back into the property as repairs and maintenance. When completing repairs, use long-term value-conscious products. Be mindful to not over-improve. It doesn't matter what you would prefer to live with, this is for a resident, not you! I mitigate these expenses by using long-term products that have warranties and are area appropriate.

One example would be installing hard flooring throughout your unit, eliminating carpeting everywhere you can, will save you time and money down the road. Always install waterproof products and make sure they allow you to replace one piece without taking apart a full room. Look for 25-year warrantied peel and stick luxury vinyl plank flooring. Using a heat gun allows you to quickly remove and replace one plank in the middle of the room, which saves a lot of labor hours and material costs during turnover. To eliminate annual labor hours on turn over sealing tile grout lines, spend a little more when tiling and use an epoxy-based grout. When updating rooms or installing drywall, use a texture that can be easily matched during future patching. Annually service the existing HVAC to extend the life of your big-ticket items and try to assign that tech multiple work orders while they're on site. Depending on your rental's location and quality, decide between installing formica, tile, or concrete countertops. Unless you have a unique situation, never install granite in a rental. Consider xeriscaping when possible, to eliminate landscaping and water costs. Also, eliminate locks that require a locksmith for rekeying to save time and money securing the unit between residents.

- Material suggestions: order your faucets, sinks, lighting fixtures, medicine cabinets, door hardware, etc. online! You'll save a lot of money by avoiding last-second purchasing of these items from big box stores. Save money on labor by NOT ordering the cheapest materials. Don't buy the cheapest option every time, purchase materials you expect to last (especially for sink and shower faucets). Watch a YouTube video on pouring concrete countertops and send the link to your handyman; it's easy and cheap if done correctly. Labor is the bulk of the cost. After your handyman watches the video, ask them to bid this job. If the job is rushed and measurements aren't taken correctly then they won't fit, and he'll have to start over. Always buy used appliances in place of new! When homeowners update their personal household's kitchen, they often eliminate functioning appliances because of the color. This is an easy opportunity to save a lot of money! Consider buying all used appliances in the same color so they can be purchased when available and stored for a time you need. If you create a standard and buy the same color appliances for every unit then you can move appliances around in an emergency and they'll always match. Take advantage of new trends by buying the old trends for your rental. Every $1,000 you save is $1,000 you can leverage into another asset. Overspending on materials and maintenance will compound and set you back years!

- Property Management (PM) expenses: Approximately 10-12% of your collections will be retained by your PM for their cost of service. Your PM will likely advertise anywhere from an 8-15% fee on collections. A PM's role is vital to your success. There are a lot of moving parts to their job and there are a lot of places to hide fees. Communicate that you want them to collect fees from your applicants and don't fight them on their collection's percentage; you want them on your team and motivated to collect as much money each month as possible. Pick a great PM; don't pick the cheapest one. Also, don't nitpick the property manager for their application, lease up, or marketing fees. If the property manager lets you handle maintenance, increases rents to market rates, has good collections, handles evictions cost effectively, and is responsive to your requests, then let them make their percentage of income and fees. The best thing you can do for your properties' performance is to motivate your PM by helping them make more money. Giving a PM the opportunity to make more money if they make you more money helps everyone and aligns interests.

After getting these numbers together and plugging them into your spreadsheet, revisit the first two qualifying factors above. Can the building produce $300 per month per door of profit once occupied? Can you pay your bills while maintaining 50% occupancy? Determining if the property can cash flow and hit your needed metrics will guide you on how to proceed. Use numbers not emotions when making acquisition decisions. Determine at what price the project makes sense and make an offer! It's okay if they say no; you're abiding by your numbers not emotions. If they say no, move on, and make more offers. When you get a property under contract for the price that you're comfortable with, then you are set up for success.

My lender once told me, "You make your money at the time of

purchase." This is a powerful statement that I've thought about a lot. I partially disagree with this statement. Simply put, what my lender was saying was that not every property could be made profitable. She was correct when applying the statement to a short time window, but time is on every owner's side. Yes, recuperating 100% of working capital is hard or impossible to accomplish in 18 months if you overpay on day one.

Overpaying for a property in 2008 before the big crash was painful for many years, but if the owner cash flowed as a rental and waited until 2021 to sell, they probably did pretty well for themselves. What is the long-term trend of real estate values in America? Long answer short, the values have increased since 1900 at a similar rate to inflation, which can be approximated to 3% annually. If you overpaid when purchasing in 2008 with the plan of making quick renovations and selling the asset, you probably lost money. Alternatively, if you overpaid in 2008 but evaluated the property to hold and cash flow, the lost equity was not a loss because you didn't sell. The amount of equity you build into an asset is greatly hinged on the initial purchase price but monthly cash flow doesn't depend on equity. If you overpay on day one, penny pinching during renovations to make up for the loss probably won't solve your problem. What will solve your problem is buying for cash flow, maintaining that cash flow with good management, and holding the asset long term. Luckily, if you evaluated the property correctly, it's easy to hold the asset and cash flow long term! After all, your residents are paying all the bills and some.

On top of determining your cash flow, you need to make sure the asset will suit your proposed exit strategy. We will discuss exit strategies later, but the takeaway here again is to always evaluate for cash flow. In a worst-case scenario, you can hold the property long term. If the property cash flows and the market dips, you can afford to be patient, and patience has historically led to restored property values. Give yourself TIME because TIME is a property owner's friend. Another way to look at this is the idea of a buoy. Money in the bank doesn't fluctuate like a buoy but your assets do. The market is going to fluctuate, but if the long-term trend is upward, then let your buoy ride the wave. Don't fight inflation, plan for this by investing in an asset that buoys with the market.

Real estate values can adjust rapidly, but the demand is ever increasing and the replacement cost, AKA cost to build, is also ever increasing. If you can create a position of leverage with your dollar and acquire an asset that fluctuates with the market, the question you need to ask is if the market, as a whole, is going to improve over time. That's for you to decide. Where does housing fall on Maslow's hierarchy of needs? It falls on the first tier,

Physiological Needs. These needs include food, water, clothing, sleep, and shelter! Housing will always be a need and in high demand, obviously in higher demand when in desirable locations. With this in mind along with increased replacement costs, anticipate home values and rents will continue to increase with the existing 100-year trend. Additionally, depending on the rate of inflation, values may increase faster than they have historically. Think through it, plan, hypothesize, ACT, problem solve, plan, hypothesize, and ACT again. Do not be static, make a plan, execute your plan, review the progress, and make changes if needed.

Lastly, how to position debt and payments so you can qualify for more debt and payments. If you've ever looked at qualifying for a home loan, then you'll be familiar with DTI. DTI is your debt-to-income ratio. This is a critical qualifying factor that lenders must calculate to approve a borrower for a loan. Debt-to-income ratio is a simple calculation; it's all of your monthly debt payments divided by your annual income before taxes. Debt payments are all of your bills that go towards paying for borrowed money. Debt payments don't include your utility bills, food, or hobby costs. Some examples of debt would be credit card payments, vehicle loan payments, student loan payments, mortgage payments, and rents. In calculating your DTI, your lender is proving to their underwriter that your income is high enough to support additional debt, AKA more borrowed money! Minimizing your debt payments by choosing longer loan payback terms is an easy way to extend your borrowing potential. When making offers, always consider the impact to your DTI. How can you structure the deal in a way that benefits this ratio? If you're purchasing a property with healthy cash flow, it should lower your DTI, AKA improve your DTI. After running the numbers, ask your lender if you should keep cash in the bank or pay off lines of credit. Maintaining this ratio along with your liquidity is a balancing act that you should coordinate with your lender! Do not pay off a debt to see a $0 balance, pay off debt based on the implications it has on your DTI.

Chapter 7: Exit Strategies!
Consider the Velocity of Your Money

You need to consider exit strategies when evaluating a purchase. Evaluating exit strategies at time of purchase is NOT putting the cart before the horse. This is a critical component to your long-term success. The exits you'll consider are refinancing after repositioning, selling, or leaving the acquisition debt in place long term. All these options hopefully work out to a net-positive outcome, but which one will provide the most favorable long-term benefit to your bank account? Let's go through them below:

Exit Strategy One: Refinance to return your capital while keeping the asset.

This is always my goal. We've already determined that the property cash flows during pre-purchase analysis, so why not keep the asset? At a minimum, you want your out-of-pocket cost to be $0 by month 18. This allows you to keep the money working while the acquired asset cash flows, depreciates on your taxes, and appreciates in value over time. When I say $0 out of pocket, I mean $0 out of pocket. You want to have all of your invested renovation capital and down payment money back in the bank and available for another deal. We are not factoring in your monthly payments to keep the property; those monthly payments should be covered by rent collections. You can do this with an owner-occupied loan then an owner-occupied cash out refinance after the work has been completed.

Alternatively, this can be accomplished with an investment loan if you're not the owner occupying the property and there is enough equity. To accomplish this short-term reposition on an investment property, I often utilize high-interest funds via hard-money or private lenders to acquire and renovate. To utilize high-interest debt, you need to have an exit strategy in mind and confidence in the asset's value-add potential. Hopefully, your cash flow covers 100% of the high-interest payments, but either way, you need to get out of that money quickly. Even if rent covers your carrying cost, high-interest debt negatively impacts your borrowing potential and absorbs your cash flow. You need to refinance and pay off that high-interest loan as soon as possible so your cash flow is feeding your bank account and available to leverage. You will accomplish this by promptly renovating after closing, increasing rents to market rates, fully occupying the building, and starting on a bank refinance. The renovations and high rents, hopefully, justify the after-renovation value you were anticipating!

Depending on the asset, you may need to establish leases then let them season for six to 12 months before a bank will consider refinancing the asset! If you get stuck with a seasoning period, then make additional calls and try to locate a lender that does not have the same seasoning requirements. A mortgage broker could be an asset in these situations. A mortgage broker will gather all of the pertinent information for your refinance and present the deal to a large number of lenders to see who may be an available option. Using a broker typically costs one or two percent of the total loan amount but saves you time and headache speaking with lenders. That broker can also save you months of high-interest payments if they get you to the closing table quickly. Required seasoning periods on lease income is an important detail; make sure you clarify the seasoning time with your lender. Your lender will likely be able to establish a maximum of 70-75% loan-to-value (LTV) for your refinance.

For number crunching purposes, let's assume you're refinancing with a 75% LTV mortgage. That 25% equity requirement imposed by the bank can be in the form of your added equity! If you purchase an asset for $250,000, and after renovations, your asset is appraised at $350,000, then the bank will lend 75% of the appraised value, $262,500. Not only will you not be bringing money to the closing table, but they'll also cut you a check for the excess $12,500. Any excess equity you can cash out at closing is considered as being borrowed from your lender. Since you're paying back those funds, that money is debt and is 100% tax free! This is an amazing tool and is always the goal; however, you may need to be creative to access a cash-out option— which we will discuss in a later chapter.

Prior to refinancing with a bank, you can have a hard-money lender or private lender put a loan in place for 75% of your expected appraised value. After establishing this new note at 75% of your expected appraisal, you can go to your bank and refinance with a typical rate and term loan. In structuring the deal this way, you're taking the excess funds out before your long-term bank debt is established instead of taking the excess funds from the bank directly. Now, what happens if the asset you purchased for $250,000 appraises for $300,000 and you're using that same 75% LTV loan? Seventy-five percent of $300,000 is $225,000 and the bank won't lend more than that amount. If you don't build enough equity, you'll be required to bring $25,000 to the closing table when refinancing to meet the investment loans 25% equity requirement. If the property doesn't match your goals and you can't afford to refinance this loan, the solution to save money may be to move into the asset and refinance with an owner-occupied product.

As discussed earlier, there are lots of different down payment requirements based on the loan type. Owner-occupied loans can range from $0 down to 20% of the purchase price as a minimum down payment requirement. In addition to owner occupied loans qualifying for higher loan-to-value ratios, you can expect lower interest rates, easier underwriting, and they typically allow for a cash-out option. A cash-out refinance option will increase your interest rate slightly, but it's still worth doing. That increased interest rate likely increases your monthly payments by under $75 per month and that $75 per month is being paid with OPM. Your goal is to always have your money back and available as working capital for future investments. Let OPM pay your bills. When running the numbers to determine an exit strategy on an investment loan, your goal is to add a minimum of 25% equity by the time of appraisal. This equity can be gained with property improvements, increased rents, or, occasionally, by taking advantage of market conditions. Why do investment loans require at least 25% equity to be left in the asset? This is for the lender's security in the event that a foreclosure takes place. In the event of a foreclosure, the bank can discount the asset and resell it at 25% under market value to recuperate the money they lent.

Example: You're buying a property for $200,000 that will take $50,000 to renovate. You expect the property's after-renovation value (ARV) to be $350,000. You want to get all of your invested capital back out and maximize your debt position when refinancing but the investment loan doesn't allow cash-out refinances. Instead of borrowing $200,000 to purchase the asset, you borrow 75% of the $350,000 ARV. You can do this before or after renovations. In this example, let's say you did it before renovating. You borrow 75% of $350,000, $262,500. At closing, you are cut a check for the difference between the purchase price and borrowed funds, $62,500. You set up automatic payments for your debt servicing and get to work on renovations immediately. After renovations are complete, you establish leases and go to your lender to start the refinance process. When pulling the title on the house, your lender sees the existing $262,500 note in place. The property appraises, as you expected, for $350,000 and the lender's maximum 75% LTV allowance on the loan is, drum roll please, $262,500. This is great news! Now, at closing, your lender pays off the $262,500 note and replaces the private high-interest renovation debt with long-term low-interest bank debt. After buying and renovating, your all-in cost was $200,000 for the purchase and $50,000 for renovations, a total of $250,000 was spent. There was some additional money spent on debt servicing, utilities, and taxes but these are smaller expenses that aren't avoidable. You spent $250,000 to buy and renovate but borrowed $262,500 when closing on the property. This means you probably paid for those additional expenses with OPM and pocketed any unspent money! That excess $12,500 was borrowed at acquisition, paid back during the bank refinance, and is 100% tax-free money, since it's being paid back to the lender with interest.

Additionally, you qualified for a long-term loan at a low interest rate instead of a cash-out refinance. Cash-out refinances aren't always available, but when they are, they're always subject to a slight interest rate increase. This is one of many creative structures that could allow you to work within the confines of your loan requirements while accomplishing your goal of returning 100% of your capital. This strategy also allows you to retain the asset, spend $0 of your own money, and maximize your cash flow long term by replacing high-interest debt with low-interest debt using a rate and term loan option (not a cash-out option which is subject to increased interest). The important takeaway from this example is to work backwards from your exit strategy to reach your goal! If you act without planning, your options are limited.

Exit Strategy Two: Sell the asset.

Selling is always an option, but it's my least favorite option. Yes, there are scenarios where you build a lot of equity in a few months and it's tempting to sell, but that profit is on paper, not in your bank account. After selling, the asset's cash flow can't help you qualify for loans; you've eliminated a depreciable asset that shelters income and the potential of building equity over time. Additionally, the taxes you pay on these capital gains are substantial! If you plan on selling, ask your CPA how to minimize your tax liability. A few options are holding the asset for at least a year to complete a 1031 exchange, utilize a lease option, or structure a seller financing strategy to combat those losses.

A 1031 exchange requires you to purchase another "like kind" asset with the proceeds within 180 days, instead of retaining the funds and paying taxes on the gains. Selling properties to generate working capital results in a final check and a loss of leveraged time. If you can refinance and keep the asset, even if you leave 20-25% equity in the building, you have the opportunity to generate cash flow for the rest of your life. Is it worth selling a renovated performing asset to make a one-time check? That's up to you and your needs. I only sell when I can transition that capital into a better performing, cash flowing asset.

Example: I purchased an ugly property for $120,000 that needed a full renovation. I expected the ARV to be $250,000 and found a lender that was willing to lend 70% of the ARV, $175,000. I borrowed $175,000 to acquire the asset and quickly began renovations. After renovating, I moved in, rented out the second unit, and got it refinanced with an owner-occupied loan. The property appraised for $250,000, and I got a $225,000 loan, 90% LTV since it was owner-occupied. At the closing table, my initial $175,000 loan was paid off, and I was cut a check for $50,000 (the difference between my 90% LTV loan of $225,000 and my outstanding $175,000 note). A few years later, I moved out and kept the asset for cash flow. This was fine until I wanted to access the equity. I couldn't establish another 90% LTV loan because I had moved out and it was now going to qualify as an investment property. The highest leverage position I could refinance up to was 75% LTV. Due to this limitation, I decided to sell the property and 1031 all of the proceeds into a larger cash flowing asset. I sold the house for $320,000, paid off the remaining balance of my 90%LTV, $225,000 loan and pushed all of the proceeds via 1031 exchange into another asset. The following asset was a 17-unit building. Selling in this way allowed me to pay $0 in taxes because the capital gains were deferred. Taxes on the capital gains were deferred because the capital gains taxes from the ugly property would now be paid to the IRS when I sell the 17-unit building ... unless I 1031 the proceeds into another asset.

Exit Strategy Three: Leaving the financing in place after repositioning.

You locked in a great rate, you're in a strong leverage position, you improve the property with minimal cost, and you've established good cash flow. You hit the income metrics you expected and want to leave the debit in place long term. This is a great scenario, and you may be right to leave the debt in place. Based on your cash flow, how long will it take to return your investment? After renovations, what is the LTV ratio? You're trying to determine if you're leveraging your dollars well. If you've completed the project and the cash flow will return your capital in 18 months or less, it may be the right move to leave the debt in place. If you finished the project and it cash flows well but hasn't gained a great deal of equity, again, it may be worth leaving alone. Alternative reasons to leave the debt in place would be if interest rates increased, if your credit score decreased resulting in you no longer qualifying for bank loans, if market values decreased, or if the loan conditions only allow you to refinance to a lower leverage position.

An example of loan conditions only allowing you to refinance to a lower leverage position: You purchased a property with an owner-occupied loan at 96.5% LTV then moved out, and you now want to refinance but it's now going to be an investment loan. Investment loans on this specific asset allow a maximum leverage position of 75%. Open your PITI payment calculator. If you access the equity and increase your debt position, how much does your payment fluctuate? Can you cash out? Make a decision based on numbers, not based on emotions or ease. A lot of work goes into refinancing properties, and many people avoid this step due to the headache. Never avoid refinancing for this reason. Be excited if you get to refinance and reposition your debt.

Having multiple exit strategies provides a nice safety net, but don't overlook red flags because the numbers look great. Even if the numbers work out and you believe you're getting a great deal, the property may be undesirable for resale or refinance. An example of this would be purchasing an asset with environmental hazards. Yes, maybe you got a great deal and established cash flow, but what if your acquisition and renovation capital is stuck in the asset? Example: You find a 4-plex with low rents, in a busy part of town that has deferred maintenance and a low purchase price. You pull the trigger and submit an offer immediately knowing you can increase rents and add equity with simple renovations. Lastly, you decide you'll exit the investment with an owner-occupied 30-year loan, which would return 100% of your invested capital and cash flow $300 per door per month. After going through this analysis, you pat yourself on the back and wait until closing. Right? No!

Spend money and time making sure you don't overlook red flags. Worst case, you lose a couple hundred dollars. Hire an inspector? No, hire a plumber, electrician, and structural engineer for an hour to come do an inspection and bid any repairs. Why not hire an inspector? Typically, inspector's reports identify where possible issues are located and, in the report, suggest hiring a licensed professional to assess. Skip this step, save the money, save the time, and bring in licensed professionals to assess from the beginning. Next, order a phase 1 environmental report. Maybe you'll find contaminated soils from a historic gas station. Maybe you'll see a history of methamphetamine production. Maybe you'll learn there was an underground cellar used to store pickles in years past (true story on the pickle storage). Who knows what you'll find out, but you should know what you're buying.

Did you run your numbers and build an exit strategy that required an owner-occupied or investment loan? Maybe the following loan conditions aren't accomplishable with the property's history. This is one of many possibilities but if you didn't identify the issue prior to closing, then your money may end up stuck in your project because you missed an important piece of information. That knowledge could have helped you negotiate a lower purchase price, guided your exit strategy, or signaled you to avoid the purchase altogether. This "good deal" could handcuff your working capital and set you back years. Leaving funds trapped in an asset will impact the speed at which you can acquire more assets.

Nevertheless, interest rates are at an amazingly advantageous place to establish long-term cash flow. How much lower will interest rates go and when will they rise? I have no idea, but I do know that I can run the numbers and earn a healthy cash flow based on today's rates. Plan for the future, lock in long-term, low-interest debt, and establish long-term cash flow. Act now while the debt is cheap! Much like long-term appreciation, I don't factor cash flow improvements into my analysis, AKA increased rents. If long-term appreciation is the cherry on top, then the large pile of whipped cream right below that cherry is annual rent increases. When I run the numbers to qualify a purchase, I'm determining today's potential cash flow not tomorrow's. However, I expect my properties' cash flows to increase over time due to rent increasing. Whether it's supply and demand driven or due to inflation, it doesn't matter. What matters is that rent will increase over time as it has historically, and if I'm in a desirable market, it may increase faster than inflation. While rents continue to increase annually, your fixed mortgage payments stay the same. You're anchoring your largest expense, while your highest revenue generating line item, rent, buoys with the market. This is very powerful over time!

Example: You vet a $350,000 4-plex, input the numbers, and determine you can cash flow $300 per month per unit with today's income and expenses. This analysis provides a snapshot of your immediate potential; it doesn't forecast the future. The numbers work and you close the deal. After you lock in a fixed interest rate for 30 years, your monthly payments are nearly static for 30 years! The expenses that change your monthly PITI payment are taxes and insurance. Taxes and insurance should be expected to fluctuate annually but typically are smaller line items that minimally impact on your PITI payment. Alternatively, market rents, your largest income line item can be expected to increase by 3-5% each year. Your reward for maintaining the property and increasing rents to market rates is increased cash flow year over year.

Chapter 8: Protecting Yourself as a Landlord

Once you've located a property, run the numbers, vetted the condition, determined you can handle the needed renovations, closed, and turned the reins over to your property manager, what else can you do to protect yourself?

I'm sure you've heard of people's nightmarish experiences with residents. In time, you may have one as well! People break up with significant others and wreak havoc, some punch walls, some may even decide to light fireworks off in their bedroom or bring a bar-b-que into their living room …. The list goes on. It feels like the landlord may be at a disadvantage trying to protect their assets while dealing with residents, but there are precautions to take such as security deposits, cosigners, thorough screening, long-term products during renovations, and insurance coverage.

Implement a security deposit (S.D.) insurance policy. For many years, I required a 1-2x rent amount as security deposit, which was collected at the time of lease signing. This security deposit is held to replenish lost rent and required repairs once the resident moves out. At first glance, a security deposit looks like a great thing! Unfortunately, few people discuss the negative implications of requiring a security deposit. What does the perfect resident look like? Would you rent to yourself? Hopefully, you're saying, "Yes, I'd love to rent to myself!" Now ask yourself how motivated you'd be to rent a property that required 2x rent as your security deposit. To me and many other highly qualified applicants, this is an unappealing cost of entry. What if you chase away the most responsible, highly qualified applicants because of this barrier of entry? Are you causing yourself to collect applications from bottom-of-the-barrel residents? I would argue that you're not setting yourself up for long-term success and should make an immediate change. Also, if you're self-managing, do you want to hold S.D. funds, issue itemized charges to your move-outs, and issue security deposit refund checks within the allotted time frame? Do you have the time to deal with collections actions if you're left with a deficiency? How much more efficient can the process be and how do you capture the best applicants?

My property manager advertises a $0 security deposit for my units, as this would be appealing to me. You want to increase the size of your funnel to help locate the best possible residents. In place of a S.D., require a S.D. insurance policy with limits to be 3-5x the rent amount in coverage. This coverage amount can be applied to lost rent, fees, or repairs once the resident moves out. These policies never require you to account for S.D. funds, never require you to issue a refund check to past residents, and eliminates the need for collections work by having higher policy limits. Once a resident moves out, my bookkeepers upload a ledger of the resident's payment history, upload a copy of the resident's lease, send a list of repair bills, and the claim is submitted. I've had great success with this model and typically have my S.D. claim approved and funded within 3 days.

Offer to add a cosigner or additional tenant to borderline or failing application packets. What is the difference in adverse actions you can take against a cosigner vs. additional tenant? They're the same, simply adding a cosigner. I've heard the argument made that an additional tenant can provide additional securities, but this isn't the case in my state. Speak with a state-specific real estate attorney to work through finer details. At the current time in the beautiful state of Colorado, you can hold both parties equally responsible, but by making a cosigner, you eliminate additional paperwork and notice requirements for additional tenants. While you don't have to provide cosigners notices, that cosigner has made a personal guarantee and is along for the ride on any adverse actions! If a resident doesn't qualify for a unit due to bad credit or low income, push for a cosigner to be added to the lease. The cosigner is required to submit a rental application and goes through the same screening process as an additional tenant. After completing screening on all parties, credit scores are averaged and reviewed.

Example: The first applicant has a 500-credit score, and the co-signer's credit score is 700, the average of these two scores is 600. You need disqualifiers when screening an applicant for lease approval, and an average credit score of under 580 is one of my disqualifiers. In the event that you're left with bills at the end of their tenancy from lost rent, repairs, lease violations, etc., all lease signers will be held responsible and can be sent to collections. If you did a good job qualifying residents and required a security deposit or insurance policy, hopefully, you avoid the need for collections and are quickly reimbursed for all delinquent funds with one of the securities you implemented. Collections aren't fun and are rarely collected in full. Also, of the funds that are collected, a large percentage of that money goes to your collections company. I strongly suggest leveraging collections actions as a threat to have your resident deposit a one-time settlement, establish a payment plan, or vacate early and respectfully. Always advertise that collections actions will be taken and give an alternative if they act immediately. Time is money! If you waste 30 more days evicting a resident, and then send them to collections, you've lost another 30 days worth of rent in today's money. It depends on your collections service and renting demographic, but I expect around 30% of what is sent to collections to be recuperated, and of that 30%, 25-50% is retained by the collections service for payment. With this percentage of recovered funds dropping to 20%, a one-time prompt payoff at 30% and the resident vacating immediately without destroying the place is a victory for the landlord.

Market analysis, demographics, and filling the need. Where does your community thrive? Do you have a high percentage of young professionals? Retirees? Lower income? Students? Don't fight the market, serve what's in demand. Don't work toward owning more products that YOU would live in; you aren't making money off yourself. Who are you serving and what niche can you fill? You want to generate as many leads as possible and approve the best of them. The ability to be picky and lease to highly qualified residents will decrease economic vacancy over the life of your investment property. If your product isn't producing leads, that means you messed up! The value is in appealing to the masses; creating a competitive environment for your product so you can avoid settling for one semi qualified applicant and hoping for the best. There are lots of niches and you do not determine the niche your property fits into; your market and the location of your investment will determine that niche. Renovate to suit that niche.

Example: Did you find a deal close to a hospital? I bet you have traveling nurses. There is a specific product for that resident, 3-month lease terms, all bedrooms with on-suites, and options to rent by the room. Is your town a retirement community with a VA Hospital? If that's the case, did you buy close to the VA, renovate with handicap accessibility in mind, and allow pets? If you do, I bet you have an abundance of applications.

Spread your risk between as many doors as possible. You have already partially done this by purchasing a property that can meet all debts while maintaining 50% vacancy. Now, apply this concept across multiple properties. This is hard to accomplish initially, but by year two, you should have the advantage of spreading your risk. No matter how much background work you do, you're still dealing with people. Good luck predicting the next life crisis, or drinking habit, break up, or fit of rage that required punching through walls and kicking down doors. Expect this because you're leasing real estate to people, and soon, lots of them. Spread your risk across many units, you have security in numbers. Secondly, if you're leasing to problem residents more than 10% of the time, change your screening requirements!

When acquiring or renovating your unit, consider cost-saving layouts and products. A simple example would be acquiring units with 1.5 bathrooms instead of one bathroom. The extra half bath allows a clogged toilet at 10 pm to be a next-day work order as opposed to an after-hours emergency. Having a plumber make an emergency service call after hours is an expensive work order. That half bath will save you a lot of money over time. Another layout suggestion is straight countertops in the kitchen instead of corners. I specifically like this for concrete applications. Whether you decide to pour concrete countertops or buy a finished product to install, straight runs will save you time, money, and headache. For installation, defer to that handyman you vetted. Use him repeatedly and ask for suggestions to mitigate long-term maintenance expenses. Additionally, use his referrals if the work is beyond his capabilities. He should know handymen in other trades and may be able to get you discounted rates and priority since he can vouch for your quick payments. Treat your team well, refer business to them, help them where you can, always ask them how they're doing before you give work orders, and pay them promptly. If you do those things, they'll keep an eye out for you and, hopefully, be honest. Occasionally, you'll even get a real estate deal referred from an unlikely place. Always treat people well and let everyone make money.

To incorporate, or not to incorporate ... that is the question

Own your assets in entities and consult with a real estate attorney on the structure of those entities. There are a lot of reasons to do this, and I've briefly discussed this earlier in the book, but a recap follows. You can watch videos, read articles, and do your own learning, but getting your questions answered by a well-versed local real estate attorney is worth the money. Take notes and ask as many questions as possible in your allotted time.

You want to provide yourself security from your renters and your asset security from the outside world. Your entity should provide you privacy and peace of mind! You can even register your entity in a state that provides additional anonymity. Again, have questions ready for your attorney and take notes; you want to minimize their billable hours. There are tax advantages to holding a title to an entity, but some loans won't allow you to purchase using an entity. That asset is now part of your business, and you want to keep your personal life and business separate, so what do you do? You quitclaim that asset into the correct ownership after closing. The process isn't hard, but you have to complete paperwork and file documents. After getting your questions answered, have the attorney help you establish your first set of entities and follow that process again on your following acquisitions. It's simple to file the forms to establish a business, but seeing the process completed correctly should save you time and headaches when filing for yourself.

I established a new LLC for each of my individual properties, they also have a parent entity registered, with my attorney as the agent. I also go to IRS.gov and establish tax ID numbers for each of my entities so a separate bank account can be formed. These business accounts typically come with an automatically approved 0% credit line and, depending on the season, a stuffed animal for opening a new account. As your portfolio grows, you'll be establishing a lot of these businesses and probably accumulating a lot of stuffed animals! Stay in compliance with your entities and file your paperwork before an incident happens. Keeping your entities in good standing with the secretary of state along with executing operating agreements for each entity takes very little time and cost. Get your automated email reminders sent to an email address, one that you check, and act when that email is received. It requires 5-10 minutes of time and $10 in my state to file the required periodic reports. If I miss that email and it becomes delinquent, it costs $50 or more to get it back into good standing. It doesn't take much time or money; it takes knowing what to do, checking your emails, and submitting updated paperwork in the allotted time.

Insurance coverage, insurance coverage, insurance coverage. You need to be covering yourself and your entities with insurance policies. On top of my standard vehicle and owner policies, I have an umbrella that provides extra coverage for me and my personal assets. As mentioned above, some lenders don't let you purchase real estate with an entity. They want the guarantors name, your personal name, on the title of the property and on the loan documents. When this is the case, complete your financing requirements, then quitclaim the asset's ownership into an entity after closing. A quitclaim deed is a simple document that can be completed with your title company or by going to the county clerk and recorder. It's a cheap, fast, and a simple process to go through, which quickly provides advantages. Do it promptly! To learn more about the process you can research quitclaim deed requirements for your area or call your preferred title company. If you tell your title company before closing that you want to quitclaim into an entity's name after signing loan documents, they'll likely have a completed form waiting for your signature at the closing table. Once you quitclaim a property, be sure to update your insurance provider with the name of the entity on title.

The name on title needs to match the name on your insurance policy. Additionally, your legal name needs to be listed as additionally insured. If your name is not present, there is a chance your lender will reach out to get the property quitclaimed back into your name or impose other requirements. Policies can name your entity first followed by "care of Your Name." If you're the signing officer of your entity, then you shouldn't run into claims being denied due to insured party name conflicts. Confer with your favorite insurance agent. I've had a few claims denied over the years but since changing to State Farm, I've had all submitted claims pay out. As long as your property is in compliance with the terms of your policy, your protection is based on your limits; you'll have to determine where these limits need to be set, and they'll increase over time as your portfolio grows. At the end of the day, I hope your claims get paid out, not fought over! It's a massive stress to deal with a major issue along with a fight with your insurance provider to cover it. Since nobody likes talking about insurance, here's a quick example to explain coverages.

Say you have $250,000 auto insurance coverage and a one-million-dollar personal umbrella along with your real estate owner policies in the names of your assets-holding entities. All assets aside from your personal residence are in the name of LLCs for this example. If you get in a car crash and you're sued for $1,500,000, what happens? First your $250,000 auto policy is paid out in full, then your $1,000,000 umbrella is paid out in full, followed by a remaining balance of $250,000 owed. Can your cash flowing assets be attacked? They could attempt this but likely won't be able to take any assets due to your limited exposure by owning in the LLCs' names. That $250,000 owed will likely be attached to something owned in your legal name. If you can't pay it out, you should expect a lien on your primary residence and possibly garnishes to your wages. This would be a very painful process to go through, but, in the end, you maintained your cash flow and will figure out how to keep growing your portfolio.

Never plan to pay your own mortgage. If you ever catch yourself analyzing a deal that doesn't have the potential to carry its own liabilities, it's not an asset; this is a liability. If you justify a purchase saying, "Yes, it loses money every month, but it will be worth X dollars in a few years," then you're convincing yourself to buy something with the hopes of appreciation. Not only is that equity fictitious, but when the asset finally appreciates to the value you're hoping for, how much money have you spent holding the asset and how much stress have you created in your life? You may have to sell the asset if you can't support it long term; you may need to sell the asset once it appreciates to recuperate the invested capital, and you'll NEVER recuperate the lost years of your life caused by the stress you created. Plan to make money monthly so your property buys you time and you can retain the asset long term. Time is your friend! Aim to buy assets that can cash flow $300 per month per door, so you can afford to extend your borrowing power and grow a portfolio. You should be entering every deal knowing your residents are paying the assets monthly expenses.

The world is dynamic, anticipate market cycles and use that expectation to your advantage. There are opportunities in every part of the cycle, but you'll need to change strategies. Such as rising interest rates. When interest rates are up, there is an opportunity! Whenever the institutional lending environment becomes less favorable, figure out how to acquire assets with lease options or owner-carry terms. Purchasing an asset with creative structures can be advantageous for both sides. You can structure the deal to lower the taxable burden on capital gains, replace down payment money with traded goods or services, avoid underwriters, the list goes on. There are entire books addressing creative acquisition strategies. Learn from other people's experience! Also, when interest rates increase by 1%, purchasing power decreases by approximately 10%.

Example: When interest rates are 4%, you qualify for a $350,000 loan, but when interest rates increase to 5%, your loan qualifications will decrease by approximately $35,000 leading to a new loan approval of $315,000. Why does this matter? In high interest rate environments, there are fewer qualified buyers which leads to less competition. Gain knowledge from experience and structure deals in a way that gives you an advantage over other buyers. When market conditions change, find a book to help you navigate your investment path. Learn the pros and cons of applicable strategies so you can appeal to sellers and acquire cash flowing assets.

Lastly, as your portfolio grows, it becomes more important to find a real estate oriented CPA. I expect we've all heard the famous quote by Benjamin Franklin, "The only two certainties in Life are death and taxes." This suggests we have no option but to pay taxes. This is marginally true, there are some taxes you won't be able to avoid, but you can lower your taxable burden on income. The tax code has been drafted specifically to incentivize our economies growth, so work within it! Ask a CPA; the tax code provides a manual on how to avoid paying taxes, so make a plan to work within it. Use this to your advantage and leverage your CPA's knowledge. Discuss deal structures with your CPA prior to executing contracts.

Before moving forward on deals, ensure your structure will minimize the taxable burden you'll encounter at the end. The verbiage and structure of your contracts has more implications on your taxes than you may realize. Just like insurance, get ahead of surprises by having the conversations before suffering the consequences. For those of you who pride yourselves as tax paying patriots, I don't argue that paying taxes isn't patriotic, it certainly is. What I argue is that it's more patriotic to provide housing, jobs, and continuing to make investments grows our economy. If you grow the economy in a way the government is incentivizing, you can reap the benefits by minimizing your taxable liability. Why would our country reward financially savvy patriots by minimizing taxes? By minimizing taxes, the country has maintained liquidity amongst individuals that will make additional investments! Every dollar kept liquid is a dollar that can be leveraged for our own benefit and the benefit of our nation's economy.

Investment Dos and Don'ts Lists

Dos:
- Talk with a lender and get a pre-approval letter!
- Be open and willing to move! Owner-occupied loans are the easiest and best debt to acquire.
- Ask your lender how to increase your loan approval best and DO WHAT THEY SAY.
- Change your habits. Poor people have poor habits!
- Read and discuss real estate daily. Always share info and help where you can; it comes back.
- Look at properties and make lots of offers. Most offers won't be accepted, and that's okay!
- Always use the lowest down payment option for low-interest loans.
- Replace carpets and maintenance headaches with long-term products

91

like waterproof flooring.
- Show as much income (tax strategy).
- Set everything you can on autopay to free up time for deal hunting.
- Inspect your handyman's work.
- Set up a cash or credit account as a contractor to save on material costs.
- Minimize new debts and live below your means until you've built a portfolio (house hack).
- Hire a great property manager, instead of self-managing.
- Screen your applicants well and make sure they qualify before signing a 12-month lease.

Don'ts:
- Don't waste money that could be liquidity for investing
- Don't commit to using friends and family who work in real estate; you need to work with the best.
- Don't buy an investment property with an HOA if possible.
- Don't move friends and family into your rentals.
- Don't give your handyman a check to go buy materials, pay with credit over the phone.
- Don't pay off debts and drain your bank account without talking to your lender. It may be more important to have money in the bank than less debt.
- Buy multifamily properties with owner-occupied loans; renovate and refi if possible.
-When moving into your rental property, don't be too proud to move into the cheapest unit.
- Don't hound your property manager about their fees. Offer them more money if they collect more money.
- Don't quit your job after a few good deals; talk to your lender first.
- Don't split the difference when negotiating; determine the price that works and hold to it.
- Don't rush to pay off your real estate! Keep your low-interest debt in place and buy more assets.
- Don't be frustrated if all the money coming in is going out. If the asset is self-supporting, then it will be a financial win in the following years.
- Don't sign short-term leases. Your lender wants to see 6-month and 12-month lease terms.
- Don't give up after a few bad residents.

And lastly ...
If you're buying an asset with an owner-occupied loan, then move into it!

Do not lie about your intent to occupy the property! Lying to obtain a loan by claiming you will occupy the asset violates your loan conditions along with state and federal laws.

Chapter 9: Stories to Solidify

Yes, there will be home runs, but expect to hit your conservative pro forma numbers. I'm going to lay out the numbers on a deal that met expectations, not exceeded them. Again, there will be home runs, but don't build pro formas with these expectations; be conservative when running your numbers to avoid strikeouts. Consistent singles and doubles will make you rich! I'm not trying to marginalize a success because the following stories are successes. I just consider these successes to be singles or doubles. Throughout this book, I've talked about spreading risk, leveraging money, maintaining a high velocity of your money, and protecting yourself along the way. Hopefully, you've decided that multifamily investing is a direct path to wealth accumulation that provides many safe havens.

The following stories are about two 4-plex purchases completed in my first 12 months of investing and how those deals played out in the following years. Unless otherwise stated, I will be providing approximate annual numbers based on 12 months of collections. The dates of acquisition, dates of reposition, and numbers along the way have all been rounded but provide true representations of the outcome. This is a simple overview that can provide a solid long-term perspective. Work through these numbers to help you understand deal analysis! The power of time is obvious when analyzing the numbers below, remember the fact that each year the building created cash flow while the residents paid down the principal balance.

If you're listening to an audiobook, the following pages will be hard to follow. I've included a spreadsheet summarizing the following text to help your understanding.

First 4-plex:

Purchased in early 2013 for $229,000, it was 75% occupied, there were two 3-bed 1.5-bath units and two 2-bed 1.5-bath units. Rents ranged from $650-700 per month.

The building was purchased with an FHA loan at 4.75% interest, with a 30-year term, and 3.5% down payment. 3.5% down payment worked out to just over $8,000. The resulting PITI payment including mortgage insurance was $1,350 per month. Prior to closing, one 3-bedroom unit was vacated to renovate, and owner occupy, resulting in 75% occupancy. I used a minimum down payment loan option that required me to owner occupy the property to qualify. Total rents after vacating one unit vs. monthly cost: $2,025 per month income minus $1,350 per month PITI payment = $675 per month profit during renovations with one vacant unit. I renovated the vacant unit in about 45 days at a cost of $6,500. I moved into one of the bedrooms in the newly renovated 3-bedroom unit and leased the other two rooms to friends for $350 per month on 12-month lease terms.

PITI payment cost vs. rental income after renovating and fully occupying: $2,725 per month income minus $1,350 per month PITI = $1,375 per month initial cash flow ($343.75 cash flow per unit per month).

Please see the summarized financial breakdown below. It has missing line items, but it shows the bulk of the expenses and income. Property one is calculated on 12 months of ownership, please recall that mortgage payments are made in arrears while rent is charged in advance. This little fact equates to one extra month of rent collections vs. mortgage payments in year one. Follow the year-by-year breakdown to understand the compounding profits realized by purchasing a cash flowing asset and holding it long term. This is a simplified 6-year financial analysis that should provide a helpful 10,000-foot view of the process and outcomes. For those of you who would prefer to review the number in a table format, a table is included at the end.

Year One:
Rents left the same plus roommate rent of $700 per month added
Total Rental income: $2,725 per month which equals $32,700 per year
Renovated one unit: $6,500 expense
PITI Payment: $14,850 per year ($1,350 per month * 11months)
Water, sewer, trash: $1,700 per year

17% of collections retained by PM to cover management fees and maintenance: $5,559

Year One Profit: $4,091

Year Two:

Rents on three units increased to $725-750 plus roommate rent of $700 per month

No units renovated

PITI Payment: $16,200 per year ($1,350 per month * 12months)

Water, sewer, trash: $1,700 per year

17% of collections retained by PM to cover management fees and maintenance: $5,926

Year Two Profit: $11,034

Year Three:

Rents on three units increased to $775-800 plus roommate rent of $800

Renovated one unit: $6,500 expense

PITI Payment: $16,200 per year

Water, sewer, trash: $1,750 per year

17% of collections retained by PM to cover management fees and maintenance: $6,436

Year Three Profit: $6,974

Year Four:

Friends move out and rents on all four units increased to $825-875 per month

Renovated one unit: $7,500

New roof installed with insurance claim: $2,500 deductible

PITI Payment: $16,200 per year

Water, sewer, trash: $1,800 per year

17% of collections retained by PM to cover management fees and maintenance: $6,936

Year Four Profit: $5,864

Year Five:

Rents increased to $910-960 per month on three renovated units and $850 per month on nonrenovated unit

No units renovated in year five

PITI Payment: $16,200 per year

Water, sewer, trash: $1,850 per year

17% of collections retained by PM to cover management fees and maintenance: $7,507

Year Five Profit: $18,603

Year Six:

Rents increased to $975-1,025 per month on three renovated units and $875 per month on nonrenovated unit

No units renovated in year six

PITI Payment: $16,200 per year

Water, sewer, trash: $1,900 per year

17% of collections retained by PM to cover management fees and maintenance: $7,854

Year Six Profit: $20,246

Now, let's get to the cherry on top of this cash flow. By the year 2020, I had 6 years of positive cash flowing ownership, three of the four units had been renovated, one original tenant remained in the building, the roof was replaced, and rent paid for all of this! Additionally, the monthly mortgage payments I made were funded by rent collections and paid down my principal loan balance. This building, along with all 4-plexes in my town, saw minimal appreciation over the first 4 years of ownership, but in years 5 and 6, the demand had grown, replacement cost had greatly increased, and values were up. Building one was refinanced in year six of ownership with a conventional loan at 70% LTV. This is how the numbers played out.

Appraisal in year six: $368,000

Outstanding principal balance on the loan: $195,000

70% LTV on $368,000 is $257,600. This means the loan amount could be up to $257,600.

The difference between my outstanding principal balance of $195,000 and the new debt of $257,600 is $62,600. These funds are given to me, the property owner, at closing and are TAX FREE since the money is debt. It's debt because I'm responsible for paying this money back with interest over the 30-year loan term.

New PITI payment: $1,360 per month

After refinancing, the building was cash flowing $2,700 per month, and it had just cashed out $62,500! That tax free $62,500 was now available for me to reinvest and grow my asset base.

Second 4-Plex:

Low and behold, the neighbor across the street was being foreclosed on. It was obvious there were problems by the accumulating pile of trash leaning against the building. I spoke with my agent, and she told me it was in pre-foreclosure; it would need to be purchased as a short sale. In trying to purchase a house via short sale, you need to have your offer accepted by the property owner and the bank holding the note. Building two's purchase started four months after closing building one but took approximately five months to close. It was financed as an investment property which required 25% down payment, and a rate increase due to it not being owner occupied. Breakdown from 2014 purchase to refinance in 2020 is outlined below.

Purchased as a short sale in 2014 for $170,000, it was fully leased, two 3-bed 1.5-bath units and two 2-bed 1.5-bath units. Rents ranged from $575-650 per month. The building was purchased with a conventional investment loan, which required 25% down payment, had a 5.25% interest rate, and a 30-year loan term. A 25% down payment on $170,000 purchase price was $42,500. I also knew that I had a large exterior cleanup expense waiting for me after closing.

This down payment and cleanup took my bank account below $10,000, which was very concerning, but I expected to cover the monthly building expenses with rent collections. This purchase didn't meet my 18-month cash-on-cash rule, but I entered the deal thinking it was my only option to execute the purchase. The lack of knowledge I had at the time of purchase led to this strategy as opposed to a strategy that leveraged OPM (Other People's Money). If I had acquired with private financing, my cash flow would have been decreased, but my liquidity would have allowed me to renovate more aggressively along with maintaining my purchasing power. I purchased this building conventionally with 25% down, which accomplished my goal of buying the building but didn't leverage a strategy that allowed me to maximize the velocity of money.

The property was acquired with a non-owner-occupied investment loan at 75% LTV. The lower purchase price and 25% down payment left a much smaller principal balance being financed than 4-plex One but it was financed at a higher interest rate because it was not owner occupied. The resulting PITI payment was $1,100 per month ($250 less per month then 4-plex One). Most of the inherited leases were month to month, so I gave the worst resident a 30-day notice of non-renewal with the plan of vacating one unit at a time for updates. Vacating and renovating one unit of the building at a time allowed 75% of the building to remain occupied and paying. As each unit was updated and released, rents were increased to market rates. I didn't like the idea of vacating units to renovate due to my decreased reserves but knew the increased cash flow was important to long-term stabilization and success. True to the broken glass theory, as units were updated the remaining residents started taking better care of their homes. I only attempted to vacate one unit at a time for renovations so I could ensure the monthly liabilities would be covered by rent collections not my savings.

Total rents vs. monthly cost at time of purchase: $2,445 per month income minus $1,100 per month PITI = $1,345 per month initial cash flow.

Let's review the following simplified six-year financial breakdown:

Year One:
Building two was purchased in July, so five months of rent collections and four months of mortgage payments were recorded in year one. Rents were left the same and no units were vacated in the initial months, but exterior cleanup and exterminations were completed.
PITI Payment: $4,400 per year ($1,100 per month * 4months)
Water, sewer, trash: $708 per year
Grounds cleanup: $1,500
17% of collections retained by PM to cover management fees and maintenance: $2,078
Year One Profit: $3,538

Year Two:
Rents on four units increased to $650-700 per month
Renovated one unit: $7,000 expense
Water, sewer, trash: $1,750 per year
17% of collections retained by PM to cover management fees and maintenance: $5,508
Year Two Profit: $4,942

Year Three:
Rents on four units increased to $700-750 per month
Major unit fire: $5,000 deductible for $30,000 insurance claim payout. Payout covered a full unit renovation and all lost rent.
Water, sewer, trash: $1,800 per year
17% of collections retained by PM to cover management fees and maintenance: $5,916
Year Three Profit: $8,884

Year Four:

Rents on four units increased to $775-850 per month

Renovated one unit for $7,500 expense

New roof installed by insurance claim: $2,500 deductible

17% of collections retained by PM to cover management fees and maintenance: $6,630

Year Four Profit: $7,320

Year Five:

Rents increased to $875-1,000 per month on three renovated units and left at $850 per month on nonrenovated unit

No units were renovated in year five

17% of collections retained by PM to cover management fees and maintenance: $7,548

Year Five Profit: $21,752

By year 2020, the building was owned for nearly 6 years, three of the four units had been renovated, a new roof was installed, and one original tenant remained in the building.

Again, this building, along with all 4-plexes in my community, experiencing a marked increase in value by year 2020 due to demand and increased replacement costs. With values up, I had building two refinanced with a conventional investment loan at 70% LTV. This is how the numbers played out.

New appraisal: $368,000

Outstanding principal balance on the loan: approximately $100,000

70% LTV on a $368,000 value is $257,600, so the loan could be up to $257,600.

The difference between my outstanding principal balance of $100,000 and the new loan amount of $257,600 is $157,600. These funds are given to me, the owner, at closing and are TAX FREE since the money is issued as debt, and I'm subject to repay with interest.

New PITI payment: $1,360 per month

After refinancing, the building now cash flowed $2,275 per month after making the monthly PITI payment AND provided $157,600 of usable funds.

Financial breakdown in the following chart:

	Purchase Price	Monthly Rent Range	Rent Collections (Monthly)	Rent Collections (Annual)	Utilities (water, sewer, gas)	PITI Payments (Annual)	Renovations & Deductibles	17% of Collections to Mgmt/Maint	Annual Profit from Cashflow
1st 4-plex									
Year 1	$229,000	$650-700	$2,725	$32,700	$1,700	$14,850	$6,500	$5,559	$4,091
Year 2		$725-750	$2,905	$34,860	$1,700	$16,200	$0	$5,926	$11,034
Year 3		$775-800	$3,155	$37,860	$1,750	$16,200	$6,500	$6,436	$6,974
Year 4		$825-875	$3,400	$40,800	$1,800	$16,200	$10,000	$6,936	$5,864
Year 5		$910-960	$3,680	$44,160	$1,850	$16,200	$0	$7,507	$18,603
Year 6		$975-1025	$3,850	$46,200	$1,900	$16,200	$0	$7,854	$20,246
2nd 4-plex									
Year 1	$170,000	$575-650	$1,019	$12,225	$708	$4,400	$1,500	$2,078	$3,538
Year 2		$650-700	$2,700	$32,400	$1,750	$13,200	$7,000	$5,508	$4,942
Year 3		$700-750	$2,900	$34,800	$1,800	$13,200	$5,000	$5,916	$8,884
Year 4		$775-850	$3,250	$39,000	$1,850	$13,200	$10,000	$6,630	$7,320
Year 5		$850-1000	$3,700	$44,400	$1,900	$13,200	$0	$7,548	$21,752

Amts rounded to nearest dollar

Second Story to Solidify

This example was referenced above in regard to changing life circumstances requiring a prompt qualification for an alternative owner-occupied loan but also display's a creative financing strategy. This strategy allowed me to maximize my leverage position, minimize my down payment requirements and helped the sellers retain more of their capital gains.

I located the sellers of three adjacent 4-plexes who were motivated to sell the properties as a group. I knew there was deferred maintenance, and a conventional loan to acquire the properties would demand at least 30% down payment. The owners had owned the properties for approximately 10 years, and I anticipated that they would have a large amount of capital gains subject to taxes. If the sellers were to take the profits from all three 4-plexes in the same year, they would be pushed into a much higher tax bracket. My goal was to minimize my out-of-pocket expense and minimize the sellers' taxable capital gains. If I could save them $50,000 in capital gains, I could justify negotiating down the purchase price by a portion of that savings. Once I established the goals, I worked backwards toward a mutually beneficial purchase offer.

The sellers wanted around $385,000 per building in as-is condition. This was a fair market price for the buildings based on current condition. I expected each of the buildings to appraise for $450,000 once they were renovated. I projected $42,000 in needed renovations on each building to reach this $450,000 appraisal, and I expected the ending PITI payment to be around $1,850 per month. I located the buildings personally and was comfortable writing my own contracts on DORA (Department of Real Estate) approved forms, but alternatively, I could have hired an attorney to draft contracts for $500. I knew I had room to negotiate by eliminating a 6% real estate agent's commission expense, and by minimizing their capital gains expense.

I proposed purchasing all three 4-plexes for a total of $1,081,000 which averaged out to $360,000 per building. To minimize their capital gains expense and my out-of-pocket cost for down payments, I would purchase the first 4-plex of the three (the building that was in the best condition) in December for $450,000 and the following two buildings, in January of the following year for $308,000 on owner-carry terms. This purchase strategy allowed for the sellers to spread their capital gains between 2 years; this kept them in a lower tax bracket and generated additional gains by providing interest payments on their owner-carry financing. The average purchase price was lower than they were asking at face value, but I worked through the numbers to explain their savings as I'll do next for you.

- 6% savings to the sellers by eliminating real estate agent commissions. 6% of the $1,081,000 purchase price is $64,860, or $21,620 per building.
- Taxable gains will now fall into the 24% bracket instead of the 35% bracket. This allows the sellers to retain a large portion of their capital gains that would have been paid in taxes. I had to make assumptions based on their date of purchase as to how much equity was in the buildings and approximated this savings at $50,000.
- Sellers would also generate additional gains from providing a short-term owner carry due to interest collected and pay down the principal balance with my funds during their owner-carry term.
- Lastly, no repair expenses would be required for the sale.

Once adding back the savings listed above, the sellers were actually realizing around $40,000 in savings per building. With this number calculated, the sellers knew they would need to sell the buildings for an average price of $400,000 to match the financial advantage of my offer.

Now that the sellers' advantages have been listed, let's talk about the buyer's advantages.

My strategy to purchase the three buildings while minimizing down payment money was to purchase the nicest of the three buildings with a highly leveraged owner-occupied loan and the following buildings with owner-carry terms followed by investment loan refinances. Due to the first building being purchased with an owner-occupied loan, I could reach a maximum leverage position of 96.5% LTV. The following two buildings would be financed long term with an investment loan; those loans' leverage position are maxed at 75% LTV. By decreasing the purchase price of the investment loans, the buyer would realize a huge savings in required down payment expense.

The first of the three buildings closed in December for $450,000 with an owner-occupied FHA loan that required 3.5% down payment. To reach a total of 96.5% debt leverage, I needed to ensure the property would appraise for the purchase price of $450,000, or I would be forced to come to the closing table with additional funds. To accomplish this appraised value, I would need the building renovated. We established a 60-day purchase contract that would close in December, and I included a clause that required the sellers allow the buyer access to the property for renovations prior to closing. In the event that the contracts were cancelled, and the closing didn't occur, the sellers would have to reimburse me for all renovation expenses or I'd lien the property. This was a risky move on behalf of the buyer, but I was confident in the deal because all parties benefited. More importantly, I was protected because appropriate contracts were drafted to reflect the agreed upon terms.

We executed all necessary contracts, and I started renovations on the building immediately. In the following 60 days, I had three units renovated, replaced the old yellow appliances with used white appliances, a metal roof installed, and some cosmetic exterior work completed. The appraisal was pushed back as long as possible to allow for these renovations to be completed. By the time of appraisal, we had completed, enough work to reach a $465,000 appraisal! FHA loans do not allow for cash out, but I could fully utilize the available 96.5% LTV term and minimize my cost to close. Additionally, the $465,000 appraisal helped to establish an ARV on properties two and three of the deal. The cost to close building one was around $16,000 for a down payment plus renovation expenses of $37,000 plus the cost of moving into a unit. We moved our things into one of the renovated units and spent very minimal time there. We actually used the unit more as a storage unit than a livable residence. After moving in our things, we went on a multi-month RV trip around the Florida coastline while the other three units paid for our living expenses and generated cash flow. It was a fantastic trip, and we got to experience most of the Florida beaches and coastline parks while minimizing our out-of-pocket expense back home. If I had purchased building one with an investment loan at 75% LTV it would have costed 75% of $360,000, $90,000 just for the down payment! After this large down payment, I would still need to pay for the renovations and deferred exterior repairs.

Buildings two and three were closed two weeks later in the first week of January with owner-carry terms. A note and deed of trust was established on both properties that required me to make interest only payments to the sellers with an eight-month term. I needed to renovate and refinance both buildings and pay off the notes within eight months or I would be in breach of contract. If I breached the contracts, I could lose all of my invested capital and lose my opportunity to purchase the properties. My goal was to refinance within the allotted eight-month window and minimize my long-term out-of-pocket expense. I knew that the ARV was going to be $465,000 with equivalent renovations, as building one and the market stayed strong. I also knew an investment loan could be leveraged up to 75% LTV if it wasn't cash out. Working backwards from this number, 75% of $465,000 is $348,750.

$348,750 of debt would be available if no funds were being cashed out.

Buildings two and three's purchase price was $308,000 and I had $348,500 available in debt so $40,500 was available for renovations. On buildings two and three, I borrowed $348,000 from a separate private lender, paid off the sellers' $308,000 notes, invested the remaining funds finishing renovations and refinanced with my rockstar lender. I now had replaced my private lenders high-interest $348,000 note with a low-interest 30-year-termed bank loan. By over-borrowing before going to my rockstar lender, I was able to finance my down payment, renovations, and closing costs into my long-term low-interest loan. Buildings two and three cost $0 out of pocket by month eight and the resulting PITI payment was $1,800 per month. These buildings greatly exceeded the $300 per month positive cash flow rule, returned all my invested capital in under 18 months, and will now provide our family spending money for the foreseeable future.

You can read book after book and go to seminar after seminar, run deal after deal through your spreadsheets, but you'll NEVER find a deal if you aren't making offers. Make a lot of offers and start soon! This book isn't very long, because it doesn't need to be. The shortest distance between two points is a straight line; make a plan, follow the path, and maximize the velocity of your money! Good luck sticking to your path!

If you have read the book and still have questions, please email me directly at maptomillionsinrealestate@gmail.com. I'm happy to help!

Printed in Great Britain
by Amazon

13573336R00068

THE

HISTORY AND ANTIQUITIES

OF

FOULSHAM,

IN NORFOLK.

BY

THE REV. THOMAS QUARLES, M.A. R.N.

CHAPLAIN TO THE RIGHT HON. THE EARL OF MORTON.

Nescio quâ natale solum dulcedine cunctos
Ducit, et immemores non sinit esse sui.
Ovidii Epist. ex Ponto Lib. 1. 3, 35.

Curabo, igitur, . . . ut Folshami nomen volitet doctorum per ora virorum.
Leland. Commentarii de Scriptoribus Britannicis.

LONDON:

JOSEPH CUNDALL, 12, OLD BOND STREET.

NORWICH: CHARLES MUSKETT.

1842.

Madeley. litho. 3. Wellington St Strand

NORTH WEST VIEW OF FOULSHAM CHURCH.

PREFACE.

A more careful research into the history of our small towns and villages than has been usually hitherto devoted to such subjects, would doubtless tend to throw much additional light on the manners, the mode of living, and the characters of our rustic forefathers. The same researches would also enable us much more satisfactorily to trace to their source many ancient customs, which, notwithstanding the great changes brought about by the lapse of ages, and more especially by the unprecedented facilities of communication opened to us during the last half century, still linger in our rural districts, and of which each succeeding year is either abridging a portion, or involving the origin in greater obscurity.

Though the parish of Foulsham may offer but little which can entitle it to any particular notice as far as the elucidation of these interesting points is concerned, yet, by those who feel a pleasure in the investigation of village lore, the present attempt to set forth the history of the place more fully than has been hitherto done, may perchance be considered as one step gained towards the accomplishment of so desirable an object.

Blomefield's invaluable History of Norfolk has furnished ample matter for the earlier part of the History of Foulsham. And though it is to be lamented that this author's life was not spared to complete the Herculean task which he had undertaken, and the continuation of the work, in which portion is the description of Foulsham, was therefore entrusted to others, who have not prosecuted the subject with that care and attention which Blomefield bestowed on those parts published under his own immediate superintendence ; yet the general accuracy of the information, somewhat hastily put together by his successors, is such, that it must always serve as the ground-work for any future and more enlarged history of the numerous small towns and villages whose outlines have been so faithfully given by them.

To the antiquary, some of the remarks introduced into the present work may seem superfluous ; but in order to connect the more recent history of the place with what is mentioned concerning it in the earliest records to which recourse can be had for information, and to present this connexion to the general reader, and to those resident in the country and attached to rural objects in a form as intelligible as the obscurity of such subjects will admit of, these apparent digressions could scarcely be omitted. With respect to those points, unsupported by MS. or printed authority, which the author has advanced as his own opinions, he has given to them all his best consideration ; and, wherever the case allowed, entered into a minute personal examination before coming to a decision. Notwithstanding this care, as exceptions may still be made to some of his conclusions, he is ' content to intermedle his own opinion simplie, ' without eyther prejudice of any other man's that shall ' judge otherwise, or pertinacitie in his owne when he shall ' hear a better.'

Regent Street, London,
 May, 1842.

SUBSCRIBERS.

Aldridge, J. Esq. London
Allen, Dr. Haslar Hospital, Gosport
Astley, Rev. H. M. Rectory, Foulsham
Astley, Rev. H. N. East Barsham, Norfolk
Aufrere, G. A. Esq. Burnside, Boroness, Kendal, Westmoreland
Austen, Mr. Watts, Foulsham

Balls, Miss, Honingham, Norfolk
Barnwell, Rev. F. H. Turnour, Bury St. Edmunds
Barton, Thos. Esq. Threxton, Norfolk
Bircham, Mrs. Wm. The Ollands, Reepham
Blencowe, Rev. E. E. West Walton, Wisbeach
Briggs, Rev. J. Chaplain of R. N. Dockyard, Devonport
Bulwer, Rev. James, Aylsham
Bulwer, Mrs. Dr. Aylsham (2 *copies*)
Burcham, J. B. Esq. Hare Court, Temple (2 *copies*)

Carthew, G. A. Esq. East Dereham
Clarke, Mr. R. Foulsham
Collison, Rev. H. East Bilney Rectory, Norfolk
Cooper, Rev. J., H.M.S. Camperdown
Crofts, Rev. T. B. Little Walsingham
Cundall, Mr. Norwich

De Mountenay, Barclay, Esq. London
Dench, Robt. Esq. Foulsham
Dench, L. Esq. Ely (2 *copies*)
Dew, Mrs. Guist, Norfolk
Drake, Mrs. Tyrwhitt, Paul's Walden, Bury, Herts
Drake, Miss Tyrwhitt, Paul's Walden, Bury, Herts
Dunne, Rev. J. Haslar Hospital, Gosport

Emms, Mr. H. Foulsham
Everard, S. Esq. West Bilney Lodge, near Lynn
Ewing, W. C. Esq. Eaton, Norwich

Falls, Rev. J., H.M.S. St. Vincent

Gaines, Charles, Esq. London
Gardiner, Rev. Wm. Rochford Rectory, Essex (2 *copies*)
Gayton, Captain, R.N. Bromley, Kent
Geddes, Dr. London
Girling, J. A. Esq. London
Girling, C. Esq. Foulsham
Girling, Barry, Esq. East Dereham
Grigson, Rev. W. Saham, Norfolk
Gurney, D. Esq.

Hamerton, C. Esq. London
Hamerton, Mrs. London
Hardy, Rev. C. Vicar of St. Paul's, Welden, Herts
Harris, Quarles, Esq. London
Hastings, the Rt. Hon. the Lord, Melton Constable Hall,
    Norfolk
Hennah, Rev. W. V. East Cowes. Isle of Wight
Hoste, D. Esq. Barwick House, Norfolk
Hudson, Rev. G T. West Harptree, Somersetshire (2 *copies*)

Jacob, Mr. J. Foulsham

Kingston, G. Esq. London
Kitson, John, Esq. Norwich
Knights, Mr. F. Foulsham

Leamon, Mr. C. Foulsham
Leamon, Mr. E. Foulsham
Leeds, Miss, Foulsham
Le Mesurier, Rev. J. T. Chaplain to the Forces, Malta
Lloyd, Miss, Bawdeswell, Norfolk (2 *copies*

Marshall, Rev. J Portsmouth
Mays, Miss, Foulsham
M'Callan, R. Esq. London
Morton, Rev. D. Harleston, Northampton
Munton, Mr. J. Foulsham
Muskett, Mr. C. Norwich

Neville, Rev. C. East Grinstead, Sussex
Norfolk and Norwich Literary Institution
Norris, Wm. Esq. Wood Norton, Norfolk, (4 *copies*)
Norris, Rev. D. G. Kessingland, near Lowestoft
Norris, C. Esq. Bracon Lodge, Norwich
Norwich, the Rt. Rev. the Lord Bishop of

Packe, Col. Twyford Hall, Norfolk, (2 *copies*)
Petman, Rev. E. Harrietsham, Kent
Pike, Capt. Great Yarmouth
Pratt, E. R. Esq. Ryston Hall, Norfolk
Pratt, Mr. S. Foulsham

Robins, Mrs. Aylsham
Robinson, Miss, Stoke, Devonport

Salter, Rev. E. M. Wood Norton, Norfolk
Scott, Rev. W. Shapwicke Vicarage, Blandford

Siely, Rev. J. T. H. London
Slight, Rev. H. S. Octagon, Plymouth
Smith, Mr. W. Foulsham
Spurdens, Rev. W. T. North Walsham
Stewart, Rev. J. V. Vicarage, Portsea
Storey, Andrew, Esq. London
Stoughton, Mrs. Aylsham
Stoughton, Miss, Aylsham
Surridge, Rev. J. E. Devonport

Thornthwaite, J. J. Esq. London
Townshend, the Rt. Hon. the Lord James, K.C.H. &c. &c.
    Yarrow, Guist, Norfolk (2 *copies*)
Townshend, the Lady James, do.
Tupper, F. B. Esq. Guernsey

Wade, R. Esq. London
Watts, Lieut. R.N. Stoke, Devonport
Wodehouse, Edmund, Esq. M.P. Norwich

HISTORY AND ANTIQUITIES

FOULSHAM.

FOULSHAM is a small market-town in the eastern division of the county of Norfolk, in the hundred of Eynsford, and at the distance of 111 miles N. N. E. from London. Its name is found differently spelt at different periods—Fold-isham, Folesham, Folsham, Foulsham ; but since custom has now for a considerable time sanctioned this last as the orthography, her decision on this point will always be considered the correct one, in the present attempt to throw some light on the history of the town.

The origin of its name, like that of many other places, may be traced to the monosyllable *Ful* or *Fol*, and the very common adjunct, *ham*, a home or dwelling : hence also, according to Blomefield in his description of Foulsham, Fulham, Foulden, Foulmere. The first of these three places, on the authority of the Anglo-Saxon Dictionaries, is derived from *ful*, foul or dirty : " Fullenham, or Fulham,

B

a foul or dirty habitation.," If the same derivation is to
be assigned to Foulsham, however appropriate it may once
have been, the peculiar force of its application is no
longer to be discerned from any thing denoted by the present appearance of the place.*

Foulsham is situated in a fertile and well-wooded valley,
through which run several nameless streams, emptying
themselves into the river Wensum; the main street of the
town, or rather the only one properly deserving the name
of a street, sloping gently from north to south. On the
north it is bounded by Hindolvestone and Wood Norton,
on the south by Foxley, on the east by Guestwick and
Themelthorpe, on the west by Guist, Twyford, and Bintry,
and is looked upon by the inhabitants of these villages as
the little metropolis of their neighbourhood.

The earliest period to which reference can be made for
any information connected with the history of Foulsham,
is the latter half of the eleventh century, when Domesday
Book was drawn up by order of William the Conqueror,
and finished in the year 1086. This invaluable record is

* Eynsford hundred took its name from some ford over the little
river Eyn, which was, it is said, at Reepham. There is also an Eynsford
in Kent, so called from a noted ford over the river Darent. This last-
mentioned Eynsford is somewhat memorable from its connexion with
the quarrel between Henry II. and Thos. à Becket, Archbishop of
Canterbury, which ended so fatally for the latter. In this sovereign's
reign, Wm. de Eynsford held the manor and castle of Eynsford, in
Kent, of the Archbishop: at which time Becket, having given the
church of Eynsford to one Laurence, Wm. de Eynsford dispossessed
him of it: for this he was excommunicated by Becket, which was one
of the first bold measures he ventured on in his struggle with the king.
See Hume's History of Henry II.

still preserved, in two volumes, in the Chapter House at Westminster. Essex, Norfolk, and Suffolk, which form the second, or lesser volume, of this great survey, probably contain transcripts of the original Rolls; whereas the officers of the Exchequer are said to have compiled the first, or greater volume, with more brevity, leaving out some, and abridging other, articles.

In Domesday Book Foulsham is described as royal demesne, being one of the lordships of which King Edward the Confessor died possessed. In King Edward's time it consisted of 12 carucates of arable land and 3 acres—there were then 30 villains, at the present survey 33—then 38 bordarers, now 44—40 acres of meadow, 2 carucates in demesne, now 3—18 carucates among the tenants, now 20—paunage, or woodland with right of feeding, for 400 swine. In the time of Edward the Confessor there was 1 mill, now 2, and a church endowed with 16 acres when King William came into possession. There was then 1 runcus, or horse for work, now 2—3 cows, now 12—47 swine, now 50—with 60 sheep, and 50 goats, now as then. In King Edward's time there were 30 socmen, now 24—with 11 acres of arable land, and 5 carucates 5½ acres of meadow. Walter Giffard, at this survey, had 6 of these socmen. The manor in King Edward's time was worth £13. by tale, *ad numerum;* and 13 sextaries of honey, a customary duty, and 23lbs. by weight. It now paid £11. and 10s. refined money, *blancas,* for the honey. It was 1 leuca long, and 1 broad, and paid 8½d. to the king's gelt. The church had now 22 acres. To this manor were added 2 freemen by Ralph Talibosc, in the time of King William, as the hundred witnessed; 14 acres of arable

land, half a carucate, and 1 acre of meadow, separately
worth 4 shillings.

The following is a literal copy of the description of
Foulsham in Domesday Book:—"Terra Regis. H. de
Ensford. Folsha'. tenuit. E. Rex. 12 car' træ. et 3 ac. tc.
30 vill. p'. et m°. 33 tc. et p'ea. 38 bord. m°. 44. et 40 ac
pti. tc. et p'. 2. carr' in dnio. m°. 3. tc. et p'. 18. car' hom.
m°. 20. silva. ad 400 porc. tc et p'. 1. mol. m°. 2. 1 eccla.
16. acr. Qndo recep. 1. r. m°. 2. tc. 3. an' m°. 12. tc. 47
porc. m°. 50. et m°. 60. ov. semp. 50 cap'. tpr. r. e. 30.
soc. m°. 24. 1. ac' træ. et 10. ac'. semp. 5. car. et 5. ac'.
et dim. pti. Et 6 de his ten. et m°. Walter' gifard. Tnc.
val 13 lib. ad numeru'. et 13 sextarios mellis cum consue-
tudine et 23. lib. ad pensu'. m°. et 11 lib. et 10. sol.
blancas p. melle. et. ht. 1. leu. in long. et 1. in lato. et
redd. 8. d. et obolu' in gelto regis. 1. eccla. 22 acr'. Huic
manerio adjuncti snt. 2. libi hoes p. radulfu' talibosc. t. r.
W. hoc. testat' hundred. 14. ac' træ. sep. dim. car et. 1.
ac' pti. sep. val. 4 sol."

Manning and Bray, in their History of Surrey, have
multiplied the sums mentioned in Domesday Book by 60,
in order to reduce them to something like the present
value of money. If such a calculation be near the truth,
what the King received from the township or manor of
Foulsham may be calculated thus: £11. × 60=£660.;
10 sh. × 60=£30.; 4 sh. × 60=£12.—Total £702.—
See Manning and Bray's History of Surrey, Vol. I. p. 114,
note x.

Whatever difficulties may occur in explaining the details
of this account, it is clear that in the short interval between the time of Edward the Confessor, who died in 1066,

and the compilation of Domesday Book in 1086, there had been a general improvement in the manor or township.— More land had been brought into cultivation; the stock on it, as well as the tenants, with the exception of the socmen, had increased. There were now two mills instead of one. Sir Henry Ellis, in his Introduction to Domesday Book, remarks, that wherever a mill is there specified, we generally find it still subsisting; and though the two present mills at Foulsham are of modern erection, the site of one more ancient may probably be traced, from the appellation "Mill-hill Lane" being still applied to a cross-road at a short distance from the town. Mills in these early times belonged to Lords of Manors, and as the tenants were permitted to grind only at the lord's mill, this made them a source of considerable revenue. There was an increase also of six acres in the land belonging to the church, which, singularly enough, according to the Terrier, still possesses the same quantity of glebe as it did in the time of William the Conqueror.

Though the manor in King Edward's time was worth £13., and at this survey the annual worth is stated to be only £11., yet this cannot be taken as a proof that its value had deteriorated, since the former yearly rent was paid by tale, *ad numerum ;* while the latter was discharged in coin of the purest kind, *blancas,* which in all likelihood more than made up the difference. This seems to indicate a great depreciation of the currency at the time of the Survey; for when the money which formed the payment was offered at the Exchequer, it was a very usual custom for the receivers there, either to melt a sample of it, or receive a certain sum over every pound in lieu of actual combustion. The money so melted, or having the supplemental payment added, was said to be *dealbated* or *blanched;* and when Domesday Book was compiled there was always a fire ready at the Exchequer for this purpose. The payment for the honey was no longer made in kind, but in actual money, a change which had in many instances been effected since the time of Edward the Confessor. What was the exact measure of the sextarius, it is not easy to decide. Blomefield inclines to the opinion that it corresponded to the old Roman measure of the same name, and contained something more than our pint; while Spelman and Selden assert, that when this measure is applied to honey, it contained 4lbs. and answered to our quart. Judging from the quantity of honey, and the corresponding weight, in the description of Foulsham, the former supposition would appear the more correct one. In most of the entries of Domesday Book in which it occurs, it is mentioned as a measure of honey, and in two or three instances only is it applied to flour. Mead being so favourite a beverage of the age, a large stock of bees was then a very valuable acquisition.

Supposing the leuca of the Survey to contain about two miles, a distance which, on a rough calculation, corresponds with it well enough in the present measurement of places in Norfolk, the ordinary mile, as computed in the country, being in general considerably more than the statute one, the boundaries of the town in the eleventh century were not very different from what they now are.— How Walter Giffard became entitled to six socmen in the manor, we are not informed; though it could scarcely have been by any other means than by the gift of the King. He was no less a personage than the Earl of Buckingham, one of the followers of the Conqueror when he invaded England, and a great favourite with this monarch, who rewarded his services with very large possessions and this distinguished title. He was also one of the Commissioners, or, as they were called, King's Justiciaries, appointed for adjusting this Survey; those for the midland counties at least, if not for all, being Remigius, Bishop of Lincoln, Walter Giffard, Earl of Buckingham, Henry de Ferers, and Adam the brother of Eudo Dapifer, who probably associated to them some principal person in each shire.

The quantity of land contained in a carucate, which was the term employed by the Normans for what was called by our Saxon forefathers a hide of land, varied in different counties, according to the nature of the soil, and the different modes of agriculture. In some places a carucate consisted of 60 acres; in others, of 80 or 100; and according to Agard, 5 acres even sometimes constituted a carucate. It was considered to be as much arable land as could be managed with one plough and the beasts belonging thereto, in a year; having meadow, pasture, and houses for the householders and cattle belonging to it. Whatever might have been the quantity intended to be expressed by it in respect to this parish, even if we could ascertain it precisely, it would be difficult to say how much land was actually in a state of cultivation at the time of the Survey, within the present boundaries of Foulsham, as the manor then included part of the villages of Twyford, Themelthorpe, and Bintry. The three carucates in demesne were farmed either by the king himself, or rather by some royal bailiff, who accounted to the monarch for their profits; and the town was moreover taxed with an annual payment of 8½d. to the king's gelt. This gelt, which occurs so frequently in Domesday Book, but which is met with there only once under its original name of Danegeld, began to be collected in Ethelred's reign; either, as some think, to induce the Danes to desist from ravaging the land; or, as others suppose, for the hire of Danish ships to oppose the incursions of foreign invaders. Originally it was an annual tax of two shillings on every hide of arable land in the kingdom, though this sum was afterwards doubled, and even trebled, and was in its nature a land-tax, the first stated tax of that kind mentioned in our history. It was always grievously complained of; and one reason of the memory of Edward the Confessor being so fondly cherished by the native English, was, his having remitted the payment of Danegeld. William the Conqueror, very soon after coming into possession of the throne, re-enacted this unpopular tax, though at the period of Domesday Book there were numerous exemptions from it. The demesne lands of the king and queen, and those in the hands of their immediate tenants and farmers, though assessed, did not pay it: the demesne lands of the church, &c. were also exempted. Like many other things, it retained its name long after it became appropriated to uses entirely different from its original purpose, and continued to be collected as low as the 21st of Henry II., and possibly later.

With reference to Domesday Book generally, it must be remembered, that it was not a complete survey of all the lands in the kingdom, but limited to estates upon which the Crown had claims. It was not a parochial survey, or a census of population, but a mere rent-roll of the particular lands which owed rent, suit, or service to Edward the Confessor, or to William the Conqueror. Hence several towns, now considerable for wealth and commerce, are omitted, as not being held of the king or his tenants in capite, but by their under-tenants. Neither is the number of women and children given, or even that of socmen, villains, &c., unless in such manors as belonged to the king or his chief tenants. The distinction between the three classes of persons mentioned in the extract under the head of Foulsham, by the appellations villains, bordarers, and socmen, must have been strongly marked at the time of the Survey, and the tenure by which they held their possessions was then undoubtedly very clearly defined; but the lapse of so many ages has wrought such changes in this respect, that the present titles to the lands in this, as well as in other parishes, fail to give such information as might enable us fully and satisfactorily to trace this distinction.

The clearest idea of the tenure of villains is perhaps to be obtained from Sir William Blackstone's Commentaries. According to Blackstone and other high authorities, villains were either *regardant*, annexed to the manor or land; or, *in gross*, annexed to the person of the lord, and transferable by deed from one owner to another. These last held some portion of land by way of sustaining themselves and their families; but it was at the mere will of the lord, and by services not only base, but uncertain as to time and quantity. Their tenure was called pure villanage, and from thence our copyhold tenures are lineally descended. Notwithstanding such weighty authority, there are numerous entries in Domesday Book, which seem to indicate that the villains of that period occupied a higher grade in society than this; since they were associated with the Sheriffs, the Lords of each manor, and the Bailiffs, in this Survey; six of their body being selected from each vill or manor; and these in conjunction, and upon oath, formed the Jury, or Inquest, which made the Domesday returns. A villain might be enfranchised in various ways: by a deed of manumission on the part of his lord; by a man's binding himself in a bond to his villain for a sum of money; by his giving him an estate in fee, for life or years; for this was dealing with him on the footing of a freeman. There were also several other methods by which a villain might become enfranchised, and which, when disputed, the laws seem more frequently to have decided in his favour. It appears, indeed, to have been the general policy of the government to countenance manumission.

What gave the finishing stroke to this species of servitude, were the confusions occasioned by the two contending houses of York and Lancaster, when the whole kingdom was divided, and every lord was obliged, even for his own security, to take part with one side or other. Villains were therefore emancipated in prodigious numbers, in order to becoming soldiers. Tenure in villanage was virtually abolished in the reign of Charles the Second; and at that time there was hardly a pure villain left in the nation. For Sir Thomas Smith testifies, that in all his time, and he was Secretary to Edward the Sixth, he never knew any villain in gross throughout the realm; and the few villains regardant, who were then remaining, were such only as had belonged to bishops, monasteries, or other ecclesiastical corporations, in the preceding times of popery.

The bordarers of Domesday Book appear at various times to have received a great variety of interpretations. Lord Coke calls them "boors holding a little house with some land of husbandry, bigger than a cottage." It would seem they were very little more than cottagers, for in the Ely MS. we find *bordarii*, bordarers, where the Breviate of the same entry in Domesday Book itself reads *cotarii*, cottagers. Their condition was probably different on different manors, distinct from that of villains—persons of less servile condition, who had a bord or cottage, with a small portion of land; tenants who paid poultry and other provisions for the lord's board or table, as Blomefield interprets the word.

Socage, in its most extensive signification, seems to denote a tenure by any certain and determinate service.— It is of two sorts: free socage, where the services are not only certain but honourable; and villain socage, where the services, though certain, are of a baser nature. The socage tenures were probably the relics of Saxon liberty, which escaped the general fate of other property, partly out of favour to their particular owners, and partly from their own insignificancy; as the number of socmen soon after the Conquest does not seem to have been very considerable, nor their possessions by any means large. Socmen, says Nichols, were those inferior landowners who had lands in the *soc* or franchise of the lord; who, though their tenures were absolutely copyhold, yet had an interest in them equal to freehold. Their services were fixed and determinate. They could not be compelled to relinquish their tenements at their lord's will: et ideo, according to Bracton's expression, denominantur liberi. Such were

actually freeholders, and a certain number of them were
necessary in every manor, to hold the pleas of the manor
court. Socmen were, therefore, those who owed suit and
service to the lord's court; and it is from the word soc,
which gave them their name, that we must derive our
tenures in free and common socage. In this instance
again, Domesday Book exhibits different conditions of
socmen, sometimes enjoying the usu-fruct with the soke
freely, and sometimes performing certain inferior services
of husbandry.

Perhaps, therefore, we may not be far wrong in supposing, that in the Domesday-Book description of Foulsham at least, the villains, in respect to their grade in
society, may answer to the labourers of the present day,
if the fact of a certain number of this class alone having
been summoned out of the rest of the parishioners, to form
part of the jury of whom the king's commissioners were to
inquire into the particulars of each township, weigh not
too heavily against such a supposition. The bordarers
may be classed a little higher in the scale, and the socmen
said to correspond with the owners of moderately sized
landed estates. If such a supposition be correct, it may
serve also to account for the decrease in the number of
socmen since the time of Edward the Confessor; as it is
well known that the character of the Norman policy was to
deprive the native English, as far as possible, of all independence, a greater share of which, according to the above
description, was enjoyed by the socmen. Six of these
were now transferred from the King to Walter Giffard, Earl
of Buckingham.

The remark of a very deeply-read writer of the present

day, that "no diligence can recover the unrecorded history of a single village during the middle ages," is fully confirmed by the instance of the parish of Foulsham. During the interval between the compilation of Domesday Book and the reign of Richard Cœur de Lion, or in other words, from the conclusion of the 11th century to the end of the 12th, we know nothing whatever of its history—there is not a single record in existence, as far at least as our researches have been able to discover, which can afford us a syllable of information on this subject. There were probably no material changes in the place during these hundred years, and the township continued to form part of the domains of the Crown, till King Richard, the hero of his age, the theme of many a gay troubadour's lay, at whose name the children of Palestine yet tremble,* after being released from captivity in Austria, where he had been basely detained a prisoner, among the many sacrifices he was constrained to make in order to raise the sum stipulated for as his ransom, granted it with its appurtenances, the Hundred of Eynsford, and many other possessions, to Baldwin de Betune, Earl of Albemarle and Holderness. Richard had remained a year and a half in captivity, and one of the conditions which restored him to liberty was, that seven months after his delivery, he would send Eleanor, sister of his nephew Arthur, into Austria, in order to her becoming the wife of the son of Duke Leopold.

* A short time since, a gentleman attached to the English Consulate in the Island of Cyprus assured me, that he himself had heard the nurses in Palestine hush their children, by threatening to send King Richard to them, if they were naughty. The name of the celebrated Governor, Warren Hastings, is still used in India for the same purpose.

The learned Benedictine, Lobineau, in his Histoire de Bretagne, says, that Richard, on recovering his liberty, was in no haste to execute the conditions of the treaty, especially as the Pope had declared his imprisonment to have been an unjust one, and had excommunicated Leopold for having detained the King. Leopold, however, had no idea that the thunders of the Vatican could authorize a prince to forfeit his word, especially as he held hostages for ensuring the fulfilment of it. He therefore sent Baldwin de Betune, brother of the Earl of Flanders, to acquaint King Richard, that he would kill his hostages if he did not faithfully fulfil all the conditions of the treaty. On receipt of this message, Richard, who well knew the determined character of Leopold, set himself in good earnest to satisfy his demands, and sent him all he had promised, together with the Princess Eleanor. While, however, Sir Baldwin was on his return into Austria, the Duke had the misfortune to break his leg, and died a short time after in consequence of the injuries he had received, so that the marriage did not take effect.

Sir Baldwin de Betune married Hawys, daughter and heir of William le Grosse, Earl of Albemarle, and conjointly with her, by deed without date, granted to Robert Constable a hundred shillings per annum out of his lands in Holderness. His seal to this deed was . . . . . on a chief . . . . . three bendlets . . . . . armed cap-à-pied, on horseback in full career, sword in hand. The issue of this marriage was an only daughter, Alice, who married William, Marshal of England, and Earl of Pembroke, to whom Baldwin, with the licence of King John in his fifth year, gave the manor of Foulsham in free marriage. One of the

Figures in the Temple church, London, represents this William Marshal, Earl of Pembroke, whose arms per pale Or and Vert, a lion rampant Gules armed and langued Gules, are on the shield. Of this ancient family Sir William Dugdale has given a succession of seven descents, from Henry III. to Edward II. Our William obtained in marriage from King Richard I. on his first coming to England after his father's death, Isabel, daughter and heir of Richard de Clare, surnamed Strongbow, second Earl of Pembroke, which title passed with his daughter to her husband. He died at an advanced age at his manor of Caversham, near Reading, 3rd Henry III. 1219, and was solemnly interred in the Temple church in the month of April of the same year. He left by his first wife five sons, who all died without issue, having succeeded one another in their father's lands; and five daughters, to whose heirs his possessions eventually descended. By his second wife, Alice, daughter of Sir Baldwin de Betune, Earl of Albemarle, he had one daughter, who also died without children. After her decease, it seems King John re-seized the manor, and gave it with its appurtenances, to William Marshal, son of the said Earl of Pembroke, and his heirs. This William gave the manor, hundred, &c. to John Marshal, and William Marshal, who succeeded this John, held the manor, &c. during his life, and after his death, Elizabeth his widow, who was living in the 3rd of Edward I., had two portions of it as her dower. The remainder, John de Bretanie then held, as guardian of John Marshal, till he came of age.

Such is the descent of the manor down to the commencement of the reign of Edward I., according to the infor-

mation derived from the Rolls, denominated the Hundred
Rolls, which contain Inquisitions taken in pursuance of a
special commission issued under the Great Seal in the
second year of this monarch. During the turbulent reign
of his father, Henry III., the revenues of the Crown had
been considerably diminished by tenants in capite alien-
ating without licence. Edward I., who was on his return
from the Holy Land when his father died, did not reach
England till towards the latter end of the second year of
his reign; and these abuses remained uncorrected till his
return. One of his first acts after his arrival in England,
was, to inquire into the state of the demesne lands, &c.,
and concerning the conduct of the sheriffs who had de-
frauded the king and greatly oppressed the people.

When this Inquiry was made, Foulsham seems to have
been considered the chief place in the Hundred of Eynsford. At the close of the Inquiry into the affairs of this
district, the commissioners observe, that they had still
much information before them; but owing to the shortness
of time allowed for digesting it, and the despatch they
were consequently obliged to use, they were unable to
insert all the intelligence which had been communicated to
them. It is deeply to be regretted that such haste should
have been required of them, since nothing now can ever
recover the information which more leisure would have
furnished them with the means of imparting to us, from
the materials they had already at hand.

John Marshal was found to die seized of the manor with
the advowson and Hundred of Eynsford, in the 6th of
Edward I., and in the 15th year of the same King, the
jury found that William, son of John Marshal, held it of

the Earl of Gloucester and Honour of Clare, who held it in capite. William was then a minor, claimed a weekly market on Tuesday, view of frankpledge, assize of bread and beer, a gallows, and stated the lordship, including these appurtenances, to be then worth forty pounds per annum.

John Marshal, son and heir of this William, died lord in the 10th of Edward II., without issue, leaving Hawyse, his sister and heir married to Sir Robert de Morley, who became lord in right of his wife. The manor remained in the Morley family till Alianora, daughter and heir of William, Lord Morley, brought it by marriage to William, a younger son of William, Lord Lovell of Tichmarsh, who died seized of it in 1475. Henry Lovell, Lord Morley, his son and heir, who was killed at Dixmude in Flanders, in 1489, left no issue by his wife Elizabeth, daughter of John de la Pole, Duke of Suffolk; so that the lordship came by Alice, his sister and heir, to her husband, Sir William Parker, and was held of the Honour of Clare. Edward Parker, Lord Morley, his descendant, who disposed of the greater part, if not all his patrimonial possessions in Norfolk, sold this manor, and Hundred of Eynsford, on the 4th of September, 1582, to Sir Thomas Hunt, Knight, of the Fishmongers' Company in London, whose grandson, George Hunt, Esquire, of Hindolvestone, sold it to Sir Jacob Astley, Bart., and his descendant Sir Jacob Astley, Bart., of Melton Constable, recently elevated to the peerage by the title of Baron Hastings, in right of his descent from Sir John de Hastings, who sat in Parliament in the reign of Edward the First, is the present lord.

The general eagerness which prevailed in England, as

c 2

well as in most other countries of Europe, for joining in
the Crusades against the Infidels in Palestine, tended
greatly to the distribution of landed property in the kingdom.   The nobles being restless and turbulent, with few
or no resources within themselves, many of them unable to
read, and many more ignorant of the art of writing, the
wilder sports of the chace or war being their only pursuits,
the idea of an expedition to the Holy Land, which,
whether successful or not, they felt fully persuaded would
ensure their path to Heaven, was what above all other
things was most likely to charm their active spirit.   But
as a large outlay was necessary to equip themselves and
their vassals in a manner suitable to so distant and
hazardous an enterprise, it was a natural consequence for
them to endeavour to dispose of, or mortgage, many of
their domains to the religious houses, which then possessed
much of the ready money of the kingdom, or to those persons, who from their commercial pursuits, had a supply of
specie at command.   By the time of Edward I., who
ascended the throne in 1272, this subdivision of manors
had been carried to a very great extent, and had caused no
little confusion in ascertaining what services were due to
the sovereign from them, according to the tenure by which
the original possessors held them.   It therefore became
necessary in the eighteenth year of this sovereign, 1290, to
enact the well-known statute, Quia Emptores, by which a
stop was put to their farther multiplication.   So that all
manors, which are in existence at the present day, may
date their origin from a period antecedent to the statute
Quia Emptores; and no new ones have since been made,
though many of those which were then in being have

since, from various causes, been lost. Such was the case with respect to the present manors of Foulsham. They were all originally included in one, viz. the royal manor which Richard I., on his return from captivity, granted to Baldwin de Betune; and from this original one were derived the three manors now existing: the manor of Foulsham, that of Foulsham Dulencross, and that of Christ's College on the part of Foulsham.

THE MANOR OF FOULSHAM.

This represents the original royal manor, and is still by far the largest manor of the three; the two others being merely parts and parcels severed from it. The General Court Baron for Foulsham manor is held in the Autumn, but since the death of the late Steward of this manor in 1829, the Court Leet has been discontinued. Its emoluments were trifling, and its duties were therefore performed by a deputy Steward. At this Court Leet, which was held on old Michaelmas-day, and included Foulsham, Bintry, Twyford, and Themelthorpe, each of these places, as a token of their having been once comprehended in the royal manor, and entitled to the privileges which such a position gave them, appointed their respective constables and pinders; and at these meetings, the parish of Foulsham expended five shillings, the others half-a-crown each. The custom of this manor is Gavelkind, its fines certain, and the tenants are at liberty to use their possessions as they will, on performing due homage at the Lord's Court at the time of their admission to them. The house on the farm belonging to Lord Hastings, is still known by the name of the Manor-house. His Lordship is the present lord.

DULENCROSS MANOR.

This manor, which was anciently called Walsingham Priory Manor, formed part of the original royal manor given by Richard I. to Sir Baldwin de Betune; the latter having granted to Giles de Cotys 100 sh. rent, which the prior of Walsingham held of him in pure alms. It was afterwards augmented by John Marshal, lord of this town, who granted to the prior, for his soul's health, and that of Oliva his wife, William Earl Marshal and Isabel his wife, John Marshal his father and Alice his mother, 60 acres of land in his wood at Foulsham, by the perch of 20 feet, with a way on the west towards Norton, 2 perches broad, common of pasture, and the soke of Foulsham. These gifts were still farther increased by Oliva Marshal, who by her deed and fine levied in the 35th of Henry III. gave to the same priory, 12 acres, 100 sh. rent in this parish and in Bintry, with a fold-course, right of fishing, &c. The temporalities of this priory here, in 1428, were valued at £4. 12 sh. per annum. At the period of the Reformation, when such a vast mass of ecclesiastical property was transferred to other hands, King Edward VI., April the 11th, in his 4th year, granted this manor to Thomas, Bishop of Norwich, and his successors, with a parcel of land called Little Divillings, or Dallings, and Dove-house close. It remained attached to the See of Norwich till the time of the Commonwealth, when on the sale of the Bishop's lands, it fell into the hands of Major-General Philip Skippon, one of the most experienced of the Parliamentary generals, then owner of the Hall at Foulsham, and the estate belonging to it; and continued in the possession of the general's family till the episcopal possessions were restored to that Order at the restoration of Charles the Second. The annual value of the manor of Dulencross and its appurtenances, at the time when Edward VI. gave them to the bishop of Norwich, was £9. 0s. 4d. The annual rental of its quit-rents amounted, some few years since, to £4. 11s. 2¼d. Gough, in his Antiquities of the Parish of Myddle, interprets the word Divlin, which was often in former times applied to a wood or lane, to mean 'a deep plain among woods,'—*dive, dep, depen,* and *deep,* being the same with what we term *deep ;* and the chief city in Ireland, he continues, was formerly, and is to this day by some, called Divilin—*len, lene,* and *laune,* signifying a plain place among woods. This definition of the term may perchance have been aptly applied to the Bishop's lands here, though they are no longer known by their original appellation. In writings, however, of the last century, the orthography of the lands belonging to the See had varied only in a trifling degree, and they were then still called Great and Little Dullins. Till within a very recent period Sir Richard Paul Jodrell, of Sall House, Bart. was the lessee of this manor, which is now rented of the bishop of Norwich by William Norris, Esq., of Wood Norton. The origin of its present name cannot be satisfactorily traced. Its fines are certain, with the customary suits and services.

THE MANOR OF CHRIST'S COLLEGE, ON THE PART OF FOULSHAM.

This manor, formerly called Creke Abbey Manor, was portion also of the original royal manor, having been

created by William Marshal, Earl of Pembroke, lord of
this town, in right of his wife Alice daughter of Baldwin
de Betune, granting to Alan de la Hythe 100*s.* rent of
lands per annum, by the service of 1lb. of pepper, which
the abbot of Creke then held by the same service. From
him it came to John Marshal, who gave it to the priory
of Walsingham, with three marks and a half rent per
annum in pure alms. William de Camera also had twenty
acres of land here, which the abbot of Creke then held.
John de Havering and Joan his wife granted to Geoffry,
abbot of Creke, 14 marks, and 40 pence in Foulsham and
Bintry, by fine, 55th Henry III. This John was the son
of Richard de Havering, who settled on him and his wife,
in tail, £9. 10*s.* rent per annum, here and in Havering
and Bocking in Essex. At the dissolution of Creke abbey,
this lordship was given to Christ's College, Cambridge,
and is still possessed by that College. There is but little
land in Foulsham held of this manor, the far larger portion of its lordship lying in the adjoining village of Bintry,
where the manor courts are always held. Its fines are
certain, with the customary suits and services.

Blomefield, in his history of Foulsham, mentions also
another manor, called Swanton's Manor. There is, however, no such manor in the present limits of Foulsham;
the greater part of the lands held of the manor so called,
lying in the neighbouring parish of Twyford, a portion of
which was originally included within the boundaries of
Foulsham lordship. It was created by Baldwin de Betune
granting, out of the royal manor of Foulsham given him
by Richard I., 60*s.* in land and rent per annum, to Geoffry
de Hesseltone, to be held by the service of a sixth part of

a knight's fee. In the 3rd Edward I. it was held by Warine de Thymelthorp, and in the 9th Edward II. the heir of John de Swanton was lord of it; from whom in all probability it derives its name. This lordship came into the possession of the Townshend family in the reign of Henry VIII., and having since that period passed through the hands of the Grimes, Wards, Holls, and Savorys, is now the property of Colonel Packe, of Twyford Hall.

The temporalities in Foulsham assigned to the little priory of Coxford at the time of its dissolution, amounted to 7s. 6d. per annum, arising from lands conveyed to John, the prior, and to the convent, in the 35th Henry III., by Roger Scot and Margaret his wife. Nothing more is known respecting these lands, nor does it appear to whom they were granted when the convent establishment was broken up.

It has been already stated that in the 15th Edward I., William, son of John Marshal, who was then a minor, held the lordship of Foulsham with the advowson and the Hundred of Eynsford of the Earl of Gloucester and the Honour of Clare, who held it in capite; and that in the year 1489, when Sir William Parker succeeded in right of his wife to the lordship, &c. it was still held of the same Honour. In the Inquisitiones post Mortem, Vol. 1, 270, Gilbert, Earl of Clare and Hertford, in the 8th Edward II., was found to die seized of one knight's fee in Banham, Foulsham, and Wood Norton conjointly; and the same fee was held in the 16th Richard II. by Thomas, Earl Stafford, Inquis. post Mortem, Vol. 3, 154; and afterwards in the 4th Henry IV., by Edward, Earl Stafford.

In this last volume, p. 117, William de Norton, in the 13th
Richard II. was found to die seized of lands in Foulsham
and the adjoining places, with 50s. rent, which he held of
the Honour of Clare.

It is somewhat singular, that after these positive notices
of the connexion which subsisted for so many ages between Foulsham and the rich and extensive Honour of
Clare, all traces of such connexion should now have
ceased. And this is the more remarkable, because, courts
for the Honour of Clare continued to be held at Foulsham,
till within about the last sixty or seventy years, a solicitor
from some place in Suffolk presiding at them as steward.
For this statement I have the authority of a gentleman of
the parish, recently deceased, who had himself been present
at these courts in his youth, though he could not recal
to mind over what lands, or in what other way, they exercised jurisdiction. His opinion was, that the holding the
courts had been dropped in consequence of the fines not
being sufficient to cover the steward's expenses. It appears,
that all the manors of Walter Giffard, Earl of Buckingham,
who at the time of Domesday survey, had six socmen in
Foulsham, came by the marriage of his granddaughter, to
the Earls of Clare, who were capital lords—and further,
that William Marshal, who had for his second wife, Alice,
daughter of Baldwin de Betune, and through her became
lord of the manor of Foulsham, had married, as before
mentioned, first, Isabel, daughter and heir of Richard de
Clare, Earl of Pembroke, and with her had obtained that
Earldom, and all the lands and rights of her father. Such
must have been the origin of the connexion. In the list
of the possessions of the Honour of Clare, Foulsham,

Wood Norton, and Banham, are usually given conjointly as one knight's fee, and according to the Returns preserved in the Augmentation Office, under the head of "Manor of Wood Norton," this royal manor extended over some small part of Foulsham in the reign of Henry VIII., and the lands in this latter place, then included within the lordship of the Crown, were charged with a trifling quit rent. In the time of the Commonwealth, when the royal manors were sold, the small-reserved rent arising to the Sovereign from his manorial jurisdiction in Foulsham, was disposed of. The name of the purchaser, however, is not mentioned, and the sale is so mixed up with others, that the price it fetched cannot be ascertained, though it was certainly but small, as the amount of the entire sale is inconsiderable.

From the presentment of a bridge at Witchingham, it is proved that in the reign of Henry VI., the Hundred Court was held at Reepham. It was, however, at some time posterior to this removed to Foulsham, its authority being limited to the recovery of debts under forty shillings' amount. From the pleadings and other remarks on its proceedings still in existence, it would seem that about the year 1770, Sir Edward Astley, Bart. the then lord of the manor, transferred the office of its judge to a solicitor at Wells in this county; shortly after which it fell into disuse. Some twenty years after this date, on application, Sir Edward consented to its being renewed; but as it was then found impossible to discover either its official records or its seal, the proposed design was never carried into effect. Thus, within, as it were, the memory of man, the Hundred Court has ceased its functions, and within the brief space

D

of less than fifteen years, the Court Leet has abandoned its petty jurisdiction!

The church of Foulsham is a rectory, in the diocese of Norwich, in the archdeaconry of Norfolk, and in the deanery of Sparham. It is dedicated to the Holy Innocents, and in the work called the Norwich Domesday Book, which was compiled in the reign of Edward I., it is valued at forty-nine marks, had a vicarage *indecimatum*, or unendowed, valued at four marks, and paid eight pence halfpenny Peter-pence. The tenths were £9. 2s. Deducted 52s. This Peter-pence, of which such frequent mention is made in the histories of parish churches, was originally an annual tribute of one penny, paid at Rome out of every family, at the feast of St. Peter; Ina, the Saxon King, when he went in pilgrimage to Rome about the year 740, having given it to the Pope, partly as alms, and partly in recompence for a house erected there for English pilgrims. It continued to be paid generally until the time of Henry VIII., when it was enacted that, from thenceforth, no persons should pay Peter-pence, or other impositions, to the use of the bishop or see of Rome. Polydore Virgil, well known as the historian of this country, resided in England many years as collector of these papal dues. In the same book the Archdeacon's procurations are valued at 7s. 7½d., and the synodals at 21d.

It may seem strange in the present day, that after the mention of a vicarage here, we should find only one solitary vicar in the list of incumbents. It is to be remembered, however, that in those early times a vicar often signified no more than a curate, and was removable at the rector's pleasure. When churches were appropriated to monasteries, and the monks were obliged to set out a portion of the glebe and tithes for the maintenance of a vicar, such a one is called *a perpetual vicar*, made presentative and institutive; but there are no traces of any other nominations to the vicarage of Foulsham, which is expressly said to be *indecimatum*, or unendowed with tithes. Not but what the rector might, with the consent of the bishop and patron, have created a vicarage, and made his own share a sinecure, as was done at East Dereham, and other places; and in the diocese of St. Asaph there are such separations of tithes made, and vicarages erected, as low as Henry the Eighth's time.

Its present value in the King's Books, according to the survey made in the 26th year of King Henry VIII. is £27. 14s. 9½d., and it pays first-fruits and tenths.

There have been three taxations of ecclesiastical preferments in England. The first, called the Norwich taxation, was made in 1254, and is so named from Walter de Suthfield, bishop of Norwich, who, by command of Pope Innocent when he granted the king the tenths of ecclesiastical goods for three years, drew up a description of all the clergy's revenues in England.

The second, called the Lincoln taxation, or the taxation of Pope Nicholas IV., was begun in 1288, when the Pope granted the tenths to King Edward I. for six years, towards defraying the expenses of an expedition to the Holy Land, and finished as to the province of Canterbury in 1291, and as to that of York, in the following year; the whole being under the direction of John, Bishop of Winchester, and Oliver, Bishop of Lincoln. This taxation is a most important record, because all the taxes as well to our kings as to the popes, were regulated by it, until the survey made in the 26th year of Henry VIII.; and because the Statutes of Colleges which were founded before the Reformation, are also interpreted by this criterion, according to which their benefices, under a certain value, are exempted from the restriction in the Statute Henry VIII. concerning pluralities. In this Lincoln taxation the rectory of Foulsham is valued at £30. At the same period the temporalities of the prior of Walsingham, arising from the property his priory possessed in the parish, were valued at £4. Those of the abbot of Creke, at £1. 17s. 4d. Those of the prior of Coxford, at 7s. 6d.; and those of the prior of Norwich at 2s.

The third and last of these ecclesiastical taxations, is the existing valuation, commonly known by the title of "The Value in the King's Books," and was made in the 26th Henry VIII., when upon the king's quarrelling with the pope, he directed an ecclesiastical survey to be drawn up, with a view to ascertain the value of all the first-fruits and tenths of the kingdom.

In Domesday Book it is stated that there was then a church at Foulsham, whose glebe, by a recent addition, amounted to twenty-two acres. Whether the existing edifice occupies the same site as that did which is mentioned in Domesday Book, can only be matter of conjecture; since there is no vestige left which would in any way authorize so high an antiquity being assigned to any portion of the present building. It may be fairly presumed, however, from there being no tradition to the contrary, nor any name of any place in the parish indicating a different locality for the church, that the edifice mentioned in Domesday Book occupied part of the present churchyard.

The gentle rise on which the church stands, and the uniform appearance which it presents when viewed from a distance, give it an imposing effect from several points in the neighbourhood, and would lead a stranger to suppose that the town to which it belongs, is one of more importance and greater size than it really is. The edifice consists of a nave, with a north and south aisle, separated from the body of the church by arches; a south porch, and a chancel—all roofed with blue tiles. At the western extremity of the nave, is a square embattled tower, of four stories besides the basement, with a clock. The lower part of the tower, to the height of some eight feet, is cased with well-wrought flint; the upper portion is built with the common unwrought flint-stone of the country. It has diagonal buttresses of an equal number of stages with the stories of the tower itself. The ornamented compartments of the embattlement were renovated some few years since, and at each of the four corners rises a crocketted pinnacle.*

Over the arch of the doorway at the western end of the tower outside, are the arms of France and England quarterly, and those of the Lord Morley, *argent*, a lion rampant, *sable*, crowned, *or*. In this device of the arms of

* Our churches, almost invariably, stand east and west, but *why* is by few persons exactly known; nor, that the degree of deviation from due east often noticeable in the ancient ones was determined, in each particular case, by the point in the horizon, at which the sun rose upon the day of the Saint to whom the church was dedicated.

France, there are only three fleurs-de-lis—a proof that they must have been placed there after the time of our Henry V., who ascended the throne in 1412; since before the reign of this king, the fleurs-de-lis were always semée. On a buttress also at the western angle of the north aisle, are the same Morley arms. These are the arms which in the year 1395, gave rise to a curious and protracted suit in the Court of Chivalry, in which Sir John Lovell, Knight, was the plaintiff; and Sir Thomas de Morley, defendant—an interesting account of which trial may be found in Blomefield's Norfolk, Vol. 2, p. 436. 8vo.

The length of the church in the interior, from the western door of the tower, which is open to the nave, to the chancel archway, is 102 feet, and its breadth, including the two aisles, 46¼ feet. The length of each aisle measured in the inside, is 78¼ feet. The chancel, which is separated from the body of the church by an arch, and has an elevation of one step, measures from this step to the interior of its eastern extremity 44 feet, and is 20 feet broad. There were in the tower up to the year 1770, when a fire committed dreadful ravages both in the town and in the church, five bells, which chimed every four hours; the sweetness of whose peal is said by those who then heard their notes for the last time, to have been singularly increased by the heat communicated to them by the destroying flames—like the fabled notes of the swan, sweetest in the hour of their destruction! Similar observations have been frequently made on the additional sweetness imparted to the music of bells by the action of heat, and in the Gentleman's Magazine for February, 1838, there is stated to have been a like effect observed in the chiming of the bells during the destruction of the Royal Exchange by fire.

The south porch, the only one attached to the church, appears from the architecture of its doorway arch, and from the mullions of the window in each of its side walls, to be nearly coeval with, or little later than the lower part of the chancel, the most ancient portion of the church, and of an earlier date than the exterior architecture of the nave and aisles. This porch has now no upper story, though previously to the fire, it had a chamber in its roof, which had served as a school-room from time immemorial. At the entrance of the porch is an ancient stone slab, gradually decreasing in size from the head to the foot; and as such spots were often chosen in former ages as the places of interment for the founders of churches, or benefactors to them, this stone might possibly be intended to serve some such purpose. Within the porch are also two other oblong stone slabs, whose inscriptions are entirely obliterated.

Opposite the south door of the nave, which is screened by the entrance porch, elevated on two steps, stands a neatly ornamented circular font of white marble, supported by a stone pedestal, both of modern workmanship. The former font, which was irreparably injured at the time of the fire, was of stone, with a handsome wooden cover, opening below, and displaying in the inside a painting of the four Evangelists. The nave is neatly paved with flag-stones, the aisles with brick pavements; and from the uniformity of the pews, which are confined to the aisles, and of no great height, their appearance does not offend the eye, as the view is not broken by any of those unsightly "sleeping boxes," whose preposterous elevation so often disfigures the interior of country churches. This

uniformity is to be attributed to their having been erected
at the restoration of the church after the fire.　Before this
period, the seats of the congregation were principally open-
backed wooden benches, of which there are still many
remaining examples in the sacred edifices of this part of
the kingdom; and which have been often introduced into
the recently-erected places of worship with the happiest
effect; since they are generally acknowledged to be much
better adapted for hearing than enclosed seats.*

At the period of the fire, the chancel was roofed with
tiles, to which circumstance it may be in great measure
owing that this part of the building suffered less than the
other portions of it.　The nave and aisles being covered
with lead, this metal, when it became liquified by the
flames, poured down in one continual stream, and entirely
gutted the body of the church.　The sight was an awful
one, as an eye-witness some years since feelingly described
it.　Every effort was made to save as much as possible
from the fury of the element.　At length the stream of
melted lead rushed down much too thickly for any farther
exertions to be made, and the collected crowd was constrained to stand by, passive spectators of the conflagration,
while the bells fell, each separately, from their height,
with a fearful crash!　The metal was afterwards sold to
aid in defraying the expenses of rebuilding the structure,
and at present there is but one bell in the tower of the
church, with the addition of what, from its diminutive

* The interior of the church at Leigh in Essex, which owes its restoration in great measure to the activity, good taste, and unusual munificence of the Rev. — Eden, the present incumbent, is a perfect model
of this style.

size and peculiar tone, is aptly enough denominated the
"ting-tang."

Foulsham never having been the residence of any of its
early lords and patrons, nor apparently of their connexions,
it is not likely that its church should ever have been
enriched with many monuments or monumental brasses.
At the time of the compilation of Blomefield's History,
there were, however, two of these latter memorials.   One
with the following inscription :

> Orate p. a' i' ab ; Tho. Thymbelthorp et Johanne uxor ej.
> qui obt, Feb. 25, 1526.

Themelthorpe was formerly considered a hamlet of
Foulsham, and several of this name were buried here.

The other thus inscribed :

> Orate p. a' i' a. Nichi. filii et heredis Robti Popi, gen.*

These brasses are both gone, having, as I presume, either
been lost or destroyed at the time of the fire.   The only
one which now remains, is a small oblong brass at the foot
of the reading-desk, commemorating the death and chari-

---

* As orthography in proper names was far from being strictly ad-
hered to by our ancestors, it seems not unlikely that Alice the wife of
Sir Robert Townshend, who died seized of considerable property in this
neighbourhood, in the reign of Philip and Mary, was a descendant of
this Robert *Popi*. See Blomefield's Norfolk, Vol. 8, 215. The recent
controversy on the name of Shakspeare proves that in the 16th and
17th centuries, one and the same person was meant, though the spelling
of the name at different times of the party's life varied much more than
in the present instance. This family of Poppy possessed the lordship
and advowson of Twyford for a considerable period, till by the marriage of the above-mentioned Alice, they came into the Townshend
family. The name of Poppy is now become extinct in the neighbourhood.

table bequest of Richard Fenn, in these somewhat quaint lines :

> Of all I had this only now I have,
> Nyne akers wch unto ye poore I gave.
> Richard Fenn who died March 6, 1565.

In the body of the church there are several stone slabs to the memory of substantial inhabitants of the place, but these have all been laid down since the year 1770. One is to the memory of Robert Toll, gent., who died 1779, aged 56 years, and bears the arms of his family. Another, to the memory of Absalom Parrant, who died 1794, aged 72, has this inscription: 'Hèlas! Il est alle. O! Sacre Enterer préservèr sa Desosseres.' We must hope that it was the error of the stone-cutter, occasioned by his utter ignorance of every language but his mother-tongue, which gave rise to such egregious blunders; for surely, no one who had ever gone through the French accidence, could have sent him a written epitaph for his guidance, so wofully loaded with mistakes as this is!

Robert Temple died, 1760, aged 57 years. Mary, his wife, died, 1792, aged 82 years.

John Temple died, 1765, aged 19 years – William died, 1777, aged 42—Thomas died, 1793, aged 48—Mary died, 1815, aged 76—Robert died, 1833, aged 82 years. The Temples were, for several generations, tenants of the manor-farm here belonging to the Astley family.

Nicholas Back died, 1749, aged 70 years. Alice, wife of Thomas Back, died, 1790, aged 68. Thomas Back, died, 1798, aged 86.

William Ivory died, 1789, aged 66. Barbara his wife died, 1812, aged 81.

The Backs and Ivorys were substantial tradesmen in the parish.

John Drosier died, 1793, aged 63, and Margaret his wife died, 1803, aged 73. Mr. J. Drosier was also a substantial tradesman here.

John Pike, Gent., died, 1788, aged 72. Susanna Rebecca his wife died, 1806, aged 62; and near them lies buried an infant daughter.

William Mays, Gent., died, 1805, aged 84. Mary his wife died, 1797, aged 66. Eleanor Colvin, their daughter, died, 1791, aged 40 years; with others of the same family. The Mayses were the occupiers of the Hall Farm for many years.

Charlotta Parrant died, 1768, aged 24; Elizabeth Parrant died 1770, aged 20; daughters of Absalom and Mary Parrant. Charles Parrant died, 1774, aged 18 years.

Mary, daughter of John Athill, Gent., and Judith his wife died, 1783, aged 54, and lies interred with her ancestors near this place. Near the above is also a small brass to the memory of James Athill Seppings, son of Dey and Ann Seppings, who died, 1788, aged 9 weeks. The arms of the family of Athill are given.

Of mural monuments in this part of the church there are but two, and these very plain. One, to the memory of Nathaniel Cooper who died, 1777, aged 69 years; the other, to that of the Rev. James Athill, many years curate of the parish, who died in 1799, aged 73, and Anne, his wife, who died, 1805, aged 75 years.

From the present appearance of the building, there is nothing to denote its ever having had any chapel or chantry attached to it, though at the east end of the south aisle is a niche in the wall of the Decorated style of architecture, which may have contained the image of some saint, as there were lights formerly burnt here in honour of St. Catharine, St. Mary, St. Nicolas, St. Peter, and St. Margaret.

Edmund Ryx in his will directed that his corpse should be buried in this church; and in 1504 gave to the new guild of Jesu 6s. 8d., and £20. to the repairs of the church, ordering also at the same time that 'the boke of ' the service of the transfiguration of Christ be bought on ' my coste, a chrismatory of silver, and one acre of land ' to his obit.' Reg. Rix. fol. 1. Who this Edmund Ryx was, or what property he possessed in the parish, is not known.

Here was also the guild of Holy Trinity, and the guild of St. Catharine. These guilds, or social confederations, may be traced as far back as the times of the Anglo-Saxons, and are more frequently mentioned in contemporary judicial codes than in Domesday Book. In the present age we may perhaps think lightly of them, but at a period when there were neither poor-laws, nor savings-banks, they must have been admirable institutions, resembling what we should now call, benefit societies or clubs. Persons of rank and wealth not unfrequently enrolled themselves in the list of their members, and many guilds possessed considerable real property devised to them by different brethren, which enabled them to erect halls for their public meetings, or to annex chapels to their parish churches, whither they were wont to repair on set days for the purposes of devotion. And then, as well as now, a merry-making, or dinner, was the usual termination of the ceremony. At the Reformation these societies seem to have generally disappeared. The remembrance of the name still survives in the familiar term "Guild-hall;" and before the enactment of the Corporation Reform Bill, the day on which the mayor of the city of Norwich entered upon his office was called the guild-day, when his worship regaled the nobility and gentry of the county and city in St. Andrew's hall there, with such unbounded hospitality, and with such a praiseworthy disregard to political opinions, that it is to be regretted so time-honoured a custom should have been deemed necessary to be superseded. There was a fraternity, or guild of St. George, established in the Black-friars' church at Norwich in 1385, to which Sir John Fastolf gave 'an angel silver, silver and guylt, berying the arme of St. George;' query, his cross or his limb? This fraternity subsisted as late as the year 1731, when being deeply in debt, they surrendered their effects to the corporation. An amusing account may be found in Blomefield, vol. 1, 534, of a new guild instituted at Attleburgh, as recently as the year 1628, the proceedings of which, as there recounted, are in exact accordance with the description just given.

According to the MSS. of the industrious Dr. Tanner in the archives of the Bishop of Norwich, there was a pilgrimage to St. Botolph of Foulsham in 1506. Rix, 373. I have not discovered any farther particulars of this 'famous image' of St. Botolph, as Blomefield calls it, nor in what part of the church the figure was placed. The usual situation of such shrines was in the east part of the chancel, behind the high altar. St. Botolph's image might have stood in one of the niches which are yet to be seen

E

there, and probably if so, there was some figure to correspond with it in the other. But whether, if it did actually occupy such a position, it withstood the shock of the Reformation, to experience the tender mercies of the parliamentary fanatics at the time of the great rebellion, or whatever else its fate may have been, there is now not even the shadow of a tradition left respecting it. Neither is there any thing connected with the history of this saint, or with that of Foulsham, which might afford reason for conjecture as to why his name should have gained so great a celebrity here. St. Botolph, it appears, was an English Saxon, to whom Ethelmund, a prince among the South Angles, gave Icanhoe, then a desert place, a short distance eastward of Lincoln, where Botolph, in the year 654, began to build a monastery. According to Camden, the town of Boston, more truly called Botulph's-Town, derived its name from him. He died in 680, and was buried in the monastery which he had founded. There his relics remained, till the Danes invaded England, and wasted all holy places with fire and sword ; when by the care of St. Ethelwold they were translated, part to the monastery of Ely, part to that of Thorny, and a third part was by King Edward the Confessor conferred on the church of St. Peter in Westminster. His memory is celebrated in our martyrology on the 16th of May, and he is usually pictured with a church or monastery, in reference to the great zeal he had for such sacred houses.

At the eastern end of the nave stands the pulpit, with the reading and clerk's desk below it; all of Virginian walnut-wood, in a plain, but well-finished style of workmanship. These were the gift of the late Sir Edward

Astley, Bart., of Melton Constable, Norfolk, the patron of the living ; to whose munificence after the fire, the inhabitants, as well as the church, were very greatly indebted, the chancel having been repaired solely at his cost. By their unanimous desire, his name was inscribed on a transverse beam over the east window of the chancel, with the date of the year 1770, where it still remains. Sir Edward, while he represented the county in parliament, was one of the two or three singular members, of whom the well-known fact is recorded, that on their entering the House of Commons, neither the minister of the day, nor the opposition, knew on which side their votes would be given.

These arms, which were formerly in the different windows of the church, have long since disappeared ; vert, an escutcheon, and orle of martlets, argent, Erpingham ; crest on an helmet, a chapeau, or, and a bunch of ostrich feathers, issuing out of a ducal coronet, gules ; cheque or and sable, a fess, argent, Thorpe, and Lord Scales.

The church was built, according to Blomefield, or rather according to his continuator, Parkin, by the Lord Morley. As the name of Morley was so long, and so intimately connected with the lordship of this town, and the patronage of the church, it is difficult to say precisely which of the Lords Morley enumerated in the list of its patrons was intended to be marked as the founder of the edifice. From the circumstance, however, according to the same authority, of the arms of Morley, Lovell, and Parker, having formerly been in the east chancel window, it is certain that some part of the fabric must have been built or repaired after the year 1489. Since in that year, Sir

William Parker, Knight, in right of Alice his wife, only
sister and heir of Henry Lovell, Lord Morley, who was
killed at the battle of Dixmude in Flanders, was the first
of the Parker family who became entitled to this manor
and advowson.   But I apprehend from the Decorated style
of architecture, which clearly prevails in the lower windows
of the chancel, in the church porch, and in all the doors of
the building, that Sir Robert de Morley, who died in France
in 1359, must have been the founder of the most ancient
part of the present fabric.   And this supposition is singularly strengthened by the positive testimony, which will
be hereafter noticed, of the incumbent who was presented
to the living by this same Sir Robert de Morley in 1334,
having contributed his share of expense to one at least of
the most ancient windows in the chancel.

The assertion, therefore, that the church was built by
the Lord Morley, is confessedly very indefinite, and at the
same time, as a very casual observation by any one at all
conversant with the different styles of architecture will
discover, decidedly incorrect ; since it is clear that this
church, like so many others in the country, was not all
built at the same time, but reduced to its present form, or
rather appearance, by a series of operations carried into
effect at different periods, yet all worked out according to
the original ground-plan ; there being nothing left at least,
to indicate any deviation having been made from the
design first laid down for its erection.   Though the
ground-plan, however, remains apparently the same as it
ever was, the alterations which the building has undergone
in other respects, are nowhere more clearly perceptible
than in the chancel, where the lower tier of windows are

in the Decorated style, while the upper, or clerestory ones, are in the later Perpendicular or rather Tudor style,* according with those in the body of the church over the arches which separate the nave from the two aisles, as well as with the windows in the aisles themselves. What might have been the form or fashion of the church which is mentioned as existing here at the time of Domesday Book, it is now impossible to say; but there is certainly no part of the present structure which can warrant us to assign to it a higher antiquity than the age of Edward III. It was then probably built or re-modelled mainly at the expense of Sir Robert de Morley, the lord and patron, and partly at the cost of Fulco de Montepinzoun, the incumbent of the rectory; for according to Dr. Tanner's MSS., which Blomefield used as his authority, attested by his private mark, "In the bottom most Westerly of yᵉ North" "chancel windows," were the following rhyming Latin verses :

> Fio Fulconis Montpynson lux ego donis.
> Nunc orare velis, maneat quod denique cœlia.

Which may be rendered into English thus :

> By Fulke Moutpynson's bounteous care,
>   Was made this window-light :
> Pray, then, his soul may ever share,
>   In Heaven's glories bright.

* The Decorated style of architecture began about 1307, and reaches to the end of the reign of Edward III., in 1377, and perhaps from ten to fifteen years longer. The Perpendicular style, which follows this, appears to have been in use, though much debased, even as late as 1630 or 1640, but only in additions. Probably the latest whole building is not later than Henry VIIIth's time.

This Fulco Montpynson, or de Montepinzoun, was presented to the living by Sir Robert de Morley, in 1334. It
may therefore be positively assumed that this the oldest
portion of the existing fabric was raised in the reign of
Edward III.; and the style of architecture agrees exactly
with that which is the decided characteristic of this period.
Of the same date is the small northern chancel door, the
arch and its columns separating the chancel from the nave,
and that which divides the tower and nave. Of a subsequent date, are the more obtuse arches which separate the
aisles from the body of the church, in the later period of
the Decorated style of architecture, together with their
supporting pillars, whose appearance, however, has been
considerably altered, as the present forms of some of their
bases evidently indicate. The same late date may be
assigned to the north and south aisle doors, to that which
forms the western entrance to the tower, to the porch, and
to one solitary window at the west end of the north aisle,
the only window probably left of those originally inserted
in the present nave and aisles.* In short, it would seem
beyond a doubt, that the old building raised in the time
of Edward III. was precisely of the same form and dimensions as the present one; and that in the reign of Henry
VII. or Henry VIII., about the period when Edmund Ryx

* I have not unfrequently observed that the west window of the
north aisle of churches is of a different character from most of the other
windows of the edifice; though I am not aware that any reason has
been suggested for this distinction. In some churches the north aisle
is still called the *dark* aisle, from having formerly had no windows.
Such an arrangement might have added to the warmth of the building
by excluding all draughts from the north.

left £20., a very considerable sum for those days, to the repairs of the church, which were then in all likelihood going on, the outward appearance of the fabric underwent much change, at least as far as the windows are concerned; those portions of the ancient church just now enumerated being left in their original state, while the windows of the aisles and nave, as well as the upper tier in the chancel, were inserted in a style of architecture corresponding with that of the age. At this latter period, I conceive, the Morley arms and those of France and England, were fixed over the western door of the tower, the windows in it left as they now are, and the battlements added. It might be too at this period, on the completion of the repairs of the church, though it is mere matter of conjecture, that some circumstance occurred which led to the pilgrimage to the famous image of St. Botolph, in 1506. That there was no material alteration made in the mullions, tracery, or arches of the windows, when the church was restored subsequently to the fire, I have had the repeated testimony of several persons well acquainted with the fabric both before and after the conflagration.

In the large east window of the chancel were the arms of Parker, Lord Morley, with his quarterings; argent, a lion passant, gules, between two bars, sable, charged with three bezants, 2 and 1, and as many bucks' heads caboshed in chief, of the 3d; Parker, quartering Lord Morley, and barry, nebuly, of six, or and gules, Lovell; azure, a lion rampant, and semée of lis, or, Holland; gules, a bend, lozengy, or, Marshall; crest, a bear, sable, muzzled, or, supporters two antelopes, argent, armed chained and collared, or. All these arms have long since vanished.

Judging from the appearance of this window, it must in its original state have been in perfect keeping with the lower tier of lights on the north and south sides of the chancel, and have greatly added to the effect of the entire building.   But the alterations it has undergone have wofully diminished its former beauty, and left it to the imagination only to judge what it once was.   Notwith-standing this drawback, and the discordance between the upper and lower chancel windows, the tracery of these latter is so bold, sharp as when it was first cut, and yet retaining sufficient delicately-painted glass to shed at least the semblance of a "dim religious light," that it imparts to the whole a soft and highly pleasing effect.   Of this stained glass it is astonishing that so much has been saved as is still remaining, and its quality in general is extremely good.   A careful examination with a telescope is often, from its distance from the eye, essential to a proper ap-preciation of its value.   Fortunately, this portion of the church did not suffer very materially from the fire.   Its walls, for nearly their whole length, are lined with a wood panelling to the height of about seven feet, carved after what is termed the linen pattern, a pattern very usual in the time of Henry VIII.

The Communion table, at the east end of the chancel, stands on an elevation of one step, and the railing by which it is enclosed was another gift of Sir Edward Astley; having been brought together with the wood panelling, as it is said, from the Hall at Thornage, one of those numerous old mansions which formerly served for the residence of the owner of the surrounding estate, but which have now, many of them, fallen into the possession of more wealthy

proprietors, and are occupied by some of their substantial
tenantry. Over the table are the royal arms, surmounting
an inscription of the Lord's Prayer, the Ten Commandments, and the Apostles' Creed; and at the back of these,
on either side of the east window, is a trefoiled niche. In
the floor of the chancel are stones to the memory of the
Rev. Henry Rice, rector of the parish, who died in 1771,
and others of his family, with their arms, ... a
chevron sable charged with three cinquefoils, between
three stags' heads horned proper. Within the rails of the
Communion table is a slab to the memory of the Rev.
Thomas Astley, and Ann his wife. He also was a former
rector, and died in 1743. A mural monument is erected
to his memory on the south chancel wall by his brother,
Edward Astley, Esq., with the arms of the Astleys of
Melton Constable. There is also in the body of the
chancel a small brass with this memorial: "Here lyeth
the body of Sr Thomas Hunt K^t. Lord & Patron of this
church and mannor who departed this lyfe ye 5th day of
Januarie 1616." The monumental ornament, the most
remarkable in the whole building, is that of this same Sir
Thomas Hunt in armour, fixed in the north wall, over the
small entrance-door into the chancel, with his three wives
kneeling behind him. The inscription, which time has
somewhat injured, runs thus: "Here lyeth interred the
body of Sir Thomas Hunt, knight, lord and patron of this
church, who died January 5, 1616, and gave £10. for ever
towards the maintenance of the organs of this church;
53 sh. 4d. for ever, to the poor of Hilderston in this
county; and £20. per ann. for ever, to the poor of the
worshipful company of fish-mongers of London; and

53 sh. 4d. for ever, to the poor of the parish of St.
Dunstan in the East, London ; and 53 sh. 4d. for ever, to
the poor of Camberwell in Surry : he had 3 wives ; first,
Margaret, widow of John Warner of London, merchant ;
the 2d. Jane, widow of Thomas Grimes, Esq. ; the 3d.
Dame Elizabeth, widow of Sir Francis Cherry, yet living ;
He had by Margaret 2 sons, William Hunt of Hilderston,
Esq., son and heir ; and Nicholas of London, merchant, by
the providence of God, deceased before him." On the monument are these, his arms ; per pale, vert and or, a saltire
counterchanged, on a canton, gules, a lion passant of the
2d, impaling, gules, on a fess, between four lis, or ; . . . .
or, three barrulets, gules ; argent, on a fess, between four
barrulets, wavy, azure, three lis of the first.

According to his will it appears that Sir Thomas had
caused this monument to be erected some time before his
death, and the figure of the knight is still found kneeling
there in nearly as perfect a state as ever. By him, agreeable to a very general custom of those times of hanging a
sword over the grave of a knight, rests his weighty weapon,
covered with the rust of ages.* Behind him are his three
wives in a kneeling posture ; their necks arrayed in that
never-failing appendage to a lady's dress in the days of
good Queen Bess, and for some while after, the wide
stiffened ruff. Sir Thomas's second wife, Jane, widow of
Thomas Grimes, Esq., was the daughter and co-heiress of
Thomas Muschamp, of Peckham, Esq., and was interred at

* No trophy, *sword*, nor hatchment o'er his bones.—*Hamlet*, Act 4,
sc. 5.

It was a custom in the time of our author, to hang a sword over the
grave of a knight.—*Johnson's note.*

Camberwell, in Surrey, November the 13th, 1604. Her painted effigy remained in Camberwell church till its recent destruction by fire, with a poetical epitaph, printed in Manning and Bray's History of Surrey, but more correctly in the Gentleman's Magazine, xcv. ii. 519. Sir Thomas was married to his third wife, the Lady Elizabeth Cherry, at St. Olave's church, Hart Street, London, on the 28th of November, 1609, by licence. The bride was the widow of Sir Francis Cherry, of London, knighted at Chatham, July the 4th, 1604. There is also this following entry in the Register of Camberwell: 1607, April 3. John Primero, baptized, a negro. Witnesses, Sir Thomas Hunt, Mr. Cox, and Mrs. Mary Grymes. (1614-15, Feb. 13, buryed Jhon Primero fr. Sʳ. Thomas Hunt.)

It will be seen by the above inscription on his monument, that Sir Thomas Hunt left 53 sh. 4d. for ever to the poor of the parish of Hilderston, *alias*, Hindolvestone, in this county. Up to what period after the death of Sir Thomas, this payment continued to be made, cannot be ascertained; but after having been suspended so long, that the recollection of such a bequest was almost lost, it was very unexpectedly to the parish renewed in 1811, and has been duly remitted ever since. These 53 sh. 4d. left by Sir Thomas Hunt to the poor of the parish of Hindolvestone are charged on certain lands in Kent Street in Surrey.

By a bond, dated 4th June, 1811, reciting the will of Sir Thomas Hunt, and reciting that the vicar and church-wardens of the parish of Hindolvestone had agreed to accept £25. in full for all arrears of the said rent-charge up to the 31st December, 1810, Edward Pickard of Homerton, in the parish of St. John, Hackney, became bound in the penalty of £100. to the Rev. John Lloyd and two others, the vicar and churchwardens of the parish, and their successors, on the condition that the said Edward Pickard and the trustees for William Henry Whittell, or the persons interested in the estate in Kent Street, charged therewith, should pay the said annuity of 53s. 4d. without any deduction, every 31st December, to the vicar and churchwardens for the time being.

This yearly sum is now received from J. C. Cameron, Esq. of Verulam Buildings, Gray's Inn, as one of the trustees of the will of the above-named Edward Pickard. We are informed by Mr. Cameron, say the Parliamentary Commissioners in their Report, printed in 1835, that this is the interest of a sum invested in the three per cent. consols, for the purpose of providing the annual payment. It is now, together with 50s. paid from the town land, distributed at Easter among all the poor belonging to the parish, whether resident in it or not, in sums of 9d. each.

This bequest is thus expressed in Sir Thomas Hunt's will : I give to the vicar and churchwardens of Hilderston, where my house standeth, to the poor there for ever, 53 sh. 4d. a year, for six poor men and women, 2d. a-piece every Sabbath day in bread ; to the sexton or clerk for setting the bread on the table, the odd 16d. ; to the churchwardens for distributing the same, a pair of gloves ; and these poor after service, if they be willing, and have no convenient lett, shall come every Sabbath-day to the stone where my father lieth, kneeling, and shall say the Lord's Prayer, and pray to God for the King and Queen then reigning over them, and for no other use.

From this, and other notices of the family in Hindolvestone church, it is highly probable that Sir Thomas was born there.

The annuity of £2. 13s. 4d. to St. Dunstan in the East, Sir Thomas gave to the parson and churchwardens of the parish, for the use of the poor, to be issuing out of his lands in Kentish-street in the county of Surrey, on condition that the parish would let his son renew the lease he then held under the church, for the same money another would give, which lease was renewed accordingly. In consequence of disputes in Chancery relating to the estate, out of which this annuity was payable, it had not been received from 1737 to 1805. In the latter year, Mr. Edward Pickard being in possession of the estate, agreed to pay £105. for all arrears then due, and to transfer to the minister and churchwardens as much stock in the three per cent. reduced annuities, as would produce yearly dividends equal to the annuity. He accordingly transferred £87. 19s. 4d. in that stock in the names of the Rev. Dr. Coryton, and Messrs. George Mackenzie and Joseph Ray, the then rector and churchwardens for this purpose; and the before-mentioned sum of £105. was laid out in the purchase of £175. of the same stock in the same names. Mr. Ray is now the only surviving trustee. The annual dividends arising from these two parcels of stock, are united, making in the whole £7. 18s. 4d.—Parliamentary Commissioners' Reports. Charities in England and Wales, IV. 98. Printed in 1820.

The 53s. 4d. a year were given by Sir Thomas to the vicar and churchwardens of Camberwell, to the use of the poor for ever; and he willed that this legacy and that to Hindolvestone should be taken out of all his land in Nor-

F

thumberland-alley, except his wife's jointure, till such time
as Mrs. Sare should die, and Brown's lease should end; after
that they should discharge his lands in Northumberland-
alley, and take it for ever out of his lands in Kentish-street,
in the county of Surrey, which John Brown held by lease.
The £2. 13s. 4d. a year have been received until lately, from
Mr. Edward Pickard, as the proprietor of some houses in
. . . . court, in Kent-street, Southwark, which are understood to have been formerly the estate of Sir Thomas Hunt.
Mr. Pickard is lately dead, and it has not yet been ascertained to whom the premises now belong.   In the application of this annuity the trustees have adopted the directions
given by the testator, with respect to his legacy to the poor
of Hilderstone, distributing six twopenny loaves every
Sunday to as many poor persons of the parish.   The remaining 1s. 4d. is carried on to the general Donation Fund.
Parliamentary Commissioners' Reports.   Charities in England and Wales, XVI. 333.   Printed in 1826-7.

As these several annuities are derived from the same
property which Sir Thomas Hunt charged with the annual
payment of £10. for the maintenance of the organ at
Foulsham, in addition to the above clear statement respecting them, it appears from the parish records of Camberwell,
that on the lands in Kentish-street, now called Kent-street,
in the parish of St. George the Martyr, Southwark, houses
have been built, which are in the occupation of W. H.
Whittell and others.   The £2. 13s. 4d. were received, till
within the last few years, from Mr. Wm. Guise Stevens,
solicitor, No. 30, Walbrook, on producing an order or receipt from the vicar of Camberwell.   This sum however is
now regularly paid by Mr. Whittell himself, who is a wool-

stapler in Staple-street, Bermondsey, to the vestry-clerk of Camberwell on his application for it at each Christmas.

Unfortunately for the parish of Foulsham, its organs are no longer in existence; and there is no proof to show that the payment of the ten pounds for their maintenance was ever made for a single year, though it can hardly be supposed that such is the fact. This circumstance, with innumerable instances of a similar kind, must lead us to regret, or rather strongly to deprecate, the careless manner in which in bygone times the records connected with charitable bequests to a parish were too often attended to. It is owing to the same strange negligence on the part of former parish officers, that some of the land anciently bequeathed for the benefit of the poor of Foulsham, is so intermixed with private property, that it is a subject of dispute both as to its quantity, and as to where it really is!

How the organs, for the plural noun instead of the singular was formerly used by us, as it still is by the French, came into the church, there are now no means of ascertaining. That they were not presented by Sir Thomas Hunt, appears pretty certain, from the circumstance of his not having mentioned such to be the case in his will, which he most probably would have done, had they been erected by him. It is likely the annual payment of £10. was regularly continued till the troubles in Charles the First's reign; for among the changes which the Puritans then made, one was the abolition of the liturgy, and another the destruction of organs. The liturgy was denounced in 1644, as a superstitious ritual, and spontaneous prayers were ordered to be used instead of a pre-arranged form of service; while with respect to music, psalm-singing, unaccompanied

by the organ, was ordained. So completely was this latter
order obeyed, that when, after the Restoration, the old
form of worship was resumed, organs, organ-builders, and
organists were almost equally rare in England: some of
the organ-builders had been constrained to become carpenters and cabinet-makers during the Commonwealth, there
being no demand for organs. In the reigns of Henry VIII.,
Edward VI., and Elizabeth, church music rose to a brilliant
height in England.

The current belief in the parish some fifty years since,
was, that a fire had consumed the houses on which the
payment was secured, situated, according to Sir Thomas
Hunt's will, in Kent-street, in the Borough ; and this accident, if true, may have increased the difficulty of substan-
tiating the claim, were any demand made for the renewal
of the legacy subsequently to the restoration of Charles II.
The remains of the organs were certainly in being at the
time of the fire at Foulsham, in 1770, by the general testimony of the old parishioners on the subject many years
since.   Whether in the event of another organ being erected
in the church, there could be any just claim made for the
renewal of the annual payment of the ten pounds in aid of
its support, may perhaps be a matter of doubt.   Yet it is
clear, from the following circumstance, which occurred in
the year 1811, the same year in which the parish of Hindolvestone recovered its right, that the then owners of the
property chargeable with the payment did not consider
·themselves exonerated from such a charge.   In that year,
at a meeting of the parishioners and the commissioners
under the Act for Inclosing the Commons and Waste Lands
in Foulsham and Themelthorpe, a solicitor from London

presented himself, apparently totally unexpected on the part of the meeting, stating that he was instructed to offer to the parish £25., on condition that the minister and churchwardens were willing to give him a discharge in full or the annual legacy of £10., which Sir Thomas Hunt had left by will, for the maintenance of the organs formerly in the church. This proposal, as might reasonably have been imagined, was not accepted; though there would seem to have been some further transactions in the affair, as an unexecuted document, drawn up on the occasion, is still preserved in the church chest. The following is a draft copy of this record:

" Sir Thomas Hunt, Knight, citizen and fishmonger of London, by his will dated 28th April, 1615, and duly proved in the Prerogative Court of Canterbury, after referring to certain lands in Kentish-street, otherwise Kent-street, in the county of Surrey, belonging to him the said Sir Thomas Hunt, then in the possession of one Mrs. Sayer, but leased in reversion after her decease to one John Brown, at the yearly rent of £26.; and reciting that he had before given and devised £20., part of the said rent of £26., for certain purposes in his said will mentioned, ordered and directed that the sum of £6. per annum, the remainder thereof, should go to the parson and churchwardens of Foulsham, towards the maintenance of the organs there for ever, so as they used them; and if they did not, then that the said £6. should go to his heir for ever. And the said testator further willed and directed, that after the expiration of the lease by him granted to the said John Brown, that £4. a year more should go to the parson and churchwardens of Foulsham aforesaid, so as they used the organs

to the glory of God; and if they did not, then to the heir
of him the said testator for ever out of his said land in
Kent-street. And Edward Pickard of Homerton, in the
parish of St. John, Hackney, in the county of Middlesex,
and Eleanor Martha his wife, or one of them, being entitled
to the fee simple and inheritance of certain premises in
Kent-street, supposed to be the lands on which the said
annuity of £10. was intended to be charged by the said
Sir Thomas Hunt, by indentures of lease and release, bearing date respectively the 23rd and 24th June, 1806, conveyed the same to William Henry Whittell and Henry Dudin,
and their heirs, for the use, upon trust, or for the benefit of
the said William Henry Whittell, his heirs and assigns for
ever. And the said Edward Pickard, by a bond dated
24th June, 1806, became bound in the penal sum of £1000.
for indemnifying William Henry Whittell and Henry Dudin
against all claims, &c. And whereas it did not appear that
any claim or demand of the said annuity of £10. had ever
been made upon the said estate or the owner thereof, by
virtue of the will of Sir Thomas Hunt or otherwise, or that
any organ or organs whatsoever had been set up or used in
the said parish church of Foulsham, by reason whereof
great doubts were entertained as to the right and title of
the said parson and churchwardens to the said annuity,
and as to the premises out of which the same was intended
to issue; but the said Edward Pickard, to prevent any
breach in the condition of the bond so entered into with
the said William Henry Whittell and Henry Dudin, by
reason of any claim, &c. which might be made or instituted
by the said parson and churchwardens of the parish of
Foulsham of or for the said annuity, and for wholly ex-

onerating the said premises, and all persons in respect to
the possession thereof from the same, and all claims relating
thereto as aforesaid, proposed to pay into the hands of
the said parson and churchwardens
of the said parish of Foulsham, the sum of £25., upon
their agreeing to accept the same in full payment and satisfaction of the said annuity, and all arrears and other claims
and demands in respect of the same."

      " (Indorsement.)   Dated   1811.

  " The Rev.   parson and churchwardens
of the parish of Foulsham, Norfolk, to Edward Pickard, Esq.
and others.

  " Draft.   Release of a rent-charge of £10. per annum,
issuing out of an estate in Kent-street, Surrey.

      " Wm. Guise Steevens, 30, Walbrook."

For reasons, which are not easy to be ascertained, as
there is not a single one of the original deeds known to be
in existence, Sir Thomas Hunt, in the year 1602, granted
to several of the copyhold tenants in the parish, leases of
their houses, orchards, &c., for the term of 500 years; and
according to his will, dated April 28th, 1615, and duly
registered in Doctors' Commons, besides his valuable possessions in Foulsham and the adjoining places, he was the
owner of very considerable property, amassed, as it would
seem, by success in trade as a soap-boiler. The £20.
a-year, mentioned in the monumental inscription, he gave
to the poor of the Company of Fishmongers, upon the
uses following, that is to say: That the Company should
build an hospital, containing houses for six poor men, who
should be free of the Company of Fishmongers, and have
the six houses rent free, &c.; the Wardens of the said

Company to have for their pains, 10s. a year, and a couple of capons, to recreate them yearly, out of his land in Kent Street.

The Company receive the said annuity of £20. yearly from Mr. Whittell, woolstapler, who is understood to be the proprietor of several small houses on the east side of Kent Street, on which the annuity is charged. A further annual sum of 10s. is received from Mr. Whittell, as a charge on the above-mentioned property, under a sub-sequent clause in Sir Thomas Hunt's will, for a purpose not connected with this charity. In the Returns of Charitable Bequests made to Parliament in 1786, and printed in 1816, it is stated that Sir Thomas Hunt's estate in Kent Street, Southwark, had then been in Chancery many years, subject to a decree in favour of the Fish-monger's Company for a debt due to them, which was not paid off; so that the parish of Camberwell had received no benefit from Sir Thomas's bequest for many years. There were fifty-three years' arrears due on Lady-day, 1786, amounting to £141. 6s. 8d. This annuity, however, it will be seen, has now been recovered by the parish of Camberwell. Sir Thomas was knighted July 23rd, 1603, and is described as then of Norfolk. In 1610, he served the office of sheriff for the counties of Surrey and Sussex, and died at Camberwell in 1616. He is erroneously styled, " Knight and Baronet," in an inscription at the Fish-mongers' almshouses. Sir Thomas in his will, which is commenced in a form of great solemnity, writes himself of Lambeth Dene, Knight, and free of the Worshipful Com-pany of Fishmongers, and desires to be buried at Foulsham, " in my church, where a monument is there made already. '

He also left two or three articles of plate, to be used by the Company on their banquetting days; as well as a small donation to be distributed among the poor of the parish of Foulsham, and directed that a sermon should be preached in the church there every Tuesday morning for the space of a year from the time of his decease, either by his relation Richard Hunt, the then rector; or, in case of his being unable to fulfil the request, the discourse was to be delivered by some other divine; and for each of these services a remuneration of six shillings and eightpence was to be made him. The hour named for the commencement of the service was eight o'clock in the morning, in order, according to the wording of the will, that the congregation who should attend the church, might not be prevented from repairing to their occupations in the market, whose busy time then began at nine in the forenoon. There must, therefore, at that period have been a considerable traffic carried on on market-days; and, indeed, within the memory of man, there used to be a respectable show of cattle, and a fair sale of corn; though a few years since, when the market died, as it were, a natural death, it had dwindled away to a mere nothing, and the very trifling business that was transacted did not commence till rather a late hour in the evening. Such complete revolutions does time bring about in the petty affairs of an obscure market-town, as well as in the mighty concerns of states and empires! Sir Thomas by his first wife was father of William Hunt, Esq., of Hindolvestone, who had two sons, Thomas, of Sharington in Norfolk, and George, his second son, of Hindolvestone, who sold this manor and advowson to Sir Jacob Astley, Bart. The Reverend Edward Hunt

Holley, the present rector of Hackford next Reephane, with
George Hunt Holley, Esquire, of Burgh, near Aylsham, the
patron of his brother's rectory, are the representatives, in
this neighbourhood at least, through a female branch by
marriage, of Sir Thomas Hunt, who purchased the advowson of Hackford of Sir Christopher Heydon, and first presented in 1589.

Under the clerestory, or upper tier of chancel windows,
along each side wall, at regular intervals, runs a line of
curious letters, each surmounted with a coronet, and precisely similar in character to those on a highly interesting
altar monument of stone in the churchyard, which has
been engraved by the Society of Antiquaries, from a drawing by Mr. Edmund Prideaux, a Norwich gentleman,
elected F.S.A. on the 13th of April, 1720, and relation
probably of Humphrey Prideaux, Dean of Norwich, though
with an unaccountable mistake in one of the letters, the
second S. This is the more strange, since the first S. of
the inscription is rightly copied. The words on the altar
monument are these: Robart Colles Cecili his Vif. This
Robert Colles, according to Blomefield, Vol. 8. p. 208, was
witness to a deed of Ralph Bateman of Foulsham, and
Alice his wife, living in the 20th year of Henry VII., 1505.
From the exact similarity between the letters on this tomb
and those in the chancel, the fair conclusion is, that their
age must be nearly the same, and that these latter were
placed there in the end of the 15th, or in the beginning of
the 16th century, when the present upper lights of the
chancel, and the windows of the body of the church were
inserted; and about the same time also, when Edmund
Ryx left £20. for the repairs of the church. Besides the

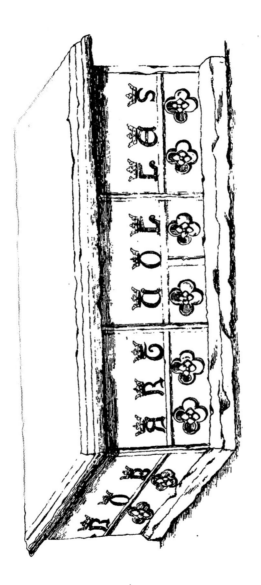

Roɓart Colles certli his wife.

Published ... Strand

proof which the fact of Colles's signature to the deed above mentioned affords, as to the date of the coronetted letters on his own tomb, in that splendid work, Shaw's Illuminated MSS., the latter part of the 15th century is assigned as the date to letters corresponding with those in the chancel, and those on the tomb; a date which, in round numbers, agrees with that here attributed to them.

In the Philosophical Transactions for the year 1687, No. 189, is an account of some Saxon coins found in Suffolk, communicated by Sir P. S., Fellow of the Royal Society, with some remarks thereon by Mr. W. W., likewise F.R.S. In this same No. also, it is said, " In the churchyard at Foulsham, in Norfolk, there is a tomb-stone with this inscription, which some of the learned in these curiosities may perhaps explain." Then follow some rude characters, bearing little or no resemblance to those on the tomb, and which may well defy interpretation! The writer of the above notice was beyond doubt the son and heir of General Skippon, the former owner of Foulsham Hall, Sir Philip Skippon, Knight; who from this would appear to have occasionally resided at Foulsham, and to have devoted a portion of his "learned leasure" to the examination of this curious piece of antiquity. At the same time, something better than this meagre account might have been expected from a gentleman and scholar, who in his other writings evinces no little talent and research; especially as the inscription on the tomb is by no means difficult to be deciphered. Besides the engraving of the tomb in this Number of the Philosophical Transactions, it is copied, but not deciphered in the Magna Britannia, Vol. 3, p. 282. A more accurate engraving was published by the Society of

Antiquaries, which has been already noticed; and it is again given in the second volume of Gough's edition of Camden, plate 2, fig. 5.

But to return to the letters in the chancel. The situation of these letters is singular; at least I have never in my numerous visits to country churches observed any thing which might help to explain their meaning. Could they have been fixed on what served as the corbels to a more ancient roof than the present one? For, besides the different styles of architecture observable in the upper and lower windows of the chancel, the circumstance of the point of the arch which separates the nave from the chancel being now buried in the roof, is a decisive proof that the original height was not the same as it now is; corroborating also the fact of the *true ancient* pitch of church roofs, being higher than the modern builder's *true* pitch. Yet though I have spent days in endeavouring to discover their meaning, I am under the necessity of adding, that hitherto I have been unable to elicit any thing satisfactory from them. Some of the letters are mutilated; but there is sufficient left even of these, to allow of their being traced with certainty, or nearly so. From the position of the letters themselves, they must clearly follow each other in one or other of these two orders; either beginning at the south wall from its east end—O. H. N? I. W. R. I., and continuing along the north wall from west to east, E. Q. N? O? .... H. G. or T. Or supposing the beginning to be at the west end of the north wall, they would run in this order: E. Q. N.? O? .... H. G or T.—O. H. N? I. W. R. I.

It could not but prove highly gratifying to discover

what these letters are meant to signify, as it might throw some curious light on the history of the church. But I almost despair of any such good fortune, and must, therefore, reluctantly leave the subject in as great obscurity as ever, scarcely venturing to indulge in the hope that at some future time the mystery may be unravelled.

Opposite the monument to the memory of Sir Thomas Hunt, in the south wall of the chancel near the altar, are three raised canopied stalls, ornamented with crocketted work and finials, with a corresponding niche adjoining, divided into two compartments, but without any drain-hole or hollow for holding water, having been intended to serve merely for the receptacle of some of the utensils made use of at the altar. The chaste style of the Decorated Order of architecture which pervades all these, and the fashion of the head-dresses of the figures at the lower points of the canopies, denote that they were erected about the time of Edward III., when the lower part of the chancel was built, and when also this Order was in its greatest beauty. It is to be wondered, that hitherto it should not have been precisely ascertained to what uses these stalls were appropriated. They are frequently found in churches, generally three in number, occupying the same position with those now in question, the south side of the altar, called the Epistle side, from the priest standing there to read the Epistle. Some have imagined that they were set apart for the lord of the manor, who was in most cases the founder of the church on his domain, and his retinue. Others have asserted that they were originally intended for the use of the bishop and his attendants when he consecrated the church, or visited it. Others again will have it, that they were reserved for the rural dean at his visitation; and others, that the stalls were designed for the use of the priest, deacon, and sub-deacon, in the Roman Catholic times. Since therefore the opinions on this subject are so conflicting, and even those, who have made the deepest researches into it, differ so widely, it is by no means an easy matter to deduce a positive conclusion as to what was their peculiar use.

Were there nothing else which might be advanced in aid of such a supposition, the churchyard would appear even from its elevation alone above the paths which lead through it, to have served for the last resting-place of the inhabitants of the parish from time immemorial; but with the exception of two noble old sycamore trees near its western boundary, whose spreading branches nearly reach the cottages on the opposite side of the highway, and the altar monument of stone, which marks the spot where Robert Colles and Cecili his Vif lie interred, there is nothing in it which can lay claim to any particular attention. The oldest gravestone in it is to the memory of John Gouldspring, who died in 1681. From the expense which must have been incurred in the erection and workmanship of Colles's monument, he was doubtless a person of wealth and repute in his neighbourhood, though there are now no other traces of his existence than this tomb, and his attestation to Bateman's deed. But whatever may have been the wealth or station of Colles, his is not the only name over whose history oblivion has thrown her veil; there are myriads of others, personages who, in their day, enacted a far more important part on the stage of this life than he probably ever shared in, " quos fama obscura recondit."

RECTORS.

Anselm le Gross occurs rector in the 3rd Henry III., 1219, presented by William Marshal, Earl of Pembroke. Probably this Anselm le Gross was some churchman connected with Alice, the Earl of Pembroke's wife, who was grand-daughter of William le Grosse, Earl of Albemarle. In 1207, John Marshal, who married Aliva or Alice, daughter and co-heiress of Hubert de Rhye, or Rye, baron of Rye in Norfolk, had a grant from King John of the Marshalship of Ireland. Le Neve says he died in 1234. He gave Themelthorpe church to the canons of Walsingham. John, son of this John, had the advowson of Foulsham in the same year, and died in 1242.

1307. *Robert de Bodekesham* instituted vicar, presented by Robert de Say, rector. It has been already observed that there was formerly an unendowed vicarage here, valued at four marks, and that in these early times a vicar was frequently nothing more than what would now be called a curate.

1310. *Philip de Wanton*, rector, presented by Hawyse le Mareschal, assignee of William le Mareschal.

This William le Mareschal, or Marshal, came of age about 1300. His mother's name was Hawyse or Alice, and he had also a daughter named Alice. In 1309 he was summoned to go against the Scots. His residence was at Hingham, and he wrote himself Lord of Hingham. He died in 1314, and left his estates to John le Mareschal his son, who died in 1316. Hingham was the usual residence of the Marshals, and of their successors the Morleys, and was always reputed the head of their Barony of Rye. John le Mareschal contributed to the building of Hingham church.

1321. *Roger de Swathyng,* rector, presented by Sir Robert de Morley.

Sir Robert de Morley married Hawyse or Alice, sister and heir of the above John le Mareschal. Sir Robert was resident at Swanton Morley, one of his manors in the neighbourhood of Foulsham, in 1335, was present at the famous battle of Cressy, and died in France in 1359; having married a second wife, Joan, daughter of Sir Peter de Tye, Knight. She, on his death, took the veil, and died in the same year as her husband. This Sir Robert de Morley was, as I conceive, the founder of the most ancient part of Foulsham church now existing; not only from the style of its architecture corresponding with the age in which he lived, but also, because soon after 13th Edward III., when Magna Charta was confirmed, many parish churches are known to have been built. Sir Robert was succeeded by his son, Sir William de Morley, who, in 1360, confirmed his father's donation of lands in Bintry, Foulsham, Guist, and Guestwick,* to the prior of Walsingham. His will is dated in Halingbury, in London diocese, 1379, and proved in the same year. He ordered his body to be buried in Austin Friars' church, Norwich; and left £46. 13 sh. 4d. to seven priests to say mass for his soul for one whole year next after his decease; one of whom was to do this office at the church of Foulsham. He also left 10 marks and his gilt cup towards the building of Swanton Morley church.

* Mr. Godwin, author of Caleb Williams, &c. was a native of this secluded village. His father was minister of the old-established dissenting place of worship here.

1327. *Bartholomew de Godelesford,* by Do.
1331. *Richard de Blacolvestre,*   by Do.
1334. *Fulco de Montepinzoun,*   by Do.

The arms of the Montepinzouns are, argent, a lion rampant sable, on his shoulder a martlet or. These arms were in Great Ryburgh church, Norfolk. A Fulco de Montepinzoun had also formerly a small manor there. The family of Montepinzoun, Montepinzun, or Monte Pincernon, was of considerable eminence in the 14th and 15th centuries, and had possessions in Great Ryburgh, Ingoldsthorpe, and other places in the county. It was this rector, Fulco Montpinzun, who gave one of the chancel windows, the lower one at the west end of the north wall, to Foulsham church.

1384. *Henry Curson,* by William and John Curson.

The Cursons held at this period the manor of Swantons, extending over part of Foulsham and Twyford. In the 2d. Edward IV. Sir John Curson had divers lands and tenements, called Hastings, in Bintry, Twyford, Guestwick, &c., and there is still a manor in Bintry named Hastings. On a grey marble in Bylaugh church, is the portraiture of a Sir John Curson, Knight, who died in 1471, with that of his wife in brass, and their armorial bearings much mutilated. This family is now become extinct, at least that branch of it which resided in this neighbourhood; except, indeed, its descendants are still to be recognized in a family bearing the same name, who have been inhabitants of Foulsham for several generations, following the occupation of letter-carriers to the next post-town. I am induced to suppose that this is somewhat more than idle conjecture, from having traced the name of Curson in writings relating to Foulsham, and these several neighbouring villages, from a remote period, to the middle of the last century, when the connexion with the then postman seemed clear. On the heads of some of the seats in Billingford church, rudely carved, are, or were, the arms of the Cursons, ermine, a bend compony, argent and sable. The same arms were also formerly in Foxley church windows, and in the east window of Twyford church.

1399. *William Cave*, by Thomas, Lord Morley.

This Thomas, Lord Morley, grandson of Sir Robert de Morley, appears to have had no trifling dealings in the Court of Chivalry; for, besides the cause in which he himself was personally concerned against Sir John Lovell, Knight, concerning the arms of the family of Morley, see Blomefield's Norfolk, Vol. 2, p. 437, he was pledge for his friend and neighbour, Sir Edward Hastyngs, Knight, in a cause between Sir Edward and the Lord Reginald Grey of Ruthyn in the same Court, where he was produced as a witness, being at the time sixty years old. In 1402, according to an enrolment in the Close Rolls, Rot. Claus. 4 Henry IV., his debts were considerable, which may have induced him to assign the previous presentation to the rectory of Foulsham to the Cursons. His son Robert died during his father's life-time, and was buried in the same church as his grandfather, the church of the Austin Friars at Norwich. In 1408, Thomas, Lord Morley procured an exemplification of the grant of the office of Marshal of Ireland, made by King John, to John le Mareschal and his heirs; in 1412, he was residing at his manor of Aldby; in 1414, he obtained a writ, under the king's seal, directed to the mayor, &c. of Norwich, telling them that Hingham and

Foulsham were ancient demesne, and that the tenants by virtue thereof, were excused paying toll in all England, and, therefore, he commanded them, that they should demand no toll of his tenants in Hingham and Foulsham, for any goods bought or sold in their city. This is entered in an ancient court-book of mayoralty, begun 3d. Henry V. After having escaped the dangers of the sea-fight before Harfleur, where he behaved with great gallantry and courage, he reached Henry V. at Calais, and died there the 25th of September, 1415, and was buried in St. Mary's church, Calais, the King of England and the Emperor Sigismund attending his funeral.

1405. *Mr. Maurice de Campeden,* by Thomas, Lord Morley.
1408. *William Peck,*   ditto
1409. *Walter Thetford,*   ditto
1412. *John Birlingham,*   ditto
1418. *John Pelle,* by Anna, Lady Morley.

Anna, Lady Morley, second wife of Thomas, Lord Morley, was daughter of Edward, Lord Despenser, and widow of Sir Hugh Hastyngs of Elsing and Gressinhall, Knight. She survived her second husband, and died about 1426. In Blomefield, 8vo. edition, Pelle is said to have been presented to the living in the year 1413, a typographical error for 1418. It seems somewhat extraordinary that within thirteen years there should have been no less than five different rectors. I have not been able to discover any probable cause for so rapid a succession.

1437. *John Lesyngham,* by Isabel, Lady Morley.

Isabel was the widow of Sir Thomas, Lord Morley, who, in 1415, succeeded his grandfather, Thomas, Lord Morley, being then twenty-three years of age. He was à distinguished commander in the French wars of Henry V., and died in 1435, seized, jointly with Isabel his wife, of the whole estate, and was buried in Hingham church, under a noble monument against the north wall, which still remains ; Isabel, his wife, being interred by him. This splendid monument is not noticed either by Weever or Gough, but an engraving of it is given in Cotman's Architectural Antiquities of Norfolk.

Thomas Wode, without date or name of patron.

1481. *William Lambert,* by John, Duke of Suffolk, on the minority of Henry Lovell, Lord Morley.

Sir Thomas, Lord Morley, and the above Lady Isabel, left a son Robert, Lord Morley. This Robert died in 1442, leaving an only daughter, Alianora or Eleanor, who inherited her father's whole estate, and married William, a younger son of William, Lord Lovell of Tichmersh, who, in her right, became Lord Morley : he died in 1475, leaving Henry Lovell, Lord Morley, his son and heir, then a boy eleven years old, who was placed under the guardianship of John de la Pole, Duke of Suffolk, whose daughter, Elizabeth, he afterwards married. In 1489, this Henry settled Hingham, Buxton, and Forehoe Hundred on trustees to pay his debts, and was killed the same year at Dixmude in Flanders. Leaving no issue, his estate descended to Alice his sister, then twenty-one years old, and the wife of Sir William Parker, Knight, of London.

1492. *Mr. Michael Diacony,* S.T.P. by Sir William Parker, in right of his wife Alice, Lady Morley.

In the 8vo. edition of Blomefield, London, 1808, with reference to this presentation, the year 1497 is a misprint for 1492. So also it ought probably to be *Alice,* Lady

Morley, and not Elizabeth; at least, Alice seems to have been the Christian name of the wife of Sir William Parker. The abbreviations Eliz: and Alic: might easily have been interchanged.

1494. *Thomas Larke*, by Sir Richard Guildford and Sir Thomas Lovell.

After the death of Sir William Parker, which happened between 1504 and 1507, his widow married Sir Edward Howard, second son of Thomas, Duke of Norfolk, who as Admiral of England, was killed before Brest in the 5th Henry VIII. I know not how Sir Richard Guildford and Sir Thomas Lovell came to have the right of presentation. From the name of the latter, he was in all probability connected with the family of Sir William Parker's wife. Sir Thomas Lovell was a Knight of the Garter, and one of the executors of King Henry the Seventh's will. He built the gate-house at Lincoln's Inn, and East Harling Hall. He refounded Halliwell, near which he had a stately house; and dying at Enfield in 1524, was buried at Halliwell, a priory dedicated to St. John the Baptist in Shoreditch, by Norton Falgate, London.

1515. *John Wisdom*, by Alice, Lady Morley.

The Lady Alice died about 1518. She was buried in the chancel of Hingham church, and by her will directed that £26. 13s. 4d. should be expended on a gravestone to be laid over her.

... *Mr. F. Seymour*, S.T.P. without date or name of patron.

1551. *Christopher Meltham*, by Henry Waller, M.D. assignee of Henry, Lord Morley.

This Henry, Lord Morley, was son and heir of Sir

. William Parker. In the 21st Henry VIII. he was summoned to Parliament by the title of Lord Morley, Baron of
Rye. He married Alice, daughter of Sir John Bletso,·
Knight, had a son whom he outlived, and died in 1556.
It is probable his lordship had released the patronage of
the living to Henry Waller; since under the description
of the village of Bergh, of which he was also lord and
patron, Blomefield, 10, 196, I find he released the patronage
of that rectory for forty years to Oliver St. John, who presented in 1597, and in 1604. In the Archæologia, vol. 25,
p. 496, under the article Household and Privy Purse Accounts of the Lestranges at Hunstanton for the year 1530,
is this entry respecting the "mynstrells" of his Lordship.
"Itm. in rewarde the Vth day of June to my Lord Morley's mynstrells, 3s. 4d."

1556. *Charles Parker*, by Henry Parker, Lord Morley,
and Sir Henry Morley.

Blomefield states him to have been presented by Lord
Morley alone ; Dr. Tanner's MSS. in the Bishop's Registry
at Norwich give it as I have done. From the name, one
might infer that this incumbent was connected with the
family of his patron. At the christening of Edward VI.,
the Lady Elizabeth, afterwards Queen Elizabeth, then only
four years old, was borne by the Viscount Beauchamp,
with the assistance of Lord Morley. In the list of the
personages who assisted at this ceremony, he is called
Sir Henry Parker.

1572. *John Cooke*, S. T. B., by Margaret, relict of
Nicholas Carr, M.D. assignee of the Lord Morley.

The present Lord was Henry Parker, Lord Morley, who
succeeded his grandfather, the late Lord, whose son died

during his life time. By an Inquisition taken at Norwich in 1561, he was found to be Lord Morley, Baron of Rye, heir to the hundred of Eynsford, &c.; being then about 24 years old. He married Elizabeth, daughter and heir of Edward Stanley, Earl of Derby.

1585. *Edward Grant*, S. T. B., by Thomas Hunt, Gent.

Edward Grant, besides holding the living of Foulsham, was master of Westminster School, had a prebendal stall at Ely, and another at Westminster! To which last he was admitted in 1577. He died in 1601, and was buried in the Abbey. He was one of the early Greek scholars in England. In 1575, he published a Greek grammar, under the title of Græce Linguæ Spicilegium, intended for the use of the Westminster scholars; and in 1581, he superintended an edition of Constantin's Lexicon, probably in the abridgement, under the name of the Basle printer, Crespin, enriching it with four or five thousand new words, which he most likely took from Stephens's Thesaurus. In 1597, Camden published a grammar for the use of Westminster school. This grammar by Camden was probably founded on that of Grant. Smith, in his Life of Camden, says, that Grant's grammar was extremely deficient. Does the Greek grammar in present use at Westminster school retain any traces of that of Grant? From a somewhat superficial examination of Grant's Greek grammar, it seems to me to deserve rather a better character than Smith gives it; at least, it appeared to be not much inferior to the Eton Greek grammar still used in many of our schools.

Thomas Hunt, Gent., the present patron, became afterwards Sir Thomas Hunt, Knight, whose history has been already given. In 1582, he purchased the manor and advowson of Foulsham of Edward Parker, Lord Morley, son of the last-mentioned Lord. It was this Edward who divided and sold most, if not the whole, of the ancient estate of the Lords Morley in this county. He was one of the peers who gave judgment of death on the unfortunate Mary, Queen of Scots, at Fotheringay. So also upon Philip, Earl of Arundel, in the 32nd of Elizabeth; as well as upon Robert, Earl of Essex, the celebrated favourite of this Queen. He married Elizabeth, sole daughter and heir of William Stanley, Lord Monteagle, and died in 1618, leaving three sons and three daughters. The youngest of these, Frances, married Christopher Danby, Esq. of Leighton, in Yorkshire, who, joining with the Earl of Essex in his insurrection, suffered imprisonment for the aid thus given to this gallant, though rash nobleman, in his strange attempt to disturb the peace of the kingdom. William, his eldest son, bore the title of Lord Monteagle from his mother. He it was, to whom, in his father's life-time, that eventful and enigmatic letter was delivered, by which the Gunpowder Plot came to be discovered; the contents of it being intended to warn this young Lord from coming to Parliament that session, which was to commence on the 5th of November. Intimating that those who should sit there, would receive a terrible blow, and yet not see who hurt them. This letter being shown to James I., the king, though others slighted it, caused search to be made in the cellars under the House of Lords, which eventually led to the discovery of the renowned Guy Fawkes.

Thus ended the connexion between the Morley family,
and the lordship of Foulsham, together with the patronage
of its church; a connexion which had been continuously
carried on, either by lineal descent, or by marriage, from
the time when Richard I., in the 12th century, after
returning from his Austrian captivity, severed them from
the royal demesne, up to the period, 1582, when they came
by purchase into the possession of Sir Thomas Hunt. The
Parkers, Earls Morley, of Saltram, in the County of
Devon, trace their descent from the ancient lords of this
township.

1594. *Richard Hunt*, instituted by the Lord Archbishop of Canterbury, the see of Norwich being vacant.

Richard Hunt was nephew or cousin of Sir Thomas
Hunt, and according to the desire expressed by the latter
in his will, was, if no great hindrance prevented him, to
preach the sermon which he directed should be delivered
in Foulsham church on each succeeding Tuesday morning,
for the space of one whole year next after his decease.

1620. *Henry Burton*, by Stephen Burton, patron for
this turn only.

, According to Walker, in his Account of the Sufferings
of the Clergy, Burton held the living of Themelthorpe also,
and was sequestered during the great rebellion in Charles
the First's reign.

. . . *Philip Tenison*, S.T.P. without date or name of
patron. Probably a connexion of Archbishop Tenison,
whose father was incumbent of Mundesley, in 1640, ejected
for his loyalty.

Blomefield says Tenison died in 1660. Between the in-
cumbency of Burton, and that of Tenison, there appears to

have been another sequestration, for Walker notices *Brown* as having been sequestered, and one Richard Worts, as having been put in here by sequestrators in 1654. It is evident from Walker's account of Brown, that the succession cannot be very satisfactorily traced during this disturbed period. By the Returns made in 1655, according to an Act of Parliament passed in 1649, and which are deposited in the Archbishop of Canterbury's Palace at Lambeth, Foulsham is described as a parsonage presentative. The executors of Sir Edward Astley, Knight, deceased, were patrons thereof. Mr. Richard Wortes, "a preachinge minister," was the incumbent, and the living was then valued at £70. a year.

1660. *Herbert Astley*, LL.D. by William Cooke, trustee of Sir Jacob Astley, Bart.

Herbert Astley, son of Herbert Astley of Plymouth, was a constant attendant on Charles I.; after whose death he travelled into France, Italy, and Turkey, whence he returned about the time of the Restoration, and in 1662, was installed a prebendary of Norwich cathedral. Sir Jacob and Sir Isaac Astley acknowledged him as their kinsman, preferred him to the rectory of Foulsham, as well as to that of the neighbouring village of Themelthorpe. Afterwards marrying Barbara, daughter and heiress of John Hobart, of Waybread in Suffolk, Esq., only son of Sir John Hobart of Hales, he was by the Hobarts' interest promoted to the deanery of Norwich in 1670. He died in 1681, aged 63, and was buried in the nave of the cathedral, and by him was interred his wife. The inscription over his grave on black marble, which has since been removed to another part of the cathedral, gives him a high character. On the

north side of the door entering into the anti-choir of the
cathedral, is a mural monument to the memory of his wife,
who died in 1692, with the arms of Astley in ·a bordure
engrailed, and a crest for difference, impaling Hobart.

1681. *Charles Spicer*, aliàs *Helder*, by ditto.

In 1671, Charles Spicer, without the aliàs attached to
his name, occurs as rector of Melton Constable, presented
by Sir Jacob Astley.

1713. *Henry Colman*, S.T.B. by Sir Jacob Astley, Bart.

1721. *George Featherstonhaugh* died rector, and

. . . *Richard Warner* was then presented by the same
patron.

George Featherstonhaugh was rector of the neighbouring
parishes of Bintry and Themelthorpe, and lies buried in
one of these churches. Richard Warner had also the living
of Betely. He died in 1722, and in that church, near the
communion table, is a stone slab to his memory.

1722. *William Selth*, by ditto.

1724. *John Tompson*, by ditto, resigned.

. . . *Thomas Astley*, by ditto.

Thomas Astley died in 1743, and his monument in the
chancel has been already mentioned. This rector's name
is omitted in Blomefield's Norfolk.

1743. *Henry Rice*, by ditto.

The reverend Henry Rice was rector also of Betely, and
died in 1771. The stones to the memory of him and his
family have been previously noticed. Mr. Rice kept a close
carriage, not of the most modern style of the equipages
even of that day. This carriage was the lion of the town,
and every one ran eagerly to catch a glimpse of it, as it

rumbled slowly through the street, drawn by two strong coal-black steeds.

1771. *John Astley*, M.A. by Sir Edward Astley, Bart.

The reverend John Astley was also rector of Thornage, and brother of the patron, Sir Edward Astley, the great benefactor to the church and the parish after the fire in 1770.

1803. *Henry Nicholas Astley*, M.A. by Sir Jacob Henry Astley, Bart.

The reverend H. N. Astley, the present incumbent of East Basham and Little Snoring, and the brother of his patron, resigned the living of Foulsham in 1833, and was succeeded by his son,

Henry Milles Astley, A.B., the present rector, presented by his cousin, Lord Hastings, then Sir Jacob Astley, Bart.

The tithes, by the recent commutation, are valued at £780. per annum.

The late clerk of the parish, Edmund Carrison, a carpenter by trade, who died at an advanced age in 1827, was a journeyman workman in London in the time of the too celebrated Dr. Dodd, and was the person who actually constructed the pulpit in which the Dr. used to preach at his chapel in Charlotte Street, Pimlico.

Earlier than the new Registers commencing in 1813, there remains at Foulsham the Register of Baptisms and Burials, 1713-1812; that of Marriages, 1746-1812. The Register of Baptisms and Burials is defective in 1700 and 1710. The following brief notice is extracted from the Register of Burials for the year 1762. " Novr. 20. Ann Strange, a Foundling." The name here given was not an inappropriate one. The child was discovered early one morning, lying at the door of the house then, and still, called the Ship Inn. The clothes in which she was wrapped were of such a quality as led to the inference that her parents must be at least respectable. Round the neck of the stranger-infant was a ribbon, with a wafer very carefully suspended to it, whence she was more commonly known among her townmates by the name of Martha, or Matty Wafer, than by her baptismal name. Her age at the time of her decease does not appear in the Register, but it is evident from the entry that she died unmarried. According to the traditional accounts of her, she was very masculine in all her habits, and would ride, leap, or climb with the boldest youth in the parish! It seems somewhat extraordinary, that no traces of her kindred should ever have been discovered.*

The Baptists have a place of worship here, which was erected about five-and-twenty years ago.

In 1838 a national school was built for children of this and the adjoining parishes, the piece of land on which it stands having been generously given by Col. Packe, the owner of Twyford Hall. According to the Parliamentary Grant for Schools in England and Scotland, it was calcu-

---

* Parochial Registers were first introduced by Lord Cromwell, when Vicar-General in 1538; but many of the clergy, either through ignorance or prejudice, evading compliance, the injunction was enforced in 1547; and by a canon in 1603, every incumbent was enjoined to complete his register from the law's first taking place, or at least from 1558, 1st Elizabeth. Many of these invaluable records, after having safely weathered the political and religious storms of the 17th century, have been since lost.

lated that there would be an average attendance of 190 scholars. The estimate of the expense of the school-house was £260., of which sum £170. was raised by subscription, and the remaining £90. supplied from the funds voted by Parliament.

We may thus at length indulge in the hope, that the wish of the poet may 'ere long be realized:

> " O for the coming of that glorious time
> When, prizing knowledge as her noblest wealth
> And best protection, this Imperial Realm,
> While she exacts allegiance, shall admit
> An obligation, on her part, to *teach*
> Them who are born to serve her and obey;
> Binding herself by Statute to secure
> For all the children whom her soil maintains
> The rudiments of Letters, and inform
> The mind with moral and religious truth,
> Both understood, and practised."
>
>   WORDSWORTH.

THE HALL.

The only house in the parish which can lay claim to any particular interest, either from its antiquity or otherwise, is The Hall, one of those "capital messuages or mansions" built in what is now termed the Elizabethan style, about the year 1520; and generally distinguished, among other marks of peculiarity, by their stacks of ornamented chimnies. Several of these chimnies of the Hall are still standing, and though the lapse of ages has deprived them of their capitals, the lower parts remain in such good preservation, that the delicate designs of the moulded brickwork may be clearly traced. Portions of

Madeley. litho.

REMAINS of CHIMNIES at FOULSHAM-HALL.

the ribs of the panelled ceilings with their bosses may yet
be distinguished in one or two of the rooms; but the many
alterations which the old house has undergone at different
periods, have so changed its aspect, that it is impossible to
form an adequate conception of the appearance it must
have presented in its former palmy days, when there was
an approach to it through the adjoining pasture, by an
avenue of spreading oaks, which have since yielded to the
fell stroke of the axe; surrounded too, as it once was, by
its dove-house, its malt-house, its mill-house, its brew-
house, and its hop-grounds; all of which, the usual appendages to the residences of the wealthy gentry of the olden
time, have now vanished. The existing Elizabethan building was not, however, the original mansion belonging to
the Hall estate, the more ancient one doubtless having
stood within the enclosure of a moat in the meadow which
runs up to the wall of the present garden, this being the
position usually chosen for such dwellings in the earlier
and more unsettled periods of our history, when for safety
some such protection was required. This moat is now
choked with bulrushes, &c., but, by a little care, a dry-shod
passage over it may be effected on its northern side. That
this was the site of the former mansion, there is positive
corroberation from the fact, that the space within the moat
was found, on recently digging it up, to be strewed with
the rubbish of building materials, all the more valuable
portions having probably been worked up in the new mansion and its out-buildings; while the old surface of the
moat enclosure, having been carefully levelled, appeared to
have been planted with ash trees, some of which were
standing within the memory of man.

The earliest owner of the Hall and its estate, whom I have been able to trace, is Major-General Skippon, one of the most active, as well as one of the most experienced among the generals on the Parliament side, during the Great Rebellion in the time of Charles I. From the general, the estate descended to his son Philip, afterwards Sir Philip Skippon, Knight; whose son Philip, aged 22 in 1692, disposed of this property to the Athills, a family which seems to have raised itself to considerable affluence by trade, as there is in the possession of Colonel Packe of Twyford, a copper token, brought to light not long since, issued by John Athill, who thereon describes himself, grocer of Foulsham. From the Athills the estate passed into the hands of the Aufreres, and is still occupied by their tenant. The arms intended to be represented on this coin, are those of the Grocers' Company, argent, a chevron gules, between six cloves in chief, and three in base sable. A few years since also, on pulling down an old house, a farthing token, now in the possession of Mr. Richard Pratt, was dug up, with the inscription: Edward Benn, Mercer, Foulsham, 1668, the Mercers' arms, and the initials, E. R. B. This last has been inserted in the "Norfolk Lists." It has been asserted by some authors, that of the birth and parentage of Skippon little or nothing is known for certain. Clarendon, in his History of the Rebellion, assigns him a mean origin, and it is even pretended that he was once a waggoner to Sir Francis Vere: but it is proved from the Register of King Charles the Second's knights, that in the reign of Queen Elizabeth his family were persons of considerable property, residing at Weasenham, in Norfolk, and entitled to bear arms. The major-general

Coin in possession of Col: Packe,

Twyford Hall.

Facsimile of the Autograph of Maj: Gen: Skippon.

Philip Skippon.

Day & Son. 5 Wellington St Strand.

bore upon his seal 5 annulets, 2, 2, and 1; with the crest, an arm embowed in armour issuing out of a ducal coronet and brandishing a sword. Probably, he had, a grant of these arms, as they are not mentioned in the list of those enumerated in the Heralds' Visitations made during this Queen's reign.

It is certain, at all events, that he was a soldier of fortune under the Parliament standard, and that his merit soon raised him to great eminence. So entirely did he contrive to win the good opinion of the Long Parliament, that he was selected by their orders to attend with a portion of the London Militia to be their guard, when they refused one under the command of Lindsey, which the King had offered them; and when His Majesty sent to demand Skippon's attendance upon his person, he had the boldness absolutely to refuse obedience.*

The first notice of his military career in England, which was afterwards of such essential value to his party, is in 1642, when the five accused Members were brought in triumph to Westminster. He was then captain of the Artillery Garden, and on this memorable occasion the Parliament appointed him major-general of the militia of London. According to Clarendon, who cannot be supposed to have drawn the character of one who was so prominently opposed to the King's cause, in too favourable colours, Major-General Skippon had served in his youth

* This matter is thus entered in the Journals of the Parliament : " Die Martis, 17 Maii, 1642. Resolved upon the Question, That the command of his Majesty to call Captain Philip Skippon, Sergeant-Major-General of the Forces of London to attend his Majesty's person at Yorke, is against the law of the land and the liberty of the subject."

with much reputation in the Netherlands, under the Prince of Orange. He was looked upon as a good officer, was a man of order and sobriety, and untainted with any of those vices, which the officers of his party were exercised in ; and had recently quitted his foreign service upon some exceptions he had to it ; and coming to London, was by some friends preferred to the command in the Artillery-Garden, where his duty was to teach the citizens the exercise of their arms. He was altogether illiterate, and having been bred always abroad, brought dissatisfaction enough with him from thence against the church of England, and so was much caressed and trusted by his party.

Such was Skippon as portrayed by Clarendon, whose masterly skill and discriminating touches in the delineation of those characters, who played a conspicuous part in the stirring events of the Great Rebellion, are universally acknowledged. There is, however, one expression in this sketch of the general which must be understood with considerable modification. On what authority Clarendon asserts that he was altogether illiterate cannot now be ascertained ; but the following list of works by the general will surely exonerate him from such a charge. Salve for every Sore ; or, a collection of Promises out of the Book of God. London, 1643, 8vo. True Treasure of XXX Holy Vows, containing all that concerns the Christian Centurion's conscionable walking before God. London, 1644, 8vo. The Christian Centurion's Advices and Resolutions. London, 1645, 8vo. Skippon's Petition to the City of London. London, 1659, fol. These works, though abounding in the affected Scripture phraseology so current at the time, and evincing no depth of learning, yet are far from being like the productions of one altogether illiterate. It might even be suspected, from the style of expression adopted by Clarendon, that he himself was acquainted with the first of these works, the best known of all the general's publications; and if such be the fact, the circumstance of his charging him with being altogether illiterate is yet more unaccountable than ever.   Among some verses introduced both at the beginning, and at the end of the "Salve for every Sore," and which, if they do nothing more, prove at least the correctness of Clarendon's statement as to Skippon's having been bred abroad, the general thus assigns his reason for having left the "beyond-sea service:"

> Much have I lost, and still may lose,
> Farewell to all; these, these I choose.
> Beyond-sea service me undid,
> Because to shark conscience forbid.

According to Walker, however, in his History of Independency, he was not long in retrieving his losses. "Skippon," says this author, "hath got above £30,000 into his purse, besides £1000. a-year of inheritance given him by the Parliament.   He hath secured his personal estate beyond sea, and his wife and children, and thereby withdrawn all pledges of his fidelity both out of the power of the Parliament and City, and is here among us but in the nature of a Soldier of Fortune."

In 1643, at the siege of Reading, the chief care of the approaches was committed to Major-General Skippon, "an old officer, and of good experience in the Low Countries," who was now made sergeant-major-general of the army, in the room of Sir John Merrick, by the absolute power of the two Houses, yet without the cheerful concurrence of the Commander-in-Chief, the Earl of Essex. This same year also, at the battle of Newbury, the London train-bands, of whose inexperience of danger, or any kind of service, beyond the easy practice of their postures in the Artillery-Garden, men had till then too cheap an esti-mation, behaved themselves admirably, and were the preservation of the army. For, when their wings of horse were scattered and dispersed, they kept their ground so steadily, that though Prince Rupert himself led up the choice horse to charge them, he could make no impression upon their stand of pikes, but was obliged to retreat: of so sovereign benefit and use is readiness, order, and dex-terity in the use of arms, which was then too much neglected! Warburton's concise and expressive note on this passage from Clarendon, is highly complimentary to General Skippon. "A most judicious observation," says the bishop, "which later times have abundantly sup-ported. Skippon had disciplined these men in the Artil-lery-Garden, ever since the first beginning of the quarrel." In the year 1643, Grafton House in Northamptonshire was also taken by him.

In 1644, near Foy, his glove and sleeve were shot through, and his buff in two places; and when the Earl of Essex escaped with the cavalry out of Cornwall, the foot, amounting to nearly six thousand, were left under the command of Major-General Skippon, "a good and punctual officer," who had fought like a lion, but was constrained to send to the king's general, the Earl of Brentford, to treat and offer conditions, which were granted. These conditions were: That upon delivering up their arms, and ammuni-tion, they should have liberty to return to London, with as much baggage as they carried upon their backs; and for protection, they had a guard of horse to conduct them to a place appointed. This agreement was executed on the 2nd of September, and though all care was taken to preserve them from violence, yet, first at Listowel, where they had been long quartered, and in other towns through which they had formerly passed, the inhabitants, especially the women, who pretended to see their own clothes and goods about them, which they had been plundered of, treated them very rudely, even to stripping some of the soldiers, and many of their wives. Of the six thousand who marched out of Foy, there did not a third part come to Southampton, where the king's convoy under the command of Lt. Col. Adrian Scroop, left them; to whom Skippon gave a testimony under his own hand, "that they had carried themselves with great civility towards them, and fully complied with their obligations." It was on this occasion that the general is reported to have ridden up to his sovereign, who was standing by to see the soldiers pass, disarmed, in such haste as to be in part undressed, and to have reproached him with having violated the terms of the surrender, in such forcible language, that seven out of nine of the offenders complained of were instantly hanged. This ill success, however, was amply compensated for by the great advantages which he gained for the Parliament in other actions in which he signalized himself during the war.

When the self-denying ordinance passed, Skippon was among the number of those officers who were allowed to retain their commands, and on a debate in the Commons on this subject, his arrears of pay were ordered to be cre-

dited, and £500. advanced to him.   On the new modelling
of the army, and the command of it being transferred from
Essex to Fairfax, he was also selected to reconcile these
changes to the troops then stationed at Reading; which
difficult charge he executed with such success, that after he
had addressed each regiment, all shouted, That they would
live and die with Fairfax and Skippon.   The happy termination of this critical affair was mainly attributed to the
prudence of Skippon, to whom the Commons sent a letter
of thanks for this and his other good services.

On the 5th of May, 1645, the Commons ordered that
Fairfax and Skippon should join Cromwell, and watch the
King's motions at Oxford; and on the 16th of June in this
same year was fought the memorable battle of Naseby, the
death-blow to Charles's hopes.   Among the Parliamentary
leaders at this important juncture, there were only two vete-
ran officers, Major-General Skippon and Colonel Vermyden,
the latter of whom, who commanded a regiment of horse,
a day or two before the engagement had resigned his commission, on the plea of his presence being required abroad.
Major-General Skippon, therefore, being considered the
most experienced among the leaders on the Parliament's
side, was directed to draw up the plan of this decisive conflict, the issue of which fully justified the confidence which
his colleagues had thus reposed in him.   The direction of
the plan of the battle of Naseby was, on the part of the
King, entrusted to Sir Jacob Astley, sometime before created
Lord Astley, ancestor of the present Lord Hastings of
Melton Constable, who, in an engagement near Stow in the
Wold, was afterwards taken prisoner, when his papers fell
into the hands of his captors.

On this fatal day, Fairfax and Skippon commanded the main body of the army opposed to Sir Bernard Astley. Shortly after the commencement of the action, some of the Parliament's horse having lingered awhile about pillage, and being thrown into some disorder, Skippon brought up his foot seasonably to their assistance; and in this charge, as he himself related the circumstance to Sir Bulstrode Whitelocke, was shot in the side, though some have supposed that he was wounded accidentally by one of his own party.

Thus by one of those strange coincidences, which the merest chance sometimes brings about, and which has hitherto apparently passed unnoticed, the two plans, which regulated the operations of the opposing armies on the field of Naseby, were drawn up by two Norfolk gentlemen, near neighbours of each other; that which prescribed the order of battle to be observed by the King's troops being designed by the Lord Astley, and that which directed the movements of the Parliament's forces, by Major-General Skippon. After Lord Astley's capture at Stow in the Wold, he retired to the Hemp at Maidstone, and was allowed to compound on easy terms. Sir Bernard Astley was son of Lord Astley, and died at Spa from wounds received at the siege of Bristol.

In a letter, written by Fairfax, after the battle of Naseby, 'to the Honble. Wm. Lenthall, Esq.' Speaker of the House of Commons, in the postscript he adds,—" Major-General Skippon was shot through his side; but, notwithstanding, he continued in the field with great resolution; and when I desired him to go off the field, he answered, he would not go so long as a man would stand, still doing

his office as a valiant and wise commander." The original
of this and two other letters was found in 1754, in a wall
nine feet thick, on pulling down a house in Palace-yard,
Westminster, in order to build an office for the clerks of
the House of Lords. They were, however, printed by order
of Parliament in 1645, and republished in Rushworth's
Collections. In another from Harry Leighton and Thomas
Herbert, the committee residing with the army, Skippon's
conduct is highly commended, and he is said to be shot in
the side, but not dangerously.

As a mark of the high estimation in which they held
him, four days after the battle, the Commons sent a letter
of thanks to Major-General Skippon, and Dr. Clarke, a
physician, to visit him; and desired Sir Thomas Fairfax to
take care that the "chirurgeons" of the army might use
their best endeavours for his recovery. On the 30th of the
month, letters were received from the major-general, conveying the most favourable report, and the Commons therefore ordered £200. to be sent to him as a testimony of
their favour, and £200. more for the payment of his
"doctors, chirurgeons, apothecaries," and other expenses.
By the 16th of July, he was so far recovered, as to be
enabled to be brought to London, "when as he passed by
the brewhouse near St. John's-street, a devilish mastiff
flew at one of his horses, and held him so fast that the
horse grew mad as a mad dog; so that the horse-litter, in
which the major-general was being conveyed, borne between two horses, tossed him like a dog in a blanket."
Shortly after this, on the petition of the inhabitants, he
was made Governor of Bristol, where he exhibited his usual
activity, and had £1000. per annum voted him by the
Parliament.

At the close of the year 1646, he was nominated Governor of Newcastle and Teignmouth, and allowed to retain the command of Bristol by deputy. At the same time also he was appointed to command in chief the convoy of the £200,000., for which the Scots basely agreed to deliver up King Charles to the Parliament; and for his extraordinary charges in this business he had £500. voted him. On the 3rd of February following, the mayor of Newcastle presented the keys of the town to him, and he took formal possession of his new post.

Major-General Skippon's superior military skill was not the only point in his character which recommended him to the notice of his party; for though he was distinguished for a strict attention to discipline, yet he was no less remarkable for the popularity which he enjoyed among the soldiers. This had been manifested on several previous occasions, particularly in the earlier part of the war, when, marching at the head of the city-bands to join the Earl of Essex at Turnham Green, after the battle of Edgehill, he had urged them onward by repeatedly exhorting them, " Come, my boys, my brave boys, I will run the same hazards with you. Remember, the cause is for God.— Come, my honest brave boys, let us pray and fight heartily, and God will bless us." These, and similar such short, bluff exhortations, told wonderfully in his favour with the common soldiery. It was mainly in consequence of this his singular popularity, that in April, 1647, he was appointed commander-in-chief of the forces in Ireland, with the title of Field Marshal, and the pay of £6. per diem; the Parliament hoping that by their selection of him for this post, the troops would more readily engage in this service, to which they had shewn themselves extremely averse. And though the general did consent to take this command, and received the thanks of the Commons for his compliance, and had £1000. voted for his contingent expenses, yet it is evident from his letters which are still extant among the Tanner MSS. in the Bodleian library at Oxford, that he was very reluctant to charge himself with it; and eventually, in a letter addressed to the Speaker, declined the appointment. His friend, Sir Bulstrode Whitelocke, of whom he entertained a very high opinion, was to have been sent to Ireland at the same time as Lord Chief Justice; which appointment he too refused on the score of age and infirmities. At this period, Skippon was in constant communication with Cromwell, and, in conjunction with him and others, was engaged in conducting the negociations which were going on between the Commons and the Army at Saffron Walden. Were it compatible with the thread of this history, it might possibly be shewn that the deep-laid policy of this party influenced him, more than he was willing openly to acknowledge, in refusing the Irish command.

In the year 1648, he was constituted major-general of all the forces within the lines of communication, and the city of London allowed him £600. per annum. Upon information that the King's party were enlisting troops there, £5000. was voted for raising a regiment of horse to be commanded by him. Notwithstanding these honours which were so thickly heaped upon him, he did not escape the virulent sarcasms of the lampooners of the day, and in order to refute the aspersions thus thrown upon him, the Vindication of Major-General Skippon against a scandalous libel was ordered to be posted up in London. He was shortly after this, February 1649, chosen one of the thirty-eight members of the council of state, with powers to command and settle the militia, navy, &c. These powers were to continue for a year, and he was re-elected to the same office, as long as the council existed. It was about this period, probably, that he became possessed of much of the property which he devised by will, for on the 9th of June in this year, it was referred to a Committee of the Commons to consider how £1000. per annum might be settled upon him and his heirs, and in the August following an Act was passed for settling £2000. a year on Major-General Skippon. From this time he appears to have led a comparatively retired life, residing, for the most part, at Acton, in Middlesex, and perhaps occasionally visiting his estates in Norfolk. He continued, amid all the jarring interests of the times, to enjoy the confidence of Oliver Cromwell, who seems to have considered him the fittest person to be placed in the command of those troops which were more nearly connected with his own personal safety. For, in March, 1655, the lord-mayor and common council of the city of London having been sent for by the Protector, he told them formally the reasons for his having appointed major-generals in the several counties, and that he now thought fit to appoint Major-General Skippon for the same end in the city. In 1657, the year before Cromwell's death, when the other House of Parliament, as it was called, or a House of Peers, was formed by the Protector, Skippon's name was inserted among those of the sixty members who composed it.*

* Among the Tanner MSS. in the Bodleian library at Oxford, are several letters written by Major-General Skippon. Some of them,

Though he had refused to sit, as Noble in his Memoirs of the Cromwells asserts, as one of the commissioners to try King Charles, his pensions were ordered to be paid yearly out of the receipts at Guildhall, until forfeited lands could be settled on him to their full amount. It is supposed that Bleekly, in Buckinghamshire, a manor of the Duke of Buckingham, was given him in part of them, as he was in possession of it at the Restoration. Skippon, however, on the authority of Walker in his History of Independency, voted that the King should be brought to trial, and "did actually sit as one of the Judges upon the Tryall of his Majesty," their number being seventy-three. Yet his name does not appear among those who sat in judgment on Charles I. when sentence of death was pronounced on him, according to the Proclamation made 18th of May, 1660, respecting the regicides; neither is it to be found among the signatures of those whose names are attached to the king's death-warrant.

When the self-denying ordinances passed he was Member for Barnstable: he served in the Parliaments held in 1654 and 1656, for King's Lynn, and on the death of Oliver the Protector, as one of the Privy Council he signed the Pro-

perchance, might throw additional light on his private life and history. The knowledge of their existence unfortunately came too late to allow of their being duly consulted in elucidation of the present work. By a strange error, Mr. Cary, in his recently published "Memorials of the Great Rebellion," constantly subscribes him *Charles*, instead of Philip Skippon—substituting the abbreviation Ch : for Ph : For the corroboration of this statement, I am indebted to Dr. Bliss, the learned editor of Wood's Athenæ Oxonienses, who kindly consulted the original MSS. whence Mr. Cary drew his information.

clamation proclaiming his son Richard, Lord Protector, but proved unfaithful to him by revolting to the restored Long Parliament. His death happened immediately after the Restoration, and on July 1st, 1661, his estates were confiscated with those of twenty-one others who were then dead.

The general's will, dated February 20th, 1659, proved October 25th, 1660, is a very lengthy one, and in the opening contains much of the Scripture phraseology which characterized the times in which he lived. He left considerable property to his second wife, Dame Katharine Skippon, whose name before her marriage with him was Philips, and expresses himself very particularly respecting her legacies. He had a town mansion in Long Acre, which at the time he made his will was let to the Lady St. John, and the "lodgings" which he himself occupied when in London, were in the Mews, near the site on which the National Gallery now stands. He possessed property in Buckinghamshire, in Suffolk, and at Wroxham, Shottisham, Wood Norton, Guist, Guestwick, Gately, and other places in Norfolk. Three daughters are named by him; Mrs. Bragge, who had been the widow of Col. Rolfe, by whom she had a family; Mrs. Meredith, and a single one; as well as two sons-in-law; one named Fowell, the other ————. His lands and "capital messuage or mansion" at Foulsham, with its dove-house, malt-house, mill-house, brew-house, hop-grounds, &c he bequeathed to his son Philip, whom he had by his first wife; with the exception of that piece of pasture in Foulsham, containing by estimation 70 acres, called Becklizard, *alias* Becklezar, *alias* Couldham Close, *alias* Sterninge Close, which was left to his single daughter, for whom he appears to have entertained a very great regard. The estate at Foulsham was then in the occupation of his tenant, William Partlet, as well as the property which the general states he had lately purchased of — Cayley, Esquire, at Themelthorpe. To his single daughter he also left "the Palace at Norwich, late belonging to the Bishop of Norwich," which had either been given him by the Parliament in order to make up the income voted him, or been at some recent period purchased by him; for, though among the purchases which the general made, this is not mentioned, yet as many notices of the sales of church property have not been hitherto discovered, he in all likelihood became possessed of the palace by one or other of these means. According to the list of church lands disposed of in these times of trouble, as given in the Collectanea Topographica et Genealogica, the names of General Skippon, Esq. and William Webb occur, as the purchasers of the manors of Neteshead, Shottisham, &c.; for which they gave £1115. 4 sh. 11¾d. As these estates were generally sold at an appraisement barely equivalent to the materials of the mansion-houses and timber on the grounds, the purchase may be presumed to have been an advantageous one. It must have been by virtue of his right to this portion of the See of Norwich, bequeathed to his unmarried daughter, that he became entitled to the manor of Dulencross in Foulsham, the lordship of which he held at the date of his will, and which reverted to the Bishop at the Restoration, and is still leased of this prelate.

From the tenor of his will, the general's establishment appears to have been on a large scale, and with an eye perhaps to any untoward event befalling him, should a change of government take place, which he might deem to be within the range of possibility, he kept carefully treasured up in one of the rooms of his usual residence at Acton, a hundred pounds in twenty-shilling gold pieces, which he left, if there should be no such need of them, as part of the provision of his wife. Scobell, the well-known Clerk of the Parliament, was his intimate friend, and from the names of the subscribing witnesses, the will was evidently made, or at least executed, at Acton. Among other legacies, was one of £5. to the poor of the parish of Foulsham, and another to his brother, Luke Skippon, vicar of South Lynn.

Annexed to the will, are two codicils, dated respectively the 24th and 26th of June, 1660, by which he directs, that £1600. in cash should be given to his single daughter, who was then on the point of marriage, in lieu of the preceding bequests made to her. Of this sum too he had in store £1000. in hard money, deposited in a trunk at Acton. Both these codicils were made at this place when the general seems to have been on his death-bed, which renders it next to certain that he died here very shortly after they were penned.

His house at Acton was near the church, and in the year 1686, his son, Sir Philip Skippon, sold it to Sir Hele Hooke, Bart. It appears to have been built in the year 1638, by Sir Henry Garway, and after having passed through various hands, was, when Lysons published his History of Middlesex, in 1792-6, the property of James Stratton, Esq. Lady Derwentwater is said to have resided there at the time of her husband's execution. The learned

and excellent·Sir Matthew Hale, Lord Chief Justice of the
King's Bench, had a country seat at Acton in the year
1670, and tradition says, that he was proprietor of Mr.
Stratton's house, which formerly belonged to Major-
General Skippon. Sir Matthew's name does not occur in
the title-deeds, but it is not improbable that he was Sir
Philip Skippon's tenant. Bowacke, who wrote an account
of this place in 1705, says, that the memory of Sir Matthew
Hale was still dear to the town : he adds, that his house
which was situated near the church was then pulled down.
Mr. Stratton's house appears in a great measure to have
been rebuilt at that time.

In the valuable collection of Pamphlets and Newspapers
relating to the period of the great Rebellion, which was
presented to the British Museum by his late Majesty
George III., Major-General Skippon's name is often found,
as having been very actively employed in the campaigns of
the civil wars. His actions, of course, are there differently
coloured, according to the line of politics adopted by the
respective writers, but not even those who are loudest in
their reproaches of the proceedings of his party, have ventured to advance any thing which can impugn the courage,
zeal, and good faith of this Republican general. In the
Mercurius Melancholicus, of July 17, 24, 1648, a newspaper
in the King's interest, the editor has thus exercised his wit
at the expense of Skippon : "Major-General Skippon hath
sent 1500 men to recruit the decaying beleaguers of Col-
chester. He is made of a pretty piece of timber, is
fashionable, and will be made a fiddle I believe."—The
full force of this piece of satire I have yet to discover. In
the same valuable collection is also a highly encomiastic

poem of about 200 lines, printed in 1648, and called Truth's Triumph, or a just Vindication of that Renowned and thrice noble Patriot, Maj. Genl. Skippon, against the late aspersions of scandalous Pamphlets, and seditious Slanders. The following is a specimen of it :—

> How sweetly doth thy harmonious soul unite,
> Valour with Virtue, virtue with delight,
> In such a system too as none can paint
> Thee right, who art both Soldier and Saint.
> How doth thine innocence upbraid the crimes
> And loose corruption of our looser times, &c.

The monument to the memory of 'Mary the late worthy and well beloved wife' of the Genl., 'who passed through death to life the 24th day of the 11th monethe (vulgar January),' 'the 54th of her age 1655, and after our marriage 34 years,' is still to be seen in the North aisle of Acton church, having been removed thither from the South chancel wall when the edifice, a few years since, underwent considerable alterations and repairs. Then follows a long account of her life and piety in English verse, subscribed Philip Skippon; and in the middle aisle is a large black stone, under which she lies buried. It was by this *Mary* his wife, as I conceive, whom Noble in his Memoirs of the Cromwells erroneously, if my conjecture be well grounded, calls *Elizabeth*, that he had Sir Philip Skippon, of Horsham in Norfolk and Stafford, and Wrentham in Suffolk; since there is no reason for supposing that the General had more than two wives, this Mary, and the Dame Katharine Skippon mentioned in his will, who survived him.

Arms in Acton church :—Gules, five annulets Or, for Skippon or Skipton ; quartering, 1. Az. a chevron between

K

3 crosses patée Or. 2. Barry of 8 Arg. and Vert, a griffin rampant Or, and impaling Erm. three lions passant in pale Gules.

Extracts from the Register of Acton.

Tuesday, 5th of April 1655, Richard Meredith, Esq. eldest son of Sir William Meredith of Leedes, in the county of Kent, Bart. was married unto Mrs. Susanna Skippon, daughter to the ~~Right Honourable Major Generall~~ Philip
_{Traytor}   _{Knave}
Skippon, by Sir John Thorowgood, in a public congregation, within the parish church of Acton, in the county of Middlesex; Mr. Philip Nye at the same time praying and teaching upon this occasion.

Mary the wife of the ~~Right Honorable~~ Philip Major
Gennerall Scipon, was buried in the chancill of Acton, the 31st of January 1655-6.

It is not improbable that these alterations in the register were made by Bruno Ryves, whom King Charles II., after the Restoration, appointed to this living. He was one of the King's chaplains, Dean of Chichester, and author of the Mercurius Rusticus, a narrative of the sufferings of the Royalists in various parts of the country, and of several sermons. At the breaking out of the Rebellion, a Dr. Featley was the incumbent of Acton, and suffered severely from the Parliament soldiers quartered there in 1642. He was afterwards imprisoned by order of the Parliament, and on obtaining a certificate from his Physician that he could not live long, if he had not some fresh air, he petitioned these 'soul-enthralling tyrants,' and at last had their leave

to go to Chelsea College for six weeks, upon good bail, to
recover his health ; he died, however, on the 17th of April,
1645, which was the very last day of the six weeks limited
for his return.   The Mr. Philip Nye, who prayed and taught
upon the occasion of the marriage of Mrs. Susanna Skippon,
was one of the most popular preachers of the day, and had
the living of Acton given him by the Parliament.   This
Independent preacher was very remarkable for the singularity of his beard, which furnished Butler a subject for
these satirical lines in his Hudibras :—

> With greater art and cunning rear'd,
> Than Philip Nye's thanksgiving beard.

. After he had succeeded Dr. Featley in the living of Acton,
he rode thither every Sunday in triumph, in a coach drawn
by four horses.   There was a curious pulpit and paper war
carried on between him and the famous Lilly, the astrolo-
ger ; and for his exertions in this strange contest he was
rewarded with the office of public preacher upon thanksgiving days.   So notorious was the peculiarity of Philip
Nye's beard, that it is honoured with an entire poem in
Butler's Remains, published by Thyer.

Philip Skippon, Esq., the son of the general, was knighted
by Charles II. at Whitehall, April 19th, 1674, and was one
of the Fellows of the Royal Society at its institution, or
immediately after.   In 1663, he left Dover for Calais, in
company with the Rev. John Ray, the eminent naturalist,
F. R. S., who dedicated his Travels to his Honoured Friend,
Philip Skippon, Esq., Mr. Willoughby, ancestor of the
present Lord Middleton, and a Mr. Bacon, on a tour
through Europe.   That Sir Philip was possessed of great
ability and learning, will appear from the excellent journal

of his Travels, which is published in Harris's Collection. In the enjoyment of an ample fortune, he travelled solely for the sake of improvement and amusement, and was therefore extremely inquisitive wherever he went. He kept so exact an account of every thing he saw, and designed so accurately every engine or machine that he thought worthy his notice, that it is to be wondered, considering the pains he took in viewing things, how he found time to describe them so carefully, and to accompany them with his reflections. His work is voluminous, and there is one very striking passage in it. He says, that the Secretary of the Republic of Switzerland constantly took off his hat, whenever the name of Oliver Cromwell was mentioned ; holding his memory in the greatest veneration, as the patron and protector of the Reformed religion, calling him, Olivarius beatæ memoriæ.

On his return home, he led a retired, or at least a studious life, as appears from the books which composed his library. In the title page of each of them is his name, and the year when they were bought or given to him, written in a very fair Italian hand ; and many of them have very learned notes, judicious corrections, or pertinent or pleasing remarks upon their margins. Thus much, adds Noble in his Memoirs of the Cromwells, I thought due to the mention of this gentleman, as having seen many of these books and possessed some. Sir Philip returned to England in 1666, and thus concludes his journal :—

Deo
Omnipotenti
Maximas reddit
Gratias
P. S.

Mr. Hallam, whose works evince the vast stores of erudition which he has at command, in his Literary History of the 15th, &c. centuries, has noticed the volumes of Ray and Willoughby, but has omitted the productions of Sir Philip Skippon's pen. This last author, in point of talents, industry, and accuracy, was not inferior to either of his fellow travellers; but as his journal was drawn up for private use only, it might from this cause have been deemed by the learned historian to be beyond the compass of research which his labours embrace.

Sir Philip married, first Amy, daughter of Francis Brewster, Esq., of Wrentham, Suffolk, by whom he had a son, Philip, born 1670, who died unmarried, and was buried at Edwardston, in Suffolk, 1716. By his second wife, Mary, daughter of Sir Thomas Barnadiston, of Kediton, he had a daughter, Mary, married to Joseph Brand, Esq., second son of Sir John Brand, of Edwardston. There appears, however, to be some error in the name of one of these his two wives, otherwise he must have married a third time, of which there is no proof, since in a deed respecting the sale of Northwold manor, dated June 8th, 1685, when he sold this manor to Thos. Holder, Esq., his wife is called Anne. Sir Philip Skippon, when he received the honour of knighthood, is described as of Foulsham, in Norfolk, and Stratford, in Suffolk, and lived at Wrentham. Le Neve says he died in 1692, but the place of his burial, like that of his father, does not seem to be known. Philip, his son, sold the property left him by his father, part of which, the Hall and estate at Foulsham, was purchased by the Athills, and by them sold to the ancestor of the present G. A. Aufrere, Esq.

The Skippons were originally of Weasenham in Norfolk. In the 18th of Eliz. a Bartholomew Skippon was living there. In Weasenham church on the screen under the rood loft, which was well painted and ornamented (probably in the reign of Hen. 6.) with the figures of Saints was this inscription: —

Orate p. a'iab; . . . . . D'ni vicarii.

Thomæ Fusant, Martini Skyppon, Joh. Davy, et Ric. Hovel. et Thomæ Scorth qui istam . . . . . fieri fecerunt.

It would appear from the Registers of Weasenham that the family of Skippon or Skyppon, for the name is variously spelt, migrated thence at the close of the 16th century, and left no trace behind. Bartholomew Skippon, above mentioned, married Anne, daughter of Robt. Davey of Stanfield. A Hammond Skippon of Weasenham married Jane, daughter of Robt. Tenison of Burnham Westgate, and was living in 1563 The entrance-door to the Rood Loft in Weasenham church, now blocked up, is all that remains of it, and the Skreen has entirely dissappeared.

From the Register of Weasenham St. Peter.

Elizabeth Skippon was buried the 30th of March 1581. Luke Skippon was buried the . . . . Septr. 1584. Robert Skippon the son of . . . . . Skippon was baptd. . . . . . 1583.

Alice the daughter of Hamond Skippon was bapti. 17th of March 1586.

William Stanford & Elizth Skippon were married the 13th of Septr. 1590.

From the Register of Weasenham All Saints.

Thomas Skippon the . . . . was buried the 6th of Octr. 1585.

Olyve Skippon widow was buried the 13th of Ja. 1586.

In the North aisle, near the door of South-Lynn church, is a gravestone : In memory of Ann, one of the daughters of Luke Skippon, D.D. Rector of Wissingset, who died . . . . . of January 1694, and sometime vicar of this parish.

Luke Skippon was presented to this vicarage in 1662. No patron is named.

On a stone in the pavement of Swaffham church :

Here lyeth the body of Mary Skippon, daughter of the Revd. Luke Skippon of Mileham, D.D. Master Elect of Peter-House, Cambridge, Convocation Clerk for the Diocese of Norwich, eminent for his Piety, Learning, and Loyalty, She departed this life the 28th of May, 1713, aged 71 years.

If this inscription be true to the letter, the politics of the divine, eminent for his *loyalty*, must have been widely different from those of his brother the general. John Goodriche, rector of Wissingset, compounded in 1642. No other name of any of the rectors occurs till 1718, when Willm. Peartree was presented to the living.

The present appearance of the old Hall, the wreck of its former grandeur, with its stacks of ornamented chimnies, its standing alone at a short distance from the town, its being still shaded on one side by the spreading branches of ancient trees, high walls enclosing its extensive yards and gardens ; all this may well lead one to suppose that strange tales are attached to its history. Accordingly, there is, or rather was, in the opinion of many, not a shadow of a doubt of its being haunted ! It was the current belief that there existed an under-ground passage running from the moat and the house, communicating with the church porch ; which passage, it was maintained, might be very plainly traced by the parched colour of the grass, whenever an un- usually long drought occurred.   And in corroboration of a remark made by Mr. D'Israeli in one of his works, that, in the youthful days of the last generation, many traditions connected with the stirring events of the Civil Wars were rife among the people, about the middle of the past cen- tury, it was, as it were, fresh in the memory of, and uni- versally asserted by, the inhabitants of the parish, that the last owner of the Hall, who occupied it in person, was one of Oliver Cromwell's generals. He had retired here, as the same authorities went on to say, when King Charles II. was restored to the throne, and lived in such strict se- clusion, and in so great dread for his safety, that he was never seen, except on one occasion, by any individual, besides two or three trusty domestics, who were ever silent on all subjects which had the least reference to their master. The unlooked-for occasion which disclosed a sight of his per- son, was this : An old woman, to whom a daily portion of milk was given at the Hall, having repaired thither at a somewhat earlier hour than she was commonly wont to do, was utterly amazed on entering the inner court-yard, to find herself suddenly in the presence of a tall gentleman, advanced in years, erect in figure, enveloped in a costly dressing-gown, with hair as white as snow, enjoying the freshness of a summer's morning ! It need not be told that this was, according to the report spread by the ancient dame, no less a personage than general Skippon !

I had imagined from this tradition being so prevalent, and from one or two other circumstances connected with the tale, that, though somewhat embellished in detail, the substance of it might be correct, and that general Skippon, from the retired situation of Foulsham, might have chosen it for his retreat at the period of the Restoration, when he had good reason to fear, not only for his property, but also for his personal safety. But the codicils to his will, and the date of the administration to his effects, are positive proofs, that this traditional report of his having taken up his residence here on the king's return, is without foundation.

This letter, rendered doubly interesting by being of an entirely private nature, addressed to Henry Cromwell, Lord Lieutenant of Ireland, may serve to shew the style of language usually employed by the general in his familiar correspondence. The crest and arms, still preserved on its seal, are the same as those which have been before described:

May it please yr. Excellency.—This worthy gent. my very loving friend (Judge Advocate Whalley) being willing at my request to put himselfe to the trouble of bringing a Turkish Semiter from mee to be presented unto you, upon noe other accompt but to testify the very great heart-affectionate service that I owe unto you; be pleased favourably to accept thereof, though neither the giver nor the guift be worthy of soe much: Not to flatter, but to encourage you; I rejoice, with thankfullnes to the Lord, for what I, and other good men heare yr. Exly. labours after, for the publique safety, peace, and comfort of honest men; and it is, and shall be through the grace of God, my daily earnest prayer, that he would please still to stand by you, to be your guide and strength, and good successe in

soe reall a worthy way. I have of late bin very weake by
reason of a very sudden and sore visitation my God pleased
(though in much mercy) to lay upon mee, that I have not
bin abroad about any publique businesse in a moneth's
time; and am in noe very good condition at present, to
indite, or write unto yr. Exly. which I humbly pray you to
excuse: And further to accept of the tender of my very
humble aud hearty service to yr. Right Honble. Lady;
and if I durst presume my kind love to Mr. Brewster: And
soe the Lord God our Heavenly father watch over you and
yrs. allways and in all things for good, which is the very
humble and earnest prayer of,

<table>
<tr><td></td><td>Your Excellencys most</td></tr>
<tr><td>16 March 1656.</td><td>humble and faithfull</td></tr>
<tr><td>Mewes.</td><td>Servant</td></tr>
<tr><td></td><td>Ph. Skippon.</td></tr>
</table>

For his Excellency the Lord Henry Cromwell Commander
in Chief of all Forces in Ireland – These humbly present.

Mr. Brewster, to whom the General with some diffidence
presumes to send his kind love, according to a letter of his
dated Norwich, Feb. 8, 1658, was Nathaniel Brewster,
apparently from the tenor of this epistle a native or former
inhabitant of that city, attached to the Lord Lieutenant in
the capacity of chaplain, and might be connected with the
Brewsters of Wrentham in Suffolk, into which family Sir
Philip Skippon married.

With respect to the subterraneous passage, which, it was
said, led from the Hall and the moat to the church porch,
though of course, little or no belief was given to the story,
yet the farther investigation of this matter lately became
an unexpected object of interest from the following circum-

stance. It was positively reported by some labourers of
the parish, that while they themselves a few years since
were at work in the pasture to the North of the Hall, the
ground there had suddenly sunk under them, and they
found themselves all at once precipitated into an arch or
tunnel. And that, moreover, a bricklayer, had actually
groped some distance along the tunnel on each side of the
aperture through which they had sunk, till he was stopped
by the earth and rubbish which choked the interior.

Under the impression that something might perchance
be discovered which would set the matter at rest, or otherwise repay the curiosity of the antiquary, as the evidence
seemed to run so strong on the side of the opinion which
for ages had been handed down by tradition, on the exact
position of the spot being pointed out, by the permission
and ready assistance of the occupier of the farm, a minute
search was made. The issue of which was, that considerable remains of foundations of buildings were found, but
without any of those peculiarities being recognized which
had been so positively assigned to them ; and on recourse
being had to more particular inquiries and researches
among old records relating to the affairs of the town, the
spot proved to be the site of some cottages once parish-pro-
perty, which had been taken down when the poor-house
was erected, and the ground on which they stood, either by
sale or exchange, thrown into the Hall pasture. These
researches, however, though they failed in the main object,
were not entirely without fruits, since on examining the
court-yard on the eastern side of the Hall itself, the foundations of several of its outbuildings, which are no longer

standing, were discovered, and at the depth of about three
feet from the surface of the soil a well was laid open, the
mouth of which had been carefully overlaid with a flag-stone
when the spot was brought to its present level.

Nearly in the centre of the market-place once stood a
Cross, which, in the days when the market was much more
numerously resorted to than it was at the time when it
fell into desuetude, some fifteen years since, served as a
shelter to the venders of butter, eggs, and poultry. The
foundations of the cross may still be distinctly traced every
hoar-frosty morning. Its form was that of a hexagon, in
humble imitation of those fifteen beautiful hexagonal
crosses, called ' Eleanor Crosses,' erected to the memory of
Eleanor, queen of Edward I,; three of which are yet remaining ; that at Geddington, another at Northampton, and
the third at Waltham. Whether the erection of Foulsham
market-cross may be assigned to so early a period as this,
is not positive, though the fact of there being a weekly
market held here on Tuesdays previously to the 15th year
of Edward I. has been already noticed. The lowest stratum
of the foundations, on a recent examination of them,
denoted very considerable antiquity. It was evident, however, that considerable repairs had been made to the structure
at different intervals, as the superincumbent layers were
formed of bricks some trifle longer, wider, and thicker
than the standard size now in use, such probably as were
employed in the 15th century, for before the beginning of
this century bricks, resembling the modern ones, will
scarcely be found in private or small buildings. About the

middle of the last century the fabric fell into such decay, that it was then decided on taking it down, and disposing of the materials to the best advantage. Of the exact period of its demolition no record is left in the parish, though one of the oldest inhabitants of the place some three years since, without being able to charge his memory with having seen the cross actually standing, was fully convinced of its having been taken down but a short time beyond his recollection, from having frequently, in his childhood, heard his parents allude to the circumstance with expressions of regret and recount the unusual fact of their having once seen two *men* spinning in it for a wager.

About noon, or a little after, on Friday the 15th of June, 1770, a fire broke out in an outbuilding belonging to a house on the west side of the market-place, and speedily consumed all the houses on that side of the street, northward of the one whence the fire originated. Among these there happened to be the tenement of a general shop-keeper, on whose premises was a quantity of gunpowder, which, in the alarm and confusion of the moment, had been neglected to be removed. The explosion of this powder having carried some of the burning fragments as far as the church and parsonage, the former edifice was in consequence very materially injured, and the latter, then a thatched house, destroyed. The flames now took a totally different direction, and spreading themselves along the east side of the street, consumed all the buildings there, till they reached as far as the public-house, now known by the name of "the Bull," which was the last that fell a prey to their fury. The great and singular ravages made by this fire, may be accounted for by the houses being then generally roofed

I.

with thatch, a brisk wind blowing at the time, and the
want of an engine. The nearest one was that belonging to
Sir Edward Astley, Bart. at Melton Constable, which arri-
ved in the course of the day, and by deluging the Bull
public-house which was then burning, and the northern ga-
ble of the adjoining one, prevented the flames from spreading
farther. Had it not been for the aid of this engine, the
destruction must have been much greater than it actually
was.

. The origin of the fire was very satisfactorily traced to
the carelessness of a servant-girl, who had emptied some
live embers on a dunghill which was heaped against the
wall of a thatched outhouse. No less than fourteen dwelling-houses were consumed, and the total damage was estimated at several thousand pounds.

Though the calamities attendant on all fires must ever
be deplored, yet in this case, as in numerous others, some
good at least resulted from the evil, since the way was thus
paved for the demolition of several small unsightly shops,
which were any thing but an ornament to the market-place,
and the new houses, which were erected on the site of
those which had been destroyed, were much superior both
in size and in look to their predecessors. It is owing to
this also that the present appearance of the town is neater
and more uniform than that of the generality of places of the
same size.

The outbuilding, in which the fire originated, stood in
the yard belonging to the house occupying the site of
that in which Mr. Saunders, surgeon, at present resides.
This and the adjoining one, where is now the butcher's shop,
were the first consumed. The destruction of these was

speedily followed by that of all the houses on the west side of the street towards the church, together with the church itself, the parsonage, the house now occupied by the Misses Leeds, and the Bull Inn. The gable-end of the house next to this last was injured, and some of its outbuildings fell a prey to the flames. The tenements which were totally consumed, were, at the time of the fire, occupied by the following persons; this mark * being attached to the names of such of them as were considered proper objects to partake of the subscriptions raised for the sufferers. Mrs. Burgis,* Butcher. John Layton,* Peruke-maker. Arthur Browne,* Brazier. Dorothy Collison,* Widow. Edward Barron,* Whitesmith. William Ivory, Shopkeeper. Michael Hall, Shoemaker. Ann Groom,* Widow. James Matsell,* Labourer. William Collison, Collar-maker. Elizabeth Roome, Widow. Thomas Bambridge,* Inn-holder. Mr. Pike, Builder. The Reverend Henry Rice, Rector.

The greatest sufferer among those who were deemed fit objects for relief, was Thomas Bambridge, landlord of the public-house then called the King of Prussia, afterwards the Bull and Dog, now the Bull. By the inventory of his effects, he appears to have united the trade of a wheelwright with that of a publican. His losses amounted to £121. 11s. 9d.

The estimate of the loss of John Layton, peruke-maker, was £108. 12s. 6d. In the list of his stock in trade are some items which give us an idea of the value of perukes and false hair, which, according to the prevailing fashion of the times, were then so generally worn. Two new wigs, £2. 2s. Curled white goats' hair, 1¼lbs. £1. 10s. Curled white and grizzled horse-hair £1. 4s.   Other stock of hair curled and uncurled £10. 4s.

The loss of Mr. Edward Barron amounted to £84. 6s. His ' books in many sciences' and account books were estimated at £2. 2s.

The loss of Arthur Browne, brazier, amounted to £45. 8s 8d. In his inventory are mentioned, Three pairs of ' plaited sleeves,' two pairs of Bristol-stone buttons, which, with some other articles, are valued at 5s. 6d.—his ' library of books' and book of accounts, 4s !

The loss of Widow Groom was £65. 1s. 6d. including her dwelling-house valued at £30.—with a deduction of 11s. 7d. for melted metal found in the ruins.

The Widow Collison's loss was £13. 8s. 4¾d —James Matsell's, £8. 19s. including 4s. for buskins and 'dannacks': Mary Strutt's, £7. Mrs. Burgis's, £8. 3s. The loss sustained by Gregory Wright, apprentice to Mr. Ivory, on whose premises the gunpowder exploded, was £5. 6s. That of Robert Copeman, his journeyman, £10. 10s. That of Elizabeth Wilson, his maid-servant, £3. 0s. 10d. That of James Buck, servant to Mr. Collison, £5. That of Ann Royston, Mrs. Johnson's maid-servant, £2. 10s. That of John Rudd, £1. 3s. Besides these sufferers there were two or three others who received some small sums.

A portion of the property destroyed seems to have been insured in the Sun Fire Office, the Directors of which, on being consulted after the fire as to which was the best construction of the engine, with which the parishioners were now about to supply themselves, presented them with one dozen of the water-buckets which were furnished with the engine. The most active measures were immediately resorted to for alleviating the distress into which many of the poorer inhabitants of the place had been thus suddenly thrown. A petition was drawn up, and after being attested by several magistrates, was carried round all parts of the county with the most gratifying success. A play also was acted at Norwich for the benefit of the sufferers, and in the course of five months from the time of the fire, the nave at least of the church, and probably the chancel too, was roofed in, and considerable progress made in rebuilding the different private dwellings.

Copy of the Petition : —

Norfolk, to wit, The Petition of the farmers, occupiers, and other inhabitants of the parish of Foulsham in the County of Norfolk—HUMBLY SHEWETH, That on Friday the fifteenth day of June 1770, about one o'clock in the afternoon a dreadful fire broke out and consumed divers houses and buildings in the said parish : and the wind being very high, the flames which raged with irresistible fury, by some accident, were communicated to the church, and no fire engines being at hand, or to be had in time, the church and steeple, together with five bells, the clock and chimes, were entirely demolished and destroyed ; nothing being left standing but the bare walls, so that your petitioners are utterly destitute of a place for divine service. AND WHEREAS the charge of repairing the said church and s'eeple in the most frugal and cheapest manner, consistent with decency, amounts to the sum of eight hundred and ten pounds twelve shillings and one penny halfpenny, exclusive of the bells, clock andchimes ; which sum your petitioners, being farmers and occupiers of the said parish hiring their farms at rack rents on short leases, and many of them having large families, are unable to raise, without impoverishing and ruining their said families. BUT, not-withstanding being desirous that themselves and all other the inhabitants of so large a parish, containing about six hundred souls old and young, should enjoy the comfort and benefit of the public worship of God, they have begun the reparations of their said parish church, by ordering the same to be roofed as soon as possible for the security of the walls. And being unable to proceed in the further neces-sary repairs thereof without assistance from others —

Your petitioners, therefore, humbly implore the aid and contribution of all charitable and well disposed Christians toward the completion of so good and pious a work. And your petitioners shall ever pray, &c. &c &c.

As the contents of this petition have been certified to us and appear to be undoubtedly true, We do (as far as by Law we may) recommend the same to the charitable con-sideration of all good people. Signed—Edward Astley, John Turner, Henry Lee Warner, E. Rolfe, Junr., Pinckney Wilkinson, Wm. Wigget Bulwer, Richard Milles, Thomas Greene, Samuel Rash, Edward Pratt.

The following account of the fire was given in the Nor-folk Chronicle for the year 1770, June 15th. A terrible fire broke out at Foulsham, which consumed 14 dwelling-houses, also the church, chancel, and steeple, leaving only the bare walls standing. The inhabitants are reduced to the greatest misery, many not having had time to save their money or apparel. The damage is estimated at several thousand pounds.

The same newspaper of Saturday, April 13th, 1771, announced that for the benefit of the poor sufferers by the fire at Foulsham, at the Theatre Royal, by his Majesty's Servants, on Monday April the 15th, will be presented a Comedy, called The Suspicious Husband, with Entertainments of Dancing between the Acts. To which will be added, The Padlock. A prologue on the occasion will be spoken by Mr. Griffith. To commence at a quarter after six o'clock. Vivant Rex et Regina. N.B. The proprietors intend giving the charges usually paid for the use of the Theatre to the benefit of the sufferers.

Through the medium of the Norfolk Chronicle of April the 20th, 1771, The poor sufferers by the fire at Foulsham return their most grateful acknowledgments to the proprietors of the Theatre Royal in this city, Norwich, for their kind and humane indulgence of a Play, free from any charge of house or salaries, given last Monday night for the benefit of the said sufferers ; their sincere thanks are also due to the audience that night, who by their contributions there so kindly assisted, in relieving the necessities of the unfortunate and distressed. They are also obliged to the managers of that theatre, and to every individual thereof, for their endeavour to carry the Proprietor's favour into execution.

Summary of monies collected for Foulsham Church and Poor, with the Payments.

RECEIPTS.

	£.	s.	d.
Collected in Norfolk - - - - - -	1120	13	4
Do. of Travellers in trade - - - - -	31	8	3
Do from the Play at Norwich - - - -	32	12	9
Lead sold - - - - - - - -	206	13	6
Split Bell sold - - - - - - -	41	3	8
Bell metal sold - - - - - - -	96	7	4
Old iron do. - - - - - - -	5	17	0
Old stuff, pavements, do. - - - -	3	7	0
	£1538	2	10

PAYMENTS.

	£.	s.	d.
Sufferers for present relief - - - - -	9	9	0
Indigent sufferers for losses - - - -	477	16	0
Faculty from the Bishop - - - - -	3	18	6
Church repairs, ornaments, bells, &c. - - -	811	9	0¼
Expenses of collecting, Collectors Committee meetings, &c. - - - -	168	17	6
A mare bought for collecting - - - -	12	0	0
Clock, &c. - - - - - - -	32	0	0
Four parish pews - - - - - -	13	13	0
Joints, &c. - - - - - - -	0	19	9
	£1530	2	9½
Balance of £8 paid towards an engine - - -	8	0	0
	£1538	2	9½

But few of the original contracts made for the building of parish churches have come down to our times. Of these few, however, some are extremely curious, from being very early, if not the earliest documents drawn up in the English language. There were, generally, two copies of these contracts; one in Latin, which was retained by the founder of the church, whether he were a lay or monastic person ; the other, in English, was delivered to the builder who undertook the work, and who from his ignorance of the foreign tongue, would not otherwise have understood the terms of the agreement into which he had entered. Such, at least, was the usual method of proceeding when the builder was an Englishman. Though there is no such early record connected with the building of Foulsham church known to be in existence, yet the most satisfactory particulars of the repairs it underwent after the fire are fortunately preserved. These details of the sums collected and disbursed on behalf of the sufferers, and the church, will be found in the appendix to this volume. For the lucid arrangement of this valuable information, the author is indebted to the kindness of John Andrews Girling, Esq. a gentleman whose researches into matters respecting the history of Foulsham have proved of material service in the compilation of this Work.

The church rate made for the half year commencing at Easter and ending at St. Michael, 1770, was 6d. in the pound, and amounted to £28. 10s. That from Easter 1771, to Easter 1772, at the same rate, produced £28. 15s. Among the churchwardens' disbursements about this period are several entries of 'hedge-hogs,' for the destruction of each of which 2d. was then the usual payment. Another entry is for 'caddows' killing; such being the common name in this part of the kingdom for jackdaws. According to the same authority, the Altar was put up by Sir Edward Astley's carpenters, May 21st, 1774, a Degrees of Marriage Board, June 30th, and the Font, in the month of November of the same year.

In the year 1784, a poor-house was erected at the distance of about half a mile from the town, on a piece of waste land called Cockle Green, and vested in the Churchwardens and overseers for the time being. The site of it was granted by the Lord of the Manor on lease for a term of 500 years, at a nominal rent. Since the present Poor Law Bill came into operation, Foulsham has been included in the Aylsham Union, and the Poor-house being in consequence no longer needed, has been converted into four or five dwellings, and is now tenanted by several families.

A fair is annually held here on the first Tuesday in May, and is usually well attended by toy and gingerbread venders, as well as by dealers in horses and cattle. The right of holding this fair, like that of numerous others in all parts of England, rests most probably on prescription alone, as no notice of any charter for such a privilege is to be found. Easter Tuesday was the appointed time for holding it up to as late as about the middle of the last century, when the day was changed for the present one, in consequence of its interfering with some of the neighbouring wakes. On the Tuesday before old Michaelmas-day are held the Sessions, or as they are otherwise called, the Statutes, at which in former times, the farmers and housewives of the town and its vicinity hired their domestics for the ensuing year; but the original uses for which these Sessions or Statutes were instituted are now nearly altogether neglected, and the few booths erected on the occasion are resorted to chiefly by children, eager to possess themselves of some of the sweetmeats and gaudy articles which are artfully displayed on their counters. The magistrates acting for the Hundred of Eynsford meet here also in Petty Sessions every alternate Monday.

· There are in the town, besides several retail beer shops, three houses of public entertainment, which may come under the denomination of country inns. The most ancient of these is that known by the name of the Ship Inn, which for ages has gone by the same appellation. According to the prevailing custom of modern times, a lettered signboard is now attached to the house, which was once distinguished by a painted representation of a ship under sail, after the model of a man-of-war in the reign of William

and Mary, which conveyed by no means a bad idea of what
such a vessel was at that period. The existence of the
present Bull Inn, under its former name, The King of
Prussia, may be dated as far back as the commencement of
the eighteenth century, when Prussia was raised from an
electorate to the rank of a kingdom; or at least, traced to
the earlier part of the reign of its monarch, Frederick the
Great, whose celebrity made his portrait a very favourite
sign for public-houses in this, as well as in other parts of
the country. The other inn is called the King's Arms.
There stood, till within the last ten or fifteen years, on the
south side of the market-place, a clay house, roofed with
thatch and having a projecting wooden porch, sure indica-
tions of considerable antiquity. This house, up to the
close of the last century, was known by the sign of the
King's Head, and was probably the most ancient of all the
inns of the place. It was in pulling down this structure
in order to make way for the range of new buildings which
now occupy its site, that the copper token of Edward Benn,
the mercer, was discovered.

From the comparatively retired situation of Foulsham,
and there being no main county thoroughfare passing through
it, one would be led to imagine that many traces of old customs might still be found lingering there; but such a
a supposition will be found to be incorrect. The only
one to which any particular singularity attaches, as far
as my researches have enabled me to discover, is the following: It was the custom some few years since, with the
dames of the place, to pass their children, when afflicted
with the hooping cough, three times round the body of
a donkey, and to repeat the same operation a set number

of days. If duly performed, this ceremony was considered
an infallible cure for the malady. Whether from lack of
faith, however, or from some other cause, this method of
healing the sick child is now but rarely practised.

At Worsted, a village in the neighbourhood of the market-town of North Walsham there is, or was a short time
since, a custom prevailing, equally, if not more singular
than this. A young ash-tree was slit from top to bottom,
and a sort of hoop formed of the two parts as they stood,
through which the diseased infant was passed a certain
number of times, and its cure was then looked upon as
certain. I had sometimes thought that the origin of this
custom might be traced to the Flemings, who settled at
Worsted and the adjoining places in considerable numbers
as early as the reign of Henry II., and who, introduced
among us the manufacture of the yarn which has immor-
talized the name of this village. But it would appear that
its origin must be assigned to some other source than this,
as Sir John Cullum mentions to have twice seen a similar
operation performed in his own garden at Hardwick.
" For this purpose," he says, " a young ash was each
" time selected, and split longitudinally about five feet ;
" the fissure was kept open by my gardener while the friends
" of the child, having first stripped him naked, passed him
" thrice through it, always head foremost. As soon
" as the operation was performed, the wounded tree was
" bound up with a packthread: and, as the bark healed,
" the child was to recover. The first of these young
" patients was to be eased of the rickets ; the second,
" of a rupture. About the former I had no opportunity
" of making any inquiry ; but I frequently saw the father

of the latter, who assured me that his child, without any other assistance, gradually mended, and at last grew perfectly well.".

As late as the beginning of the present century, it was not an unusual custom with the women of the place to wear round their necks a narrow strip of black velvet, which was supposed to be possessed of some peculiar virtues. This usage may be traced to a considerable antiquity, and among other notices of a similar superstition, in a very scarce and elegant poem by T. Cutwode, entitled, "Caltha Poetarum," or The Humble Bee, 1599, 4°. the heroine of the piece is introduced attired by the goddess Diana, who "ties a necklace underneath her chin," which was to protect her from harm, and enable her "to walk full warily." At the risk of the remark being looked upon as somewhat puerile, I may be allowed to observe that in few places did those ridiculous appendages to the head-dress of the male sex, pigtails, maintain their ground longer than here. The origin and antiquity of these strange incumbrances, which the all-powerful sway of fashion for a length of time decided should be a necessary part of a gentleman's attire, are involved in some uncertainty, but Mr. Repton in vol. 24. of the Archæologia, suspects with great reason, that they came into use much later than the reign of Charles I. This absurd fashion continued to be followed till the commencement of the 19th century, when by the good sense of the age it was nearly exploded.

The memory of the ancient "Curfew toll" is still retained here by the ringing of the larger church bell during a portion of the winter season, commencing on the 15th Novr. and ending the 14th of Feby. For the performance

M

of this service the sexton of the parish receives a small annual payment.

The quality of the land at Foulsham, though not very rich, is in general good. Some portions of it indeed towards Themelthorpe are stiff and cold, while others in the direction of Guist are light and sandy. A nameless brook, or beck, * as it is more generally called, which takes its rise in Melton Constable park, and empties itself into the river Wensum at Guist, renders some of those parts of the parish through which it flows, damp and marshy; but with these exceptions the lands here are good and easily worked. Over this rivulet were thrown two brick bridges, each of a single arch, at the time of the inclosure of the commons.

The botanical productions of the place are in no way distinguished from those of the neighbourhood, except that, it is said, a rare species or two of the orchus tribe is sometimes met with in the pastures to the east of the town towards Guestwick. Among the various trees with which the old hedgerows abound, the elm is that which is most frequently met with, shooting up spontaneously, as it were, in every direction. From some cause, however, this tree generally suffers from a premature decay at its core, and, although so plentiful here, seldom attains any very great size.

* Beck. In modern Dutch, beek. Wendish, bec. In lower Saxony a small brook is called a riche—one of a larger size, a beke. Beck, a mountain-stream, or small rapid river. Burn, a brook which winds slowly along meadows, whereas a beck proceeds with a rapid stream, according to an ancient Glossary of words used in the West Riding of Yorkshire.

In the parish there are five or six farms of considerable
size; the rest of it is divided among a number of smaller
proprietors and occupiers. Among these larger estates, is
one called the Keeling Hall Farm, the house attached to
which is on a large scale, and appears from its style to have
been built in the early part of the last century, by one of
the family of Sendal, if my information on this point be
correct. Since that period the property has passed through
various hands, and is now possessed by J. Francis, Esq., of
Twyford. The situation of Keeling Hall itself was formerly
very bleak, Themethorpe common running nearly up to its
front; and it seems difficult to conceive what should have
been the inducement to fix on such an exposed position for
the site of the house, as there are many other spots on the
property which would appear far preferable. This bleak-
ness is now, in a great measure, done away with by the
quick growth of the trees which were planted about it at
the time of the Inclosure of the common in 1811. The
house attached to the estate of the late John Andrews
Girling, Esq., which has now passed into other hands,
though much modernised, was built in the year 1677, by
one of the Crome family, whose initials, and the date, are
yet remaining on it. Nearly the same date may be assigned
to that belonging to the late Mr. J. Berwick. This too
has undergone material alterations. The other houses in
the parish, with the exception of two or three ancient clay
cottages, are of a comparatively modern date.

In the year 1811, in pursuance of an Act of Parliament,
the waste lands and commons of Foulsham and the adjoining village of Themelthorpe were inclosed, and according
to the award then made by the Commissioners, the value

of houses and lands in Foulsham was £4571. The value of the tithes was £627 per annum, and the number of acres in the parish was 3189. 3 r. 8 p. In 1814, the value of the lands, according to their actual admeasurement, including the tithes, was £5378, and the number of acres stated to be 3179. 0 r. 4 p. In the Population Returns for 1831, it is stated that there are in Foulsham 3100 statute acres, and that the annual value of real Property, as assessed in 1815, was £4026. The amount of money expended for the maintenance and relief of the poor for the five years ending 25th March 1825, 1826, 1827, 1828, and 1829 respectively, was in 1825, £1,392. 11s.; in 1826, £1,063; in 1827, £1,023. 12s.; in 1828, £890. 10s.; in 1829, £1,118. 5s.

At the last survey, in conformity with the provisions in the Parochial Assessment Act for the purpose of assessing it to the poor rates, the estimated rental was £5549. 11s. 10d., and when the tithes were commuted, there were found to be in Foulsham, 2002 ac. 0 r. 35 p. of arable land, with 1224 ac. 0 r. 5 p. of pasture, including the sites of buildings, gardens, and roads.

The total amount of poor-rate collected in 1841 was £407. 7s. 6d. The amount of Assessed Taxes raised by the parish for the same year was £183. 9s. 8d. The amount of Land Tax assessed on the parish is £176.; of which £41. 16s. have been redeemed; consequently £134. 4s. is the net annual charge on lands and tenements. The County rate, which is ever varying, for the last quarter of the year 1841, amounted to £13. 9s. 4d.; and the police rate for the same period was £8. 1s. 4d.

Foulsham may lay claim to having given birth to two

theological writers, whose productions were once held in no trifling estimation, though they have now long been consigned to oblivion, the names even of their publications being scarcely known, except to a few of the learned. One of these authors, Richard de Foulsham, a monk of the monastery of St. Benedict, at Norwich, was a great favourite of Arundel, Archbishop of Canterbury, and lived much in the Pope's court at Rome, where he was highly esteemed by John XXII., to whom he addressed several epistles, twenty-eight of which he published in one volume, besides others in another. He flourished in the reign of our Henry IV., and was living in 1410, but the time of his death is uncertain. The titles of his two works are, Epistolarum viginti octo, 1 vol., and Epistolæ Naticiæ, 1 vol. His character both as a man, and as a writer, is highly commended by Pits in his treatise, De Illustribus Angliæ Scriptoribus.

The other and earlier author, John de Foulsham, who derives both his birth and his name from this place , seem to have enjoyed in his day a much wider reputation than the former, and published a greater variety of works, all connected with theological subjects. John de Foulsham was prior of the Carmelite monastery at Norwich, and provincial of all England. He was educated at Cambridge, where he had the degree of Doctor of Divinity conferred on him. According to Leland, Pits, and Bale, he was a divine of eminent superiority in talents and acquirements, and strictly exemplary in all the duties of life. This last writer, in his work, De Scriptoribus Illustribus, is so enthusiastic in his praises of John de Foulsham, and allows himself to be carried away into such an hyperbole of en-

comium, that his panegyric can scarcely be read with a
serious countenance. "John de Foulsham was so deeply
versed in syllogistical reasoning," says his enraptured biographer,—

.... his tongue
Dropt manna, and could make the worse appear
The better reason.

"that he could turn black into white, and men into asses!"
Bale, however, shortly after this excess of commendation,
as if fearful that these laudatory expressions might be taken
in an equivocal sense, adds in italics, and in an altered tone
more suitable to the seriousness of history, that John
de Foulsham was an eloquent and unflinching opponent of
the corruptions of the times, and for his treatise, De Matrimonio, which is his best known work, is deserving of
very great praise, for having in it zealously undertaken the
defence of the marriage of priests, in an age so debased, and
when such a doctrine was totally at variance with that advocated by the authorities of the Church of Rome. He
probably engaged in this work at the instigation of John de
Baconsthorpe, a monk of the Carmelite monastery of
Blakeny, a voluminous and popular writer of the same age
and neighbourhood as himself.

His other work, which, next to his treatise De Matrimonio, brought him the greatest share of reputation, is that
entitled, De Arte Prædicandi, or, On the Art of Preaching.
In this he strenuously urged the necessity and utility of
public preaching, which was but little practised in that
age of ignorance and superstition. He himself also is
reported to have been a model of pulpit eloquence. He
wrote several works evincing much learning, the catalogue
of which is as follows :—

Isagogen metaphysices,
Quæstiones theologiæ,
Moralitates rerum,
De arte prædicandi,
De matrimonio,
Flores ex Chrysostomo,
Collationes per annum,
Super Anselmum indices,
Commentarii in quosdam Salomonis libros,

and died in a great pestilence, in 1348, by which more than 57,000 persons perished. These are the only instances, which have come within my knowledge, of persons deriving their surname from Foulsham; with the exception of a family of the same appellation, who, some five and twenty years since, were resident at Norwich, though recent enquiries have failed in discovering any of the name still in existence there.

In the description of the church, it has been already noticed that several of the family of Themelthorpe were buried here. This old family, of wealth and repute, were residents at Foulsham for many generations, and the name is to be traced there nearly to the beginning of the 18th century. A Nicholas Themelthorpe was appointed "one of the shoers" to Queen Elizabeth, in right of which office he was allowed to add a horse-shoe to his armorial bearings. It might be, perhaps, from some circumstance connected with the Queen's visit to Norwich in 1578, that this post was conferred upon him. The Themelthorpes were allied by marriage with the family of the Bulwers of Wood Dalling, the ancestors of the author of Pelham, &c.,

whose works have made the name so universally known.
As early as the reign of Henry III., a Walter de Themelthorpe resigned to the prior of Walsingham the presentation to Themelthorpe church in a dispute between them,
the prior claiming it by right of a grant from the Mar-
shalls; and in the 1st of Edward VI., George Themelthorpe bought the manor of Themelthope and the advowson,
which continued in the family till the end of the 16th
century. A part of the family about this period removed
to Worsted. In the 3rd and 4th of Philip and Mary, Bertram Themelthorpe leased the manor of Worsted of the
bishop of Norwich, and in the 8th of Elizabeth, Thomas
Themelthorpe bought a manor in Worsted. In the 7th of
James I., Edmund Themelthorpe also purchased lands in
Worsted, where Charles Themelthorpe was living in 1664, ·
who had two daughters; and in North Walsham Church is
a stone to the memory of Mary, wife of Edmund Themelthorpe, who died in 1685. In the chancel of St. Stephen's
Church, Norwich, is this memorial : Edmund Themelthorpe
of this parish, gent., died 21· Dec. æt. 70, 1714; Elizabeth,
his first wife, daughter of Henry Watts of Norwich, Esq.,
June 14, 1682; and their four children, two Edmunds,
Mary and Hannah, all died young, and are here buried.
Martha, his second wife, daughter of Ric: Chamberlain
of Warwickshire, Esq., June 19, 1695. Ric: the son
of Edmund and Martha, buried here, March 19, in the
19th year of his age, surviving his father only three months.
This is the last of the name whom I have been able to
discover. It does not follow from the above mention of
two Edmunds that they were both alive at the same time,
though in former ages, however different the modern usage

may be, it would seem to have been no uncommon circumstance for parents to give to two living children the same baptismal name.

Among the losses at the time of the fire at Foulsham, it is believed that several of the old register books fell a prey to the flames, or were destroyed in the alarm and confusion attendant on the conflagration, which may account for the scanty notices left of the Foulsham branch of this ancient family. The Themelthorpes bore, Sable on a fess between three antelopes' heads erased, or, three crescents gules. Crest, a demi-ostrich erased, or, wings argent, in beak a horse shoe argent.

There is, however, some doubt at the Heralds' Office as to whether the crest ought to be a demi-ostrich with a horse-shoe or annulet in its beak; but the emphatic notice made in one of the pedigrees of the appointment held by the family under Queen Elizabeth, seems to be decisive in favour of the horse-shoe.

In the Parliamentary Commissioners' Reports is a very clear and satisfactory account of the charity lands connected with this place, which altogether now amount to 40 ac. 2 r. 22 p. It is there stated that Richard Fenn, in 1565, according to the inscription on the brass tablet in the church, left to the poor nine acres. This property is situate in Guestwick, and is freehold, but there are no deeds relating to it. In 1786, it was vested in James Athill, and was then of the clear yearly value of £5. 19s. 4d. In 1835, it was held by John Berwick, under a lease granted by the trustees of Semicroft's Charity, for eight years, from 5th April, 1829, at a good yearly rent of £22. 10s.

These rents are carried to the same account as Semicroft's Charity.

Semicroft's Charity.

Henry Semicroft, in 1693, gave by will to the poor, land vested in 1786, in Thomas Manning, William Manning, Thomas Back the younger, and Thomas Parrant, of the then clear annual value of £5. 12s.

At a court held for the manor of Foulsham, 12th Jan'y., 1819, it was found that at a court held 9th Jan'y. then last, William Manning, the Rev. Henry Nicholas Astley and eight others, were admitted, on the surrender of the then surviving trustees, to a close called Harrison's, containing six acres, in Foulsham, and to an allotment of 1 a. 2 r., set out on the inclosure, upon trust to demise the same for any term not exceeding seven years, and to distribute the rents and profits on Christmas-day yearly, to the poor inhabitants of the parish of Foulsham, according to the directions of the Will of Henry Semicroft, dated in or about the year 1693.

The old inclosure, now in two pieces, containing 4 a. 1 r. 15 p., and 2 a. 1 r. 39 p. was, in 1835, held by John Bird under a lease granted to Benjamin Nobbs, for a term of eight years, from Michaelmas 1830, at a good yearly rent of £19.- 10s.

The allotment of one acre and a half forms part of a piece of ground, containing 5 a. 3 r. 38 p., being several allotments put together, and let to William Jordan, on lease for eight years from Michaelmas 1827, at the yearly rent of £10.

Out of the rents of Fenn's and Semicroft's Charities, and

the allotments held therewith as above-mentioned, amounting to £52. there is paid for land tax and quit rent, 15s. yearly. The residue is distributed between Christmas and Easter, among poor persons belonging to the parish, whether resident in it or not, in sums varying according to the different description of the objects ; persons who have become aged and infirm, and have supported themselves and families without parish assistance, have the largest proportions ; others receive according to the number in family ; persons of bad character have been occasionally excluded for a year, but put on the list again.

The distribution is made by the churchwardens, generally in the presence of some of the trustees.

Chapman's Charity.

John Chapman in 1661, gave by will for gowns to poor widows yearly, land vested in 1786, in the same four persons who were the trustees for Semicroft's Charity, and of which the clear annual value was then £8 15s. 6d.

At a court held for the manor of Foulsham, 1st Jan'y., 1819, the same trustees as had been admitted for Semicroft's Charity were admitted also to a close called the Carr, containing by estimation seven acres, and a piece of pasture thereto adjoining, containing by estimation six acres, and also to two pieces of land set out on the Foulsham and Themelthorpe inclosure, containing respectively 3 a. 2 r. 12 p. and 3 r. 23 p., upon trust to demise the said pieces of land for any term of years not exceeding seven ; and to pay over the rents and profits to the churchwardens and overseers of the parish of Foulsham, to be by them laid out in the purchase of gowns, all of one colour, to be distributed by them between Michaelmas and Christmas among the poor widows and other poor women of the said parish of Foulsham, according to the directions in the Will of John Chapman, bearing date 10th Octr. 1661.

The old enclosed land held in trust for this charity, though described on the court rolls as containing by estimation 13 acres, and consisting of two parcels adjoining each other, contains only 10 a. 2 r. 6 p. according to the map annexed to the award of the Commissioners of inclosures, and it consists of two inclosures separated from each other by a close of 5 a. 1 r. 37 p., marked as Sir John Lombe's, whose estate now belongs to Edward Lombe, Esq.

As it appeared in evidence that upwards of 40 years ago the charity land was in the occupation of Simon Rackham, who was also tenant of the intervening field of Sir John Lombe, and that when he gave up the land the fences were pulled down, and upon the parishioners interfering, the present boundaries were set out, a suspicion arose that part of the charity land had been lost, but it is evident from a map of Mr. Lombe's estate made in 1766, that there has been no material alteration since that period.

The charity land in 1835 was held by John Austin under a lease for eight years from Michaelmas 1830, at a good yearly rent of £24.

The allotments made in respect of this land are included in the lettings mentioned under Semicroft's charity.

The rents are received by the churchwardens, and disposed of about Easter, among all the widows of the parish equally.

Gowns and flannel petticoats are given away every year, and blankets generally every alternate year in addition.

It seems to have been erroneously considered that all the

widows of the parish, whether poor or not, were entitled to this charity; and there appeared to be upon the list one or two individuals who it is stated were in good circumstances; we recommended, say the Parliamentary Commissioners, that such persons should no longer be permitted to participate in the charity.

On 12th March 1834, there was a balance in the hands of the churchwardens of £10. 4s. 8d., which was kept in hand as a fund for the purchase of blankets in the ensuing year.

Chime lands.

In a terrier of 1784 are mentioned under the head of Town lands—Four acres called Chime lands at a place called Sandhills; and also four pieces of land, containing together three acres, and bounded as therein mentioned; without any statement as to the trusts on which they are held.

There are also two allotments set out to the churchwardens and overseers on the inclosure containing 3 r. 24 p. and 36 perches.

The land called Sandhills was in 1835, let to Edward Mallett and Thomas Case as joint tenants, on lease for eight years from Michaelmas 1833, at a good yearly rent of 10l.

The allotments are let in small parcels to poor persons at rents amounting to 2l. 14s. per annum.

The other lands were represented in 1835 as lying intermixed with lands of John Berwick, John Craske, and George Cooke; no rent had been paid for any of these lands since 1829, but the churchwardens intend taking steps for ascertaining the boundaries and obtaining possession of the lands, or letting them on fair terms.

The rents now received are carried to the churchwardens' general account.

Walfred de Save was found to have died possessed of lands in Foulsham, Bintry, &c. 28 Hen. III.

Lands in Foulsham were confirmed to the Prior of Walsingham, 39 Hen. III.

The manor of Foulsham formerly belonging to Wm. de Marescall was found to be ancient demesne, 50 Hen. III.

Wm. Goreberge, or Gerberge, had lands confirmed to him in Foulsham and other neighbouring places, 53 Hen. III.

The Prior of Walsingham had free warren in Foulsham, 28 Ed. I.

In 1315, Eynesford Hundred belonged to John le Mareschal; and of Foulsham cum Themelthorpe the lords were, John de Roselyn and John Gerberge heirs of John de Swanton, and the Prior of Walsingham.

Joanna, formerly wife of Wm. Roscelyn, was found to have died possessed of the manor of Foulsham, 1 Ed. III.

Wm. de Norton had lands, &c., in Foulsham and the adjoining places, with 50s. rent, held of the honor of Clare, 13 Rich. II.

Foulsham was allowed to be ancient demesne on the authority of Domesday Book, 20 Rich. II.

Humphrey, Duke of Buckingham, as heir of Wm. Marshal, held one fee in Banham, Foulsham, and Wood Norton, 38, 39 Hen. VI.

Sir John Curson had divers lands and tenements, called

Hastange, in Bintry, Twyford, Guestwick, and Foulsham, 11th Ed. IV.

Thos. Brampton had lands in Foulsham, 21 Ed. IV.

Besides the names of lands cited in the Terrier, almost every field in this, as well as in other country parishes, has its distinguishing appellation. In Foulsham there is little or nothing peculiar in the derivation of any of them, which might render their enumeration interesting. The following is a list of some few of the names of fields, &c., which occur in old writings relating to the town.

Botshill—a grazing-ground, near Keeling Hall.

Basham's, near the workhouse. . . . . Basham, accord ing to some ancient deeds, died shortly before the year 1688.

Clergyman's Widows Land.—This is the name errone-ously given to the land bequeathed by John Chapman in 1661, for charitable purposes before noticed.

The Carr, near the clay pits—The lane called Primrose-lane leads to it.

Batt's Close, otherwise Fenn's Land, near a farm-house, called Skitfield. This is the land left to the poor by Rich. Fenn, in 1565. Whence Skitfield derived its name does not appear.

Lawe's grazing-ground. Hawys's.

Brick Field—a field adjoining the town. Many of the bricks used in rebuilding the place after the fire in 1770, were obtained from this field.

Cawdle Close—near a part of the parish called Bate's Moor.

Curson's Close—belonging to the Keeling Hall Farm.

The Woodrow—land on the left of the road leading to

Themelthorpe, a field there, called Fishpit Close, forms a part of it.

The Marsh—part of what was once the common land, lying at the bottom of the field, on the south of a pasture, called the Eyle. A portion of the marsh was named Holl's Mouth, and a drift-way with a falgate led to it from the lands on its eastern side.

Lower, Upper, and Middle Bayley's—lands adjoining the road leading to Hindolvestone.

The Great Moor. Langley's Close.

Death's Hole—by Guestwick Green. Could this place have derived its name from having been used as a burying-ground during any plague?

Holl Lane, or Town-Close Lane—was once a hollow way, lined with oaks, through the field leading to the lonely cottage, formerly occupied by — Nobbs. The trees were felled and sold when the workhouse was built, and the road levelled. This field is town-land, and there is still a foot-path through it.

The Lizards—these are probably the lands mentioned in Genl. Skippon's Will by the name of Becklizard, &c., and bequeathed to his daughter.

De Manason's Pightle—a field belonging to the manor-farm of which the present Lord Hastings is the owner.

Dulencross Meadow - by Skitfield. This meadow probably derives its name from the same source as the Dulen-cross Manor. There was a monastery in Staffordshire called Diewlencrease, alias Delacresse. Could the name of the monastery, as well as that of the manor, be a corruption of the French words, "Dieu l'engraisse?"

Paradise, a piece of old pasture-land with a cottage on it.

In all likelihood this was once considered as what we should now term the lawn of the house, belonging to the late Mr. Girling, such ornamental grounds being formerly so called. The word Paradise is of eastern origin, and occurs in the Greek writers, signifying a park, or hunting-seat, of the kings of Persia.

According to the Norfolk poll-book for the year 1734, the number of freeholders in Foulsham, who voted for the County Members, was 20.

In 1768, the freeholders who voted were 8 in number. In 1802, 14. In 1806, 11. In 1817, 17. In 1832, after the passing of the Reform Bill, 42 persons voted. In 1835, 46. In 1837, according to the altered arrangement of the poll-book, there were, home-voters, 42; out-voters, 1; and the present number of persons entitled to vote at the County elections is 61.

It appears from the Parish Register, that the number of baptisms, marriages, and burials for the years 1800, 1810, 1820, 1830, 1840, and 1841 respectively, stands thus;

	1800.	1810.	1820.	1830.	1840.	1841.
Baptisms,	9.	13.	20.	27.	19.	26.
Marriages,	3.	1.	3.	4.	5.	4.
Burials,	19.	18.	13.	8.	16.	21.

Since the commencement of the present century there has been a steady increase in the population. In 1801, there were 101 houses occupied by 101 families, and 2 uninhabited houses. Males, 290, females, 315. The persons chiefly employed in agriculture were 110, those chiefly employed in trade, 61. Other persons not included in the two preceding classes, 434. Total number of inhabitants 605.

In 1811, there were 105 houses occupied by 146 families, 1 house building, and 1 uninhabited. The families chiefly employed in agriculture were 73, those chiefly employed in trade, 64, and the other families not included in the two preceding classes, 9. Males 327, females 355. Total number of inhabitants, 682.

In 1821, there were 131 houses inhabited by 180 families, 2 houses building, and 7 uninhabited. The families chiefly employed in agriculture were 94, those chiefly employed in trade, 69, and the other families not included in the two preceding classes, 17. Males 410, females 425. Total number of inhabitants, 835.

In 1831, there were 143 houses inhabited by 219 families, 2 houses building, and 8 uninhabited. The families chiefly employed in agriculture were 66, those chiefly employed in trade, 70, and the other families not included in the two preceding classes, 83. Males 474, females, 484. Total number of inhabitants, 958.

At the last census in 1841, the population amounted to 1048, shewing an increase of 90 in the previous ten years, and an increase of no less than 443 since the year 1801. By the same census it appears that the number of inhabitants in Foulsham is greater than that of any other single parish in the Hundred of Eynsford.

A TRUE TERRIER of all the Glebe lands, Messuages, Tenements, Tythes, Portions of Tythes, and other Rights belonging to the Rectory and Parish Church

of Foulsham, in the County of Norfolk, and Diocese
of Norwich, now in the use and possession of The
Reverend Henry Nicholas Astley, Rector there, or his
Tenants, taken, made and renewed, according to the
old Evidences and knowledge of the antient Inhabitants, at a vestry held this Eighth day of June, in the
year of our Lord, one thousand eight hundred and
twenty-seven, pursuant to due and legal Notice, given
in Church on Sunday last for that purpose, and
Exhibited in the Ordinary visitation of The Right
Reverend Father in God, Henry Lord Bishop of Norwich, holden at Norwich, in the Cathedral Church
there, on the fourteenth day of June, one thousand
eight hundred and twenty-seven.

One Acre, three roods and eight perches of Land, with
the Parsonage House, Barn, Stables and other out Buildings standing thereon bounded by land, belonging to John
Berwick north, by land late belonging to John Mays
deceased, now of Sarah Mays east, and by land late
belonging to the said John Mays and now of Sarah Mays
in part, and the Churchyard of Foulsham south, and by the
King's highway leading from the Market Place of Foulsham aforesaid to Hindolveston in the said County west.

Also Four acres, three roods and thirty two perches of
land, bounded by a lane called Mill-Hill Lane north, by
land belonging to Anthony Aufrere Esquire, east, and on
land belonging to the said Anthony Aufrere in part, and
on land belonging to the said John Berwick in part south,
and on land belonging to the said John Berwick in part,

and on other Glebe land lately taken in exchange of the said John Berwick in part west.

Also One rood and twenty-one perches of land, lying intermixed between the lands formerly of Roger Hill, late of Thomas Cook deceased, now of George Cook east west and north, and the King's highway leading from Foulsham aforesaid to Wood Norton in the said County south.

Also Three acres, three roods and sixteen perches of land bounded 'by a Drift way leading to grazing Grounds belonging to Sir Jacob Astley Baronet north, by the King's highway, leading from Foulsham to Hindolveston aforesaid east, by land belonging to Elizabeth Tompson widow south, and by land belonging to the said Sir Jacob Astley west.

Also One acre, three roods and three perches of land called Jenkins bounded by a Drift way leading to grazing grounds, late of William Johnson now belonging to William Durrant north, by land late of the said William Johnson now belonging to William Durrant east and south, and by a lane called Jenkins Lane west.

Also Five acres, two roods and four perches of land, late part of the Common Pasture of Foulsham aforesaid, called Themelthorpe Common, bounded by land belonging to John Francis north, by land late of Mary Collison widow, deceased, now belonging to John Mussett, east, by the King's highway leading from Foulsham aforesaid to Reepham in the said County south, and by land belonging to the said Sir Jacob Astley west.

Also Two acres, one rood and two perches of land, being part of an Inclosure of land belonging to the said John

Berwick bounded by the said land called Mill-Hill lane north, by other Glebe land of Foulsham aforesaid east, by land belonging to the said John Berwick south, and by the King's highway leading from Foulsham aforesaid to Hindolvestone aforesaid west.

Also Two acres, one rood and ten perches of land, being an Inclosure called the Hindolvestone Pightle, lately belonging to the said John Berwick, bounded by land belonging to the said Anthony Aufrere Esquire north and east, by the aforesaid lane called Mill-Hill lane south, and by the said King's highway leading from Foulsham to Hindolvestone west.

The above Glebe Lands lie in eight several pieces and contain as herein before mentioned, 22 ac. 3 r. 15 p.

Memorandum. All Tithes within the said Parish are payable in kind, and we have no custom in the said Parish that we know of.

An account of the Town Lands in Foulsham aforesaid.

Six Acres of Land called Harrison's Close in two pieces, late in the occupation of Francis Thomas Quarles and Hannah Burgis and now in the occupation of Benjamin Nobbs and John Chapman Burgis, bounded by land late of William Buck, now belonging to Elizabeth England east, the King's highway or road leading from Foulsham Market place to Batesmoor west and north, and the lands of Anthony Aufrere Esquire late of John Atthill south.

Also Nine acres of land lying in Guestwick in the said County of Norfolk, late in the occupation of John Munton, now in the occupation of William Randall Walne, bounded by land late belonging to the Earl of Buckinghamshire

deceased, now of The Dowager Lady Suffield east, on land
formerly of Coulsey Savory, late of Thomas Knights, now
of Rose Cooper west, and the King's highway leading from
Wood Norton, to Guestwick aforesaid north.   This piece of
land was formerly Richard Fenn's.

Also Eight acres of land called The Carr, being Gown
land bounded by land, late of Sir John Lombe, Baronet,
now of Edward Lombe Esquire, east, on land late the
Common pasture of Foulsham aforesaid, called the Lower
Moor west and north, and the land of John Andrews Girling,
south.

Also Four acres of land called Chime land, lying at a
place called Sand-Hills, bounded by the lands late of the
Rectory, now of William Robins north, on lands late of
Margaret Drozier, now of William Robins south, on lands
late of Coulsey Savory, now of William Robins west,
and on land late of the said Margaret Drozier, now of John
Munton east.

Also One acre of land, bounded by land late of William
Sharpe, now of John Berwick east and north, and land
formerly of John Lowden late of James Archer, now of John
Berwick west and south.

Also One acre of land bounded by land formerly of the
said John Lowden, late of the said James Archer, now of
the said John Berwick east west and north, and by land
late of the said William Sharpe now of the said John
Berwick south.

Also One rood of land bounded by land formerly of
the said John Lowden, late of the said James Archer, now
of the said John Berwick east and west, upon land formerly
glebe land south, and upon land formerly of Henry Hagon

late of William Harper, now of William Harper at or nigh unto a place called White Stone north.

Also Three roods of land bounded by land formerly of Roger Hill, late of Thomas Cook, now of George Cook east, upon land formerly of Alice Back and others, late of the said William Sharpe, now of the said John Berwick west, upon land formerly of the said John Lowden, late of the said James Archer, now of the said John Berwick north, and upon land formerly of John Drozier, late of the said John Blanchflower, now of John Craske south.

Also Three acres two roods and twelve perches of land (being lately part of the Common Pasture of Foulsham called Court Green) bounded by the King's Highway leading to Kerdistone in the said County north-west, by a private road leading to Grazing grounds east, and by land belonging to William Jordan south.

Also Two acres one rood and twenty-three perches of land (being lately part of the common pasture of Foulsham aforesaid called Court Green) bounded by the Parish of Wood Dalling north, by the King's Highway, leading to Kerdistone south-east, and by land late of the Right Honorable Lord Suffield deceased, now of the Dowager Lady Suffield west.

Also Three roods and twenty four perches of land (being lately part of the Low Common of Foulsham aforesaid) bounded by land belonging to Hannah Mays, north, by land belonging to the said Hannah Mays, Robert Watts, and James Saunders respectively east, by land belonging to the said James Saunders south, and by other land belonging to the Town of Foulsham and Corbet Cooke, and a private road, respectively south-west, and by the King's highway leading from Foulsham aforesaid to Bawdeswell in the said county west.

Also Thirty six perches of land (being lately part of the Low Common) bounded by land late belonging to Thomas Stringer now of Corbet Cooke north, by other land belonging to the Town of Foulsham and the said James Saunders respectively east, by land belonging to the said James Saunders south, and by a private road west.

Also Three acres two roods and seven perches of land bounded by land belonging to Sir Jacob Astley, in part and on land belonging to Edmund Sawer in part north, and on land belonging to Edward Lombe, Esquire, on every other part.

> The above town lands lie in thirteen pieces and contain Forty acres, two roods and twenty-two perches, the rents whereof are duly paid and are applied to the purposes for which the same were left by the Donors.

An Inventory and Account of all and singular the Goods, Books, Ornaments and Utensils belonging to the Parish and Parish Church of Foulsham in the county of Norfolk and Diocese of Norwich.

One Silver Cup, one Silver Paten, two Pewter Flaggons, a Pewter Dish, one Velvet Cloth for the Communion Table, one Linen cloth and Napkin for the same, a Church Chest, an Iron Chest, one Velvet Cushion with Gold Fringe, and Tassels for the pulpit, one small Cushion with Gold Fringe for the Reading-desk, one old green Cushion for the same, two Holland Surplices, two Books of Common-prayer, a Book of Homilies, and one large Bible, two Bells as they hang with the ropes, one Fire-engine with pipes, and three dozen Leather Buckets and a Burying cloth.

The above is a true Terrier and Account.

Witness our hands,

H. N. Astley, Rector.

Hen. May Waller,
J. Berwick, } Churchwardens.

Principal Inhabitants.

William Archer.

F⁸. T⁸. Quarles.

Henry Glasspoole.

Benjamin Nobbs.

Charles Leamon, Overseer.

William Scott.

James Saunders.

Thomas Purdy.

Samuel Pratt.

William Seaman.

John Bale.

William Mays.

O

APPENDIX.

THE estimate of the Roof for Foulsham Church, all to be done with oak, with the following scantlings at £3. 4s. per square.

	inches.		inches.
The Wall-Plates,	- 8½	by	5½
Principals,	- 7½	by	5½ in the middle
Purloins (*sic*)	- 5	by	4
Small Spars	- 4	by	3

The trusses the same thickness as the principals, with a proportionate depth.

One ditto, with oak, of the following scantlings at £2. 12s. 6d. per square.

	inches.		inches.
The Wall-Plates,	- 8	by	4½
Principals,	- 6½	by	4
Purloins,	- 4½	by	3½
Small Spars,	- 3½	by	2¾

The trusses as before.

N.B. Carriage excluded.

Samuel Burcham, of East Dereham.

Proposals made by James Frost of Norwich, to roof Foulsham Church.

		inches.		inches.
Scantlings.	Wall-Plates, - - -	9	by	4 of Oak.
	Ties, - - - - -	9	by	6 do.
	Purloins, - - -	4½	by	4½ of Fir.
	King-Posts, - - -	6	by	6 of Oak.
	Do. in the Joggings,	12	by	6
	Strutts, - - - -	6	by	4 of Oak.
	Principals, - - -	6½	by	5½ do.
	Small Spars, - -	4	by	3 of Fir.

To find all materials, and to put up the roofs of the church and aisles fit for tiling (lath and carriage excepted) in two months from this day. Fir to be good red wood ; oak of heart. The price to be at the sum of fifty shillings per square.

Scantlings of the aisles :—

	inches.		inches.	
Principals,	- - - 10	by	6	of Fir.
Spars,	- - - - 4	by	3	do.

July 4th, 1770. It is agreed by the said James Frost and the Committee for repairing the said Church that the said James Frost shall execute the said roofs according to the above proposals and a plan delivered.

Witness our hands, Ts. Quarles, Thos. Back, Rich. Fleming, John Pike, John Drosier, A. Parrant, James Frost.

Memorandum made this first day of August 1770. It is agreed between the Committee appointed for the sale of the lead coming off Foulsham Church, and for the repairing the said Church, and Nicholas Sison, Brazier, of Little Walsingham, and Ann Sudbury, Widow, Glazier, of Fakenham, both in the County of Norfolk, as follows : *first*, that the said Nicholas Sison and Ann Sudbury shall in a good and workman-like manner, glaze, or cause to be glazed, the windows of Foulsham Church with the best Newcastle Crown Glass (not inferior to the sample that has been produced) and the same to be well leaded in squares according to the directions to be given, at the price of thirteen pence the foot, to be measured in the usual method, and to be finished on or before the 25th of December next, and

to do, or cause to be done, all the plumbing-work that will
be wanted about the Church at the customary prices, in a
workman-like manner.   And the said Nicholas Sison and
Ann Sudbury do agree to buy all the lead coming from off
the said Church at the price of fourteen shillings per hundred weight, being allowed seven pounds to every hundred
weight for dross, to be weighed at Foulsham, and delivered
half at Norwich, and the other half at Fakenham, to be
paid for as follows, viz :   One hundred pounds of the pur-
chase-money on the 25th of September, and the remainder
on or upon the said twenty-fifth day of December next.
As witness our hands.

A. Sudbury.

Nich. Sison.

Proposals made per Joseph Mack for making and erecting
a Church-clock for the Parish of Foulsham to be finished
and put in the steeple there, on or before the 10th day
of October, 1771, to be completely executed in a workman-
like manner to the satisfaction of a competent judge of a
work of that nature.

A Church-clock to go 30 hours, to be made of brass and
steel, with a square dial-plate of copper a proper thickness,
6 feet 5 inches square, with weights, pulleys, ropes, and a
case, with all other appurtenances necessary, at the sum of
thirty-one pounds and ten shillings, and to be allowed ten
shillings more for scaffolding and help to put up the clock,
dial-plate, &c.   And the said Joseph Mack is to keep the
clock in repair for seven years after the same is completed,
without any allowance for so doing.

I, the said Joseph Mack, having undertaken the said
clock, do agree to perform the same according to the above

proposals; and I, Nathaniel Cowper, do agree to pay the said Joseph Mack the said thirty-two pounds when the above is fully completed. As witness our hands this 18th day of June, 1771.

Joseph Mack.
Nat. Cowper.

There was also a bill for carpenters' extra work done to the Church, by James Frost, amounting to £163. 17s. 4d.

Amount of Cash received on behalf of the Sufferers at Foulsham by Fire, and of the Church.

RECEIVED.

		£.	s.	d.
	Of Sir Edward Astley, Bart. 2 Bank Notes (Church)	50	0	0
	Do. Cash for poor	21	0	0
	Rev. John Astley for Poor. . . .	3	3	0
1770	Thomas Greene, Esq	2	2	0
July 26.	Mr. Fleming and Mr. Temple collected by Petition	74	5	9
28.	Mr. Drosier and Mr. Porter collected .	35	3	11
29.	Mr. Fleming and Mr. Wood collected at Elmham, &c.	22	17	6
Aug. 1.	Mr. Fleming and George Carrison, collected at Bawdeswell, &c.	8	4	0
	Mr. Quarles and George Carrison collected at Thornage	15	17	0
	Mr. John Drosier and Richard Porter collected at Rainham	15	9	3
	Mr. Nathl. Cooper and Mr. T. Bambridge collected at Hindolveston . . .	14	19	0
3.	Mr. Nathl. Cooper and Mr. Fox collected at E. Dereham	34	1	3

o 2

	£.	s.	d.
Mr. John Drosier (for Edwd. Drosier) . .	1	4	0
4. Mr. Parrant collected at Holt, &c. . .	43	9	3
Mr. Fleming collected	0	19	0
6. Mr. Mayes and Mr. Fox collected . .	7	0	9
8. Mr. Fox and John Burgis collected . .	3	12	0
Gift of I. Temple, Thornage	0	10	6
Do. T. Bell, Bintry	0	5	3
11. Mr. Wynn, Holt	0	10	6
9. Mr. Quarles's collection at Reepham, &c. .	15	3	0
15. Mr. Fox's and Burgis collection at Letheringsett, &c.	5	13	6
16. Mr. Zankey Ladley	1	1	0
Mr. Thomas St. John, Briston . . .	0	5	3
18. Collection of Dr. Fleming at Snoring, &c. .	13	10	9
22. Collection of Mr. Fox and Mr. Barron at Clay, &c.	16	6	9
Collection of Mr. Mays and Mr. Fox at Weyborne, &c.	6	13	9
26. Collection of Mr. Drosier and Mr. Porter at Wells, &c.	33	12	6
Collection of Mr. Cooper, &c. at Swaffham .	23	15	9
28. Collection of Geo. Carrison and Fox at Saxthorpe, Oulton, &c.	11	3	6
Gift of John Ladley	2	2	0
Collection of G. Carrison and Barron at Cromer	13	2	9
Rev. Armine Styleman	3	3	0
Mr. Bell Cooke of Oulton	1	7	0
31. Mr. Quarles's and Mr. Temple's collection .	19	5	3
Septr. 1. By a further gift of the Rev. Repps Brown .	0	10	6
3. Collection of Dr. Fleming, &c. at Gressenhall	15	16	3
Mr. Drosier, from Mr. Raby of Rainham .	1	1	0
Mr. Muffet, Swaffham	0	5	0
6. Collection of Mr. Quarles and Mr. Cooper at Wymondham, &c.	22	14	9
Collection of Mr. Fox. &c. at Shipdham .	17	4	9

		£.	s.	d.
9.	Collection of Mr. Fleming and Mr. Barron at Burnham	33	12	3
	——— Medlecott of Swaffham, Esquire .	1	1	0
12.	Mr. Fleming's collection at Foxley . .	2	7	6
	Mr. Norton at Twyford , . . .	0	10	6
13.	Mr. Parrant and Mr. Hill, collection at N. Walsham, &c.	22	16	9
	Lord Buckinghamshire's Gift . . .	20	0	0
16.	Mr. Quarles and Mr. Back collected at Aylsham, &c.	15	8	1½
	Lord Walpole's Gift	5	5	0
	Sir Wm. Morden Harbord, Bart. . . .	5	5	0
23.	Mr. N. Cooper. &c. collection at Litcham, &c.	13	12	3
25.	Mr Fleming and Mr. Kemp at Tittleshall .	8	18	0
Octr. 3.	The Rev. Mr. Drake of Wymondham . .	2	2	0
	Mr. Parrant and Mr. Wood, collection at Lynn	35	4	6
	Mr. Chad	5	5	0
	Mr. Molyneux	5	5	0
	Geo. Carrison and Mr. Fox from Plumsted, Barton, and other towns in that neighbourhood	12	16	9
10.	Do. collected at North Tuddenham . .	0	12	9
	Mr. Ware of Worsted	0	5	0
	John Beck of Stanfield	0	10	6
	Robt. Porter of Hinderingham . . .	0	5	0
12.	Nathl. Cooper and Jno. Drozier for amount received of Mr. Sison on account . . .	190	0	0
Nov. 3.	Of Park Honoree and George Carrison by 3 weeks' collection at Downham, Wisbeach, &c.	46	4	9
4.	Edmund Rolfe, Junr. Esq.	2	2	0
	Mrs. Henley, Docking	1	7	0
	Mr. Custance, Fakenham	0	5	3
9.	Rev. Mr. Partridge of Cranworth, by the Rev. Mr. Lane	0	10	6
27.	Geo. Carrison and P. Honoree from Thetford, Diss, Bungay, &c.	31	4	6

Amount of monies paid to the Sufferers at Foulsham by Fire, and for the repairs of the Church.

PAID.

		£.	s.	d.
To Poor, part of Sir Edw. Astley's Gift . .		5	5	0
To Do. the Rev. John Astley's do. . .		3	3	0
1770. To Do. part of Mr. Green's do. . . .		1	1	0
July 26. To Mr. Fleming and Mr. Temple, expenses .		1	10	6
28. To Mr. Drosier and Mr. Porter, do. . .		0	4	5
29. To Mr. Fleming and Mr. Wood, do. . .		0	0	4
1. To Mr. Fleming and Geo. Carrison, do. .		0	2	2
To Mr. Quarles and Geo Carrison, do. . .		0	3	4
To Mr. Drosier and Mr. Porter, do. . .		0	2	4
To Mr. Cooper and T. Bambridge, do. . .		0	5	10
3. To Mr. Cooper and Mr. Fox, do. . . .		1	2	9
4. To Mr. Parrant, do.		0	10	0
6. To Mr. Mayes and Mr. Fox, do. . . .		0	6	9
8. Mr. Mayes and John Burgis, do. .		0	6	0
To Sufferers:				
James Matsell		2	2	0
Thomas Bambridge		30	0	0
John Layton		20	0	0
Edward Barron		8	15	0
Rebecca Burgis		20	0	0
Dorothy Collison		5	0	0
Arthur Browne		7	10	0
Mary Strutt		1	15	0
James Buck		1	5	0
Elizabeth Wilson		0	15	0
Philip Leamon, a bill of expenses . .		1	11	4
9. To Mr. Quarles's and Mr. Fox's expenses at Reepham		0	6	3
Beer at Bambridge's, for help about the bell		0	2	6
15. Expenses of Mr. Fox and Burgis at Letheringsett, &c.		0	5	6
Two skins of parchment to copy petitions .		0	2	0

			£.	s.	d.
16.	To Mr. Morphew, for faculty, &c.	. .	3	18	6
	Sufferers, Groom and family	. . .	16	2	6
18.	Expenses to Dr. Fleming	. . .	0	4	0
22.	Do. to Mr. Fox and Barron	. . .	0	14	10
	Do. to Mr. Mayes and Fox	. . .	0	12	9
	Philip Leamon, a bill for Mr. Fox, &c.	.	0	10	2
	Expenses of Committee this day	. .	0	5	0
26.	Do. of Mr. Drosier and Mr. Porter, 2 days, hobby, &c.		1	3	6
	Do. of Mr. Cooper, &c. (3 days)	. .	2	8	10
28.	Do. of G. Carrison and Fox, (2 days)	.	0	16	0
	Do. of G. Carrison and Barron, (4 days)	.	1	14	9
	Three chaldrons of lime for the church	.	1	4	0
	Help and expenses of beer, &c. to weigh the lead		0	7	9
31.	Mr. Quarles's and Mr. Temple's expenses, 2 days		0	17	1
	Guide and horse		0	1	6
Sept. 1.	Thomas Withers, a sufferer. . . .		1	5	0
	Robert Copeman, do. . . .		2	12	6
3.	Expenses to Dr. Fleming	. .	0	8	2
	James Taylor, 2,000 bricks (church)	.	1	16	0
6.	Webster, 5 loads of sand, per Hill	.	0	1	8
	Expenses of 4 people, guides, horses, &c., for 3 days and nights at Wymondham	.	4	12	8
	Expenses to Mr. Fox, Shipdham, &c.	.	1	18	7
9.	Expenses and hobby, Mr. Fleming and Mr. Barron		1	11	3
12.	Expenses, Mr. Fleming, &c., at Foxley and Twyford		0	2	6
	Gave carpenters (roofing) . . .		0	1	0
13.	Expenses, Mr. Parrant and Mr Hill, North Walsham, &c.		1	17	0
16.	Expenses of Mr. Quarles and Mr. Back, at Aylsham, &c.		0	9	6

		£.	s.	d.
23.	To Expenses, Mr. Cooper and Barron, 2 days	1	11	3
25.	Mr. Fleming and Mr. Kemp's expenses .	0	8	4
	Mrs. Burgis, a sufferer, further on account .	20	0	0
27.	Mr. Fleming and Mr. Quarles's expenses to Norwich	0	16	6
30.	John Layton, a sufferer, further on account	10	0	0
Oct. 3.	Mr. Parrant and Mr. Wood's expenses at Lynn, &c.	3	17	8
8.	Mr. Collison, a sufferer, further on account	5	0	0
	Expenses of George Carrison and Fox a week out	3	8	11
	Expenses of ditto on N. Tuddenham collection	0	10	4
	Mr. Fox, as per Bill and Receipt for collecting, 5 weeks and 3 days, and his 5 Sundays' expenses.	5	18	0
	George Carrison for two weeks and one day collecting.	1	19	0
	In part for a mare for the riding collector	10	10	0
15.	Edward Barron,	8	15	0
	Thomas Withers,	1	5	0
18.	Arthur Browne,	7	10	0
	James Buck, } Sufferers.	1	5	0
	Mary Strutt,	1	15	0
	Thomas Bambridge,	30	0	0
	Mary Neal,	0	5	0
	4 Loads Sand for the Church . .	0	1	4
22.	For 6 Drug loads, ditto carriage. . .	6	6	0
29.	Robert Copeman, a sufferer. . .	2	12	6
Nov. 3.	Expenses of Park Honoree and Geo. Carrison, 3 weeks, horses and selves. . .	12	16	9
	Park Honoree, 3 weeks' pay at 15s. a week	2	5	0
	George Carrison, 3 weeks at 18s. ditto. .	2	14	0
3.	To Mr. Fleming and Rich. Porter, expenses to Docking, Heacham, &c. . . .	0	16	3

		£.	s.	d.
Nov. 4.	To Philip Leamon, 2 bills	6	15	5
5.	John Rudd, a sufferer, in part . .	0	11	6
6.	John Layton, ditto ditto . .	2	2	0
14.	Help in weighing some lead . . .	0	0	3
21.	Men tiling on finishing the nave . .	0	2	0
27.	Three weeks' expenses, Honoree and Carrison	12	10	10
	Honoree's journey and time, 3 weeks .	2	5	0
	Ditto, . a bill . . .	0	10	8
	Carrison's horse and journey, &c., 3 weeks	2	14	0
	Henry Carrison, on account . . .	10	10	0
	Thomas Withers, a sufferer . . .	1	5	0
28.	Dr. Fleming, expenses	0	11	0
	Honoree with ditto, time, &c. . .	0	5	0
29.	Mr. Parrant, expenses	4	16	6
	Horse-hire for Mr. Williams, (10 days) .	0	15	0
	Guide, &c. at Yarmouth, &c. . . .	0	17	0
Dec. 4.	Philip Leamon, a bill	2	2	9
	Jas. Matsell, a sufferer	2	2	0
14.	John Layton, ditto, in part . . .	2	2	0
	John Collison and Wilkins, expenses .	1	5	3½
17.	John Buck and Wilkins, expenses . .	1	17	4½
19.	Edward Barron, a sufferer . . .	4	4	0
23.	John Wilkins and Sheringham, expenses .	1	15	9
	Ditto, for time in collecting . . .	3	12	0
	Philip Leamon, a bill	1	8	0
26.	Robt. Brandon, a bill for tiles and bricks .	48	0	0
27.	Robt. Hill, for hurdles, &c. . . .	0	6	0
	Mr. Thos. Back, a bill	0	9	6
	Mr. John Drosier, carriage . . .	0	17	0
	Mr. John Pike, ditto . . .	1	3	0
	Mr. Nathl. Cooper, ditto . . .	0	17	0
	Mr. Thos. Quarles, a bill of expenses .	1	15	8
	Mr. James Frost, at separate times on account	157	3	6

P

		£.	s.	d.
Dec. 27. To	Frost and Carrison, on account, steeple-work, doors, bell-hanging, &c.	60	0	0
	Mr. Drosier, Case's bill for brasses	0	11	0
	Expenses of Committee these days	1	2	0
	Widow Collison, a sufferer	5	0	0
29.	John Layton, in full of his 2nd payment	5	16	0
	James Sutton, for a hatchet lost	0	2	0
30.	Mr. Mayes, &c. expenses	1	1	1
1771, Jan.	Edward Barron pr. Jas. Foster, in full of his 3rd payment, 19th Dec.	4	11	0
6.	Mr. Charles Leamon, &c. expenses in collecting	2	0	5½
9.	Expenses at the Ship Committee, and work-men measuring	0	16	0
10.	Mr. Pond, the measurer, 3 days	2	2	0
	Mr. Saml. Burcham, three quarters of a day	0	15	0
14.	Remainder for the mare	1	10	0
	John Wilkins, for collecting to the 6th Jan.	1	5	0
20.	Philip Leamon, a bill of expenses, horse-keeping, &c.	1	17	7
	Do, a bill in full to this day	0	3	8
21.	For 3 chaldrons of lime from Edmd. Beck, and carriage	1	16	0
	Expenses at the Ship, on a Meeting	0	1	6
28.	Leamon's expenses at Yaxham, &c.	0	12	2½
Feb. 10.	Philip Leamon's expenses at Scarning, &c.	2	17	8
	John Stangroom, 6 days collecting	0	10	6
14.	Mr. Parrant, carriage	0	17	0
	Mr. Mays, do.	1	7	0
16.	Matsell, a sufferer, on account	1	11	6
	Mrs. Sudbury, on account	21	0	0
25.	Eliz. Wilson, a sufferer	0	15	0
	Philip Leamon, &c. 6 days expenses of col-lecting at Attleborough, &c.	3	0	10
	Ditto, for his time	0	12	6

		£.	s.	d.
Feb. 25.	To Philip Leamon's horse-hire . . .	0	7	6
	John Stangroom, 6 days collecting with do.	0	10	6
27.	Carrison and Co. in full	21	15	0
	Carrison, a single day bill . . .	0	16	6
March 1.	Jacob Brinton, a bill	2	0	0
2.	Philip Leamon, a bill . . .	2	0	5
6.	Stalham Carrison, a bill . . .	3	0	0
7.	Two Chaldrons of Lime from Basham .	1	0	0
	Carriage of do.	0	10	0
9.	John Ontley for sand, &c. . .	0	3	0
10.	Mr. Robert Temple's expenses and sundries	3	19	2½
	Stangroom's collecting, a week .	0	10	6
	At the Bull and Dog . .	0	1	6
17.	Expenses, Wilkins, &c. a week .	1	19	7½
24.	Do. do. do. .	1	19	0½
	Wilkins, for collecting . .	1	5	0
	Thomas Gant, do. . .	0	12	6
	Expenses at the Prussia . .	0	2	0
27.	John Buck, as per receipt for carriage .	2	13	6
30.	John Ontley, for 9 loads sand .	0	4	6
April 2.	Mr. Sison, for a bell, weighing 9c. 2q. .	44	6	8
	Do, for carriage . .	0	1	6
	Mrs. Ivory's man to measure windows .	0	1	0
	Mrs. Sudbury, glazing and plumbing on account more (vide 16th February)	128	11	10
	More to her on further account .	4	16	4
	Edmund Carrison, in part of plastering .	5	5	0
	Thomas Bambridge, 3rd payment .	30	0	0
	Mrs. Burgis, ditto . .	20	0	0
	James Matsell in full for ditto .	0	10	6
	Mary Neal, ditto . . .	0	2	6
	Robert Copeman, ditto . .	2	12	6
	Arthur Brown, ditto . .	7	10	0
	John Layton, ditto . .	20	0	0
7.	Leamon and Carrison's expenses .	2	16	0

			£.	s.	d.
April 7.	To Leamon's time 12s 6d, horse, 10s 6d	.	1	3	0
	Expenses, Mr. Fleming, &c. at Norwich, about the play, treating players, masons, &c.	.	1	7	1
15.	Blackburn, part of Mr. Ivory's bill	.	0	10	6
16.	Expenses, Mr. Cooper, &c. to Norwich, treats to manager, tickets, &c. . .	.	1	15	8
	Chaise-hire, 8th, 9th, 15th, and 16th	.	2	0	0
17.	A messenger to Walsingham .	.	0	0	6
	Expenses, Brown and Gant a week	.	1	16	6
	Gant for horsehire and time .	.	0	12	0
	Carriage of 6 chaldrons of lime .	.	1	10	0
May 4.	Jacob Brunton, a bill . .	.	0	14	0
10.	Mrs. Sudbury further . .	.	6	6	0
20.	Mr. Richard Cooper for carriage of 2½ chaldrons of lime . .	.	0	12	6
	Mare keeping from March 1 to 20 May, at different times, 51 nights, hay and corn at 1s per day and night .	.	2	11	0
	Extra corn 4½ pecks at 10d .	.	0	3	9
June 1.	Ann Royston . . .	.	1	17	6
	Expenses, Mr. Parrant and Mr. Hill	.	2	14	2
5.	Samuel Bircham for hair .	.	4	4	0
7.	Edward Barron in part of 4th payment	.	5	0	0
13.	Bambridge for beer at sundry times (Church)	.	0	4	7
18.	Expenses of the Committee at the Ship	.	0	3	1½
22.	Henry Carrison on account (Cove and Cornice) . . .	.	5	5	0
	Edward Carrison on account of plastering, &c. 10 guineas . .	.	5	5	0
29.	Five chaldrons lime, and carriage	.	3	2	6
	Beer for unloading . .	.	0	0	6
July 3.	Edward Barron, in further part of 4th payment	.	1	7	0

		£.	s.	d.
July 8.	To Expenses of Dr. Fleming and Robert Temple, at Brintou, ...	0	3	0
10.	Expenses of Mr. Parrant, &c. horse-shoeing 2s, guide 1s	1	11	10
	Mary Strutt, 3rd payment . .	1	15	0
18.	Jacob Brunton, a bill . .	0	3	4
20.	Elizabeth Wilson . .	0	15	0
22-23.	Beer (washing dust) . .	0	1	6
	John Groom for 6 loads of sand .	0	3	0
27.	Clark, the plasterer on account .	3	3	0
	Expenses, Mr. Parrant and Mr. Temple	2	17	3
Aug. 3.	Clark, the plasterer on account .	3	3	0
10.	Ditto, balance . .	13	14	0
	Henry Carrison . . .	6	6	0
	At the Bull (Committee) .	0	4	6
11.	Expenses, Mr. Parrant in the Flegg Hundred	1	13	0
13.	John Drosier's bill . .	7	3	4
	Ditto for cash expended for labour, lime, &c. and painting . . .	14	10	6
14.	Mr. Nathaniel Cooper, a bill .	2	16	6
	Two pails with irons, &c. .	0	5	4
16.	Beer, lime, and sand . .	0	0	3
19.	Plasterers on account . .	3	3	0
20.	Arthur Brown, in full . .	7	10	0
	John Layton, in full . .	20	0	0
	Thomas Bambridge, ditto .	30	0	0
	Mary Strutt, ditto . .	1	15	0
	Robert Copeman, ditto . .	2	12	6
	Thomas Withers, ditto . .	1	5	0
	Gregory Wright, ditto . .	5	5	0
	Dorothy Collison, ditto . .	5	0	0
	Widow Burgis, ditto . .	20	0	0
	Edward Barron, ditto . .	2	8	0
24.	Plasterers on account .	3	3	0
31.	Ditto, ditto . . .	3	3	0

			£.	s.	d.
Sept.	2.	To Plasterers in full	2	12	0
	6.	Committee at the Bull	0	2	0
	8.	Plasterers, on account	3	3	0
	15.	Ditto, ditto	3	3	0
		4 dozen pins for hats	0	6	0
	22.	Plasterers	3	3	0
		Spanish white and yellow ochre	0	3	9
		Matsell, in part	0	10	6
	23.	John Rudd, in full	0	11	6
		Prior, for looking after the mare	0	5	0
		Henry Carrison	3	3	0
	29.	Plasterers, on account	3	3	0
	30.	Men, scaffolding	0	1	0
Oct.	3.	Twenty-one pounds of French ochre, for stucco	0	10	6
	6.	Plasterers, on account	3	3	0
	8.	James Matsell, a sufferer	1	11	6
		Mary Neal, do.	0	2	6
		James Buck, do.	2	10	0
	21.	John Archer, for Groom, in part	1	5	0
	27.	Plasterers, on account	3	3	0
		A skep for the church	0	0	6
		Labourer, for sifting refuse lime	0	1	0
		Kenny, 2 loads sand	0	1	0
Nov.	15.	John Buck, for carriage	1	2	0
	17.	Plasterers, on account	3	3	0
		Ann Royston, a sufferer, in full	0	12	6
	24.	Plasterers, on account	3	3	0
Dec.	11.	Woodrow, fetching flagstones, &c.	0	15	9
	12.	Plasterers, in full	26	11	0
	13.	Mr. Cooper, a bill for nails and cord	1	11	0
		Mr. Dew, 20 sacks charcoal	2	0	0
	21.	Mr. Haycock, flagstones	16	15	10
		G. Lenny, for 2 loads sand	0	1	0
	26.	Carriage, to Michl. Fenn	2	4	0

		£.	s.	d.
Dec. 26.	To Mr. Drosier, a bill of sundries paid by him	9	19	11¼
	Groom's loss in full	48	7	6
	Bambridge, for beer	0	2	0
1772.	Robt. Hill, horse, journey, and carriage of a			
Jan. 6.	load of flagstones	1	2	6
23.	Beer for workmen	0	1	0
24.	At the Bull, (bell-hanging put out)	0	1	0
Feb. 3.	Charles Simpson	0	1	3¼
17.	Bambridge, beer, bell-raising	0	1	0
	Mr. Robt. Temple, for mare's keeping	0	15	0
	Mr. Quarles, a month's do. (grass)	0	10	0
28.	Henry Carrison, in part of bell-hanging	1	11	6
22.	Philip Leamon, a bill	1	8	6
	Mr. John Drosier, 6 dozen flagstones	4	4	0
	Carriage of do., loading, beer, &c.	1	13	6
March 6.	Beer, altering the small bell	0	1	0
April 6.	Do., stonemasons	0	1	0
9.	Carriage, to Aldred Raven	0	15	0
	Six dozen flag-stones, Harrison	4	4	0
	Stonemasons' beer	0	1	0
11.	Edmd. Carrison, on account	5	5	0
	Sand, 2 loads, Kenny	0	1	0
17.	Bill to Ivory, a stonemason	2	4	3
	Bill to Mr. Collison, Knacker	1	8	10
18.	Nine hundred feet pavements, and carriage	8	11	0
	Sand, 2 loads, Kenny	0	1	0
	Broom	0	0	3
May 2.	Sir Edwd. Astley's waggoner	0	1	0
5.	Carriage, 4 dozen flagstones	1	2	0
9.	Allowed Mr. Temple, for deals	1	1	0
	Do., for horse-journies, collecting	0	6	0
9.	For cleaning Fenn's brass, and studs	0	1	0
16.	To Stone-cutters, on finishing	0	2	0
21.	Dr. Fleming, for boards used as temporary			
	doors, &c.	0	17	6

		£.	s.	d.
June 8. For clock, dial, &c.	.	32	0	0
July 9. To John Buck, a bill for carriage	.	1	7	6
A new gown for the Clerk, and carriage	.	2	4	4
18 Scutcheons for pews	.	0	1	6
George Carrison allowed for freestone to repair windows of the North Aisle,	.	0	2	6
August. Thomas Bambridge's bill for beer and board of Sir Edward Astley's joiners	.	0	18	0
28. Mrs. Sudbury, balance	.	0	18	6
Sept. 1. Mr. Thomas Cossor, for pews	.	6	16	6
Mr. Drosier, for joints, screws, &c.	.	0	19	9
Mr. Henry Carrison, for pews	.	6	16	6
28. William Buck, a chaldron of lime fetched by Edmund Carrison, 15th Jan. last	.	0	15	0
Oct. 1. Freight of engine	.	0	18	0
24. Robert Carrison, for leather for size for plasterers	.	0	1	0

		£.	s.	d.	£.	s.	d.
Cost of engine	.	45	0	0			
Collected by subscription		35	19	6			
Deficiency					9	0	6

		£.	s.	d.
Carriage of ditto from Cley	.	0	4	6
Nov. 5. Stalham Carrison, job done to engine	.	0	2	0
Jacob Brunton, a bill of iron-work	.	2	19	0
Edmund Carrison's bills, balance for 15 guineas in his account before as paid,				

		£.	s.	d.	£.	s.	d.
1st Bill		24	12	7			
Deduct		15	15	0			
					8	17	7

		£.	s.	d.
Edmund Carrison, 2nd bill	.	28	1	0
Stone masons	.	11	14	10
Allowance	.	2	2	0
Balance	.	0	8	7½
Total of expenditure	.	£1538	17	3

THE END.

SINTRAM AND HIS COMPANIONS.

By the Author of "Undine." Fcp. cloth, with Frontispiece, price 3s. 6d.

Royal 32mo, cloth, 2s. 6d.; roan, 3s. 6d.; morocco, 5s.

PICTURES OF RELIGION AND RELIGIOUS TRUTH;

OR,

FAMILIAR ILLUSTRATIONS OF CHRISTIAN TRUTH AND DUTY;

In a Selection of Figurative and Emblematic Passages from the Works of Hall, Taylor, Leighton, Beveridge, Hopkins, Donne, and other eminent Writers.

This Selection exhibits a series of the great truths and precepts of religion, illustrated by appropriate similitudes from striking and beautiful objects of the visible creation, or decorated by those happy turns of thought which at once imprint their subjects on the memory and commend them to the heart. It is especially suited as a present to the young.

BOOKS FOR THE YOUNG,

In square 16mo, cloth, with many Engravings.

1. THE WINTER'S TALE. To which is added, LITTLE BERTRAM'S DREAM. 2s. 6d.

2. THE LITTLE COUSINS. (For Young Children.) 3s. 6d.

3. SPRING-TIDE. By the Author of "Winter's Tale." (In the press.)
4. LUCY AND ARTHUR. (In the press.)
5. HOLYDAY TALES. By the Rev. W. Gresley. (In the press.)

FOURPENNY BOOKS.

With numerous Engravings, suited for Presents, School-Rewards, &c.

In packets, price 2s. 6d.

THE FIRST SERIES CONTAINS,

1. The Life of Izaak Walton.
2. Hymns for Children.
3. Dialogues with a Godmother.
4. Lives of Ancient Bishops.
5. Christian Courtesy.

6. Jenny Knight and Mary Taylor.
7. The Life of George Herbert.
8. Sketches of Christian Character; selected from different stations of life.

SECOND SERIES.

1. Stories from Bede, with a Sketch of his Life.
2. The Life of Bishop Ridley.
3. Christian Lyrics.
4. A Gift for Servants.
5. The Life of Sir T. S. Raffles.

6. The Life of Lord Exmouth.
7. Conversations on the Church. By Rev. W. Gresley.
8. The English Citizen's Politics. By Rev. W. Gresley.

17, PORTMAN STREET, PORTMAN SQUARE.

The Englishman's Library:

A SERIES OF

CHEAP PUBLICATIONS, ADAPTED FOR POPULAR READING;

ON THE

PRINCIPLES OF THE ENGLISH CHURCH AND CONSTITUTION;

Suited for Presents, Class-Books, Lending Libraries, &c. &c.

Twenty Volumes of this Series have now been completed, which may be had as a set, at the subjoined prices :—

Bound in cloth, lettered..... £3 7 0	Full-bound calf, neat £5 17 0
Half-bd. morocco, gilt edges. 4 17 0	Full-bound morocco, neat... 6 17 0

The Volumes may also be had separately, in the three bindings: hf.-bd. mor. 1s. 6d. per vol.; calf, 2s. 6d.; full mor. 3s. 6d. above the price in cloth.

(A VARIETY OF BINDINGS MAY BE SEEN AT THE PUBLISHER'S.)

The following are the Subjects and Authors :—

1. CLEMENT WALTON. (Rev. W. Gresley.) 3s. 6d.
2. SCRIPTURE HISTORY: OLD TEST. (Dr Howard.) 3s.
3. Bp. PATRICK'S PARABLE of the PILGRIM. (Edited by Chamberlain.) 2s. 6d.
4. A HELP to KNOWLEDGE. (Rev. T. Chamberlain.) 2s.
5. ECCLESIASTICAL HISTORY. (Rev. W. Palmer.) 4s. 6d.
6. The PRACTICE of DIVINE LOVE. (Bishop Ken.) 2s.
7. The LORD'S PRAYER. (Rev. R. Anderson.) 2s.
8. THE EARLY ENGLISH CHURCH. (Rev. E. Churton.) 4s. 6d.
9. TALES OF THE VILLAGE. Vol. I. (Rev. F. E. Paget.) 3s.
10. CHRISTIAN MORALS. (Rev. W. Sewell.) 5s.
11. SHERLOCK on PUBLIC WORSHIP. (Edited by Melvill.) 3s.
12. The FIVE EMPIRES. (Archdeacon R. I. Wilberforce.) 3s. 6d.
13. The SIEGE of LICHFIELD. (Rev. W. Gresley.) 4s.
14. SCRIPTURE HISTORY: NEW TEST. (Dr. Howard.) 3s.
15. CHARLES LEVER. (Rev. W. Gresley.) 3s. 6d.
16. TALES of the VILLAGE. Vol. II. (Rev. F. E. Paget.) 3s. 6d.
17. The ART OF CONTENTMENT. (Edited by Pridden.) 3s.
18. TALES OF THE VILLAGE. Vol. III. (Rev. F. E. Paget.) 3s. 6d.
19. The FOREST of ARDEN. (Rev. W. Gresley.) 4s.
20. RUTILIUS; or, Stories of the Third Age. (Archdn. R. I. Wilberforce.) 4s.
21. A HISTORY of the ENGLISH REFORMATION. (Rev. F. C. Massingberd.) 5s.

LIVES of EMINENT ENGLISH LAYMEN, by the Rev. W. H. Teale, M.A. Leeds, will follow.

Several other Volumes are in preparation.

The Christian Remembrancer;

A MONTHLY MAGAZINE AND REVIEW.

COMPRISING THEOLOGY AND GENERAL LITERATURE, AND COMBINING
THE FEATURES OF THE QUARTERLY AND MONTHLY PERIODICAL.

Price 2s. 6d.

The Volume for 1842 commences with considerable additions and improvements, and an accession of new Contributors; and it is intended that no
pains shall be spared to render this one of the most interesting of the Monthly
Periodicals. Those desirous of subscribing are requested to order the Numbers
for this year, as soon as possible, through their respective Booksellers.

CONTENTS.

—Notes of a Half-pay in Search of Health—A Pilgrimage in Auvergne from Picardy to Le Velay—A Search into the Old Testament, by Joseph Hume—Episcopacy and Presbytery, by the Rev. Archibald Boyd, A.M.

Shorter Notices :

Confessions of an Apostate—Country Parson's Wife—Books by the Author of "Peep of Day"—Warton's English Poetry—Wheatley on the Common Prayer—Howett's Visits, Second Series—Prince's Letters—Jameson's New Zealand—Modern Education, by E. L.—Letters from the Baltic—Stephens's Central America—Christian Diary—

Farmer's Sonnets—Defence of the Church of England—Notes on Genesis—Petit's Church Architecture—Selby's Forest-Trees—Maitland's Pamphlets on Foxe—History of Pews—Milford Malvoisin—The Corn Laws—Stephen on the Fasts and Festivals, &c. &c.

A Letter to the Lord Bishop of Oxford, on the Formation of Colleges of Bishops' Fellows.

The Divine Right of Tithes, &c. No.V.

Prospects of the Church of England. No. III.

ECCLESIASTICAL INTELLIGENCE.

Large paper copies of the Engravings of the New Church at Streatham may be had, price 1s. 6d. each.

The Two Volumes for 1841 may still be had, price 10s. each in cloth, with Engravings. They comprise, besides the usual contents of a Monthly Magazine, a considerable number of papers of permanent interest. The following among other subjects are included :—

Ecclesiastical Music (4 Nos.)	The Divine Right of Tithes and the Offertory (4 Nos.)
Literature and Authorship in England.	The Ancient British Church.
Church Architecture, with Plates.	Presbyterianism in Scotland.
Invalidity of Dissenters' Baptisms.	Astronomy.
The Inductive Sciences.	Chapters on Ecclesiastical Law.
Life and Writings of St. Irenæus.	Convocation.
Chemical Philosophy.	Original Letters of Abp. Laud.
Illustrations of Ballad Poetry.	The Church in Scotland.
Christian Almsgiving.	Travels in Palestine.
Religious Poets of the Day.	The Parables of our Lord.
On the Sonnet (2 Nos.)	Churches and Churchwardens.
Episcopal Visitations (3 Nos.)	
Missions in the East.	

"This Magazine is now second to none of its numerous competitors. The critical notices are more searching and more impartial than any we have elsewhere met with."—*Oxford Herald.*

"In its plan, and the ability with which it is conducted, this Magazine more nearly resembles Murray's *Quarterly* than any of the other monthly periodicals."—*Britannia.*

"The articles of this first of the monthly Reviews show great ability, and some of them amusing cleverness. Church architecture, Church music, Church property, &c. will be found here discussed on the scriptural and catholic principles of the Church of England, and with a faithfulness, courage, and power, too rare in the present day."—*Church Intelligencer.*

"The most able of the monthly periodicals."—*Cambridge Chronicle.*

THE NUMBERS FOR MARCH AND APRIL CONTAIN ARTICLES ON—

Tytler's Scotland—The Witness of Methodism to Catholic Truth—Foreign Protestantism—Recent Conversions to Romanism—Arnold on Modern History—Recent Educational Works—Carlyle's Hero-Worship—Ecclesiastical Architecture (with Cuts)—Church and State, &c. &c.—with copious Notices of New Books and Pamphlets, and Intelligence as usual.

CHURCH MUSIC.

Second edition, enlarged and corrected, price 2s. 6d.

GREGORIAN AND OTHER ECCLESIASTICAL CHANTS,

Adapted to the Psalter and Canticles, as pointed to be Sung in Churches.

This work contains: (1) The 8 Gregorian Tones, with their several endings. (2) A variety of the same Tones harmonised for four voices, but so as to preserve unaltered the original melodies. (3) Miscellaneous Chants. (4) The Versicles and Responses from Tallis' Cathedral Service.

An allowance made to Clergymen purchasing quantities.

The GREGORIAN MELODIES may be had on a separate sheet, price 4d.

The PSALTER pointed for Chanting. Price 2s. 6d. cloth; 3s. 6d. roan; and 5s. morocco.

The Canticles and Athanasian Creed alone, price 4d., or 28s. per 100.

In small 4to.

SACRED MUSIC.

Selected from the Compositions of TYE, TALLIS, GIBBONS, RAVENSCROFT, &c ; and adapted to portions of the different Versions of the Book of Psalms. This volume contains several easy compositions by old Masters, suited for Schools and Churches.

THE ORDER OF DAILY PRAYER, THE PSALTER, AND THE OFFICE OF THE HOLY COMMUNION,

According to the Use of the Church of England: with the Musical Notation authorised in the reign of Edward the Sixth. Elegantly printed in small 4to, with Woodcut Borders, &c. A few copies are printed on large paper, to secure which an early application will be needful. Edited by WILLIAM DYCE, Esq., M.A. (*Nearly ready.*)

CABINET SERIES OF

NARRATIVES, TRACTS, &c.

For Presents, Prizes, Village-Schools, &c. Illustrated with Cuts.

1. Richard Morton. A Village Tale. By the Rev. W. PRIDDEN, M.A., Vicar of Broxted. 6d.

2. The Book of Characters:—the Minister,—the King,—the Bishop,—the Gentleman,—the Yeoman,—the Merchant, &c. &c. (From FULLER.) Cloth lettered, 1s.

3. A God-Parent's Gift. By the Rev. T. CHAMBERLAIN, M.A. Cloth lettered, 1s.

4. James Ford; and other Stories. 9d.

5. Conversations with Cousin Rachel. 9d.

6. Dialogues on the Te Deum. 6d.

7. A Manual of Christian Doctrine. By the Rev. J. JAMES, M.A. Sewed, 8d.; cloth, 1s.

8. What we are to Believe. 18mo, cloth, 1s. 6d.

9. Conversations with Cousin Rachel. Part II. 9d. (*Parts I. and II. may be had together in cloth, price 2s.*)

10. The Rocky Island, and other Similitudes. By SAMUEL WILBERFORCE, M.A., Archdeacon of Surrey. In 18mo, with Engravings, price 2s. 6d.

11. Prasca Loupouloff; or, Filial Piety exemplified. A true Story. 6d.

Narratives, Tracts, &c.—continued.

12. A Companion to the Fasts and Festivals (for the Young). 18mo, cloth, 3s.

13. The Book of Anecdotes. With Frontispiece. Cloth, 2s. 6d.

14. The Book of Poetry. Cloth, 2s.

15. The Book of Church History. Cloth, 1s. 6d.

16. Conversations with Cousin Rachel. Part III. 1s.

17. Christian Contentment. By Bishop SANDERSON. With Portrait, &c. 1s. 6d.

18. Abdiel; a Tale of Ammon. With Engravings. 2s. 6d.

19. The Life of William of Wykeham, Bishop of Winchester. By the Rev. JOHN CHANDLER, M.A. 2s.

20. The Life of Richard Hooker. 1s. 6d.

21. First Doctrines and Early Practice; or, Sermons for the Young. By the Rev. A. WATSON, M.A., Cheltenham.

22. Ivo and Verena; or, the Snowdrop: a Norwegian Tale.

BURNS' CHILDREN'S BOOKS.

Neatly printed in 32mo, with coloured Wrappers, and Woodcuts. Sold also in packets, price 1s. 6d.; or bound in cloth, 2s.

FIRST SERIES.

1. Good and Bad Temper. 2d.
2. Prayers at Church and Prayers at Home. 1d.
3. An Offering of Affection to a Young Child. 1d.
4. Margaret Fletcher, 2d.
5. The Pink Bonnet, 2d.
6. Jenny Crowe, the Orphan Girl. 2d.
7. The Bunch of Violets. 1d.
8. The Apple-Tree. 1d.
9. Lessons upon the Apostles' Creed. 2d.
10. Amy's Earnings. 1d.
11. Lessons upon the Calendar. 2d.
12. Lesson on Attention. 2d.
13. The Prayer-Book. 1d.

SECOND SERIES.

1. The Red Shawls. 2d.
2. First Lesson on the Commandments. 1d.
3. Second Lesson on the Commandments. 1d.
4. Out in the Dark. 2d.
5. The White Kitten. 2d.
6. Obstinacy and Passion. 2d.
7. Prayers for Children. 1d.
8. Fretful Fanny. 2d.
9. The Burial of the Dead. 2d.
10. The New Church. 2d.
11. The Two Sacraments. 1d.
12. Playing with Fire. 2d.

CARDS FOR DISTRIBUTION.

1. The TWO STATES; addressed to every one who, having been Baptised, is not a Communicant. 1d., or 7s. per 100.

2. The CHURCH OF ENGLAND and the APOSTOLIC SUCCESSION. 1½d., or 10s. 6d. per 100.

3. TEXTS for MEDITATION, before or during Divine Service. 1d., or 7s. per 100.

TRACTS ON CHRISTIAN DOCTRINE AND PRACTICE.

1. The Church of Christ. 1d., or 7s. per 100.

2. On Fasting. 1d., or 7s. per 100.

3. A Word to Parents. 2d., or 14s. per 100.

4. The Church Visible and Invisible. 3d.

5. My Parishioner Cautioned. 2d., or 14s. per 100.

6. The Presence of God. 2d., or 14s. per 100.

7. Bp. Jolly's Address on Baptism. 8d.

8. Examine and Communicate. 2d. or 14s. per 100.

Tracts on Christian Doctrine and Practice—continued.

9. The Story of Old Ambrose. 3d., or 21s. per 100.

10. A Catechism on the Church. ½d., or 3s. 6d. per 100.

11. A Few Words on Public Worship. 2d.

12. Plain Prayers, with Directions how to Pray. ½d., or 3s. 6d. per 100.

13. The Creeds of the Church. 2d., or 14s. per 100.

14. Evangelical Truth and Apostolical Order; a Dialogue. 2d., or 14s. per 100.

15. The Christian State. 3d., or 21s. per 100.

16. Robert Langley and Thomas Mott. 3d.

17. Scripture Dialogues.—No. I. On Conscience. 1d., or 7s. per 100.

18. Anglo-Catholic Piety—George Herbert. 2d , or 14s. per 100.

19. Scripture Dialogues.—No. II. Regeneration and Conversion. 2d., or 14s. per 100.

20. On Keeping the Church Festivals. 2d.

21. Baptismal Regeneration, a Doctrine of the Church of England, and its Practical Effects considered. 3d., or 21s. per 100.

22. On the Holy Scriptures. 2d., or 12s.

23. The Duty and Benefits of Fasting. 2d.

24. The Providence of God. 1d., or 7s.

25. The Death of the Righteous. 2d., or 14s.

26. Zeal for the House of God. 4d

27. Plain Remarks on Baptism and the Registration Act. 1d., or 7s.

28. Reasons for being a Churchman. 1d., or 7s.

29. Prayers for the Use of Schools. 1d., or 7s.

30. Liberty of Conscience; or, a Dialogue about Church and Meeting. 3d., or 21s.

31. On Holy Thursday, or Ascension Day. 1d., or 7s.

32. The Prayers of the Liturgy, arranged for Private or Family Use. 6d.

33. The Guilt and Danger of Sin. 2d., or 14s.

34. Instructions in Confirmation. By Robert Nelson, Esq. 2d., or 14s.

35. The Two Carpenters. 2d., or 14s.

36. The Bliss of Heaven. 1d., or 7s.

37. Man Fearfully and Wonderfully Made. 2d., or 14s.

38. The Life of St. James the Great. 2d., or 14s.

39. Reasons against Joining a Dissenting Congregation. ½d., or 3s. 6d.

40. The Honour of the Sanctuary. 2d., or 14s.

41. The Village Feast. 2d , or 14s.

42. On Absolution. 2d.

43. Church Matters. 2d.

44. A Word in Season (on the Sin of Intemperance). 2d.

45. The Gospel Invitation. (For the Additional Curates' Fund.) 2d.

46. An Address to the Parents of the Children at a Parish School. 1d.

47. Obedience to Spiritual Governors. 2d.

Vols. I. and II. are now published, price 3s. 6d. each, in cloth.

Vol. III. will be ready shortly.

BOOKS OF DEVOTION.

1. HORÆ SACRÆ: a Manual of Private Meditations and Prayers, from the older Divines. With an Introduction. By the Rev. J. Chandler, M.A., Vicar of Witley, Surrey. Third Edition, enlarged and revised. Cloth, 2s. 6d.; roan, 3s. 6d.; morocco, 5s.

This Work contains Prayers for various circumstances and occasions to a greater extent than is to be found elsewhere in the same compass.

2. PRAYERS for UNITY and GUIDANCE into the TRUTH. 2d. each, or 14s. per 100.

3. HOURS of PRAYER. Printed in black and red, with parchment wrapper, 1s., or 10s. 6d. per dozen.

4. PLAIN PRAYERS, with Directions how to Pray. ½d., or 3s. 6d. per 100.

5. PRAYERS for SCHOOLS. 1d., or 7s. per 100.

Books of Devotion—continued.

6. The PRAYERS of the LITURGY arranged for Private or Family Use. 6d., or cloth, 1s.

7. EUCHARISTICA: Meditations and Prayers, with Select Passages on the most Holy Eucharist, from Old English Divines, with an Introduction by Samuel Wilberforce, M.A., Archdeacon of Surrey. New Edition, 2s. 6d. cloth; 3s. 6d. roan; 5s. russ. or morocco.

A FRIENDLY ADDRESS on BAPTISMAL REGENERATION. By the Rt. Rev. ALEXANDER JOLLY, D.D., late Bishop of Moray. With a Memoir of the Author by the Rev. PATRICK CHEYNE, M.A., Aberdeen. Fcp. cloth, 1s.

The ORDER of CONFIRMATION; explained and illustrated by select Passages from Holy Scripture, the Baptismal and Eucharistic Offices of the English Church, and the Writings of Eminent Divines. By the Rev. HENRY HOPWOOD, B.A., of Queen's College, Cambridge. Printed in black and red. Price 8d., or 1s. cloth.

The BAPTISMAL OFFICES of the UNITED CHURCH of ENGLAND and IRELAND illustrated from "the Use of Salisbury"—the Liturgy of Herman, Archbishop of Cologne—and the sentiments of the Compilers and Revisers of the Book of Common Prayer. By the Rev. T. M. FALLOW, M.A., Curate of All Souls. 12mo. 7s. 6d.

In 2 vols, imp. 8vo, handsomely done up, price 20s.

THE VOICE OF THE CHURCH.

This Work contains a large and varied collection of Treatises, Tracts, Sermons, &c. by the older Divines; translations from the Fathers; Biography; Church History; interspersed with Poetry, Anecdotes, and short Theological extracts. The whole is illustrated by original Notes, Prefaces, and Biographical Notices, and forms a comprehensive Library of doctrinal and practical Theology, suited for the perusal either of the Layman or the Divine.

The following is an Outline of the Contents :—

Lord Bacon's Confession of Faith.
Leslie's Episcopacy defended.
Bishop Sanderson's Answer to Puritan Objections.
The Life of Bishop Ridley.
Bishop Hall's Olive of Peace.
Joseph Mede on Sacrilege.
Dean Brevint's Christian Sacrament and Sacrifice.
Waterland on Regeneration.
An Account of the Sufferings of the Clergy in the time of the Great Rebellion, from Walker.
Spelman on the Rights and Respect due to Churches, with a History of the Fate of Sacrilege.
Dean Stanley's Faith and Practice of a Church-of-England Man.
The Correspondence between King Charles I. and Alexander Henderson.
Bishop Morton's Confession of Faith.

Bishop Beveridge's Scriptural Rule for the Government of the Church.
Characters from Fuller's "Holy State."
Bishop Patrick on the Christian Priesthood.
Bishop Ken's Devotional Exposition of the Catechism.
Dean Comber's short Discourse on portions of the Common Prayer.
Bishop Jolly's Address on Baptism.
Bingham on Divine Worship in the Ancient Church.
Bishop Patrick on Tradition.
Jones (of Nayland) on the Church.
Life of the Rev. John Bold.
Original Translations from St. Bernard, Chrysostom, Theodoret, Irenæus, Athanasius, Gregory, &c.; together with a large collection of Theological Extracts, Anecdotes, and Poetry.

Vol. I. may be had separately, price 10s. 6d. Vol. II. 9s. 6d.

86, FLEET STREET, LONDON.

TILT AND BOGUE'S
Catalogue
OF
NEW AND POPULAR WORKS.

TILT'S ILLUSTRATED CLASSICS.

COWPER'S POEMS,

With Life and Critical Remarks by the Rev. THOMAS DALE: embellished with 75 fine Engravings on Wood by J. Orrin Smith, from Drawings by J. Gilbert. 2 handsome vols. crown 8vo. 24s. hf.-mor.; 34s. morocco.

" The main feature of the work is bibliopolic---the beauty of its type---the vellum-like character of its paper---the amplitude of its margins---and the number of its illustrations. In these respects it appears to us the handsomest of the editions of Cowper."---SPECTATOR.

II.

THOMSON'S SEASONS AND CASTLE OF INDOLENCE,

With Life and Critical Remarks by ALLAN CUNNINGHAM; and 48 Illustrations drawn and engraved by Samuel Williams. Crown 8vo. 12s. half-morocco; 17s. morocco.

*** Other works, in continuation of this series of STANDARD ENGLISH AUTHORS, are in preparation.

THE CHRISTIAN SOUVENIR.

Edited by the Rev. CHARLES B. TAYLER, Author of " May You Like It." The Scripture Illustrations by the Rev. THOMAS DALE; with Contributions by various distinguished Authors:---The Rev. E. Bickersteth---Rev. J. Moultrie---Rev. Dr. Gilly---The author of " The Rector of Valehead." Embellished with 12 highly-finished Line Engravings. Morocco, 16s.

THE GALLERY OF BEAUTY;

Or, COURT OF QUEEN VICTORIA. Seventeen large and finely-engraved Portraits of the Female Nobility and a Vignette Title; with Poetical Illustrations. Imperial 4to. superbly bound, 42s.

THE PARTERRE; OR, BEAUTIES OF FLORA.

Twelve large Drawings of Flowers, by JAMES ANDREWS, elaborately coloured after Nature; with Poetical Illustrations. Imperial 4to. 31s. 6d.

CHARLES SWAIN'S POETICAL WORKS,

With numerous Embellishments in the Style of " Rogers's Italy," drawn and engraved by Eminent Artists. 8vo. 24s. cloth.

THE YOUNG ISLANDERS.

The Adventures of the Seaward House Boys, their Escape from School, and subsequent Misfortunes. A Tale of the Last Century. By JEFFERYS TAYLOR. With Eight Plates by Samuel Williams. Fcp. 8vo. 7s. cloth.

" This is one of the best of the Juvenile Books that have lately appeared. The illustrations are excellently engraved from spirited and graceful designs, and the story is full of interest. Our young friends will find in this pretty volume many things to excite laughter and tears, and a whole tribe of agreeable recollections."---COURT GAZETTE.

SCENERIES, VIEWS, &c.

BEATTIE'S CASTLES AND ABBEYS OF ENGLAND,

Including Royal Palaces, Baronial Halls, Manor Houses, &c.; with Historical Details, Biographical Sketches, Anecdotes, Legends, and Traditions. By WILLIAM BEATTIE, M.D. author of "Switzerland," &c. In Monthly Parts, imperial 8vo. 2s. 6d.

SKETCHES AT HOME AND ABROAD.

By J. D. HARDING. Sixty Views of the most interesting Scenes, Foreign and Domestic, printed in the new tinted style, in exact imitation of the Original Drawings. Imperial folio, half-morocco, £6. 6s.

"A treasure-house of delight. Here northern Italy yields up its architectural glories and its lake scenery—Venice its palaces—the Tyrol its romantic valleys and villages—the Rhenish cities their picturesque beauty—and France and England their greenest spots of remembrance." ATHENÆUM.

ILLUSTRATIONS OF CAIRO.

By ROBERT HAY, Esq. of Linplum. Drawn on Stone by J. C. Bourne, under the superintendence of Owen B. Carter, Architect. With Descriptive Notices. Printed in the new tinted style. Imperial folio, half-morocco, £4. 4s.

ROME, AND ITS SURROUNDING SCENERY.

Illustrated with Engravings by W. B. COOKE, from Drawings by eminent Artists; including a beautiful Panoramic View of the City, reduced from Vasi's celebrated Print, with Descriptions by H. NOEL HUMPHREYS, Esq. Quarto, 31s. 6d. cloth; 42s. morocco.

FINDEN'S ILLUSTRATIONS OF THE BIBLE.

Ninety-six Views of the most interesting Places mentioned in the Old and New Testaments, with Descriptions by the Rev. T. HARTWELL HORNE, author of "Introduction to the Study of the Holy Scriptures." Two vols. super-royal 8vo. morocco, £3. 3s.

LE KEUX'S MEMORIALS OF CAMBRIDGE.

A Series of Views of the Colleges, Halls, Churches, and other Public Buildings of the University and Town, engraved by J. LE KEUX; with Historical and Descriptive Accounts by THOMAS WRIGHT, B.A. Vol. 1 is now ready, 8vo. 21s.; 4to. 42s.; India proofs, 63s.

FINDEN'S PORTS & HARBOURS OF GREAT BRITAIN.

Fifty large Plates, engraved in the first style of art, from Drawings by Harding, Balmer, &c. &c. 31s. 6d. morocco, elegant.

₊ A second series of this work is now in course of publication.

INGRAM'S MEMORIALS OF OXFORD.

Historical and Descriptive Accounts of the Colleges, Halls, Churches, and other Public Buildings. Edited by the Rev. J. INGRAM, D.D. President of Trinity College. With Engravings by J. Le Keux, from Original Drawings by F. Mackenzie. 3 vols. 8vo. 58s. cloth;—Quarto, £5. 10s.;—India proofs, £8.—The work may also be had in various styles of binding.

WANDERINGS IN NORTH WALES.

By THOMAS ROSCOE, Esq. With Fifty-one Illustrations, after Drawings by Cox, Cattermole, Creswick, Copley Fielding, &c. New edition, with a large Map and Table of Routes. Demy 8vo. 25s. cloth; 35s. morocco.

Tilt and Bogue, Fleet Street.

BOOKS OF PLATES.

HEATH'S WAVERLEY GALLERY.

Portraits of the principal Female Characters in the Novels and Tales of SCOTT.—Thirty-six highly-finished Plates, engraved under the direction of Mr. Charles Heath, from Drawings by Eminent Artists. Super-royal 8vo. splendidly bound in morocco, 31s. 6d.; or, with coloured plates, £3.

HEATH'S SHAKSPEARE GALLERY.

Forty-five Portraits of the Female Characters of Shakspeare's Plays, engraved by CHARLES HEATH, from Drawings by Chalon, Stephanoff, Bostock, Meadows, &c. Quarto, splendidly bound in morocco, 42s.; or with the plates highly coloured, £3. 13s. 6d.

LE BYRON DES DAMES:

The Principal Female Characters in Lord Byron's Poems. Thirty-nine highly-finished Female Portraits; with Illustrative Extracts. Morocco elegant, 31s. 6d.; with plates highly coloured, £3.

PEARLS OF THE EAST:

Beauties from "Lalla Rookh." Twelve large-sized Portraits of the principal Female Characters in MOORE's celebrated Poem, by FANNY CORBAUX. Imperial 4to. 31s. 6d. tinted; plates highly coloured, 52s. 6d.

FLORA'S GEMS:

The Treasures of the Garden; Twelve splendid Groups of Flowers, drawn and coloured by JAMES ANDREWS; with Poetical Illustrations, by L. A. Twamley. Imperial 4to. 42s. handsomely bound.

GALLERY OF THE GRACES.

Thirty-six beautiful Female Heads, illustrating celebrated Passages in Modern British Poets; with accompanying Extracts. Quarto, morocco elegant, 31s. 6d.; plates highly coloured, £3.

THE AGES OF FEMALE BEAUTY:

Pictorial Illustrations of Woman's Life, from Drawings by the most eminent Artists. 4to. 21s.; plates coloured, 31s. 6d.

FINDEN'S ILLUSTRATIONS OF BYRON'S WORKS.

One Hundred and Twenty-six Plates, in the highest style of art; comprising Landscape Scenery described or referred to in the Poems, Portraits of his Lordship and his Friends, &c. &c. New edition, 2 vols. large 8vo. beautifully bound in morocco, £3. 3s.

THE AUTHORS OF ENGLAND.

Biographical Notices of Modern Literary Characters. By H. F. CHORLEY. Fourteen splendid Portraits, curiously engraved in basso-relievo. 4to. 31s. 6d.

THE BEAUTY OF THE HEAVENS.

One Hundred and Four coloured Scenes, representing the principal Phenomena; with an Elementary Lecture on Astronomy, expressly adapted for Family Instruction and Entertainment. By CHARLES F. BLUNT, Lecturer on Astronomy. In a handsome case, resembling a quarto volume, price Two Guineas.

"We can truly recommend this handsome work to the favour of the public, and particularly to parents and teachers."—LIT. GAZ. "By its aid alone a competent knowledge of astronomy may be gained in the family circle in a few evenings, and as matter of amusement."—ATLAS.

Tilt and Bogue, Fleet Street.

BOOKS OF ENTERTAINMENT.

COMICAL ADVENTURES OF OBADIAH OLDBUCK,

Wherein are duly set forth the Crosses, Chagrins, Changes, and Calamities, by which his Courtship was attended; showing, also, the Issue of his Suit, and his Espousal to his Ladye-love. Large 8vo. with 84 Plates, 7s. cloth.

THE HISTORY OF MR. OGLEBY.

Shewing how, by the polish of his manners, the brilliancy of his repartees, and the elegance of his attitudes, he attained distinction in the fashionable world. 150 Designs, 6s. cloth.

THREE COURSES AND A DESSERT.

A Series of amusing Tales; with Fifty-one Illustrations, the *chefs-d'œuvre* of GEORGE CRUIKSHANK. In a large and closely-printed vol. 12s. cloth.

" This is an extraordinary performance. Such a union of the painter, the poet, and the novel-ist, in one person, is unexampled."---SPECTATOR.

THE COMIC LATIN GRAMMAR.

A New and Facetious Introduction to the Latin Tongue. Profusely illus-trated with Humorous Engravings. New edition, 8s. cloth.

" Without exception, the most richly comic work we have ever seen."---TAIT'S MAG.

GEORGE CRUIKSHANK AND HIS WORKS:

Being an Essay on his Genius. With numerous Illustrations, selected from the earlier as well as the more matured productions of his pencil. Reprinted from the " Westminster Review," with Additions. 3s. cloth.

TABLE-WIT, AND AFTER-DINNER ANECDOTE.

By the Editor of " Hints for the Table." Fcp. 8vo. cloth, 2s. 6d.

" The pleasantest little book of the season. It is full of the most amusing anecdotes."
SPORTING REV.

THE SPORTING ALPHABET.

Humorous Scenes and Situations in the Life and Adventures of a Sports-man. By HENRY HEATH. 3s. 6d. plain; 5s. 6d. coloured.

CARICATURE SCRAP-BOOK.

Many Hundred Laughable and Amusing Groups, illustrative of Life and Character: forming a never-failing source of Fire-side Amusement. 18s. cloth.

GEMS OF ANECDOTE,

Original and Selected. Neatly bound in cloth, 2s.

GEMS OF WIT AND HUMOUR.

With Frontispiece. Neatly bound in cloth, 2s.

GEMS OF AMERICAN WIT AND ANECDOTE,

Containing the most amusing Jonathanisms of the day. Cloth, 2s.

Tilt and Bogue, Fleet Street.

BOOKS OF ENTERTAINMENT.

THE COMIC ALMANACK, 1842.

With Twenty-four Etchings by George Cruikshank, and many other Embellishments, comprising Silhouettes, Borders, Figures, and Incidents. Fcp. 8vo. 2s. 6d.

THE COMIC ALMANACK FOR EIGHT YEARS.

Being from its Commencement in 1835 to 1842. Illustrated with 96 large Plates by G. CRUIKSHANK, and many hundred amusing Cuts. 2 vols. neatly bound in cloth, 18s.

GEORGE CRUIKSHANK'S OMNIBUS:

A Vehicle for Fun and Frolic; comprising Sketches, Essays, Disquisitions, and Jeux-d'esprit, by the best writers of the day. With numerous Illustrations on Steel and Wood. 10s. 6d. cloth.

LOVING BALLAD OF LORD BATEMAN,

With Twelve Humorous Plates by G. CRUIKSHANK. Cloth, 2s.

CRUIKSHANK'S SKETCH-BOOK.

Containing more than Two Hundred laughable Groups and Sketches. By G. CRUIKSHANK. Neatly bound in cloth, 18s. plain; 24s. coloured.

MORE HINTS ON ETIQUETTE.

For the use of Society at large, and Young Gentlemen in particular. With Humorous Cuts by G. CRUIKSHANK. 2s. 6d.

SCRAPS AND SKETCHES.

In Four Parts. By G. CRUIKSHANK.—ILLUSTRATIONS of PHRENO-LOGY—ILLUSTRATIONS of TIME. 8s. each, plain; 12s. coloured.

GEORGE CRUIKSHANK'S COMIC ALPHABET.

Twenty-six Humorous Designs. In a case, 2s. 6d. plain; 4s. coloured.

JOHN GILPIN.

With Six Illustrations by George Cruikshank, fcp. 8vo. 1s.

THE EPPING HUNT.

The Poetry by THOMAS HOOD, the Illustrations by George Cruikshank. New Edition, fcp. 8vo. 1s. 6d.

WHIMS AND ODDITIES.

By THOMAS HOOD. New and cheap edition, containing the whole of the Original Work, with 80 Plates, 7s. 6d. cloth.

" Hood's earliest, and perhaps his best, work. It contains the germ of most of his future productions."

LIBRARY OF ANECDOTE.

Remarkable Sayings, Efforts of Wit and Humour, &c. &c. With Five Engravings. Fcp. 8vo. 2s. 6d. cloth.

Tilt and Bogue, Fleet Street.

USEFUL WORKS.

THE WINE-DRINKER'S MANUAL;

And, Guide to the Choice of Wines, their Growth, and Management. By the Editor of "Hints for the Table."

"The life of mirth, and the joy of the earth,
Is a cup of good old Sherry."---PASQUIL'S PALINODIA.

SEVEN HUNDRED DOMESTIC HINTS.

Combining Elegance and Economy with the Enjoyment of Home. By a LADY. Neatly bound in cloth, 2s. 6d.

PICTORIAL FRENCH DICTIONARY.

The more important Words illustrated in a new and striking manner by Seven Hundred and Sixty Engravings on Wood. Royal 8vo. 12s. cloth.

YEAR-BOOK OF FACTS IN SCIENCE AND ART.

Exhibiting the most important Discoveries and Improvements of the Year, and a Literary and Scientific Obituary. By the Editor of "The Arcana of Science." Illustrated with Engravings, 12mo. 5s. cloth.

‡§‡ This work is published Annually, and comprises a complete and condensed view of the Progress of Discovery, being, in fact, the spirit of the scientific journals for the year systematically arranged, so as to present, at one view, the scientific discoveries, new and improved processes, &c. of the past year. Each volume is embellished with a Frontispiece and many Illustrations on Wood. Three volumes have already appeared, any of which may be purchased separately.

POPULAR ERRORS EXPLAINED AND ILLUSTRATED.

By JOHN TIMBS, Editor of "Laconics," "Year-Book of Facts," &c. Frontispiece, fcp. 8vo. 6s.

LACONICS.

Or, the Best Words of the Best Authors. Three vols. embellished with Thirty small Portraits. New and very cheap Edition, 8s. cloth.

HINTS FOR THE TABLE;

Or, the Economy of Good Living; containing New Instructions in Dietetics, Gastronomy, and the Art of Dining; including also Wine-Drinking; Coffee and Tea Making; National Dinners, &c. 2s. 6d. cloth.

TREATISE ON DIET AND REGIMEN.

Intended as a Text-book for the Invalid and Dyspeptic. By W. H. ROBERTSON, M.D. New Edition, enlarged and improved, 4s. 6d. cloth.

"As a family-book, Dr. Robertson's 'Treatise' is unequalled in the language."---SUN.

SHARPE'S DIAMOND DICTIONARY.

Of the ENGLISH LANGUAGE. A very small volume, but beautifully printed in a clear and legible type, admirably adapted for the writing desk. Morocco, elegantly gilt, 3s. 6d.; roan neat, 2s. 6d.

THE YOUNG LADY'S EQUESTRIAN MANUAL.

A Complete Book of Instruction, calculated, without other aid, to render any Lady a graceful and accomplished Horsewoman. Plates, 4s. cloth.

ETIQUETTE FOR THE LADIES.

Eighty Maxims on Dress, Manners, and Accomplishments. New Edition, with an Appendix on Court Etiquette. 1s. cloth.

ETIQUETTE FOR GENTLEMEN:

With Hints on the Art of Conversation. New Edition, 1s. cloth.

Tilt and Bogue, Fleet Street.

ELEGANT VOLUMES FOR PRESENTS.

THE ROMANCE OF NATURE;

Or, the Flower Seasons illustrated. By L. A. TWAMLEY. With Twenty-seven coloured Plates. 3d Edition, morocco elegant, 31s. 6d.

"A book of singular beauty and taste. .. Whether for tasteful decoration, originality, or grace, we have seen no superior to this beautiful volume."---LITERARY GAZETTE.

THE PILGRIMS OF THE RHINE.

By Sir E. L. BULWER. With Twenty-seven splendid Engravings, from Drawings by Maclise, Roberts, &c. New and Cheap Edition, uniform with "Rogers's Italy," crown 8vo. 21s. cloth; 28s. morocco.

SIR WALTER SCOTT'S MOST POPULAR WORKS—

Tilt and Bogue's Illustrated Editions.

1. THE LAY OF THE LAST MINSTREL.
2. THE LADY OF THE LAKE.
3. MARMION; A TALE OF FLODDEN FIELD.
4. ROKEBY.

These elegant volumes are uniformly printed in Foolscap Octavo, and illustrated with numerous Engravings on Steel, price 7s. cloth; 10s. 6d. morocco elegant, with Heraldic ornaments.

. Very cheap and neatly-printed Pocket Editions of these works form part of "TILT'S MINIATURE CLASSICS."—See p. 11.

ELIZA COOK'S POETICAL WORKS.

Beautifully Illustrated Edition. Post 8vo. 16s. cloth; 20s. morocco.

"Contains a great number of lyrical and other poems, many of which are extremely beautiful."
UNITED SERVICE GAZETTE.

OUR WILD FLOWERS.

A Popular and Descriptive Account of the Field Flowers of England. By L. A. TWAMLEY. Many coloured Plates, morocco, 21s.

EMMA DE LISSAU;

Or, Memoirs of a Converted Jewess. New Edition, with Illustrations by John Gilbert. 7s. cloth; 10s. 6d. morocco.

ROSETTE AND MIRIAM;

Or, the Twin Sisters: a Tale. By the Author of "Emma de Lissau." Fcp. 8vo. 6s. cloth.

RECOLLECTIONS OF THE LAKES;

And OTHER POEMS. By the Author of "Moral of Flowers," "Spirit of the Woods," &c. Frontispiece. Fcp. 8vo. 7s. cloth; 10s. 6d. morocco.

THE POETS OF AMERICA,

Illustrated by one of her Painters, with many beautiful Embellishments engraved on Steel, in an entirely new style. 14s. cloth; 18s. morocco.

MAY YOU LIKE IT.

A Series of Tales and Sketches. By the Rev. CHARLES B. TAYLER. New and Cheap Edition. Fcp. 8vo. 7s. 6d. cloth; 10s. 6d. morocco elegant.

Tilt and Bogue, Fleet Street.

TRAVELS IN TURKEY AND PERSIA:

With Notices of the Condition of Mahommedanism and Christianity in those Countries. By the Rev. HORATIO SOUTHGATE. 2 vols. 8vo. with Woodcuts and a large Map, 15s. cloth.

MISSIONARY TRAVELS IN CHINA,

HINDUSTAN, BURMAH, MALAYA, and SIAM. By the Rev. HOWARD MALCOM. 2 vols. 8vo. many Wood Engravings and an original Map, 16s. cloth.

LETTERS FROM PALESTINE,

Written during a Residence there in 1836-37-38; affording a complete View of the State of the Country, its Population, Resources, and Condition. By the Rev. J. D. PAXTON. Fcp. 8vo. 6s.

GLOSSARY OF ARCHITECTURE:

Explanations of the Terms used in Grecian, Roman, Italian, and Gothic Architecture, exemplified by many Hundred Woodcuts. New Edition, greatly enlarged.—*In the press.*

COMPANION to the GLOSSARY of ARCHITECTURE. 8vo. cloth, 16s.

STUART'S ANTIQUITIES OF ATHENS,

And other Monuments of Greece. With Seventy Plates, accurately reduced from the great Work of Stuart and Revett; and a Chronological Table, forming a valuable Introduction to the Study of Grecian Architecture. New Edition, revised and enlarged. 10s. 6d. cloth.

BREES' GLOSSARY OF CIVIL ENGINEERING.

A Clear and Practical Explanation of the Terms used in this Science, with References to numerous Works now in progress or lately completed, and many illustrative Wood Engravings. By S. C. BREES, Author of "Railway Practice, &c." 8vo. 18s. cloth.

PRINCIPLES OF GOTHIC ECCLESIASTICAL ARCHITECTURE

Elucidated by Question and Answer. By M. H. BLOXAM. 4th Edition, enlarged. Fcp. 8vo. 6s.

TAYLOR'S ILLUSTRATIONS OF THE BIBLE.

Confirmations of Sacred History drawn from Egyptian Monuments. By W. C. TAYLOR, LL.D. With Ninety-three Engravings, cloth, 6s. 6d.

CHROMATOGRAPHY;

A Treatise on Colours and Pigments, and of their Powers in Painting, &c. By GEORGE FIELD. New and improved Edition. Demy 8vo. 14s. cloth.

CHROMATICS.

An Essay on the Analogy and Harmony of Colours. By GEO. FIELD, Author of "Chromatography." Quarto, 21s. cloth.

WILLIAMS'S SYMBOLICAL EUCLID,

Chiefly from the Text of Dr. Simson. Adapted to the Use of Students by the Rev. J. M. WILLIAMS, of Queen's College, Cambridge. New Edition, 6s. cloth; 7s. roan.—An octavo Edition may also be had, 10s. 6d. cloth. ‡$‡ This edition is used at Cambridge and many of the Public Schools.

Tilt and Bogue, Fleet Street.

INTERESTING JUVENILE WORKS.

	s.	d.
ABBOTT'S ROLLO CODE OF MORALS	2	6
ARABIAN NIGHTS, as related by a Mother (many Plates)	5	0
BARBAULD'S LESSONS FOR CHILDREN (Coloured Plates)	1	0
BINGLEY'S STORIES ABOUT DOGS (Plates)	4	0
BINGLEY'S STORIES ABOUT INSTINCT (Plates)	4	0
BINGLEY'S TALES OF SHIPWRECK (Plates)	4	0
BINGLEY'S STORIES ABOUT HORSES (Plates)	4	0
BINGLEY'S TALES ABOUT BIRDS (Plates)	4	0
BINGLEY'S TALES ABOUT TRAVELLERS (Plates)	4	0
BINGLEY'S BIBLE QUADRUPEDS (Plates)	4	0
COUSIN WILLY'S HOLIDAYS (16 Engravings)	1	6
CURIOSITIES FOR THE INGENIOUS (Plates)	2	6
DICK THE LITTLE PONY (many Cuts)	1	6
FAMILY POETRY, by the Editor of "Sacred Harp," silk	2	6
FIGURES OF FUN; Two Parts (Coloured Plates)	1	0
FLOWERS OF FABLE (180 Engravings)	4	0
HERVEY'S REFLECTIONS IN A FLOWER GARDEN (12 col'd Plates)	4	0
LIFE OF CHRIST, New Edition (28 Plates)	4	0
LITTLE FORGET-ME-NOT (Plates)	2	6
LITTLE SKETCH BOOK FOR BEGINNERS (2 vols.) ....each	4	0
MOTHER'S PRESENT TO HER DAUGHTER, silk	2	6
PARLEY'S VISIT TO LONDON (Coloured Plates), cloth	4	0
PARLOUR MAGIC, Amusing Recreations (many Plates)	5	0
PERCY'S TALES OF KINGS OF ENGLAND (Plates)	4	6
PERCY'S KINGS OF ENGLAND, Second Series (Plates)	4	6
PERCY'S ROBIN HOOD AND HIS FORESTERS (Coloured Plates)	6	6
PICTORIAL BIBLE HISTORY (OLD TESTAMENT) (144 Plates)	4	6
PICTORIAL BIBLE HISTORY (NEW TESTAMENT) (144 Plates)	4	6
RECREATION FOR MDCCCXLII. (Plates)	5	0
SEDGWICK'S STORIES FOR YOUNG PERSONS (Plates), cloth	3	6
SEDGWICK'S MEANS AND ENDS, New Edition (Plates)	3	6
TALES OF ENTERPRISE, neatly bound	2	6
WILSON'S STORIES ABOUT HORSES (Plates)	3	6

TILT'S HAND-BOOKS FOR CHILDREN:

Each containing Forty-eight pretty Plates, neatly bound and gilt, viz. :—

	s.	d.
LITTLE PICTURE BIBLE	1	6
LITTLE PICTURE TESTAMENT	1	6
ZOOLOGICAL GARDENS, REGENT'S PARK	1	6
SURREY ZOOLOGICAL GARDENS	1	6
LITTLE BOOK OF BRITISH BIRDS	1	6
LITTLE BOOK OF BRITISH QUADRUPEDS	1	6
TOWN SIGHTS FOR LITTLE FOLKS	1	6
COUNTRY WALKS FOR LITTLE FOLKS	1	6
LITTLE ROBINSON CRUSOE	1	6
LITTLE ESOP—Fables for the Young	1	6
LITTLE HISTORY OF ENGLAND	1	6
GREAT MEN OF ENGLAND	1	6

A neat Case, lettered "MY OWN LIBRARY," *and containing eight of the* "Hand-Books," *may be had, price 14s.*

Tilt and Bogue, Fleet Street.

Tilt's Cabinet Library Editions.

1. DR. JOHNSON'S LIVES of the ENGLISH POETS.
2. BOSWELL'S LIFE of JOHNSON.
3. OLIVER GOLDSMITH'S WORKS.
4. HERVEY'S MEDITATIONS and CONTEMPLATIONS.

‡§‡ The above Works are clearly and beautifully printed by Whittingham, and each comprised in a handsome foolscap 8vo. volume. Their elegance and cheapness render them very suitable for Presents, School Prizes, or Travelling Companions. Price 6s. each, neatly half-bound in morocco; or 8s. 6d. morocco gilt.

"TILT's EDITION" must be specified in ordering the above.

ELEGANT POCKET VOLUMES,
With Illuminated Titles,
In the style of the Ancient Roman Missals.

VICAR OF WAKEFIELD.
COTTAGERS OF GLENBURNIE.
SACRED HARP.
COWPER'S POEMS. 2 vols.
THOMSON'S SEASONS.
SCOTT'S LADY OF THE LAKE.
SCOTT'S MARMION.
SCOTT'S LAY and BALLADS.
SCOTT'S ROKEBY.
SCOTT'S SELECT POETICAL WORKS. 4 vols. containing the above Poems uniformly bound.

₊ Each volume, very neatly bound and gilt, 2s. 6d. cloth; 4s. morocco.

BOOKS OF POETRY,
With Illuminated Titles.

Neatly bound, for Presents, School Prizes, &c.

THE POETRY OF FLOWERS.
POETRY OF THE PASSIONS.
POETRY OF THE SENTIMENTS.
THE LYRE—Fugitive Poetry of the Nineteenth Century.
THE LAUREL—a Companion Volume to the Lyre.

4s. 6d. each, cloth gilt; 6s. 6d. morocco elegant.

Tilt and Bogue, Fleet Street.

DRAWING BOOKS, AND WORKS ON THE FINE ARTS.

J. D. HARDING.

ELEMENTARY ART;
Or, the Use of the Black Lead Pencil Advocated and Explained. 28 Plates. Imperial 4to. 42s. cloth.

EARLY DRAWING BOOK:
Elementary Lessons. Six Numbers 1s. 6d.; or in cloth, 10s. 6d.

DRAWING BOOK for 1838:
Advanced Studies, printed in Tints. Six Nos. 3s.; half-morocco, 21s.

DRAWING BOOK for 1841.
Sketches in Sepia and Chalk. Six Nos. 3s. 6d.; neatly bound, 24s.

DRAWING BOOK for 1837:
Advanced Studies. Six Nos. 3s.; half-morocco, 21s.

HARDING'S PORTFOLIO;
24 highly-finished Sketches. Six Nos. 3s.; coloured, 5s.

SAMUEL PROUT, F.S.A.

PROUT'S MICROCOSM;
Or, Artist's Sketch-book: many Hundred Groups of Figures, Boats, &c. Imp. 4to. 24s. neatly bound.

ELEMENTARY DRAWING BOOK of Landscapes, Buildings, &c. Six Numbers, 1s. 6d.; cloth, 10s. 6d.

T. S. COOPER.

DRAWING BOOK OF ANIMALS and RUSTIC GROUPS.
Eight Nos. 2s.; or 16s. bound.

SKETCHES FROM NATURE,
Groups and Animals printed in tints. Six Nos. 3s. 6d.; bound, 31s. 6d.

GEORGE CHILDS.

THE LITTLE SKETCH BOOK: easy Studies in Landscapes, Figures, &c. Improved Edition, Fourteen Nos. 6d.; or 2 vols. cloth, 4s. each.

ELEMENTARY DRAWING BOOK: Studies from Nature, in a Series of Progressive Lessons. Eight Nos. 9d.; or in cloth, 7s. 6d.

JAMES ANDREWS.

LESSONS IN FLOWER PAINTING, Drawn and Coloured after Nature. New Edition, Six Nos. 2s. 6d.; cloth gilt, 16s.

PROGRESSIVE DRAWING BOOK of FLOWERS, in Easy Lessons. Six Nos. coloured, 1s. 6d.; cloth, very neat, 9s.

JULIEN'S STUDIES OF HEADS, Selected or Drawn from Nature. Six Nos. 2s.; cloth, 14s.

BARRAUD'S STUDIES OF ANIMALS, Lithographed by Fairland. Six Nos. large 4to. 3s.; or coloured, 5s.

ZEITTER'S STUDIES OF ANIMALS and RUSTIC GROUPS.
Six Nos. 1s.; cloth, 7s. 6d.

SHIPPING AND CRAFT.
In Progressive Lessons. By W. M. Grundy. Six Nos. 1s. 6d.; cloth, 10s. 6d.

HARLEY'S LANDSCAPE DRAWING BOOK. Six Nos. 1s.; cloth, 7s. 6d.

THE HUMAN FIGURE.
In Progressive Studies. By Thos. Fairland. Twelve Nos. 2s.; or 2 vols. cloth, 12s. each.

WORSLEY'S LITTLE DRAWING BOOK: Easy Studies in Landscapes, Houses, &c. Fourteen Nos. 6d.; or 2 vols. cloth, 4s. each.

FAIRLAND'S JUVENILE ARTIST: Figures, Landscapes, and Shipping. Eight Nos. 1s.; or cloth, 8s.

FAMILIAR LIFE: Sketches of Figures, Groups, &c. Drawn and Etched by John Phillips. Three Nos. 1s. 6d. each.

NEW PRINTS FOR FRAMING, THE PORTFOLIO, &c.

THE DEATH-BED OF CALVIN.
Painted by JOSEPH HORNUNG, of Geneva. Engraved by W. O. GELLER. Size, exclusive of margin or writing, 26¼ by 20½ high. Prints, £2. 2s. ; proofs, £3. 3s. ; proofs before letters, £4. 4s.

FAMILY DEVOTION—MORNING.
Painted by E. PRENTIS; engraved by JAMES SCOTT. 22¾ inches by 17¾ high. Prints, 21s. ; proofs, 31s. 6d.

FAMILY DEVOTION—EVENING.
By the same Artists, Companion to the above.—Same size and price.

THE INFANT SAMUEL.
Painted by Sir. J. REYNOLDS ; engraved by T. HODGETTS. Prints, 5s. ; proofs, 7s. 6d.

THE DREADNOUGHT HOSPITAL SHIP,
Moored in the Thames, off Greenwich. Painted by W. C. SMITH ; engraved by R. W. PRICE. 21s. plain ; 42s. coloured.

RALEIGH'S FIRST PIPE IN ENGLAND.
Painted by BUSS; engraved by EGAN. 10s. 6d.

FRUITS OF INDUSTRY.—FRUITS OF IDLENESS.
A pair, painted by E. PRENTIS; engraved by W. CARLOS. 16½ inches by 13½ high. Prints, 12s. ; proofs, 21s.

HOUSEHOLD PETS.
Painted by W. DRUMMOND ; engraved by W. H. SIMMONS. 12½ inches by 16 high. Prints, 8s.

JOHN ANDERSON MY JO.
Painted by KIDD ; engraved by CARLOS. 12 inches by 15 high. 8s.

AULD ROBIN GRAY.
Companion to above. 8s.

CHRIST STILLING THE TEMPEST. 11½ by 15½ high. 7s. 6d.

CHRIST WALKING ON THE SEA. Companion to the above, 7s.6d.

FALSTAFF TUMBLED INTO THE RIVER. Painted by KIDD; engraved by CARLOS. 8¼ inches by 10¾. 7s. 6d.

THE LAST SUPPER.
Painted by L. DA VINCI ; engraved by H. DAWE. 15 in. by 4½. 10s. 6d.

LAST TRIBUTE OF AFFECTION. 12¾ inches by 16. Prints, 12s.

THE MOTHER'S GRAVE.
9¼ inches by 11¾. 7s. 6d.

MY OWN FIRESIDE.
Painted by DRUMMOND. 9¼ inches by 11½. 7s. 6d.

SEARCH THE SCRIPTURES.
Painted and engraved by H. DAWE. 9¾ inches by 12. 6s.

WAYS OF PLEASANTNESS.
Companion to the above. 6s.

WIDOW'S TREASURES.
14 inches by 17. Prints, 12s.

THE WIDOWER.
Companion to the above. Prints, 12s.

A complete List of T. & B.'s Stock of Prints may be had on application.

Tilt and Bogue, Fleet Street.

CHEAP BOOKS.

THE ENGLISH SCHOOL:

A Series of Engravings of the most admired works in Painting and Sculpture executed by British Artists from the days of Hogarth: with descriptive and explanatory Notices, by G. HAMILTON. In 4 vols. small 8vo. containing nearly THREE HUNDRED PLATES, neatly bound, with gilt tops. *Originally published at £3. 12s.; reduced to 34s.*

WATER-COLOUR GALLERY;

Containing large and highly-finished Engravings of the Works of the most distinguished Painters in Water-colours, including PROUT, STEPHANOFF, COX, DEWINT, HARDING, CATTERMOLE, FIELDING, &c. 18 Plates, imperial 4to. cloth. *Originally published at £3. 3s.; reduced to 21s.*

PUCKLE'S CLUB;

Or, a Grey Cap for a Green Head. Many first-rate Wood Engravings, cloth. *Published at 7s. 6d.; reduced to 3s. 6d.*

*** This very curious book is illustrated with numerous and characteristic designs by the celebrated Thurston. It was published originally in 4to. at One Guinea.—*See Jackson on Wood Engraving.*

ADDISON'S ESSAYS;

From the SPECTATOR. 2 neat vols. cloth. *Pub. at 8s.; reduced to 4s. 6d.*

ILLUSTRATIONS OF SCOTT'S WORKS.

1. LANDSCAPE ILLUSTRATIONS OF THE WAVERLEY NOVELS. Eighty fine Views of real Scenes from Drawings by ROBERTS, HARDING, STANFIELD, &c. Two handsome volumes, super-royal 8vo. *Originally published at £4.; or India Proofs, royal 4to. £7. 7s. Now reduced to 28s. 8vo. and £3. 3s. in 4to.*

2. PORTRAIT ILLUSTRATIONS OF THE WAVERLEY NOVELS. Forty Plates from Drawings by PARRIS, INSKIPP, LANDSEER, &c. Super-royal 8vo. published at £1. 13s.; *India proofs, royal 4to. £3. Now reduced to 14s. in 8vo. and 31s. 6d. in 4to.*

3. LANDSCAPE ILLUSTRATIONS OF THE POETICAL WORKS. Forty Plates from Drawings by TURNER, CALCOTT, FIELDING, &c. Super-royal 8vo. *published at 31s.; India proofs royal 4to. £2. 8s.; reduced to 14s. in 8vo. and 31s. 6d. in 4to.*

*** The Complete Series of these valuable Illustrations are kept, *very handsomely and appropriately bound in morocco, price only Four Guineas;* forming one of the cheapest and most elegant books ever offered.

WILD'S ENGLISH CATHEDRALS.

Twelve Select Examples of the Ecclesiastical Architecture of the Middle Ages, beautifully coloured after the Original Drawings by CHARLES WILD, Esq. Mounted on Tinted Card-board. *Originally published at £12. 12s.; reduced to £5. 5s.*

1. WESTMINSTER: Henry VII.'s Chapel.	7. WELLS: West front.
2. PETERBOROUGH: West front.	8. NORWICH: Interior.
3. GLOUCESTER: View of the choir.	9. SALISBURY: Exterior view of south east.
4. YORK: West front.	10. WINDSOR: St. George's Chapel.
5. YORK: View of the choir.	11. OXFORD: Interior view of the choir.
6. ELY: Transept.	12. CAMBRIDGE: King's College Chapel.

" There never was an artist who touched on Gothic Architecture with the same severe truth and fidelity as Mr. Wild." ATHENÆUM.

Any plate may be purchased separately, 12s. mounted on Card Board; or on small paper for Framing, 7s. 6d.

Tilt and Bogue, Fleet Street.

CHEAP BOOKS.

WINKLES'S ENGLISH CATHEDRALS.

ARCHITECTURAL AND PICTURESQUE ILLUSTRATIONS OF THE CATHE-
DRAL CHURCHES OF ENGLAND AND WALES, from Drawings by ROBERT
GARLAND, Architect, with descriptions by THOMAS MOULE; containing
One Hundred and Twenty Plates, beautifully engraved by B. WINKLES.
In two handsome volumes, imperial 8vo. very neatly bound in cloth.
*Originally published at £2. 2s.; reduced to 24s. Royal 4to. India proofs
(very few left), published at £4. 4s.; reduced to 48s.*

₊ Nearly four years ago, T. and B. bought of Mr. Winkles's Assignees, the
Steel-plates and Copyright of this work, and, *being incomplete,* they reduced
the price as above. So many copies having since been disposed of, and so
urgent the requests for its completion, the present proprietors have determined to finish the work by publishing the third volume according to the
original plan. Several Numbers of the concluding volume are now published,
and the whole will be completed by Midsummer 1842, when the price of the
work will be raised.
Purchasers of the two first volumes may have the numbers of the Third
supplied as they appear, on application to any Bookseller.

WINKLES'S FRENCH CATHEDRALS.

From Drawings by R. GARLAND, with Historical and Descriptive
Accounts, containing Fifty large 4to. Plates. In a handsome volume,
bound in cloth. *Originally published at £1. 10s.; reduced to 21s. Royal
4to. India Proofs, published at £3.; reduced to 42s.*

THE GEORGIAN ERA :

Modern British Biography, since the Reign of Queen Anne; comprising nearly Two Thousand Memoirs of the most Eminent Persons
who have flourished in Britain from that period to the demise of George
the Fourth; chronologically arranged.

The work is embellished with Portraits of the four Georges, and is handsomely bound in cloth, with the contents of each volume lettered in gold;
forming a handsome and beautiful ornament to the Library. *Published at
£1. 14s. 6d.; now reduced to 21s.*

THE NOBLE SCIENCE—FOX-HUNTING.

By F. P. DELME RADCLIFFE, Esq., Master of the Hertfordshire Hounds.
With highly-finished Portraits of HUGO MEYNELL and C. LORAINE
SMITH, Esqs. and beautifully executed Illustrations of the Chase, the
Cover, and the Kennel, from Original Drawings by the Rev. C. D.
RADCLIFFE. Royal 8vo. *Originally published at 28s.; reduced to 14s.*

" A book which ought to be in the hands of every fox-hunter, and of every man who loves the
' Noble Science.' "
                                                                      BELL'S LIFE.

MUSEUM OF PAINTING AND SCULPTURE :

A Collection of the principal Pictures, Statues, and Bas-Reliefs in the
Public and Private Galleries of Europe. Drawn and engraved by
REVEIL. With Critical and Historical Notices. This splendid work,
which contains Engravings of all the chief Works in the Italian, German,
Dutch, French, and English Schools, includes TWELVE HUNDRED
PLATES, and is an indispensable *vade-mecum* to the Artist or Collector.
In 17 handsome vols. small 8vo. neatly bound, with gilt tops. *Originally
published at £17. 17s.; reduced to £6. 6s.*

Tilt and Bogue, Fleet Street.

CHEAP BOOKS.

MARTIN'S ILLUSTRATIONS OF THE BIBLE.

Consisting of Twenty large and magnificent Plates, designed and engraved by JOHN MARTIN, author of "Belshazzar's Feast," &c. In a large folio volume, cloth. *Originally published at £10. 10s.; reduced to £3. 3s. Proof Impressions (very few left), published at £21.; reduced to £4. 4s.*

MARTIN'S MILTON'S PARADISE LOST.

Imperial 8vo. Twenty-four large mezzotinto Plates. By JOHN MARTIN. Published at Six Guineas; *now reduced to £2. 2s. cloth; £2. 15s. very neat, in morocco.*

NEW READINGS FROM OLD AUTHORS.

Illustrations of Shakspeare, by ROBERT SEYMOUR. Four Volumes, containing Two Hundred and Fifty Plates. *Originally published at £2. now reduced to 20s. neatly bound in cloth.*

*** TILT and BOGUE have been enabled by a recent purchase to make up One Hundred Sets of this very amusing Work. The Drawings on the Stones have long been effaced, and the numerous admirers of SEYMOUR have this opportunity only of possessing one of his best works. The designs and drawings were wholly done by that lamented artist.

NORTHCOTE'S FABLES.

Illustrated by Two Hundred and Eighty Engravings on Wood. *Originally published at 18s.; now reduced to 8s. in extra cloth bds.*

*** This splendid volume, for the production of which the late Mr. Northcote bequeathed a large sum, may be considered as the triumph of the art of engraving on wood. The plates are unrivalled in beauty and merit.

LE KEUX'S ILLUSTRATIONS OF NATURAL HISTORY ;

Containing One Hundred and Fourteen Engravings, with Descriptive Accounts, of the most popular and interesting Genera and Species of the Animal World, drawn by LANDSEER, LE KEUX, &c. &c. Large 8vo. bound in cloth. *Originally published at 21s.; reduced to 9s. 6d. cloth.*

DON QUIXOTE DE LA MANCHA.

Beautifully Illustrated Edition, containing Eight Hundred Engravings on Wood by TONY JOHANNOT. In Three large and handsome Volumes, neatly bound in cloth. *Published at £2. 10s.; now reduced to 34s.*

THE ADVENTURES OF GIL BLAS.

In the same style, with Six Hundred Engravings, designed by JEAN GIGOUX; forming Two handsome Volumes, super-royal 8vo. bound in cloth. *Published at £1. 12s.; now reduced to 21s.*

SINGER'S EDITION OF SHAKSPEARE.

Beautifully printed by Whittingham, with a Life of the Poet, and illustrative Notes. Embellished with many Engravings by STOTHARD, HARVEY, &c. In ten vols. small 8vo. neatly bound in cloth, gilt. *Originally published at £4. 4s.; reduced to 35s.*

TILT AND BOGUE, 86, FLEET STREET.

LaVergne, TN USA
08 April 2011
223383LV00004BA/113/A

Wh

on Earth are

Yu?

a field guide **to** identifying
and knowing **yourself**

Wh
on Earth are
Yu?

a field guide **to** identifying
and knowing **yourself**

NICK INMAN

 FINDHORN PRESS

© Nick Inman 2013

The right of Nick Inman to be identified as the
author of this work has been asserted by him in accordance
with the Copyright, Designs and Patents Act 1998.

Published in 2013 by Findhorn Press, Scotland

ISBN 978-1-84409-620-6

A CIP record for this title is available from the British Library.

Edited by Nicky Leach
Cover design by Clara Villanueva
Interior design by Damian Keenan
Printed and bound in the EU

Published by
Findhorn Press
117-121 High Street,
Forres IV36 1AB,
Scotland, UK

t +44 (0)1309 690582
f +44 (0)131 777 2711
e info@findhornpress.com
www.findhornpress.com

Contents

Contents

To Clara

No sé que tienes que no tengan las demás…

Acknowledgements

No book is made by one person alone. I am especially grateful to Thierry Bogliolo, Nicky Leach and everyone else at Findhorn Press for their help and enthusiasm. I would also like to thank Emmanuelle Curbelié and her family for their indispensable support.

Preface

· · · · ·

Y ou and I, we could be twins. It's like looking in a mirror. Almost. I know there are a few differences between us but nothing that great. We are the same species, aren't we? Built to the same model. We differ only in the details.

And that goes for any two of us. If you doubt this, go and look at a beach full of semi-naked people. Get us away from our houses and possessions, make us take our clothes off and surrender our job titles, stop us talking so that we don't fudge the issue with words, and there is not much left to tell us apart. What's true of me is largely true of you, and vice versa.

But, you might protest, you are far more than you appear to be. You are *someone* within that skin. All of you is important—your trappings, too. They are not insignificant variations on a standard format. They are what makes you a you and me a me. And I would have to agree.

There are at least two ways to see a human being, and they are both implicit in the question that forms the title of this book. We are both generalizations and particularities. To explain who on earth you and I are, we must simultaneously consider what it is to be a human being (what we are we doing here) and what it means to be an individual person in these two forms.

What can I tell you about you? Not everything, that's for sure. But I can tell you much by telling you about me. On many points we will, I hope, coincide, and where we don't you can supply your arabesques for yourself.

Taking the two together, my thoughts and yours, we should be able to compose a respectable response to a question of vital importance to us all.

— *Nick Inman*

Here Or Here?
My Problem Self

1

A Challenge from My Bank

My bank has written asking me to prove who I am. Although I have been a customer for some time, the letter explains, it is obliged by new regulations to make sure that I am not a money-laundering identity thief. Otherwise, it won't be able to look after my money.

When I first received the letter, this seemed like a reasonable request, and I was ready to do my best to comply. I am used to identifying myself to interested parties. It is a frequent routine in the modern world. Their proposed procedure is a simple one. All I have to do is provide two documents—a copy of my passport and a utility bill—signed by a witness on an approved list of occupations.

Thinking about this further, what they are asking me to do makes less sense. If I were a cheat—either a lazy man or someone pretending to be me—these two documents would be easy to forge. I could recruit the first person I meet on the street to write the required text in a convincing-looking handwriting. I could even write it myself—who would ever know? For extra authenticity, I would get a rubber stamp made giving the name of a bogus solicitor or estate agent, because no one ever argues with a rubber stamp.

The bank could call to check up on my witness, but what would that prove? Anyone can pretend to be anyone on the phone. If it is going to check up on me properly it would have to find a reliable witness to witness the witness, and a witness to witness the witness, and so on. This would go on ad infinitum, or until the chain of witnessing reaches back to the official in the bank who started all this. He would then have been assured by someone he knows personally that someone known personally to the first someone knows someone who knows someone who knows someone . . . and so on around the world a couple of times and back to the starting point: me.

Even if my documents are genuine and my witness sincere, how will my bank be able to connect them to *me*? They will know that a person with my name was born and was still alive on the date given (but perhaps no longer), that he held a valid passport, and that he lived at a particular address. Any half-competent impostor could steal that kind of proof. If he wants to acquire an identity, all he has to do is intercept a letter containing witnessed documents that, by the bank's definition, guarantee that the sender is an authentic person.

I can't help feeling that my bank is on an absurd and futile quest. However, I sympathize with its predicament. It does need to check up on me, and it is in my interest that no one impersonates me. Is this really the best way to go about it? If it is not, can I suggest anything better?

This set me thinking, while the letter from my bank lay on my desk. What would I have to do to prove who I am? To answer that, don't I have to first ask how do I know who I am? Or even more bluntly, who or what am I? What makes me so certain that I know the answers?

Because I do know the answers without even asking the questions, or rather I pretend that I do. I couldn't function if I didn't.

We need ways of identifying ourselves in all human interaction. Every day we go through dances of identity, more or less formalized rituals, charming little displays of superficial and reciprocal trust. I have practised my part in these exchanges all my life and have got it off pat. I know just what to say to convince people that I am a genuine person.

We all get used to giving the responses expected of us. We rattle them off each day to new acquaintances (and acquaintances who have forgotten that they know us), employers, strangers, receptionists, bureaucrats, and anyone else with a legitimate need to know.

If we meet, you'll probably ask me some innocuous little question, so that we don't have to stand there looking awkwardly into each other's eyes. The chances are the first couple of sentences I say about myself will satisfy your curiosity about me. If you want something from me or have something to give—say, you are considering me for a job—you may want to know a little more but still within a limited range. I will have my lines prepared to make you think that I believe them.

We don't generally question what we are saying. If it sounds true, it must be true. We get used to being who we say we are.

All this is good and natural, an essential part of social life. We are a gregarious species of animal. We need to know who each other is: friend, foe, or harmless other without portfolio. There is safety and reassurance in being recognized—in knowing your place, in others knowing who you are.

The old ways of interacting work as long as you are dealing with only a few people in a reduced space, in any kind of small, traditional community, and conditions stay more or less stable. But the contemporary world largely isn't like that.

Society is more fluid than it was a generation ago. We abandon our roots on a whim, in search of freedom. We mix with people we would never have come into contact with, were it not for the fact that we have new media at our disposal. We switch banks as often as we need to, in search of better deals. Then the banks merge and morph with each other in search of profit margins, so that we don't know who we are dealing with any more. The strange, disconnected, and often identity-less freedom of the internet, in particular, makes everyone both excited and nervy.

Trust, loyalty, truthfulness, and availability seem like quaint concepts that have been swept away by globalization. Bank branches don't have their own phone numbers manned by people you know: you have to go through a central switchboard, where the staff rotates by the minute.

No one wants to be pinned down. Fixed-line phones at home are fast becoming antiquated as smartphones enable us to resume the nomadic lifestyle we gave up several thousand years ago. We could be anywhere pretending to be anyone—and we probably are.

Greater individual freedom generates an increasing level of fear. The more opportunities people have to cheat, it is reasoned, the more they will cheat and the more they need to be checked up on and curtailed. The price of planetary sociability is a paranoid level of surveillance: a vast industry of monitoring, interrogating, and recording operated by states and private companies for their own ends.

As a result, we are expected to feed the appetite of a massive and growing organic-to-inorganic data-crunching machine dedicated to making sure that we remain verified, compliant units in the economic and political orders.

My bank is merely doing its bit within all this. It is just as scared of the permanent, accelerating change that we are living through as the rest of us are. It doesn't know what else to do but to do what every other institution is doing.

There is, however, an argument to be made that the more you try to check up on people, the more you will fail. You can feed the details of a human being into a computer, but if you want to use the data you need a human being at the other end of the system to make sense of it. Automated identity hunting is really a massive detour between the same two points that were once reached with a handshake and a smile. No amount of elaborate procedures and technologies can resolve the perennial challenge for one human being to know another.

The curious thing is that my bank and I are interested in answering the same question. We go about it in different ways, with different motivations, and we are hoping for different kinds of answers, but in essence we both want to know who I am. We aren't the only ones. This question has been taxing the brains of human beings for millennia, and it has teams of experts working on it 24 hours a day. So what, we might well ask, have they come up with so far?

2

Easy Impossibility

I am not the first person to ask, "Who am I?" Learned thinkers, freed from the grind of food production by slave and labouring classes, have been asking themselves the same question since at least the time of the ancient Greeks, 2,400 years ago, and possibly for eons before then.

The question may even have been formulated (nonverbally) the second after some primitive human being pointed at his chest and invented a personal pronoun. Asking it would not have done him much good in the daily struggle to survive, but a quest had begun.

We can only suppose that during the immense stretches of time that is prehistory, tribal shamans held a monopoly on the answer, couching it in terms of deities, myth, and taboo.

Over the last two millennia, philosophy has spun many theories on the nature of being human and on the experience of being an individual. Religion has also always had a lot to say about who we are, offering dogma instead of troubling uncertainty.

The Enlightenment proposed that man not God held the answer, and that it was to be found using the rational mind and empirical exploration with the senses. Today, science is still asking the question through a multitude of specializations, especially psychology, psychiatry, anthropology, and sociology, and their subsidiaries. It is widely hoped, however, that another discipline, neuroscience, the study of the physical brain, will finally demystify the subject.

As yet, however, the immense amount of thought and research that has gone into the question has produced few if any certainties. We remain a surprisingly slippery substance, rich in ideas and insights about ourselves but poor in facts. It seems that "Who am I?" is an easy question to ask but an impossible one to answer with any confidence. There are several reasons why this should be so:

1. **It may not be a closed question with a definite answer but an open question**. There may be more than one right answer, or the answer may be multifaceted. Neither science nor philosophy nor religion may have the

complete answer: we might have to take many different, even incompatible statements together in order to make sense of ourselves.

2. **Words can get in the way.** Many terms are used to talk about human nature and personal identity, and each academic discipline invents its own terms to add to the mix. None of them have unambiguous meanings and what meanings they do have overlap.

    Even the most basic words are problematic. If I look up "me" or "I" in the dictionary, I find they are personal pronouns that can apply to anyone. What I want to know is about this self of mine: it is, I read, "a person's essential being/distinctive individuality that distinguishes them from others, especially considered as the object of introspection or reflexive action." More precisely, "myself" refers to "a person's particular nature or personality; the qualities that make up a person individual or unique."

    My identity is "the state of having unique identifying characteristics held by no other person or thing," "the individual characteristics by which a person or thing is recognized," or "the fact of being who or what a person or thing is." These definitions amount to lexicographical tautologies. I am what I am: I am the components that, taken together, make a whole me.

    We have no choice but to communicate in words, but we must never forget that they are always metaphors standing for concepts and literal truths.

3. **Every generalization is based on the assumption that we are all essentially the same, but we may not be.** Clearly we have things in common, but we also have variations. We don't know how important these variations are: trivial embellishments or fundamental differences.

    In the best of circumstances and with the most straightforward of phenomena, it is impossible to know how far any generalization can be stretched. The closer we get to the subject matter, the harder it is.

    Unlike all other phenomenon that we study we are the subject matter under observation here, and that creates a conflict of interests for any would-be expert: how do you dissect yourself? How is he to know whether any statement he makes applies to all of us or just to him? Before he makes any pronouncements he has to know himself well and persuade the rest of us that he is not just passing judgement on his own neurosis, or navel gazing.

4. **It is not necessarily a question we can answer with the head alone**. As we are dealing with ourselves, we may have to engage with the question passionately rather than dispassionately, making full use of our humanity instead of trying to minimize it in the interests of objective scholarship.

   There is also an element of courage needed—to dare to see who you really are, which might not be what you hoped or expected you would be.

5. **Knowledge, especially self-knowledge, goes in fashions in its aims and methods**. What we ask, and how we ask it, depends on the age in which we live. For most of history the question, "Who am I?" would have been unutterable. Either the answer would be presupplied by religion or, since the individual was inseparable from society, the question would have to be rephrased as a group inquiry: "Who are we?" It might not have included in its remit anyone less than full members of society. Slaves and colonized peoples may have been excluded, and probably the poor and women, too. Identity changes with the centuries, varying with socioeconomic conditions.

   For most of history, only the rich and powerful have been accorded full identities; everyone else has been permitted only as much as they need to function in their daily lives. When life was short and death more present, being someone on Earth must have felt like being in a waiting room: why waste time asking such questions if the answer wasn't going to serve you for very long? "Who will you be when you are no longer on Earth?" made a lot more sense.

6. **Like all objects we are indivisible wholes, but we can also be dismantled into our components**. Is it self-evident that the two states—the dense, undivided bundle of stuff including consciousness that operates as a person and our various body parts carefully removed and preserved in jars of formaldehyde—need to be studied in different ways? Don't we lose something, perhaps the overview, if we look too closely at the detail? And don't we miss vital information if we insist that the whole is all that matters? Is there a way to consider the whole and its parts at the same time?

7. **In all self-examination, it is easy to let your own interests or expectations get in the way of an impartial search for the truth**. You can easily see what you want to see: a materialist may see only matter,

while a religious believer may consider only such evidence as will uphold his faith.

8. We have to study the outside and the inside at the same time. As we are looking at ourselves, it is probably true that we will need to take two approaches simultaneously: to study ourselves from the outside as objectively as we can, while also observing ourselves from the inside, entirely subjectively. Do it from one side only and you risk getting only half the picture.

All of these problems are a reminder that it is possible to be too clever, too well read, too wrapped up in methods, assumptions, rules, and fear of ridicule to see what we all see in the mirror and feel behind our eyes. It is easy to write a book on the subject, full of technical terms, footnotes, and ingenious hypotheses—and to get no farther than your starting point.

The question, "Who on earth am I?" has always been treated as a philosophical, scientific, or religious one. But it is too important to be left at that—confined to lecture halls, laboratories, churches, and conferences.

This affects you and me. It is about you and me. We can go on waiting for new generations of experts and new techniques and technologies to provide better answers, but a much simpler way is to ask ourselves what we know, then see where it leads us. We could start by simply listing the incontrovertible facts about human identity before we attempt to go any farther.

3

Sure Thing

W hat can we say for sure, prima facie, about identity? It seems to me to there are several sound premises from which to start a search for myself.

Identity matters

Identity matters to all of us—personally and together as groups. I need to have one of my own, and I might need to know what yours is. It is how we get a fix on each other. It is also how we get what we want. With an identity you can make friends, get sexual partners, further your career, and earn respect and admiration. An identity also acts as a force field that tells others not to interfere in your affairs.

In some areas of life, identity is crucial. Society needs to identify people in order to catch and convict criminals and exonerate the innocent. It is essential to know who is wandering around our children's schools and hospitals; who is working with young people, the old, and other vulnerable groups; who we appoint as police, security guards, and prime ministers; and to whom we sell firearms. In wartime, identification is what allows us to decide who lives or who dies, avoiding accidents through friendly fire and unintentional harm being caused to civilians.

We are fascinated, if not obsessed, by identity in a general sense. There would be little drama in the world, fictional or true, without confusions and disputes over identity, and we would have to find something else to do with our leisure time. In daily life, we discuss people we know or know of, forming judgements about them and passing on rumours. We watch news about the famous and notorious, wondering who they are behind all the hype. The exploration of character is key to cinema, opera, and literature and fuels both comedy and tragedy.

Everyone has got one

It is almost a tautology: to be human is to be identifiable. Everyone has got an identity, however reclusive, elusive, or unworldly he may be. Every outsider, misfit, and loner has an identity. The most important person in the world has one, as has the holiest guru, lost in disembodied meditation and in a state of total abnegation of the body, having extinguished want in himself and on the point of completing all the tasks of incarnation.

No one—barring those who are in psychiatric care, perhaps—is able, let alone content, to live without an identity, to be truly anonymous, a nonentity. The response "I don't know" or "I don't care" to the question "Who are you?" would sound either pretentious and deceitful or nonsensical.

You are only supposed to have one

As regards everyone having an identity, it would be truer to say, "at least one." Under normal circumstances, identity is strictly rationed: you get one—you are who you are. I may be vague, selective, and/or deceitful about certain facts; I may enjoy pretending I am someone else in my head—or even in real situations; but I only have one coherent identity.

Even if it is multifaceted, it is still a set of inescapable, mundane facts that tie me down in certain set ways. Only spies, along with schizophrenics and pathological imposters, deploy multiple identities.

We do, however, sometimes take on partial identities of limited duration to serve specific contexts. I might, for example, have to subordinate myself to a job, particularly if it involves a badge or uniform. If I am admitted to hospital, I am temporarily converted into a patient and everything else about me becomes less important than this.

Identity is personal, intimate, and nontransferable

My identity is mine alone. It is a personal matter. Only I know all of its details, from the trivial to the transcendental. I cannot transfer it or share it even temporarily with anyone else.

I may illicitly lend my credit card to a friend, but he does not become me. If everyone can produce a copy of my passport and knows the answer to my personal questions, there is no singular entity of me any more and the notion of identity becomes redundant. My identity must remain attached to me if it is to mean anything.

A corollary of this is that no one call tell me how to be me. There are plenty of life-skill teachers and spiritual masters around who assure me that they have the secret to me being a better me, even the best me possible, but they are deluded. You can be very good at being you, but it doesn't follow that you know equally well how I can be me.

The lack of transferability of identity is key to the very important principle of human right—the right to respect and dignity at least, because you cannot help being who you are (male/female, gay/straight, poor/rich, part of an ethnic religious minority or whatever).

Information about identity appears to come from two directions: outside and inside

Each of us seems to have an inner sense of self (I think I know who I am), which is only indirectly connected to our worldly identity (what everyone else insists we are) through our senses. The nature of this inner identity is contentious and hedged about with speculation: for instance, does it merely reflect the exterior world, or does it have any innate powers of its own? For now, I merely want to acknowledge the phenomenon of self-consciousness and continue listing the points we can all agree on.

Identity depends on context

Identity is not some abstract, archetypal concept; it varies according to context, or at least the perception of it does. If I meet someone in a weekend workshop, both of us removed from our habitual environments (separated from families and work and respective pasts invisible), we will appear to each other to be very different than if we were to meet during the course of our "normal" lives. This is a debatable point: to what extent am I the same person wherever I go, whatever I do, and whoever I am with, and how much do "I" vary according to the setting?

Identity is attached to time

Were we all to live in the eternal presence there would be no need for identity. Most of us, though, have one eye on the past, one eye on the future, and only a weak third eye on the unstable present. If I am to have anything to do with you (certainly, if I am to trust you), it is important that you are the same person today as you were yesterday, and that you will be the same person tomorrow. Identity is a guarantee of continuity and reliability. Aspects of it may change, certainly. I may get married, say, or change nationality, but this becomes part of my running record not a replacement for it, with a new beginning at each change of circumstance. If I were to continually reinvent myself—pop up each year with a new name, new job, new family, say—you would find it hard to get to know me. Identity becomes meaningless if you were a different person when I last met you to the person you are today and the person you decide to be tomorrow—as the verb tenses and personal pronouns in this sentence make clear.

Identity is for the benefit of other people

The only reason I have an identity at all seems to be to serve the interests of other people. Identity is a social currency. If I live alone on a desert island I do not need to specify who I am. I don't need a name or even know any other details about me.

This notion raises some interesting questions. In particular: if my identity only makes sense when there are two people present, how much of who I am is influenced by the other person? Could it be that sometimes (or even always) who I am depends on who is asking, what they want to know, or what they want and why?

Identity is a sign of significance

Identity is not created or maintained by the holder; it is bequeathed by someone else and only sustained by continual recognition. Identity, therefore, is an acknowledgement of my existence by one or more people. Moreover, it is a recognition of my significance—to be given an identity is to be elevated from the general class of things. We give identities to people or groups of people, creatures, or occasionally things we consider worth knowing. Godlike, we are capable of according someone or something more or less "identity," according to how much we care about them. This might explain why some people get on better with pets than with their human neighbours, elevating the identities of animals they prize over those of humans in their milieu.

The apportioning of identity is power (and the opposite)

The ability to hand out or refuse identity to others as we see fit equates with power. We play with this all the time, often casually and deliberately. If you know my name and I do not know yours—or you know more details about me than I know about you—you have a hold over me already. Or if you behave as if my name is not worth remembering, you show your disrespect for me, exercising a kind of insouciant power. To successfully conceal your identity is to get away with whatever it is you have done. The courts at all levels, including international, are filled with people determined to conceal all or part of their identities. More seriously, slavery is, by one definition, the condition of having your identity decided by your economic master.

Identity is always at least two-way

Whatever the power relationship between two people, identity is always a two-way arrangement. Each is either aware of the other's identity or aware that the other is withholding it for a reason. This is true of any relationship. Good and proper dealings can only be carried out between two people who are equally open about their identities, hence the need for transparency in all dealings.

Identity is always expressed in words

There are other components to identity, but an identity always comes down to a formula of words. Words are metaphors full of nuances and double-meanings. They can and do mislead us into seeing reality in an incomplete or inaccurate way. We need to take a great deal of care when we think we are talking clearly and literally. In some contexts, poetry may be closer to the truth than technical terminology.

The ingredients that constitute identity can be ranked in different ways

Identity has many aspects to it. It can be broken down in many ways and the pieces arranged in any order. We need to be very wary about this. The order in which the ingredients are presented is important. Ideally, we allow each person to do his own ranking. So, for example, someone might want to be identified foremost as a gay man, with his nationality declared as being much less important, whereas a bigot might want to emphasize his nationality, race, or religion before everything else.

We keep most identity transactions to the lowest possible level

When we meet someone new, or want to remind ourselves of who someone is, we generally keep the transaction on the simplest, most superficial possible level. We want to find out only what we want to know and no more. We don't usually have the time or desire to go deeper than our immediate requirements. We avoid enquiring about the existential well-being of a stranger.

What we want from the other person is the correct response to suit the situation—in effect, a password. We want to be reassured firstly that he is friend not foe and then we want to know where we stand in relation to him so that we can temper our behaviour accordingly. To do that we have to label and classify him in our minds and reach a judgement: harmless, can be ignored, could be useful to us, and so forth.

Reciprocally, when I am asked for information about myself, I give the minimum. Depending on the reasons for the request, I will say enough to get what I want or to satisfy the other, so that he will stop checking up on me and go away. I don't want to bore an interlocutor or hand power over me to an undercover operative, so I keep things brief.

To each situation, there is an appropriate level of exchange of information. This may or not be the same for the two (or more) parties involved.

Most transactions are straightforward as long as my statements about myself are plausible and congruent. They usually are, because several decades ago I was trained, semi-successfully, to be a parrot.

4

Parrot Person

Although I think of my identity as now my own, and in great part shaped by me and the decisions I have made, much of it was decided long ago and not by me. Like everyone else, I was trained as a parrot: brought up to learn and repeat the facts I was told about myself.

These facts derive mainly from the world as it was when I was conceived. My given genealogy, nationality, and my language all come from my parents. While I was still a blubbery mass growing arms and legs, yet without a personality, I already had a sex, a family, an address, and a name.

For around 18 months after being born, I was not expected to do much but grow and learn the rudiments of life on the planet: how to walk and communicate with my kind. Then I began to become self-aware and to assimilate the essentials of my identity. My parents, entirely responsible for me, decided what I would be taught to treat as normality.

The idea, I realized, was to memorize the right answers to the questions that I was repeatedly asked, so that I could give the appropriate response. My identity was established by this process of instruction, regurgitation, and approving response.

As well as being expected to accept the fixed facts of my existence, I was fed with judgements about the world made by my parents and others—their beliefs about religion, their morality, their fears, and so on.

Some of this information was generalized or implicit—I was told what "people like us" do and do not do, how boys are expected to behave, and fed a long list of shoulds and shouldn'ts; but there were also personal expectations placed on me, even if these weren't always articulated.

I was not expected to think about or question the facts—nothing I was told was negotiable—but to take them on trust. My reactions were not important, except in as much as they indicated a tendency to resistance, which needed to be discouraged. I was guided in this process by the desire to please and to avoid pain. I still had my doubts, nevertheless, and had to weigh up my interests against those of society.

The right answers were reinforced by the people I came into contact with, as these people were of my own kind. I would see in their eyes whether I had given a satisfactory response. They would congratulate me or berate me accordingly.

School, family, and social life all involved a process of constant repetition of good personal traits, healthy qualities, and what could be said and what was taboo.

I learned, simultaneously, that there were people to contrast myself with, who I shouldn't want to be like. I was taught the prejudices of that time and place, both formally and informally, by various means, including through the jokes that children tell.

The objective of my training was twofold. It was mainly concerned with equipping me to fit into the various shades and levels of society to which I belonged; to be a good son and citizen. As a byproduct of this, and to create a virtuous circle, it was hoped that I would be happy within the boundaries set for me. Well-adjusted people function as autonomously as the group desires, doing their duty as required. Ideally, there is no conflict between the two: the happiness of the individual is the happiness of all, and vice versa. It's the rare society that does not rely on its members feeling good doing what has to be done.

Everything would be fine for me, I was led to believe, even if I sometimes failed the meet the standards set for me, as long as two things held true:

1. That the world didn't change and I wasn't put to some extreme test, such as having to cope with mass unemployment or being called up to fight a war. Fortunately, neither of these two disasters befell my generation.

2. That I was alright in myself; that there were no irremediable contradictions about my identity inside my own head. Unfortunately, I wasn't, and there were.

5

Rebellion Against Myself

I don't know what age I was when I realized that I wasn't happy with the direction the world was trying to steer me, but it must have been in early adolescence, the classic moment for a first identity crisis. Despite my upbringing, I didn't feel right. I didn't know how to fit in. I felt the fault was with the world not me, but it didn't seem interested in hearing what I had to say or changing to suit me. Why should it? The damage was localized—I was the miserable one—and there was no reason to suppose that even if reality could be rearranged for my benefit, I would be any happier.

I'm sure from the outside it must have looked as if I was moodily tormenting myself over nothing. Conventional wisdom declared that I would grow out of it and find my place in society.

Anyway, what did I have to complain about? I was fortunate. I was born into all the wholesome identity a person could need. I lived in a stable, moderately well-off family in a prosperous country in 20th-century peacetime. I was not part of a persecuted minority. My parents were caring people. They gave me a good education and offered me choices in life.

Whatever was going on outside me, however, inside things didn't feel right. I felt under-confident and self-conscious, and if I behaved as I had been taught to behave, I felt insincere. I couldn't see where a person like me fitted into the world. A me-shaped slot had been prepared for me, but we were mismatched.

Looking back now with detachment, I see that there were two "me's" and that I was fighting a battle between my two "selves." One way to see this is as me versus reality—a determination to make things the way I wanted to be or die in the attempt. A better way to express it might that there were two competing desires within me. One wanted to be like everyone else: to be "normal." Another self wanted the exact opposite. It considered that I was abnormal and would never fit in. All I could do, it reasoned, was champion my own uniqueness, my undiluted individuality, and live forever as an outsider. Either way lay a predictable amount of misery.

Most of this came across as rejection, If I didn't know what I wanted exactly— how I wanted to be, to live—I did know that I didn't want to:

- live in my dull provincial home town
- do what everyone else did, to be conventional
- have a job (or at least not a "proper" job)
- have any attachments or commitments
- be settled somewhere, in the sense of stuck
- be constrained, unable to move or change
- be mediocre, uninteresting, and predictable
- be passionless, unspontaneous
- be smug, docile, complacent, and materialistic
- be secure

The list went on. Any and all of these prospects terrified me.

To begin with, I devised a provisional plan for living that would put off any decision I had to make. I became a permanently temporary person and for a long time, I lived in full flight from normality, a rebel persona who would not do as he was told. I had no clear positive goal. The only important thing seemed to me not to become any of the things I had rejected. Travel and changes of abode symbolized my freedom and my sense of perpetual escape. I knew that I didn't want this self-imposed uncertainty to last forever, but to bring it to an end I would have had to create an identity on my own terms. That meant fulfilling one or a combination of three ridiculous and unconfessable fantasies that kept me going:

To be someone. I didn't phrase it like this to myself, but it came down to being successful, admired, loved, considered a genius, famous, and generally blessed with good fortune. I thought this would happen naturally once I revealed my talents to the world. I knew I would have to put in some effort, but if I did, I was convinced that the reward would follow as an overlooked birthright. I was more than the person that my upbringing had made me, and now I was going to prove that I could forge a better identity for myself through a combination of ability, merit, and destiny (which may appear to others as luck).

To be *like* someone else. Discouraged by years of striving as the first fantasy faltered, I yielded one of my core beliefs, that I could do it on my own. I was willing to accept help. I read about self-help methods, I attended workshops, I did exercises, I observed people, I thought things through. If only I followed the right method diligently enough and believed in myself I would become as well adjusted and successful as my model.

To *be* someone else. Fantasy no. 2 worked better than fantasy no. 1 but still only partially, and I felt (obviously) that trying to be like someone rather than trying to be myself lessened the satisfaction of any achievement. In effect, I was just learning to play roles successfully so that other people would accept me. But wasn't that what my upbringing had tried to do? Worse still, I could imitate other people in some aspects (say and do the right things), but I never escaped from all my own personality flaws that I dragged behind me. In disillusionment and frustration I took refuge in a third fantasy, that what I really wanted was not to be myself at all but someone else. I wanted to unlearn me entirely and be different. I wanted to be someone who was inherently interesting to other people and successful in worldly terms. I wanted to be in someone else's skin. (I was very slow to see that to be someone else I would also have to take on any pains they had, visible or invisible. I could end up putting down one set of sufferings only to pick up another.)

These fantasies sometimes came consecutively; at other times, they ran concurrently and frequently became mixed up. They also interacted with reality because I was busy doing things and learning. Even if I was sometimes confused and unhappy, I wasn't an unmitigated disaster as a human being. I had assets (not least that there were people who loved me, however moody and deluded I could be). I also made some progress. I had some modest successes—some elements of life that I did manage to change.

It took me a long time to realize that I had no choice but to reach an accommodation with myself and the world. I came to understand that inner mess and confusion wasn't some aberration that I should always strive to overcome. It is, rather, a characteristic of incarnation on Earth. I was human. I was a rich, bubbling stew.

As I searched for the answers of how to cope with my own problems, I gradually became aware that I was not the only one in this predicament. I began to wonder whether it was not part of the human condition to suffer from a perennial, smouldering, now-you-see-me-now-you-don't identity crisis.

6

Each To His Own
Identity Crisis

While I was wandering around trying to sort out who I was I talked to many people, sometimes, within weekend workshops, on a profound and intimate level. I learned that I was far from being the only one to have a slow-burning, near-perpetual identity crisis. Most of us have doubts and questions around our identity, even if we daren't voice them.

There are, it must be added, fortunate people who do not doubt who they are. They stay put, near where they were born and close to their families; they have steady jobs that they like; and they live well. For them, stability and security is the norm and rebellion never a consideration. It is of no interest to them.

Crisis is never far away from any of us. Even if you don't have your own identity crisis, the crises of other people affect you. Apparently stable individuals can turn out to be seething volcanoes of uncertainty inside. Plenty of people live in anguish, covering up their existential panic with drink, drugs, pills, or other palliatives. You may be settled in yourself, but any member of your family or one of your friends may be living in silent confusion.

How many mental disorders, I wonder, stem from self-doubt? How many atrocities are caused by loners who have entirely lost their social bearings; who would rather go out in notoriety than live any longer as a nobody?

I would be surprised if there is anyone on the planet who hasn't had the occasional doubt; who hasn't looked at the door or the horizon and asked himself what it would be like to jack it all in, walk away, and never come back; who hasn't wondered what it would be like to be someone else, somewhere else. A few people actually do it.

Contemporary living can easily alienate people from themselves. The lucky ones enjoy freedom and purchasing power while the unlucky ones wonder what is wrong with them. Weighing down on all of us are a range of forces that want to turn us into units of production and political control rather than cherish our individuality. Footlooseness and 24-hour connectivity make it harder to stick to the forms of identity that we have always known. The threat of climate change, meanwhile, seems like a question mark hanging over our entire species. It is almost as if there is a collective identity crisis brewing in the human race. If we are to survive, we may be obliged to ask the question in unison: Who on earth are *we*?

To sort ourselves out, individually and collectively, we need to come to some realizations. The first of these is that we are all much the same. We ask the same kind of questions:

- How is it that I am here at all? Where do I come from?
- Why am I as I am?
- Why are other people not like me? (and perhaps, Why can't I change them to match me?)
- What am I doing with my life? (or what have I done with my life?). How did I become *this*? Is *this* the best option.
- How far can I choose what I am? Dare I change the things I don't like? Where am I going? Shouldn't I act now before it is too late?
- And so forth.

Likewise, many of us feel the same set of emotions around identity, including:

- Victimhood and sense of injustice
- Pride in our family or our rank
- Arrogance or guilt for being born into privilege
- Contentment or resentment towards duty.
- Fear of losing our position in society, being demoted.

To make sense of ourselves and find some answers we can divide our identity into five parts:

- **Learned Identity**: the identity that we are taught.

- **Discovered Identity**: the identity that we find out about en route through life. For example, to realize that you are gay or adopted or have a talent that is revealed through opportunity.

- **Decided Identity**: the identity that results from choices we make, to take a job, get married, have kids, and so on.

- **Circumstantial Identity or Chance**: identity that derives from events not in our control, such as an accident, a decision taken by someone else, the international situation, and so on.

- **Declined or Anti-identity Identity**: the opportunities we did not take—identity defined by that which we did not do, whether out of fear or laziness. We may or may not have meant to do them, it doesn't matter: they remain in our minds parallel possibilities that were not realized. We hesitated too long, or fudged the decision, or declined outright. This is also the identity of regret or relief—a phantom form of ourselves that can haunt the present with "what ifs" or "if onlys."

Of these, there is only one that we have direct control over: the identity of decisions that we make through our own free will. This, to simplify things, reduces ultimately to a choice between two options: to stay or to go.

Given that we are social creatures and our identity is intimately tied up with the various overlapping groups from humanity downwards, we each face the same situation in different forms and contexts throughout our lives. How do act as part of each group we belong to?

We are always subject to two warring urges within ourselves when we find ourselves in a group: to fit in or to stand out. There are risks and rewards, advantages and disadvantages, to each strategy.

The normal, default option is to conform to the group. Conformity brings company and comfort. In return, it demands some compromise of individuality, the surrender of complete freedom, and most people manage this with more or less good grace. Group cohesion demands that members adhere to the rules and obey orders. They may indulge in small protests but must not take these too far.

Conformity is a form of self-denial; the alternative is to distinguish yourself in some way, to stand out from the rest—as if you were someone special, with more identity than them. This may mean promoting yourself as a leader or asserting your individuality. It can be hard work being different; it is certainly much easier to fit in than to struggle. It could go either way: you could be popular and get showered with honours, or you could be made to feel unwelcome, a misfit who has effectively excluded himself from his peer group. In which case you have to find another group that will have you.

The consequence of this is that we are cast, in our different social contexts, as either settlers or wanderers, conformists or pioneers. Every society needs both in proportion: a bulk of those stay put and get practical things done, spiced by a pinch of immigrants who arrive with fresh ideas. The newcomers prevent the host group from becoming culturally (and perhaps also in a literal genetic sense) inbred. Identity crises, which frequently cause disaffected individuals to break away and travel, could be described as the engine of human evolution. (The only catch in all this is that we cannot necessarily all rebel at the same time or else there is a risk that the structures of society may be loosened or torn apart.)

In other words, an identity crisis is not necessarily a bad thing, a traumatic process that no one sane would wish to have to go through. Instead, it can be the initiation of a period of questioning and searching. A crisis, by definition, is a turning point, which is an opportunity. If I had not been shaken loose from my moorings—or rather shaken myself loose—I would not have been able to discover new seas.

Somehow, I discovered that I didn't have to drift; I could row. Eventually it dawned on me that the question of my identity might not be an irritant in the way of my happiness but the point of life (or one of them). Doubting myself was not a symptom of a lost and neurotic mind; it was a way of getting down to my real work on Earth.

Identity ties us to the planet. Can we not see life on Earth as a cosmic treasure hunt, with a single question serving as all the clues?

Even if this question of mine cannot be comprehensively answered—and would any of us really want that?—merely by asking it we may be able to find where we want to go.

Why Would You
Want to Know?

Whether or not you are undergoing an identity crisis, there are some good reasons to get to know yourself. This might seem like an egocentric, navel-gazing way of wasting your time, but actually it is the complete opposite. To ask the question "Who am I?" is to take a step towards invaluable self-awareness. I can think of at least seven benefits to be derived from it, and certainly more.

You can't know anything if you don't know who you are

All knowledge is based on a tacit assumption that seems obvious to the point of stupidity when it is stated: that we can know facts and communicate them to each other.

The trouble is we are subjective creatures, each locked into himself, and for a fact to be known, shared, and agreed upon it must be objective. The two things—subjective self and objective fact—are hard to tally.

Our modern system of empiricism and reason (which together constitute science) depends on our being able to maintain distance from knowledge, to separate it from ourselves, so that we can make emotionally neutral pronouncements about it. We behave as if there are truths "out there" that have nothing to do with us until we come along and sweep them up.

In doing so, we gloss over the premise that there is a *who* doing the asking, knowing, and making sense. If a premise of a system is questionable, its conclusions cannot be relied upon.

Science is never impersonal. The observer is always a participant in reality. He has a life that leads him up to the point of experiment or discovery. He or someone else chooses which bit of reality to look at and how it should be looked at.

The conventional approach to knowledge works well enough for relatively simplistic phenomena—observing the inert world, chemical reactions, and mechanical processes—but it leads us into false certainty when we turn our attention to ourselves. When science makes pronouncements on human nature and human behaviour it is delivering judgements rather than stating impartial information.

This business of subjectivity is not an obtuse and trivial point. One of the greatest puzzles left in science is the mind-body problem: how the sensation of "you" inside you interacts with the physical world. All our knowledge and understanding of the universe rests on this subjective-objective split we all experience every day. We cannot put off solving it until later and still claim to be sure of what we know. We cannot have sense if we do not who is making it or how.

There is no shortcut. We need to know ourselves. At the very least we need to proceed with humility and caution and be alert for the times when self-knowledge (subjectivity) trumps learning and experimental data (objectivity).

Medicine provides a very clear illustration of this. Every patient experiences moments of knowing his condition better than his doctor, who sees it through the filter of disease classification and clinical research. Complementary medicine, for all the criticism heaped on it, recognizes this and uses self-knowledge as a tool for healing.

Another instance is climate change. Experts can present us with graphs telling us what is going to happen, but it is up to 7 billion souls to decide whether or not to take action. The solution will not only be in the facts but also in the feelings. The survival of the human world may hang on whether we each regard ourselves as worthwhile or worthless. If the latter, we may surrender to fatalism. We would do well to get to know ourselves first, before we decide.

Getting to know ourselves, therefore, cannot be left to social function after we have done the science; it must precede it, or go alongside it.

To know yourself is to be free

To get to know yourself is to become free; as free, that is, as you can be within the constraints of being human. It is to bring as much as possible of yourself into consciousness and know what choice you have. It is to know the difference between:

- speculation and fantasy, and the reality of you
- the fixed elements of your identity and those that can be changed
- your conditioning and the consequences of the decisions of your free will
- the forces within your control and those beyond your control
- psychological "projection" on other people (assuming them to be a certain way) and clear-headed social intercourse

Where you are blind and where you see clearly, giving you, for instance, the confidence to act on your intuition.

It is to become aware of your resources and your potential, and to assume responsibility for what you do with them. It is, in short, to become fully incarnate and not look for easy ways out of self-examination, such as retreating into a rigid dogma or technological comforts, or anything to avoid self-examination. It is to realize that you are on your own. If there is such a thing as security it must lie in knowing yourself, all of you.

Freeing yourself makes you a better, more effective person

Setting yourself free though self-awareness is not only good for you, it is good for the rest of us. It makes you a more effective person, able to contribute more to the world.

The freer you are, and the better you feel inside yourself, the less you have to prove, the less you need to draw attention to yourself, the less your attitude gets in the way, the less you block progress. Instead of imposing yourself on others, you look for ways you can help.

This may be as simple as making decisions with a more ample and generous perspective; being co-operative instead of competitive; looking for points of agreement, whether or not they suit you; simply keeping quiet and allowing people to speak their own truths.

To consciously "own" your own identity is to take responsibility for it—to be visible and recognized. It is not to hide in anonymity or allow yourself to be subsumed into a large organization, which acts on the world with corporate indifference.

To be effective may mean to take a pioneering, even unpopular, stance on something you believe to be right. Knowing yourself and feeling your freedom give you courage to break from the pack. No advance is possible unless some people are able to do this, motivated not by ambition but by quiet faith in themselves. Society otherwise becomes fossilized. Being secure in your identity is the only way to engage in politics without getting lost or corrupted.

On a more mundane level, knowing yourself makes you feel better about your limitations and the compromises you have to make to live on Earth. It stops you yo-yoing between two ineffectual extremes: paralyzing guilt ("I should be doing something to help other people/the planet") and devious self-justification ("What's the point?/Why should I bother?/The problem is too great, even insoluble and my contribution wouldn't make any difference to anyone").

You can't know anyone else if you don't know yourself

Knowing yourself is the precursor to sympathy and empathy: to really believe that you could have, in only a slight reconfiguration of the universe, been born in the other's skin. The separation we create between ourselves and anyone we dislike or disapprove of is an artificial one; it reassures us of our own goodness but tricks us into thinking in terms of black and white.

From self-interrogation, however, flows interest in the other, even if we don't like him, followed by understanding. It makes you see how easy it is to label someone and casually dismiss them rather than seek the truth of them.

Instead of being baffled by human behaviour, and judging and condemning it from superiority, you are able to ask yourself, "What is inside me that might help me understand him or her?"

We all have the same ingredients inside, mixed in differing proportions, but some of us choose not to know about the unpleasant ones. By admitting to ourselves who we are, we remind ourselves that things are not always as clear as they first seem. We are multifaceted creatures full of contradictions and confusions. Too often we cover up the anguish this causes by proclaiming that we are right and the other person/other community/other nation or even the world is wrong.

To comprehend your own nuances and subtleties is to grant respect, to allow the other to be as he is. It is, by extension, to allow the possibility of reform and repentance, so badly needed in most criminal justice systems.

This is not some limp excuse for all antisocial behaviour; it is merely a step toward separating the doer from the deed, to pause for a moment in order to understand by internal reference, without immediately condoning or exonerating.

The opposite of understanding is bigotry and discrimination: the denial of the equal right to have an identity to a person inside another skin, whose religion is different, who espouses ideas you disagree with. If you know who you are, you know that someone else's claim to identity does not cancel yours out.

Self-knowledge is the source of ethics

Self-understanding is the root of ethics. All moral decisions are by definition difficult. There is no right and wrong. Every situation we face is unique; every choice is ours alone. We can take advice, but no one else can know how we see things. The only point of reference we have is our inner self, what used to be called our conscience. From the outside it might look easy, as if there is no choice at all; inside, however, is entirely different. Only I know the difficulties surrounding such decisions, particularly my weak spots—how I can be tempted, bribed, compromised, or corrupted. If I don't know who I am and how I operate, what I aspire to and what I need to be wary of, I won't know how to choose between any two moral judgements. This is particularly important in the raising of children. If I haven't got my internal ethics at least a little sorted out, how can I pass them on to my offspring?

Self-knowledge fosters variety and creativity

The more I discover about myself, the more I form a conception of what I share with others and what sets me apart. I come to identify my unique talents and perspective of reality. Knowing myself gives me the confidence to be my most creative self. The best inspiration comes from our individuality; if not, we end up recycling the same ideas within a limited permissible pool. Exploring yourself is a way of drawing from a new well rather than recycling depleted waters.

From creativity—in all areas of life, not just art—flows variety, different ways to do things. Variety, in serious and contested matters, offers a choice of solutions. Knowing ourselves therefore leads to greater exploitation of the latent ingenuity of the human race.

Self-knowledge is the antidote to alienation

Modern living has a great many compensations, but it also has a tendency to alienate us—to make us feel detached from nature, society, and human caring; to make us feel that we do not matter.

To celebrate our individual identities, to remind ourselves that we are who we are not what *they* tell us we are, is the only way to combat this force.

To know ourselves is to reclaim our souls

It is almost taboo in this increasingly secular age to talk of our metaphysical natures, certainly in public, if you want to be taken seriously in a developed country. Many people are uncomfortable discussing things that aren't proven (or even provable), and the prevailing consensus is that we should keep our beliefs private.

As scientific materialism tries to reduce man to substance (only matter matters), we have literally become engaged in a war for our souls, for the right to be more than we appear to be.

We are even in danger of losing the vocabulary of higher thinking. The word "soul" (in its literal sense) has gone out of fashion among rational people. They are afraid to even whisper the word "soul" because of its religious connotations. To ignore or deny a concept, however, is not to do away with it. We lessen ourselves if we think we can do without soul or an equivalent. Replacement names, notably mind and psyche, hint at the same idea but do not quite capture it and are equally vague.

That our souls are of no interest or use to science, politicians, and marketers should be enough to make us want to go in search of them.

PART B

Outside In

8

Let Me Introduce Myself

The next chapters set out what I know about my identity, and by implication yours. Each chapter looks at a different aspect of me: a form that I am known to the world or to myself, and a way that I can describe and explain myself to you. The chapters go together in a particular order to tell the human story, from the superficial to the supernatural, but there is no reason why you shouldn't treat them as semiautonomous essays to be dipped into as you wish.

I have written the book in the first person for three good reasons:

1. I wouldn't want to suggest that I know you better than you know yourself, which would have been the effect of pitching it in the second person (you). The first person is also a way for me to own up to who I am. If, as you are reading it, you are able to think as the "I" and "me" as referring to you, the communication between my brain and yours will be that much more direct.

2. By keeping the text to the first person, I also get around a potential problem. Although I hope I am articulating some universal truths here, I do not have the power or the right to say anything accurate and meaningful about anyone else, specifically someone whose circumstances are different to mine: female, gay, wheelchair bound, and so on. I have, nevertheless, tried to at least mention as many variations on the individual human being as possible.

3. I am not putting forward a philosophy of self or a scientific theory, for which impersonal third-person register would have been more appropriate. I could have written a compilation of answers other people have given to the question, but that is not the book I wanted to write. Instead, I have based my authority on firsthand experience and knowledge. I have tried, as far as possible, to make my own observations and pursue my own thoughts. This does not mean that I have not drawn on sources of information and inspiration (cited in the notes or in the bibliography), whether to confirm my conclusions or to challenge me to rethink them.

Another problem is less easy to work around. English is automatically sexist when it comes to the use of the third person: it has to be either a he or a she. Neither is satisfactory, and all proposed solutions seem forced to me. For consistency only, my hypothetical third persons are all "he's," but I hope, as you read, that you will imagine 50 percent of them as female.

All of which has carried me a long way from my starting point. When I first read the letter from my bank, my first urge was to complain of the folly behind it. Now I see how grateful I should be to that unknown policymaker in an office somewhere for bringing such a crucial question to the front of my mind. Lessons in wisdom—or at least invitations to inner sojourns—can come from even the most unexpected source. After all those years spent in intellectual search, earnest discussion, listening to and reading about spiritual teachers, interpreting numinous texts, participating workshops, and it is my bank manager who delivers the proverbial satori slap on my face to wake me into consciousness.

"Who on earth am I?" Good question. Where do I begin to answer it? At the beginning, of course, with the habitual description of me. With that aspect of my identity that can be pronounced and printed. With the reflexive response to the question, "What do they call you?" I'll tell you what they call me, then I will tell you everything else about me. And, by extension, about you.

9

The Nominated Me

· · · · ·

READ THE LABEL

I am, to begin with, a name. It is the first thing I will tell you if we meet or that you will be told about me in my absence. It may well precede me in a phrase, such as, "You must meet . . . ," "I'm sending you to see . . . ," or You know . . . ?"

It may be the only detail you retain about me when our association ends. "The name is familiar," you say years from now, when prompted. "Didn't he live in that house, go to my school, know my sister, write that book . . . ?" Or more probably, "But I can't remember his face or anything about him."

My name sums me up. It is mine for life (unless I choose to change it), but it is not my name at all. I did not arrive with it. It predates me. It was chosen for me, prepared, waiting until I was born. It was the first gift I was given in life, whether or not I wanted it. I couldn't refuse it. It was insisted upon, and I learned to answer to it, just as a dog learns to answer when called.

Really, I have no name. I never have had, and never will. Like the stars and the birds and everything in creation, we are nameless. Just as there are no countries marked on the landscape, no indelible distinction of your tribal land from mine, so names are human contrivances for human purposes—temporary devices to make it seem as if we are the ones in charge here.

Therefore my name is not attached to *me*; it only refers to me. It is a label easily detached, a category name for the container; by itself, it tells you nothing about me.

In itself, my name is bare and describes nothing. It is a signpost, a metaphor, an arrangement of sound and lines. It is mere code, a convenience, a formula, a string of letters, a hollow sound, a meaningless proper noun, a hyperlink that leads to me as long as the code behind the icon remains correct. No wonder it sometimes sounds strange to me and there are states of mind in which it can seem like something alien, nothing to do with me at all.

I do not carry this name for my benefit. I don't use it much. I do not, myself, need a name. I am only obliged to remember it when I am asked for it or wish to claim possession of something. "I" will do for me when I am alone. You and I, together with no one else present, can manage without it: "you" would be enough; there could be no confusion. My loved ones may not need a name for me, either. To my children, for example, I am simply "Dad."

My name is therefore for other tongues to speak and hands to write; it is a convenience provided for third parties. They do what they want with it; I may have little sanction. I may try to correct them, or ask them to use it differently, but I can't oblige them to do so.

I have to trust them to nurture my name and keep it alive. It needs to be sung into use if it is to survive. It will last only as long as it is used—as long as there are human beings around who know what it means and care about it. Otherwise (eventually), it will lapse. When the material substance it refers to—me—is gone and forgotten, the batteries will run down from lack of use and will not be revived. Just as a long-held address passes into new hands, maybe some one else will one day possess my name with no knowledge of its previous owner.

I should feel honoured to be singled out in this way. It is reassuring to be awarded a name. It is a special item of language, one with a clear and specific meaning. It is a very personal and proper pronoun, and its application is duly rationed.

We cannot give everyone and everything particular names or we would forget most of them. We only give names and identities to people (and animals and sometimes objects) who are significant, however ephemeral they are.

We are quick to name a child who lives for only a few days, and we name the animals who live with us but avoid naming the animals we intend to slaughter and eat. My name humanizes me, allows me to believe that I exist and that I matter.

Because a name confers favour, we take great care how we refer to evil. Wanton villains and monsters do not usually have names (certainly not when they hunt in packs) or else we risk treating them as beings like us and sympathizing with their predicaments. Only when we are sure of our opprobrium do we name the target of it.

We retain and use only the names of beings we value and intend to have protracted dealings with. We may not bother to find out the name of the neighbour we don't like. We probably don't want to know the identity of a tramp who reminds us of our own fragile good fortune; and we cannot possibly ask for the names of the starving and dispossessed billions who we can only think of as a mass. They live and die anonymously, as far as I am concerned.

Conversely, to know my name and deliberately not to use it is an effective way to dehumanize and demean me. If this is your intention you may want to replace my name with a number, so that I can be referred to as if I were a spare part of machinery.

My name was not granted to me altruistically, without conditions. There are several reasons why I have been given it:

- **For convenience, to sum up the otherwise unidentifiable "me."** It describes and delineates me: a certified stamp on a packing case of genetic material. By the act of naming me I became a recognizable, discrete, and later autonomous entity. I was also placed in context. My name makes clear which family I belong to, which territory I came from, my social status, how I should be treated, and so on.

- **To get my attention when called or addressed in writing.** I learned as a child that people liked me to respond to my name; it made them smile, or at least made them less severe. This ensured I got fed and looked after and even loved. It also works to my benefit. Hearing my name in times of crisis, reassures me that there is a link between me and the person who is willing to utter it.

- **As an instrument of power.** If I am a dictator, I wield the power: I transmit orders in my name. In all other cases, people use it to wield power over me. In childhood it was a way of staking paternity/maternity over me, or even ownership. My parents and teachers used it as a means to tell me what to do or not to do and to chastise me when I ran foul of instructions. Bullies used it to specify me and personalize their taunts—to pick me out in order to pick on me. Since then, my name has proved useful to anyone who wants to exert authority over me, formally or informally. To hear it, isolates me from everyone else. It triggers responsibility and guilt, so that I can be made to punish myself. It is easier to pin blame on me and harder for me to shrug it off if I am named. My name can be used to caress me or to hurt me, depending on how it is said, depending on the gesture of the hand that accompanies it. The bureaucrat uses my name in a particular way. With it he arranges me, in alphabetical order, in the filing cabinet or in order of priority on a list. This is how I can be accounted for, politically controlled, and taxed.

- **To direct praise and love.** An award certificate is meaningless if it is made out to no one in particular, and I would not feel loved by someone who didn't know my name.

- **To express requests and needs.** Those who can't tell me what to do have to ask. If they ask anyone who is listening, I can pretend I am not listening. If they ask me by name, I may well feel obliged to respond.

- **To oblige me to take care of what is mine.** If I acquire a possession, it passes into my name and that is the only way its rightful owner can be identified.

- **For referring to me in the third person**, usually when I am absent. It is useful to know my name if you want to talk about me, to quote me or judge me, praise me or curse me. To say "him" or "those people" (lumping me with others in a category) doesn't have the same precision or force.

My name serves all these purposes because it has four important properties:

1. **Continuity**. It doesn't change, and as such is a way of maintaining my identity through time. Most people keep their names for life—and beyond. A name can be changed but only rarely, as it is a radical step. If I changed my name daily it would not be of much use. Anyone who truly lives in the eternal present probably doesn't need an enduring name; the rest of us do.

2. **Commonality**. My name is communally agreed upon, a currency universally honoured. A name ensures that we are all talking about the same person. Society would break down if we all used nicknames for each other.

3. **Singularity**. My name is, at least locally, unique. It sets me apart from other people, makes me an individual. It indicates me and me alone. It is synonymous with my skin. It is what separates me from everything else, the boundary between us. It is confusing to have more than one person with the same forename or surname in a group or community, and some system has to be invented to restore their divisibility.

4. **Plurality**. Depending on the culture and status, a name is likely to be adaptable to requirements. I have a forename, middle names, and a surname that can be used singly or in combinations to suit different circumstances. I can also use my initials, and I may take a pseudonym for a specific reason. Other people may give me nicknames, out of affection or frivolity or malice. In addition, my name may be embellished front and back with abbrevia-

tions to invoke a level of formality (Mr.) or to inspire respect (my university degree). That makes a lot of ways for me to describe myself or for you to address me.

In the process of living, my name is turned into a transporter of predicates. Like a magnet it attracts what is placed next to it. First, the circumstances of my entry into life are associated with it—my family, date of birth, and so on—and gradually everything that happens to me is appended as medals or scars: my schooling, my behaviour, my achievements, my work record, my addresses, my coupling and procreation, and so on. Depending on the context, the specifics don't have to be given: my name acts as shorthand for all these items.

Moreover, in people's minds (and in mine), my name crackles with emotional resonance. You hear my name and a feeling is provoked in you that leads to one of three basic reactions: a desire to see me, a need to keep your distance (out of fear or repulsion), or indifference.

My name says a lot in a few letters, but in itself it is a useless piece of information. To activate it you need to attach it to something. And that can only be one thing, because I am only one thing: some body.

10

The Incorporated Me

· · · · ·

If I have a name but I am not my name, then I can only be I this thing you can see: my body. Really the last sentence is a tautology. "I" implies that I am incarnate, but I can't shake the notion, perhaps a myth, of *having* a body rather than *being* one.

I have good reason for regarding my body as a semi-separate part of me: it seems to know what it has to do while I do not. It is as if it has been left in my possession temporarily, to look after, without me being expected to do much except top it up with food and keep it clean. For the most part, it operates entirely without my conscious supervision. It reacts before I realize what it has done. It repairs itself as much as it can. I feel as if it, rather than me, is responsible for how it is, even if I take the credit or the shame for its appearance.

Whether it is me or mine, a container or container-and-contents combined, my body is a robotic presence that moves me around the world. It is a visible object that speaks for itself. It is the always-on, giveaway me that requires no effort of interpretation on your part, no cultural tools.

Naturally, it shares the basic characteristics of all concrete objects in existence.

It occupies space (rarely the same space for any length of time) and is localizable. This may sound obvious, but it is possible (I think) for my mind not to be in the same place as my body.

Although somewhat irregular in shape, it is built to symmetric pattern and has measurable dimensions: a height that remains constant for several decades, and a number of widths. It also has a fluctuating weight, and other readings can be taken from it with specialized instruments. If I want to know the crude facts about it, I can always get a medical checkup.

It is a fairly complex object, akin to a machine, but I wouldn't push this analogy too far. As such, it is both a whole and a composition of parts. This can make a complete description of it tricky. You can take an overview, but that won't tell you much; or you can cut me open and sort and stack my organs to arrive at an inventory. There again, you won't have the whole thing any more.

It is understood through the senses: it can be seen, heard, and felt—and smelled and tasted, if you dare. Touch is a particularly good way to find your way around its contours. I must have a particular feel to me, or perhaps how I feel depends on your hands.

In its amenability to sensory explanation it is similar to a lot of other objects in existence, with one big exception: it has got me inside it.

I find it hard to be objective about my body because I am sensing it mostly from within, as the fulcrum of all its nerve endings, although I can get a sense of what you see, if I use mirrors and cameras. I have also had much more time than you to become familiar with it. I have had the chance to experience it in many different conditions. In some ways I may know it better than you, but approaching it fresh you may notice distinguishing marks that I am not aware of.

Either the overview or the anatomical dissection will make it clear that I am not just any object; I am an animate one. I grow and decay over time. My body developed without any help from an egg and sperm at conception to what it is today.

It has changed greatly since I was born, especially in the first 15 years or so, and will carry on changing until, for whatever reason, it goes over a threshold of no return. As it decomposes—as my hair goes grey or falls out, my teeth slide out of alignment or come loose, my skin wrinkles and sags, my muscles diminish—my identity will evolve. This will happen even if I protest that I still feel as if I am 29. It is curious to think that there must have been a moment of transition, a split second, when it switched from overall growth to overall decay.

This deterioration is ultimately inevitable, but the rate at which it happens and the way in which the program proceeds will not be the same for me as they are for someone else. This partly depends on my body and partly on how well I care for it.

Other events can intervene in my body, adding to its characteristics. These can include those that are out of my control, such as disfigurement, disability, and chronic illness, as well as those that I inflict on myself, such as a tattoo or cosmetic surgery.

You and I will probably agree that I am more than just an animate object; I am a human object. I hope you will not treat me merely as an example of our species. You will undoubtedly see me in your own way, your view coloured by your own interests, but I hope you will grant me individuality.

You may well vary your study of me according to whether you desire my body or are repulsed by it. Chances are that you will also compare it to your own body, and to some theoretical idea of human perfection, so that you can state how far I deviate from the norm.

I wonder how deeply you will try to see me? It takes much less time and effort to see a human being superficially than to see him as a visible body and something more.

A great deal of information passes between us without either of us being aware of it. My body behaves for the most part involuntarily, with only a little dictation from me. Its—my—behaviour has been shaped over the years, so that if you look in the right way you will be able to see particular gestures, ticks, and habits that signify me. It also traps past experience and emotion, and with insight you may be able to see where tension has accumulated. You might also want to look at what I am not. My body betrays how in or out of shape I am and which muscles I do or do not use, although for a balanced appraisal you would have to observe me in various states, active and passive. All this adds further to my dynamic physical description.

To see me, however, you will need to notice but not be overly distracted by another aspect of body identity. All of the above ignores the fact that we don't see much of each other's bodies. I usually show you only what I want you to see. Mostly, my body appears in heavy disguise, covered by clothes (including footwear). With rare moments of exception—when I am alone or in a moment of intimacy—I hide parts of my body to comply with social norms of prudery and out of practicality (for warmth and protection). Coarse clothes in monotonous colours would meet these two ends, but I never wear them. I dress myself with far more devious strategies in mind.

I clothe this body in a particular way—intentionally, if possible, but sometimes unintentionally—according to my means, my taste, and the availability of choice. See my wardrobe, and you see me.

Clothes provide me with a superbly flexible identity: superimposed, temporary, superficial, and adjustable. They are a display—a prêt-a-porter plumage—and I use them for effect: to get a reaction or discourage one. I dress partly to bolster how I feel about myself but mostly to show other people who I think I am.

Most of us pay great attention to the code of clothes. On a basic level, clothes separate us according to whether we are male or female, rich or poor, high status or low, successful or failing, powerful or subservient, members or outcasts, and so on.

Clothes undermine equality—that is the whole point of them. No two people can be equals while they are clothed differently; only nakedness strips away faked identity.

Apart from serving these distinctions, my clothes can be made to do plenty more. I may dress to hide my personality; to create a distance or to mislead, attract, or dazzle you; to make it clear what I think I am (even it's false); or to declare that I don't care what I look like.

Certain clothes come with a built-in perceived theatrical identity, but it is easy to fool us. Our expectations and behaviour change according to the costume. We wouldn't want our tribal shaman to conduct sacred rites in his everyday dress. A white coat makes a doctor, a suit and tie a businessman, conferring through the material wisdom, experience, competence, sobriety, and authority of whatever quality is required. It is almost as if the clothes replace the "real" identity of the person who wears them. This is the intention of a uniform: to suppress individuality (and with it, extracurricular personal responsibility) and instil esprit de corps in the wearer. A uniform, like a mask, enables us not only to look like someone we are not but to feel as if we have slipped into another skin.

I can change the wrapper as much as I want, because it is only temporary. I am more limited in what I can do to the body underneath. Still less can I alter two intangible products—forms of natural communication—that rise out of me and pervade the surrounding air.

11

The Vocal Me

· · · · ·

If I open my mouth you can identify me with your ears. My body is capable of making a range of sounds—mostly percussive—but it is my voice that is most versatile and distinctive. No one else has one quite like mine. What I can and cannot do with it—my control of it or lack of control: this is the me you have if you are near me but not touching me and you close your eyes.

Forget your preconceptions for a moment, and put aside the cultural overlay that makes you ready to extract information from me through your ears. To begin with, just listen to me without judgement, as a maker of sound without sense.

What you hear is my body speaking. I am capable of producing a particular range of sounds, depending on how I breathe, the emotions I feel, and how much control I try to exert. They are formed, with or without my conscious direction, by inhaling air through my nostrils and mouth, down my trachea into my lungs, and expanding my diaphragm, then exhaling air back up from my lungs and diaphragm in bellows fashion, through my trachea, larynx, and vocal chords, squeezing it out between palate and tongue, and refining it with my mouth, lips, and teeth.

I am simultaneously source, echo chamber, and amplifier. I send out waves into the air that cannot be recaptured or unmade. Sometimes I care where they go; occasionally I do not. Maybe you will get a better sense of who I am if I think you are not within earshot.

I can make a range of meaningless sounds that are particular to me. I cry and laugh in my own idiosyncratic ways, and I have a repertoire of other expressions to suit the occasion. I am capable of producing sounds that I have not yet made. You may hear them if I am forced into some extreme situation—or they may never be articulated.

I try to ensure that most of the sounds I make are deliberate. There are two uses that I reserve my voice for, as far as I can. These add immense richness to the sound picture that you can make with me.

The first application of my voice is speech. Sound is our only direct, portable form of communication—except for people who know sign language—and it is key to the transmission of complex messages that are not only full of intended meaning but also feeling. Words are a direct communication from my brain to yours, conjuring up images—more direct than writing. If I read this text to you aloud, it would have an extra dimension to it. It would be like my mind talking into yours. If I am not present to do so, you read it in your head using your own voice or an imaginary voice, not mine.

My voice may range from a whisper to a shout, but I keep those sound effects for occasions when I require them. Most of the time I simply talk more or less loudly. In this way, you can get an idea of the quality of my voice, its pitch, tone, timbre, and so on, and how well I pronounce my words. This last depends on the language I learned in childhood: I may find it hard to make the necessary sounds in a foreign language. My accent is certainly a distinguishing mark, and it could make the difference between you getting my meaning or not.

How I speak my message, therefore, may be as important as the message itself.

Sound and speech convey (or betray) our emotions. You can tell when I am nervous by the way my voice is modulated. You could almost map out my responses to different life situations according to the changes in my tone and volume of voice.

Sometimes, my sounds can reveal far more than their intended meaning. I may, for instance, recount some personal tragedy as if it were funny or present some petty fact with sadness in my voice. It is up to you to make of such confusion what you will. With intuition or training, you can learn to see the emotions behind the play-acting that I do in order to survive in the world and not be found out. If you tell me that I am angry, say, because you can hear it in my voice, I may well deny it but react instinctively by slurring or swallowing my words, or snapping back at you.

Normally, speech is a spontaneous thing of proximity. You can see me as I talk, so that sounds, words, and appearance all go together. Technology, however, has created another possibility and greatly altered our idea of vocal identity. Whereas for most of human history the farthest we could yell or yodel was across a field or from one hilltop to the next, the invention of recording equipment, the telephone, and radio did away with the relationship between sound and location. We are still learning to cope with the effects of this shift. Now there are plenty of people around, or who are long dead, who we think we know something about because we know what they sound or sounded like.

We routinely deal with people through phone lines and satellites for whom we don't have a face. If you speak to me in such an artificial manner, you will find that I have a subset of my vocal identity that I have honed for this purpose. Without visual clues, you have no choice but to take me at the "face value" of sound, and I have to be careful not to confuse you.

The other way I use my voice is to sing. We can all sing; however, it is widely held that some of us sing better than others, whether the algorithm we use is the mathematics of music (I am either in tune or I am not) or the subjectivity of human pleasure (either I am pleasant to listen to or I am not).

If you can bear to listen to me sing for any length of time, you will be able to gauge a lot about my character. My song choice; the occasions on which I sing; whether I hum or know all the words—all of these offer clues to my identity.

Unlike speech, singing is not primarily about the exchange of chat or information; it is the communication of feeling. It draws physically on the storage areas of emotions in the body. If I sing and truly feel what I am singing about, you will get the same sensation somewhere in your body, and both of us will have shared something without the need to engage our rational brains.

So far, I have been doing nothing but making noise, but there is another part to my sound identity that must be mentioned: those times when I am silent. The absence of sounds counts just as much as its presence. There are many reasons for my voice to stay silent, and behind each of them is a state of mind encapsulating a piece of who I am. I may be at peace, alone, or in company. I may be listening to you speak.

In silence, I can hear sound in my head. It doesn't sound the same as it does in my ears, but the two are close. What I notice in my head is that although sound is an ephemeral thing—mostly used for things of no lasting consequence that are uttered and then "die"—it can be profound and enduring, living on in my memory in a very primal way. I remember the voices of people I am no longer in touch with; even more than that, I remember those whom I have loved who are now dead. I can clearly hear them speaking to me: the things they said and how they said them. These people are nowhere near me in the present, nor are they sitting in front of a microphone; yet they have an ethereal reality to them, exactly as if they were broadcasting to me from some unknown location. Their voices haunt me and keep them alive for me. They are less dead as long as my memory preserves their sound. Voice is life; it is carried on the breath.

Sound, at least, can be summoned up in the memory and can also be recorded. But there is another emanation from my body that is even more fleeting and mysterious.

12

The Stinking Me

· · · · ·

COME CLOSER, DOWNWIND

One good way of identifying me is with your nose. Come close, just downwind. Lean towards me. Breathe in. Now tell me what you think. You should get something that is uniquely me.

I suppose that I smell. I couldn't tell you for certain, but I strongly suspect that I do. I know that I make smells involuntarily, such as when I am sweating. Corroborating evidence comes from other people. They either move in closer, or screw up their noses.

Human beings are animals. All animals produce body scents. Logically, then, as animals, we too produce odours; we cannot help it. To stay alive and grow we have to ingest and synthesize volatile chemical compounds that are fated to produce gases as they break down. These have got to go somewhere. Either they stay within us or leak out of us.

This thought—that we are stinking animals—seems to upset or even horrify some people. Stink is anathema to civilization. We associate it with dirt, lack of hygiene, manual labour, unrefined pastimes, and corporality. To be detectable by your smell is offensive; it drives people away.

We do our best not to smell like the animals we are. Sometime in our evolutionary past, we decided that we didn't need our sense of smell as much as previously. Maybe it was when we stopped grooming each other, or else when the smell of fire drowned out all other smells.

Having given up the skill of nasal recognition we were still left with the stench, and for most of human history only the rich could ever hope to escape it. Now that we are modern, we all claim the right not to smell like beasts. We try to hide the presence of our excreted fluids and either not to smell at all or smell of something better than ourselves.

Simply washing, we have found, changes our olfactory presence for the better. Things are improved even further by using perfumed, largely synthetic products. We then apply more purchased chemicals as sprays, powders, and creams. When

I say, "You smell good," I don't mean you—I mean you smell as your perfumer rather than your maker intended. You might sum up my reeking self, therefore, not by commenting on the functioning of my glands but on the brands to be found in my washbag and bathroom cabinet. No bad smells come through the pictures in glossy adverts in magazines or from the fantasy lives on television. That is exactly how we like it. When we envision the good life, we can pretend that bad smells do not exist.

You and I both know that our efforts to smell appetizing can only ever be temporary. The beast must come out of its lair eventually. If I go for long enough without washing, wear my clothes too long, or experience a state of panic, fear, or excitement, my natural self will emanate into the world once again.

We will always revert to our ancient selves, our automatic setting, and the best we can do is to understand the purpose of smell. Animals—other animals, that is—smell for a reason. They don't wash for the same reason. Smell is important information. They communicate identity, territories, and change of emotional state through odour, which means we must do, too, even if we are unaware of it.

Any animal will have a clear idea of my smell: a biochemical printout in its brain of exactly what I am. This is a language that my dog speaks fluently, whereas I am completely inarticulate. It's a shame he cannot tell me what he smells, but then that would be impossible not only because he lacks the power of speech but also because this is a means of communication unlike any other.

Smell is impossible to translate into our matter-orientated language. My smell is what it is: strange and ungraspable. You can't see it or touch it, and it is hard to imagine or summon up from memory. It has no shape or visible texture. It is difficult to measure—you can't estimate the concentration of molecules in the air—and catalogue without making a subjective comment (smells pleasant or unpleasant). With a sound, you can say something about it in words, but there is no onomatopoeia of smell, no figures of smell, no irony, no literature.

If we don't discuss smell, it is because we can't. When we talk about a smell, we are always unoriginal. All we can do is compare it to a repertoire of existing fragrances (and then we refer to the sources of smells as if they were the smells themselves), and mention associations or describe our reactions to it.

Smell is not even directional. You don't know where it is—it is everywhere.

You can reproduce a gesture with your body. You can hear a sound and mimic it. You can see something and depict it by waving your hands around or drawing it. What can you do with a smell except smell it?

My smell—the smell that speaks of me, that is me—is literally unutterable. It is made up of a combination of separate smells from parts of my body—my armpits, my feet, my breath. Together, they constitute a molecular identikit picture, one that is both unique and fluctuating all the time.

My body pumps out the smells of a living creature and its particular metabolism. Despite my best efforts to suppress them with contaminating layers of soap, washing powder, deodorant, and aftershave, sentences and paragraphs of code about my physical state filter through the airwaves. They transmit messages about my health, my diet, and my levels of anxiety, fear, and aggression—my receptivity to friends and enemies and whether I am on the point of fighting or hiding.

One day, I must command a master *parfumier* to recreate the exact smell of me and put it in a bottle with a label on it so that it lives on. I would have to warn users to quickly put the stopper back in: the purest essence of me will quickly evaporate, and that will be that.

Not that we need the label. Smell doesn't work like that. It is not something reducible to sense. Smell speaks to us directly, subjectively and emotionally. It bypasses the analytic brain and goes straight to where the memories and feelings are stored, and there it triggers feelings before you are even aware what is happening. So to you, I'm not really my smell; I am the feeling that sprouts from it in you.

If this lost language can speak to use directly and we do not quickly or easily comprehend, then we could ask what else we are being told without our realizing it.

There is evidence that we can recognize members of our family by smell alone, and that a two-way flow of smell is essential for a parent to bond with a new baby. It has also been suggested that we are drawn to sexual partners by our noses; that a woman unconsciously follows her nose in choosing a mate who is healthy enough to give her strong offspring. It follows that a true Darwinian would throw away his deodorant—the chemical equivalent of being in the nude—and let himself be recognized for the competitive animal he is.

My smell, then, is blatant if you allow your unconscious systems to interpret it; but for the conscious, rational mind it is altogether too vague (and I hope too subtle) to give you a clear grasp of who I am. Conveniently, you will pleased to know, my body provides an oval display screen designed to clear up all ambiguities.

13

The Recognizable Me

. . . . .

LET'S FACE IT

When you consider me with your eyes, you may look at my body but you will concentrate most of your attention on one part of it. My face may as well be me. Much of my personality and identity is concentrated there.

It is my permanent presentation, a trademark stuck to me, an interface between the pair of us. It is unmistakable to those who know me well—useless to anyone who doesn't. It acts as an instant identity card: if you see it and recognize it you take the appropriate action, welcoming me or letting me pass through a door.

So it is important that you read it accurately, that you don't get me mixed up with someone else; however, certain problems can make it more difficult to pick me out of a lineup than you might expect.

My face has one use for me and two for you. In daily life it acts as an advertising hoarding. It is seen by other eyes, and I use it to communicate with them. A variety of facial muscles attached to underlying bones pull it out of shape to create a range of expressions, voluntary and involuntary, indicating my moods.

This is important work. Animals get by without smiling or laughing, but not me. Since I was very small, I have had to use my face to convey essential messages that get me food, company, shelter, and sex. I can also convey gratitude, subservience, displeasure, and a wider repertoire of expressions.

The message of my face is not always clear if you only glance at me, and even if you stare you might not be able to tell the difference between love and hate. I generally reinforce its impact using my hands and voice.

We'd love to go further and read character and thoughts in a face, but our attempts are variable to poor. Some of us claim to be more perceptive than others. But while some perceptions by some people may be confirmed as uncannily accurate, we have no way of knowing whether we really see behind the face or just see what we want to see. The most we can do is guess or hypothesize and ask for confirmation. Entertainers, salespeople, and con artists know just how such facial trickery can be made to work to their benefit.

The other use to which you put my face is as a tool of recognition. I am unlike everyone else. I may have a doppelganger somewhere, but it's unlikely that you will see another me, so remember what I look like.

If you live in a city, chances are your facial recognition software will be overwhelmed and you might have to select whose face you remember and whose you forget. It can also be useful to know who I am not: that you can rule me out from your list of people to whom you owe obligations and debts. Even if you only see a few people each day, recognizing a familiar face is not always easy and you will have to negotiate several obstacles if you want to be sure of who I am:

- **My face is three-dimensional**. It may be the flattened front plane of my head, vaguely oval, but it is much more complicated than that. It is not just a flat map of features; it has relief and texture. It does not look the same from the side as from the front. It needs to be looked at from all angles and in all moods (my moods and those of the viewer—sometimes studiously, sometimes casually), at all my ages, in all my stages of desperation and tiredness. It is a complex piece of machinery, deceptively simple but not at all. It has texture, and the texture changes, too.

  Getting a good look at me will require some hard work and cunning. You can't just glimpse me out of the corner of your eye and know me. You may have to stare at me in good light, at medium to close range, in concentrated silence, and that may make you feel either intimate or provocative. Only lovers and psychopaths really look at people like this.

- **It grows and dies**. It changes over time with age. It has been in evolution from the moment that the foetus-me became recognizably human, and will continue to do so until I rattle my last breath. It is only ever a work-in-progress. It grows from baby to child to adolescent until it turns into my adult face. It carries on developing: sprouting hairs, drawing lines, dragging my eyes inside my head, and letting flesh sag. Experience, sadness, disappointment, and dreams are etched into its skin in some suggestive language without literal translation.

- **It is also in constant motion**. It varies from moment to moment, according to my expressions and my inner moods. I can control some of its plasticity—I can give you a cheesy grin any time I want or feign anger—but a lot of it is unconscious reflex. Its tension alters in line with pain or pleasure; it begs for the reaction that I need or want.

- **I can make temporary changes to it**. I can put on glasses, cut or grow my hair, wear a beard, and so on.

- **It can incur permanent changes**. It can change, either deliberately, through plastic surgery, or perhaps due to an accident.

- **You see in it what you do or do not want to see.** You may not be a neutral observer, someone who is able to look at my face with an open mind. If you cannot, this will distort your judgement. You may well look much longer on my face if you like it and take in more details or notice something endearingly odd about it. If you don't like my face, you may barely look at it at all and not register anything. We are apt to stare at a beautiful face, if we are allowed to, giving us chance to study it, and flick our glance away from someone we consider ugly as soon as we can.

- **My face will probably respond to yours.** If I see how you look at me my expression might change.

- **My face needs to be put in its context**. It will look different if it is shown, say, without my hair or isolated from the rest of my body, or if it has been moved from the particular habitat you are used to seeing it in. My face has to be seen where it belongs, on the front of my head.

Given that there is so much to take in, and that so much can change, it is a wonder that we recognize each other at all. We do this by rapid and astute scanning and unconscious processing. We are not methodical. There is no time for conscious calculations and estimated proportions. We gloss quickly over the features and look for signs that we recognize. In our brains we compare and eliminate suspects until we know we have found the right match.

Sometimes we allow ourselves to act on probabilities: if this person looks like me, and he is in a place you would expect to find him, the chances are it is me.

I can't give you any help with the formation of your mental image of me because I can't see what you see, and I don't know what I look like. I have never had to pick myself out from a crowd. I have never had to look into my own eyes to see if I am telling the truth, I can't guarantee that what you are seeing is me.

If I had to meet myself on a blind rendezvous I wouldn't rely on recognizing my own face: I'd much rather use my clothes, or a book, or a bag I was carrying.

I know what I look like as a two-dimensional image in the mirror looking back at myself, but this is an unnatural way of knowing myself. I'm always on my best behaviour when I am in front of the mirror, tense, scrutinizing. Usually, I am strained or in a hurry or sleepy, and invariably I pull a pose. Looking at myself demands a formal effort, and I can't do it with disciplined indifference. There is no chance of that. I am more likely to be thinking how good or bad my face looks, how it is aging; and I will probably be fixated by some detail of it, worried about my eyebrows or my chin. I doubt that what I see is how I appear to other people.

You have the advantage over me. One piece of advice I can give, however, is not to just look straight at me. Faced with this 3D facial animation, you would be well advised to try and catch it from different angles and in different situations. Unlike me, you have the opportunity to study me without my knowing it, to spy on me offguard, and to study my face when it thinks no one is looking at it.

The trouble is, when you know me there is not much you can do with this knowledge. It is hard, if not impossible, to describe my face in words. You can convey a sense of it, perhaps, but not the actual, literal face.

There are few objective things you can say: you could mention the colour of my eyes, perhaps, and any unique facial marks, as you would in identification papers like a passport. You could give meticulous dimensions for each of its features and how they relate to each other. You could attempt to work out the anatomical details involved: the occipitofrontalis muscle is 63 percent habitually distended and the zygomaticus major is under 0.01 kg/square metre of tension...

You would almost certainly want to give imprecise but perhaps necessary indicators that narrow down the possibilities. For example, my age and sex are surely relevant, even though neither precludes variety. Distinctive features would certainly help, but then you would be venturing into poetic territory: crooked teeth, bulbous nose, bushy eyebrows, and the like. This could conjure up very different images in two minds.

Mostly when we speak about or write a description of a face, we try to evoke a sense of it for the listener or reader, knowing that what we are conveying is far from the exact face in front of us. You can see me, but the other does not. The solution is obvious, of course, and we only waste time describing faces when they belong to fictional people. For anyone who really exists, like me, we have mechanisms of capturing and transmitting copies of faces, and these "likenesses" comprise an identity in themselves. Not everyone on Earth is going to meet me in real life. Unless our paths cross somewhere, you are more likely to see a picture of me, which is an entirely different thing from the original.

14

The Imagined Me

· · · · ·

PICTURE IMPERFECT

My face and an image of my face—the reality and its representation—are two different but sometimes complementary things. Each is a form of identification, but each has its limitations.

The obvious way to depict my face (and you would think the most accurate) is a photograph. My face travels only where I go, but a photograph is far more versatile. It can be copied and dispatched anywhere needed at great speed, a neutral testament to the fact of my existence.

A photograph is meant to be an exact portrayal of me, free of language and culture, as close to the real thing as you can get. But it is not as simple as that. Be wary of how far you trust it.

A photograph is always taken for a purpose, by someone and in a particular way. It is a selection from my life. It may say that I am one thing and only one thing, but that is an ingenuous claim. There are a lot of variables in any frame. It may be posed, or it may pretend to be spontaneous. Either way, one part of my way of being is lost. One omits the natural me, the other the unnatural me. To say it catches a singular me precisely is to ask too much of it. It is possible to take pictures of me that do not look like me at all because of their timing, angle, or composition. This suggests that in fleeting moments I am not me, or I am a me that I do not know.

The context for the photograph also matters. The me in the surf and the me at my desk may not seem like the same person. That is a matter of interpretation, a process that can go on for years.

Every photograph is a snapshot. It is a record of me in an instant and only that instant; it is frozen and sliced time. Through lens and film or digital sensor, I am converted into a pattern of light and shade, form, and colour that may or may not be more permanent than me. Immediately after the photograph is taken my face changes. My photograph is a historical document. Would another second chosen have shown another me?

The subject of my photographic portrait is a still life. It doesn't show the living me as living. You can't see or hear my breath. My eyes do not move. It doesn't include any thoughts and feelings. I am still, or at least stilled, in the moment the shutter blinks open and shut.

Photography is both uninhibitedly revealing and utterly opaque. A photograph of my face gives nothing away; you, the viewer, have to provide the meaning. Any reproduced image of me is imagined; it is not real—it demands the imagination to act. Even the distinction between me and the background is imposed on it. It requires a further step to see me as being worth separating out from the rest of humanity. Only then can you begin to say what the photograph shows you.

All a picture shows you is surface detail—even less than that if were you looking at the real me up close; it says nothing about the inner me. The photographer might try to get me to speak through extrovert gestures, staged symbolism, and exaggerated props. You might peer into my face and think you can divine what is inside, but you can't. Anything you read into my photograph—as with the face—is entirely your own supposition. If I had to have an honest, typical photograph taken of me, what, I wonder, would it show? How would it be? Me alone, frowning, lost in some mysterious thought? Falling asleep?

Yet, for all their shortcomings, we love photographs of ourselves. Officialdom loves them even more, and for the last hundred years or so it has demanded that we produce them periodically, in quantity, usually in duplicate or triplicate.

These photographs, for passport and the like, deliberately eschew the inner, living me. For my portrait to be valid, I have to follow a list of instructions to make me as least like me as I possibly can be.

If, in posing, I show any sign of my personality, the snap will be invalid. I am told to be impassive, as if I will be more recognizable if I first drain all the life out of my face. I must be on my best behaviour: comb my hair how they would like me to comb it, remove my glasses, and look straight ahead.

Whoever sees me looking like that? Not even myself. But they get what they want: me putting on an act for the camera.

Above all, I mustn't smile. In asking for this, they are asking me to discard a vital part of me—perhaps my best and most distinctive facial feature.

This is curious. When photography began, no one smiled for the camera. Now everyone is expected to smile, and if we find a picture of someone looking glum we throw it away.

If every photograph captures something different about me—the tense stare of the passport applicant or the semi-drunk party guest—you would be wise to ask for a selection. To get a feel for my imagined face you might want to go through my photograph collection, so that you can see me depicted in all ages and states;

compromised and rigid with the attempt to present myself in the best possible way; formally dressed and naked; with good company and perhaps bad. Amongst this pictorial record of me, you might just find the odd candid expression or telling look that reveals more than all the other pictures together.

Wouldn't a video of me serve the purpose better? It would show more of me, in motion, from a variety of angles and engaged in different activities. Wouldn't it give a more rounded view of how I appear? Not necessarily. Video's omnivision can also be its drawback. It sees all but doesn't look. It is not selective and makes the viewer lazy. It doesn't have that static, lingering, disturbing gaze of the frozen photograph. It usually gives too much reality, too much context.

Besides, video and photography suffer from the same distancing effect. To look through a lens or screen is to see your subject indirectly. Often we make the assumption that the better the technology, the better the result, and that because we have the machine available we should use it. But sometimes the old ways are better.

What I am after in an image of me is a likeness, and the best way to get that may be through hand, eye, and paper. Anyone who has ever tried to do it knows that it is not so easy—it may be a gift you are born with or not, although it improves with study. They are rarely dramatic. Mostly our faces are subtle. Everything about them is subtle.

Faces are notoriously difficult to draw. We all seem to be arranged according to the same pattern, with the same features in the same places, but when you start to look at them and measure them you realize how little one person's eye or ear differs from another. The variations in dimensions can be minute—the proportions hard to estimate—but take a step back and you see that tiny details can make one face dramatically different from another; even taking precise measurements may not produce a convincing portrait. And then there is the problem of colour, particularly of skin tone. This changes with the light, so what moment of the day do you choose for the picture to look most like me?

A self-portrait is no easier to execute. Familiarity does not help. In fact, knowing myself can make it harder. It is not just an object before me; it matters. How honest do I want to be?

Even the most skilled artistic portrait of me will show more and less than a photograph. That's because it takes much longer to do. With the time taken, there is more of the artist invested in the finished work and, hopefully, he will be interested in his work. My face is not a still life. More of me passes for longer across the field of vision, and the artist has time to change his mind, to alter his arrangement of me, to see something new. With a portrait, you can select and rearrange reality.

You can flatter or condemn the subject. But unless he paints with photographic precision, something will be missed out—the extraneous detail, the confusing cast shadow.

Art looks, and in looking tries to reveal. It inevitably takes its time, even if it is hurried and impressionistic. It takes more than a fraction of second. That time gives the artist time to consider his work carefully—to look at the model, a person, and to feel and think what he wants. He cannot be neutral, as the camera can be or can pretend to be. He has to take a stance, and to make an interpretation, whether conscious or unconscious.

It could be argued that a caricature would be a truer representation of me than a straight portrait. At least the artist who creates a caricature sees something distinctive in me, important to my appearance, and exaggerates it while keeping the whole recognizable.

Whatever the means and the medium used to capture it, a visual representation of me is useless without words attached to it, without a caption. You have to know it is me. My image may go around the globe or endure for centuries, but without a name to go with it, it could be of anyone. It is so easy for a photograph to become detached from its caption. Then who will I be? Just someone who once lived.

If, however, you keep the image and its description together, you can get to know all about me. You have the basis for opening a file and documenting me.

15

The Documented Me

· · · · ·

Why bother to ask any more questions or look further? It says here who I am. My name and my photograph lead to the vast and still accumulating mass of paperwork that exists about me.

To begin with, I can show you a wallet full of identification on request—driving licence, passport, identity card, credit card, and so on. I can back this up with drawers full of bank statements, utility bills, tax returns, and correspondence with assorted bureaucrats that bear my name. All of these papers have their counterpart in government departments and company offices. They crisply sum up who I am for administrative purposes. My documentation is an abstract of me.

These are just the papers that I know about. For all I know, there may be a huge amount of additional documentation about me in existence in various locations across the world, including places I have never been to. People and files move around, copies are made and remade. Who knows what scraps of me are held, and whether they are accurate records. I'm sure I would recall some of it, if I tried—completed and aborted transactions dutifully filed and forgotten, which someone forgot to shred. Perhaps there are sheets of paper about me wafting through shantytowns somewhere, having been blown off a rubbish heap. It would be an impossible job to track down all this ancient ancillary documentation in order to build a complete account of me.

I should feel honoured to be worth so much paper and ink. It is proof not only that I exist but that I am valid in other people's terms—if only as the target of a marketing campaign. Much of this paper trail may make rather dull reading, but the fact that we can be so literarily profligate at all proves that I represent the pinnacle of civilization. This is the dream of some Mesopotamian bookkeeping scribe come true. What started with goods and transactions being inscribed on clay tablets to keep a track of trade and tribute, and continued on papyrus and parchment for the sake of aristocrats and emperors, has now become a routine record of the doings of the common man.

The folders and drop files indexed under my surname are not kept for my benefit. The motivation behind tracking me in this manner is the same as it was for the peasant in the Fertile Crescent, and as it has been throughout history. Keeping records on people is born from authoritarianism, the desire of powerful people to control their subjects. It is a way of ruling at a distance and of holding proof of obligation for future use. It makes things impersonal and bars access to the throne. Issue me a document and I no longer have a reason to demand to see you in person; you will accept a paper version of me, instead.

Documents are a sign of mistrust. They exist to discourage transactions taking place at an informal, human level. They are intended to replace free will, conversation, intimacy, and gift-giving as a means to get things done. If you and I can help each other, with no record kept or duties paid, we will both be happier, but we will have left those who survey us out of the deal. What more do two people need, in a realm without government, than eye contact, a handshake, and their word of honour?

That we are required to record our existences and doings in some central filing depot engenders wariness and fear in us.

Put my affairs in writing and restrict access to the file and you have got your hand permanently around my throat. You have ensured that I live in fear of every police patrol and I can't get safely beyond the border without your permission.

Which of us when travelling doesn't fear that's a rule-bound guard will disappear with our passport and never come back? If that happens who will I be? When all things depend on identification papers, without the correct papers I would be irrevocably adrift. Who is going to believe my protests that I am not an impostor? I have been reduced to my papers; I am nothing but them. These inky sheets of wood pulp and size are more important than me. They may speak of me, but they are not mine. They remain the property of the issuing authority and are supplied only for my use.

Documents, however, have several weaknesses as currencies of identity. They are:

- **Flat, two-dimensional versions of me**. They don't carry as much information as I do. You can't ask them questions.

- **Always out of date.** Even if they have been issued today, this morning, any fact on them may have changed already. They are thus a kind of fossil or sloughed skin, proof only that at a time in the past my then-correct details passed across the desk of some official. Ironically, they are historical artefacts prepared and kept for future consultation.

- **Vulnerable to natural or unnatural disaster.** They can be lost or burned, or stolen or forged.

- **Portable and therefore can be transferred to someone illicitly, either temporarily or permanently.** Tie all your security to an identity card and you have to hope or assume that it stays in the right hands.

- **Open to interpretation.** They may be issued to the right individual, for the right reasons, but their reliability and effectiveness depend thereafter on the performance of the person who checks them. If an inspector is lazy, illiterate, or corrupt—or is simply distracted it a critical moment—all careful work in preventing forgery will have been a waste of time.

Control requires control of the controllers. If you are not careful you will end up with a whole chain of people checking up on each other—of command job creation and duplication, modulated by a complicated arrangement of targets and assessments. Then what do you do if you discover rife incompetence? You will be forced to waste time in purges, sackings, and show trials, which may not improve the working practices of the staff who remain in their posts but will certainly demoralize everyone involved. Totalitarians know this well: the more meticulous and seamless you make the system, the less anyone in it feels like showing imitative and the more ingenious cheats become. Meticulously filed paperwork can become an outward show of an administration that is internally rotten.

Fortunately, we now have computers to eliminate the need for both paper documentation and human beings to check it. Things are streamlined; there is no chance any more of cock-ups; and a computer can't ask for a bribe in return for letting you through a checkpoint.

Increasingly, my documentation is now stored digitally because it takes up less space (no space at all, really) and is easier to access (as long as the server isn't down).

Maybe one day the last piece of paper on the planet will be scanned and archived and the forests left to regenerate but, as of today, the paper mills still haven't closed down because of falling demand and printers are still be sold.

In the meantime, I am being converted into code as fast as possible. My paperwork, once solid, crisp, tangible, is becoming "content" or energy. One big stray burst of electromagnetism from outer space, I suppose, and my official identity will vanish as if a master switch had been thrown.

There is a way past the fragility of data. Why go on generating documents at all, either printed or onscreen? The problem with all paperwork is that while it represents me, it is not me. Technology is coming up with workarounds to address this. A growing biometrics industry is now dedicated to turning us into our own documents. If you can read the body, it is reasoned, and connect it to a database, you have no need to get anything in writing any more.

This is a control freak's dream. All we need is some unmistakable feature of me that I cannot surreptitiously hand to someone else or flush down the toilet if cornered.

Fingerprints have been used for a long time to pin criminal suspects down, and DNA swabbing is becoming an accepted part of police procedure in developed countries. It is now proposed that my hand geometry, voice, retina, and even my entire face can be scanned by machinery giving a readout onscreen of who I am (or am not).

Biometric procedures can be expensive to implement, and there are technical challenges still to be overcome. Every automated system works within a margin of error that has to be set at either falsely accusing some of those who are innocent or letting some of those who are guilty go free. Not only that, but a computer has to report back to its human operator, so we never get away from the reliability of checkers (and the loop of checkers checking up on checkers, as described above). More importantly, there are ethical issues about snooping on people. I might have got used to the idea of carrying around a driving licence because the state does not trust me to be a responsible driver, but I don't want camera beams crawling over my skin just in case I am about to do something wicked when I am out shopping.

We all want to be protected from cheats, terrorists, and dangerous people, but it is important that we don't surrender all our rights in return for surveillance. The key issue here is consent, and there is a very simple method for us to give this. Soon, though, we may have to change that "is" to "used to be" because this indicator of our identity may be about to go extinct.

16

The Inscribed Me

· · · · ·

We are living on a lexicographical cusp. Technology now permits us—if we want it—to dispense with handwriting and replace it with a smoother technique of generating phantom characters on a screen using input devices such as a keyboard and a sliding click-button. It could be that our days of scratching marks on paper by hand are over and that our forefingers and thumbs are about to evolve into agile little sticks in response to our new tapping and typing needs.

It took a lot of campaigning to make handwriting available to so many of us through education; but we may one day look back on it as a brief flowering, lasting little more than a hundred years—a charming lunacy that we engaged in while waiting for machines to catch up with our needs. Will we regret the transition from "real" writing to hyper-writing? After all, it requires us to sacrifice a crucial form of identity, the only way we have of telling a genuine document from a forgery?

Handwriting is the intimate, very personal mark of an individual. Everything we write is an expression of our brains, our personalities, or our obligations. How and what we write sets us apart from each other. On the most basic level it maps out our level of literacy, but graphologists belief that they can read our entire character through our writing.

I choose my favourite instrument, and I write how I can or want. My handwriting can be imitated or forged, but only I can write in the manner that I do, with fluidity and ease and my characteristic omissions and mistakes.

All this, however, is merely an introduction to the really important function of writing by hand. Among all the various words, phrases, and sentences I write, there is one that I use repeatedly, and it is exclusively mine: my signature. You see it, and you know I have made it—you show it to me, and I will have to admit it or tell a lie.

This ideogram that I have designed for myself through trial and error does important work. It demonstrates my past intention unequivocally. It is proof that my living hand touched a piece of paper and endorsed it. Only the dead and fictional cannot make some personal mark on their correspondence.

The act is not to be taken lightly. A signature cannot be retracted or apologized for ("I didn't mean to sign it"). It stands as my final, indisputable approval of whatever is written above. My signature can fulfill one or more important functions. Depending on the context, it signifies:

- **Consent.** "I give my approval to the act stated in this document," or "I do not dispute the facts written here," or "I will not stand in the way of a proposed action."
- **Proof of presence—or presence of mind.** "I am here, in this specified place on this particular day," or "I have read this document and am aware of its contents."
- **Ownership.** "This book or house or country is henceforth mine."
- **Responsibility.** "I will undertake to do what I hereby say I will do."
- **Promise to shut my mouth or stay away:** "I will not criticize the company/state, on pain of whatever punishment the law decides for me," or "I will never come back to my home country."
- **Confession.** "I hereby admit to the misdeeds set out above. Everything said herein is true."
- **Permission.** "I will allow this order to be carried out."
- **Instruction of authority.** "I order this action to be carried out."
- **Appeal for action or change of policy.** "I add my signature to this petition begging you to reconsider this matter."
- **Denomination of origin.** "My signature is at the bottom of this letter because I wrote it."
- **Authenticity or personalization.** "I wrote this book," or "I made this work of art."

As any totalitarian ruler knows, a signature is not a trivial addition to a document; it is a form of complicity. Each time I make my signature, an event is set in motion or blocked. I am involved, and I add something to my identity. To truly control someone you need him to accept his own subjugation, even if only nominally. It takes effort and ingenuity to get someone to sign a document he doesn't want to, but old-style oppressive regimes placed great weight on it. A confession is more authentic if accompanied by a signature; it adds a layer of public humiliation and shame to the operation.

Signatures are tediously practical things, and the very quality that made them once useful now makes them inconvenient. To sign you have to be in contact with paper, and you cannot (yet) send paper through the internet. Also, signing a letter takes time and organization. The person who dictated the contents has to be physically present.

For non-paper correspondence, we simply type our names or say nothing. Today, when busy, cost-monitoring organizations like banks and state bureaucracies write us letters, it seems to be understood that a true signature is no longer needed. A scanned signature that is cut and pasted as needed gives enough sense of authorship. Another solution is to create a pseudo-signature using a handwriting font: a transparent imitation of reality that is worse than no signature at all. In the spirit of the digital age, we have decided that it is enough to transmit appearance or impression. We don't see the point in teletransporting atoms of analogue ink from my pen held, in my hand, to your fingers and eye. What difference does it make if it looks okay?

It makes all the difference. To dismiss out signatures in this way, to let our handwriting wither, is to dismiss ourselves. It is to turn our identities into typographical flourishes, serifs of delight. If a signature becomes a worthless fraud, the signee need no longer be human nor living. We now condone not autographs but auto-forgeries: make up what you want to represent you (perhaps an animated signature cartoon?)—it doesn't matter to me.

Curiously, bureaucratic bankers who do not sign their letters still expect me to sign my application forms and get witnesses to sign photographs of me. It is as if we have not decided about the fate of the signature. Is it or is it not indispensable to literate human identity? Perhaps officialdom never cared much about it, anyway. Forcing a signature out of someone was merely symbolic. They wanted some gesture of absolute rendition, and a signature was considered the last thing any respectable person would let go of. *They* knew they could do what they wanted with people, with or without my consent. Nothing has changed; it's just that the gloves are off. If you want to control someone you get his signature as a routine . . . because you can, not because you care who he is. There's no need to discipline individuals anymore, now that we live in mass society. No longer are people seen as compliant or stubborn idiosyncrasies. Now we are just units of demographical accounting, a collection of tick boxes, with the injunction "Please do not write anything else on the form." In other words, if it's not relevant to us, it is not relevant to you.

The Categorical Me

· · · · ·

TICKED OFF

Thanks to the ever-increasing power and speed of computers, we now process almost unlimited amounts of data. I say "we," but I myself am not doing much of the processing; mostly, I am the data. If I don't like to think of myself in this way, all I can do is go off and live alone and self-sufficiently in a log cabin in the hills.

To be connected to the modern world is to be collected. Every time I agree to something—buy a car, sign a contract, see a doctor, make a tax declaration—I respond to questions, then my answers are fed, fact by fact, into a computer.

As I am digitalized, I cease to be a whole person; instead, I become a series of yesses and nos, of open or closed electronic gates, in databases of magnitudes that I cannot comprehend. The circuitry splits me up and arranges the parts into categories, so that I am counted as a member of this class but not of that one. Reverse the equation, put the classes I belong to together and work backwards, and you would have thought that you reconstitute me.

There are many possible questions, but a few of them are more useful for categorizing me than others. The following are the main ones; the order of priority can be argued over:

Alive or Dead?

To a database it doesn't make much difference; to my friends, family and me, it does. The answer is usually obvious, but the distinction does need to be made. This is one phenomenon that is purely binary: I am either switched on still, or I have switched off.

Gender?

Until relatively recently, most forms gave a choice of two categories of human gender (more of a sociological description than allowed for in the definitions of biological sex). Either I had to be in one or the other. Now, we know that humanity divides into three groups: male, female, and those who either resent having to identify themselves as one thing or the other, or claim they are of a third gender category.

Which sex I am matters greatly to other people. We don't like ambiguity. It makes us uncomfortable—probably because we know that things are much less clear than we would like to believe, and because we all feel bound by unwritten rules.

Although in my society great efforts have been made in my lifetime to even up opportunities between the sexes, we still use gender to consciously or unconsciously impose expectations of personality, character, and behaviour.

To say that I am a man doesn't tell you much except the anatomically obvious, and even there, if you will forgive the pun, men vary enormously. Just as there are more or less feminine men, there are more or less masculine women. Self-categorization may be easy for the majority of us but it denies all nuance.

I have ticked the male box all my life without hesitation, but I recognize that this says very little about me.

Nationality?

As a rule, each of us is born with a nationality. This accords us membership in a group of people, typically counted in millions, who happen to live within a defined, mapped area and are ruled by the same government. Nationality is transmitted by family status, like an geographical gene, or occasionally by place of birth.

Normally, you get only one nationality, but sometimes you are allowed to hold two concurrently, and you just have to hope that there is never any conflict between the two states you belong to.

Some people either have to, or decide to, switch their nationalities by process of naturalization, and a few unfortunates are classed as stateless because of an accident of history or persecution.

In times of peace and prosperity, nationality can be a nominal affair, a mere convention that I observe because everyone else does. It brings with it rights (although these may be minimal) and entails obligations, specifically loyalty to the national zeitgeist. This is essential in time of war, when in return for the right to bear a passport I may be asked to make a sacrifice.

I prefer to think of nationality as having two distinct aspects to it—one precise, the other inevitably less so. Most of the above fits into the definition of political nationality, whose manner of expression I may not always agree with. I am much happier with a notion of cultural nationality, a shared set of values, attitudes, and aspirations that arises from history and shared experience. The average form, however, does not allow me to specify my degree of assent to each of the two branches of nationality.

Confusingly, there is one other kind of nationality that affects some people. The normal kind of nationalism can be an umbrella for "sub-nationalities," when a country has within it regions whose residents believe themselves to have a right to statehood for reasons of political, economic, cultural, and linguistic heritage.

Ethnicity or Race?

These two terms are problematic to define but the enlightened modern view on them is that anyone should be allowed to identify themselves ethnically as they see fit, without further justification.

History has taught us clearly that to discriminate against people on grounds of race leads to injustice and great confusion. It is the same with skin colour. I'm definitely not the person to be answering questions on this topic, as I was brought up not even thinking about it. I was told, or I assumed, that I had a "normal" or neutral skin tone, since almost everyone around me had more or less the same level of pigmentation. Back then, the affairs of the world were largely decided by white men, and anyone who was non-white was expected to put up with this. Now, as an adult, I know that my colour grants me privileges by default and that it is difficult for me to fully comprehend the role that race plays in the identities of other people.

Language?

The mother tongue of a child is usually determined by nationality and/or ethnicity. I acquired my mother tongue, English, without questioning it, and it underlies all my thinking. Without it, I wouldn't be able to communicate in the way I do, or even think. This would be a different book if I had been born elsewhere. So my identity is very much tied up with my mother tongue, my mental voice, and my reading eye.

Learning foreign languages has taught me several important lessons. The first is that I become a different person when I step out of my native tongue. I become what I can be, as if there were a "me" for each language. A second lesson is that being without my preferred grammar and vocabulary humbles me. I return to the level of a child, and because I understand less with my ears I have to see and sense more. Thirdly, a foreign language is not just a collection of different sounds and irregular verbs; it is a key to another way of thinking entirely. Fourthly, I have learned how important unimportant information is. I am sure items of my identity were built simply by understanding the chat and gossip being thrown away around me. In a foreign language I have to struggle to pick up trivial, throw-away remarks.

The point of all this is that simply to declare my mother tongue and say what other languages I speak is to say very little about me. To get to know me well, you would have to observe me first in a comfortable linguistic milieu and then in one where the accents and the alphabet are new to me.

Religion?

This can be a tricky question. Why do I have to say anything on this subject? Isn't religion a matter of private conscience? How can a computer understand my answer here?

For some people, the answer may be easy, but it isn't for everyone. Religion has a tendency to fragment. Simply ticking a box naming one of the major world religions seems to imply that you accept everything associated with it, when it is more likely you are attached to some sect or perhaps have your own particular view on what parts of dogma and their interpretation are right or wrong.

No database can be designed to cope with every eventuality. The catchall categories "agnostic" or "none" are worst of all. They are devoid of meaning. They could be chosen for any number of reasons, and there is no way to distinguish between people who think deeply and constantly about religion but remain undecided and people who have never thought about religion at all and have no opinion.

Religion, or spirituality, or a professed lack of interest or a vehement opposition, can be an important part of someone's identity but if ever there was a case for "You may continue your answer on a separate sheet of paper," this is it.

Place of Residence?

This is a straightforward question accompanied by a fixed set of options. Owner-occupier or tenant? And usually a supplementary question to clarify, "How long have you lived at this address?" I'm sure this gives someone an indication of something about me, but obviously there is a lot that is left unsaid. If anyone really wants to know me, they would have to follow up this theme with some more searching questions: "Do you like the place you live?" "Who are your neighbours, and what are your relationships like with them?" "What do you feel about the community you live in, and how much do you participate in it?" and "Which DIY jobs have you not got around to doing, and why?"

Age?

Age is very duplicitous substance. For a start it is both subjective and objective. I have been on Earth for an exact number of years and if asked to select between different age ranges, I must be in one of them. Everything else we have to say about

age is subjective, and we may well disagree. Terms like young, middle aged, and old are hard to define, and generations get so mixed up that the term is almost meaningless.

What can be important to know—and this goes with age, of course—are the decades I have lived through and the dramatic world events that have occurred within the time of my memory. Age might (or might not) also determine the technology and popular culture I am most familiar with. None of this explicitly correlates with my actual age.

Education?

Adults divide up into those who went to school and those who didn't, but that's just the start of it. There are innumerable gradations to specify, each separating us into classes of education: how many years of schooling, the kind of school attended, grades, achieved, subjects taken, and so on.

Job Title?

My job title at least tells you what I do during office or factory hours, but it won't tell you any more than this unless you ask some supplementary questions.

A job title can be very misleading. It can be used to inflate the importance of its holder or completely mislead someone. Often, what we are looking for when we ask "What do you do?" is confirmation that someone else will vouch for the person we are talking to; that an employer has put him to the test, tells him what to do, and gets enough value out of him to give him money.

You won't get this from me. In my case, my employment is self-created and my working style particular to me. I don't fit easily into any category of employment.

The question, whether on the form or in person, is invariably insidious. It means, "What do you do for money?" not "How do you spend your time?" It frequently disregards or belittles unconventional or unremunerated employment statuses, such as housewife/husband, volunteer, struggling artist yet to get paid for his work, and so forth.

A job title is often a clue to two other categorizable items: income bracket and social class (a tricky concept for both human brains and automated databases).

Marital Status?

The phrase "Marital Status" sounds antiquated and seems to imply that there should be a norm in two-way human affairs. The choice used to be clear: "Unmarried," "Married," or "Previously Married (But Now Divorced or Widowed)."

Thankfully, we've created new categories to sort out how individuals behave with respect to love, commitment, responsibility, sex, and procreation. The marriage question on a form is still there, but there is a broader range of multiple-choice answers, and some of them sound almost indiscreet. We've done away with the stigma of spinsters and the louche glamour of bachelors in favour of the much more upbeat "Single." "No longer is separation or divorce any big thing. For a time it even looked as if marriage would wither away, as "Living Together" contracts re-placed the legal niceties and heavy religious overtones of marriage. But ceremonial marriage has stayed with us, as if we need it as a standard to judge things by. Now we talk of "Relationships" and "Partners," to leave room for necessary ambiguities and not trigger preconceptions.

Of course, we no longer assume that someone's partner is of the opposite sex. We may even be moving to a situation in which we admit that it is none of our business how and with whom individuals arrange their lives.

Dependents?

Families have changed, too. Whereas the typical family was once the norm, it has almost been replaced by the atypical family, if that makes sense. But any parent knows that looking after a child is a lot more than either a kinship tie or an honor-ary position.

Additional Information?

Many forms I have to fill in end with a blank box in which I am invited to write anything about myself that has not been covered by the categories above. The temptation is to use this space to write a personal message to the hypothetical human being who will read the form. This is wish and vanity. Whatever I have to say will almost certainly not be of interest to whoever has to digitalize my data. If there is no category under which to put my additional information it will not be crunchable by computer and will be classed as irrelevant and ignored. I should save any vital but unclassifiable anecdotes, self-analysis and quirky remarks about myself for more intimate forms of communication, human being to human being.

The Qualified Me

• • • • •

IRRELEVANT INFORMATION

There is a revealing phrase we ask of people, typically of someone in public life, who we would like to know more about. We can pull up their database entries on screen, but that just gives us the dry facts: name, address, education, job title, achievements, and so on. What we want to know is, "Who are you as a person?" This is not a question with any one, definite answer; it is an open enquiry, inviting ideas that we will sift through until we have a sense of what we are looking for.

I have called this aspect of my identity "The Qualified Me," because it concerns the quality of me rather than the quantity, nuance rather than full-on fact and veri-fiable precision. If you like, it consists of everything that is left off an official form, that won't fit in the database. I can only appeal to you as a fellow human being, to ask without judging; to not expect evidence and certainty; and to view me as an Impressionistic or abstract painting (or perhaps a cartoon), not a figurative portrait. So who am I as a person? Who do you need to ask to find out?

You will need to consult two sources. The first is me; the second is everyone else who knows me or claims to know anything at all about me. This includes my family, my friends, and my enemies. You can put questions to any or all of these people or let them talk freely; but there are certain things you should be aware of as you go about your investigation:

• **You will have to decide who to trust and how much.** Am I—or is the person you are speaking to about me—being honest? Is he even capable of having a clear view and saying anything useful? You may get the impression that I seem like a different person to each person I come into contact with, depending on our relationship—or at least they see a different aspect of me. You may well end up having to merge accounts and making a rather shaky composite picture.

- **It may all be emotive.** Don't discount emotions. What is said about me might be motivated by love, hate, fear, or any other feeling.

- **Don't expect precise, verifiable information.** You can compare witness statements, and you may be able to test some allegations, but you will not be able to confirm or refute most of what you are told. Consider everything here as contentious and you can't go wrong.

- **I am variable—things can change.** What may be true when you hear it may be history when you relay it to someone else. Don't expect any fixed facts.

- **All information is graduated.** It is suggestive and defies absolute statements. I'm probably not the most extreme example of whatever it is they say about me. All things come in different levels and intensities.

- **Combinations count.** Two things separately are not the same as when they are combined with my personality.

- **You can never compile an exhaustive list.** What I or anyone else tells you will be selective. There will always be something one of us forgets to mention or deliberately ignores.

- **Some of the best information may be private, and you may never get to it.** I reserve the right to keep away from some subjects. I might even see you in court if you try to investigate them. Only I know what goes on when I am alone, and I might not say.

- **At the end of your investigation, I may remain vague.** There is a risk that for all your efforts my identity is no clearer than when you started.

- **You're not neutral in this, and you are not going to reach to an objective assessment.** How I appear depends on your motivation, what you make of it all, how you assemble all this anecdotal information from your perspective, and how you apply your judgement about me. One person may gather this information to condemn me, another to praise me, another to explain my actions. Maybe you will impose a meaning, an angle, a narrative of your own on this qualified identity of mine. Maybe you will use your imagination to fill in any gaps.

- **Words will always get in the way.** Much of what I say here comes down to vocabulary: I or someone else may not have the words to describe me as they wish. They may say about me only what they feel able to articulate, rather than what they mean.

Self-Definitions

The qualified me can be divided into five broad categories with some overlap. The first of these is how I define myself.

Some "facts" that I put forward about myself are the product of realizations I make about myself, or choices, and I expect you to respect what I have to say without argument. You have no expertise in my affairs, and therefore no right to tell me that I am wrong.

There is some crossover here with categorization, in that I may point to evidence for what I tell you; but there again, I do not have to. Another variable for you to be aware of is that I may change my mind. You cannot define me today by what I said about myself yesterday.

Race and ethnicity come under this heading, to some extent. Sexuality is certainly a matter of self-proclamation—or concealment, if I so choose. You will probably never know which sex I am attracted to. Class may well be auto-defined; caste, however, certainly is not. I may also profess inclusion in some minority group, which only exhaustive research can verify.

Medical conditions and mental syndromes without visible symptoms often have an element of self-definition, in the sense that to verify them we'd have to consult the doctor who made the diagnosis. Mostly we take the information we are given on trust.

Beliefs, Opinions, and Prejudices

My religious beliefs, or lack of them, are another area of independent right, although here we are approaching grounds for debate. I may secretly hold or vociferously assert other views, especially on politics, and these clearly identify me.

There is much confusion about what constitutes a valid belief or opinion (or prejudice). What can I assert as a matter of self-definition, without being challenged, and what should I expect to have to defend in argument? The difference is partly to do with evidence—it is one thing to hold a counterfactual view that can be proven and another to claim that the facts don't matter—and partly to do with the effect of what I think on other people. All societies have to find a balance between these contesting forces. Should one person have the right to say objectionable things about another, to preach hate and violence? Or should he

be silenced for the common good? Either way, most of us work with a palette of prejudices—some of which we are aware of and others of which we remain oblivi-ous and may be unwilling to question, whatever the cost.

Personality

Here, personality intersects with identity. The former, as every biographer knows, informs the latter. Personality is a quirky, subtle thing, and there are a lot of ways to look at it from the hyper-methodical to the casual, condescending glance. Some of the parts of my personality that most distinguish me are my:

- **Likes and Dislikes.** How do I choose to spend my spare time? Where do I learn about current affairs?
- **Preferences.** Books, music, people, art, pastimes, and so on
- **Reactions to Stimuli.**
- **Moods and Emotions.** What makes me cross and how do I behave when I am angry?
- **Personal Habits.** How organized and tidy I am, and so on
- **Challenges and Fears, Including Imagined Ones.**
- **Guilt and Shame.** What causes them and how they affect me
- **Idiosyncrasies.**

Abilities

My capabilities are more concrete, although they still come in degrees. I or some-one else can tell you what I am capable of, but being able to do something and being able to do it well are two different things. A diploma on my wall may look convincing, but you would be wise to question it. You may, for instance, be told I play tennis, but you will need to cite my level or even ask for a demonstration to see whether I am any good at it. How I behave in conversation and debate; how practical I am; and what I do with my creativity, if anything, will also be relevant. My hobbies and pastimes could be included under this heading. My levels of literacy and numeracy also count.

Attitude to Possessions

You may get a clearer view of what kind of person I am through my behaviour towards "things." Do I accumulate possessions? Which do I value most among them, and why? My house and car may well say a lot about me, but some small keepsake on a shelf in my study may also have a story attached to it that delivers insight into my personality.

Effect of Place

Where I come from and where I presently live are easy categories to define me by, but how these two and other places influence me can tell you a lot about me. Pertinent questions about my geography will yield much information about me: How do I feel about certain kinds of places, such as the city or country? Do I love or fear wildness?

Which particular places do I prefer and avoid? Do I feel at home anywhere? Am I willing to change location for any reason? Do I know what it is like to live as a migrant and a foreigner?

As you look into the nature of the "qualified" me, in either the front or back of your mind must be the question, Why is he like this? If there is a single answer, it is summed up not only by place but by that other great force that shapes my life: time. I came to be who I am because I come from the past.

The Inherited Me

· · · · ·

I DIDN'T PACK MY
OWN BAGGAGE

I like to think that my present identity doesn't owe anything to my past—that I have left it behind me and made my own fortune. My history is finished with. I live in the here and now. How can things from long ago have any effect on me? I may not want them to, but they do. I am what I am because of what I have been. History is never finished. I wouldn't be here if it I didn't have a past, and it influences me still. I have an identity that I have inherited that is worth the effort to understand.

Now that we have the comfort, leisure, and means to do so, we take an obsessive interest in the past. Our enquiries take two broad forms: curiosity (we catalogue our photographs and souvenirs and enthusiastically research our family trees) and anguish (we trawl our childhoods in search of traumas and other memories to heal lingering adult hurts). In all this, it is as if we have left something behind that will explain how we are now, if we can only find it.

On the most basic level, my origins gave me my genes. This insubstantial inheritance still drives me. It shaped my body and my face, which in turn have had an effect on what I can and cannot do in life.

At birth, genes collide with reality and a battle begins that will last my whole life. Who will win out, my coding or my conditioning?

Each of us has a different childhood. Even siblings close in age brought up in the same house with the same parents will not have the same experience. It's one of the great mysteries of parenting, and an enduring question of self-examination. Broadly, from an adult vantage point, we divide into those who consider their childhoods to have been as nurturing as possible within the circumstances, causing no lasting damage, and those who still think they are suffering from the fallout. Therapists usually consider that we are all in the second category. I once took part in a workshop in which I was asked to list all the bad things about my childhood. I barely touched the questionnaire. "There weren't any," I said. That answer wasn't

allowed, and I was sent back to find some. Even after uncovering some things I was unhappy about—which felt like a betrayal of my well-intentioned parents—I still maintain that I had a happy childhood. I know this because I have since come across people who had very difficult early years.

What is true of all of us is that we are confronted with a battery of situations that are by definition unfamiliar. We have no previous experience to draw on, and we react as best we can. In so doing, we form judgements about the world, and these stay with us either for life or until we reassess them. Those judgements make up part of my actual identity.

The main issues we all face in infancy in different ways are:

- **Power.** It is clear from the baby's perspective who has power: not him. I quickly learnt that I could respond to the benevolent dictatorship of my parents in three ways: obedience, resistance, or a power struggle. I imagine I developed a dynamic blend of the three and discovered what worked for me in different situations. I am sure my current attitudes to authority and my voting preferences stem from decisions I formed when I was too young to realize I was deciding anything.

- **Imposition of Identity.** My parents used their power to stick a name on me, and an identity that suited them. I reacted by trying to be what they wanted, but I discovered simultaneously that I was who I was. The two can either flow together or clash, but ideally there is some accommodation at some time. Either way, I am spending the rest of my life working through the consequences.

- **Judgements About Me.** If I didn't develop as the model child, they let me know where I was going wrong, heaping verdicts on me, usually in adjectives such as stubborn, moody, obstreperous, and so on. A child can either accept these verdicts as undisputable truth or use them to build a rebel identity.

- **Group Dynamics.** Every childhood is a lesson in living with other people, especially other children, typically brothers and sisters, who are also going through the above three subjects. I had to learn by trial and error how to compete for attention and a modicum of power, and about the frustrations of other people not doing what I wanted or trampling on my wishes.

• **Belonging.** I learnt that I had a social location in the world. I had a place in the age and power order in my nuclear family, and I also belonged to wider family, a neighbourhood, a country, and so on. Belonging brought the security of reassurance, but it also brought challenges as I grew up. What if I didn't want to belong? Could I choose which group I belonged to and which I didn't? What if I belonged too much and was aggressive to people who were not part of my clan? Could I earn belonginess to some new group? What if they didn't accept me as one of theirs? And so on.

In some families, there is an additional lesson to learn: what to do with a physical inheritance and a psychic obligation. A family with land, or which has owned a house for generations, may place a duty on the first-born son to look after them and deny this to the second-born and to daughters. This is the lot of only a minority among us, aristocrats and royals. Their identity is decided for them by the actions of their ancestors. They may have wealth and privilege handed to them at birth, but they are not given freedom, and they may even be handed a death sentence, if society turns against them during their tenure.

I have ancestors, too, although not a superior lineage that is recognized by its peers and underclasses. I have often wondered how much it matters who came before me in my family line? Does this form a part of the answer to the question, "Who am I?," which is couched in the present tense.

The answer is, of course. But then does it matter if I know who they are? Perhaps it does, and perhaps it doesn't. Family trees tend to throw up dry reminders of lives. Whole years are telescoped into a sentence, saying nothing of the foibles of the human being. I wonder how much I am like any of them and whether they would recognize me, the adult. Perhaps they would snort at my cocky assertions of being a unique person forging his own way through life. I never knew any of my grandparents, adult to adult. If they were here now, would they look at the grownup me and say, "You're just like me."?

All the above helps me to understand who I have become, but I am not just seeking to satisfy curiosity or looking for resources to make a happier me. My identity affects other people. I need to know about my past, because I give it to my children.

Without my being able to intervene, my kids get some of the same stuff as me (the biological component) diluted by 50 percent, more or less. I select which of the rest, the social or cultural past, I want to give them, then feed it to them in dribbles, filtering and interpreting it, answering questions when I can. This then informs their identities, and so on. They go through all the old issues of power with

me, and I begin to understand why my parents were as they were.

Meanwhile, I am learning to grow into a new identity, that of father. I some-times introduce myself as my son's dad, if that makes my relevance to the situation clear. It is strange to have dependents, to never again be able to take a decision thinking only of myself.

Knowing this, what it is like to be a parent, makes it strange to meet someone new: to meet him with his children or without them (that is, not to know whether he has children at all) is to get to know two different people. It can also be impor-tant to know which of his family members are still alive and whether he still talks to them.

This led me to a wider thought: how different people can seem, according to whether we know their history or not. If tomorrow I meet someone who commit-ted a violent crime in the past, do I need to know about what he did? Can I trust my judgement about him in the present situation? What if I get to like him and then find out what he did? Would that change anything? What if the world still condemns him, but in person I find him to be a reformed and repentant person? The mass media is pregnant with such unspoken questions, but they are invariably rife with condemnation. Understanding evil is risky, they say—once bad, always bad. You'd have to be naïve to think otherwise. Forgiveness is for fantasists and fools. What's done is done. That is what gives us each another piece of our identi-ties: our reputations.

The Reputed Me

. . . . .

If I think, as I do much of the time, that I am the hub of my life, the centre of my world, I am deceived. Really, the world goes on around me. People may think about me and talk about me, interact with me and take decisions that affect me, but none of this means they are interested in me or care about me. They may be able to tell you something about me, if asked directly, but with very few exceptions, they do not have an opinion about me, per se, only about how I affect them. What one person has to say does not have much consequence, but opinions are shared around and acted upon as if true. Between them, other people manage a communally owned marketplace part of my identity, which I get only indirect glimpses of and have almost no control over. I'm talking about my reputation. This is very important to me. It not only decides whether I am liked, loved, disliked, or hated; it limits or facilitates my entire life. It determines who I am and what I can and cannot be.

In relationship to me, people can be divided into four groups:

1. **Those who know me** (subdivided into infinite shades of familiarity, from living with me every day to having met me once)
2. **Those who know of me** (that is, know one or more fact about me)
3. **Those who know me well**
4. **Those who don't know me at all**

All these people, independently and in groups, form judgements about me—even if it is that I am not worth the mental effort of judging. These judgements can be fluid and short-lived, or fixed for life and unquestionable. They can be revised at any time, or reinforced. Most of this process of continual appraisal, I know nothing about. People reach their judgements about me on whatever basis they want. They are under no obligation to be fair, and it might be impossible for them to be impartial. A few might consider me a holistic creature to be seen against the complete human

environment, but most probably look no further than whether I help or inconvenience their lives or have a negligible impact.

Independently verifiable truths are unlikely to be highest on their list of criteria,
and what they say about me may be pure fiction. They can add to the mix what
they have heard (or misheard), what they imagine about me, or what they think a
listener wants to hear.

They may or may not be lenient when they doubt me, or give me a second chance
to prove that their first impression was wrong. They will probably also base their
judgements on my past performances, without allowing me the possibility of change.
They can be as bitchy and as biased as they like, and being human themselves
their own weaknesses will get in the way. If I have a success, they might want to
pull me down out of jealousy; or they might put word around that I am just pretending to be a nice person out of twisted motives. They may even get me mixed up
with someone else, and even if they realize this, it will be too late. We're very good
at making assumptions but very poor at reevaluating them.

My defenders and accusers, and other half-attentive bystanders, communicate
their judgements to each other in a variety of ways, mainly verbal but sometimes in
writing. Gesture and silence can also speak out about me.

A chief way of communicating what we think about each other is through
gossip and rumour. Which of us is hard-headed enough to sift through every conversation for what is reliable and what is conjecture? Fuelled by feelings, rumour
usually speaks louder and more often than dull fact, and it sticks in the brain better.
We know it is never entirely true, but we suspect that it is never completely un-
founded either: we conclude that it must contain some truth, even if it is distorted.
Much is added by the context and the style of the delivery of rumour. Two
entirely separate ideas can easily be conflated in the speaker's or listener's mind,
or both, which is how wrongful accusations occur and witch-hunts are instigated.
The same person can be seen as generous or gullible, a coward or a peacemaker,
tolerant or a bad listener, depending on the person who is relaying the information
and their intentions.

Out of all this—what we know and what we are told—we distil truths about
each other that we state in simplistic terms. We forget how complex we are and
speak as if another human being can be reduced to one or two unambiguous adjectives or nouns. Low-level journalism encourages us in this. What we want are
primarily labels with which to think of the other. In the minds of others, therefore,
the sum total of me is made up of short descriptive sentences that get passed
around, encapsulating me in such a way that two people look at each other in
understanding and say, "Ah!"

I couldn't tell you what is said about me. That's because a precondition for the spread of rumour is that I not be present during other people's conversations to hear what they have to say about me, nor defend myself by presenting the facts. I only ever get to hear what is said about me indirectly, some time later, after the fact.

While I remain unaware of what is being said about me, opinion radiates out-wards from its origins circulating in interfering circles, reaching new ears, and bouncing backwards and sideways. As it does so, it forms patterns of greater or lesser stability that affect my reputation (or reputations—since I am likely to have a different one in each community or group I belong to).

An unwritten, informal consensus emerges regarding how I should be treated. It decides whether I should be fully accepted, tolerated, or curtailed in my actions … whether I should be admired, ridiculed, or shamed. What is the agreed-upon communal feeling about me, the word that best describes me and to which each of my inquisitors should adhere in order to earn his fellows' approval? How should they behave with respect to me as a member of their group? Should I be held back for the good of society, or preferred for advancement? Will they widen the circle to allow me to take my place and then let me talk? Will they vote for me, or will they pillory me, safely knowing that I am an object of ridicule?

Decisions on these matters are taken by everyone, and by no one. Rarely can I point a finger and say, "You are responsible for what I have or have not been able to become." I am the product of collective irresponsibility.

Not only am I not present for most of this, but I am powerless to act. My name and identity are at stake, yet I don't have much say over them. It is difficult, if not impossible, to correct a mistaken impression that has gained circulation, or to replace a negative judgement of me with a positive one. An accusation already implies involvement and points to blame: to defend myself is to accept my involve-ment in the matter, even if I am not to blame.

There may even be some block about me in people's minds that I can do noth-ing to budge. Whatever they think of me personally, they may not like my family (even my ancestors), my nationality, my religion, and so on—even if their informa-tion is based on error.

There are many labels that can be attached to me that are not of my own mak-ing, but I do have a little freedom to act and, as a social being, I have a stark choice to make. We each have two competing internal urges when we find ourselves in a group: should I conform as far as I am able, or should I try to stand out?

It is a risk either way. I will probably have an easier life if I subordinate my in-dividual identity to the group's interests, but then I will feel eternally emasculated. This may be the best option if members of the group are mistreating me and all I

want is for them to leave me alone. If, instead, I promote my individuality at the expense of collective obedience, in the hopes of winning popularity and success, I could risk ridicule.

It can be a complex puzzle. Should I stick with what I have or go for more? Can I have half and half? If I decide to distinguish myself, what must I do to succeed, to win over the majority and subdue the dissenters? The more visible I get, the more jealousies I will arouse, the more competitors will want what I have and seek to do me down.

This is the challenge that all politicians face, the way a political identity is formed. Every political career is built on a succession of such gambles—personal exposure increasing at every step, and with it the number of potential enemies who want to see a spectacular fall of the man who thought he was better than everyone else.

If I choose to go for promotion rather than remain on the shop floor, I will have to do my best to control the circulation of information about me, to make sure it reflects well on me, and that powerbrokers get the message that I am useful and harmless at the same time. The person who rises in the organization may not be the best liked or the best for the job, but he who knows how best to play the reputation-building game.

In wider society, the system of rumour, consensus, and promotion is magnified by the media. Extremely motivated celebrities use it, or are used by it, to boost themselves to a much higher level of fame. Celebrity is a kind of amplified or enhanced identity awarded to the deserving, lucky or unlucky. They live as best they can in a volatile stock market of reputations, having to accept that they are more than ordinary people in some way, even if they remain, at heart, ordinary people themselves.

Not long ago, there were not as many famous people relative to the population as there are today, and the means of gaining fame was largely inaccessible to the general public. A rigorous de facto selection process allowed only a few, usually talented, people to achieve celebrity, and because access to their ranks was restricted, this contributed to their mystique. Contemporary technology has brought open, supposedly democratic access to the media and created the overpopulated celebrity class we have today. With quicker routes to fame available to more people, celebrity has become devalued, and it often brings not admiration and respect but visibility and ridicule.

The Virtual Me

· · · · ·

AS SEEN ON SCREEN

One way to split humanity into two unequal parts is to divide us into those who remember a world before the internet and those who do not. The former grew up relating to people in mostly nontechnological ways. The latter largely treat the online world as an extension of themselves, a second way of being, and barely question how it is.

Use the internet, and you are assured of at least one online, or virtual, identity. But it is not hard to rack up multiple online identities, whether by choice or ob-ligation (for example, having to create a new online identity each time you want to use a new website). You can be as many people as you want to be, as long as you can remember all your usernames, passwords, and answers to security questions. It could be said that these personal access details in themselves comprise my primary internet identity.

For many internet users, this is just the starting point for a promiscuity of new identities. Like a gaming machine, some of us may think the more information we feed into the internet the more likely we are to get something worthwhile out of it. The internet offers two ways for us to be different from how we normally are. The most conspicuous of these is that the internet serves as a gallery in which the main exhibit is ourselves. It is at once:

- **a shop window,** where I can put up a curriculum vitae or a multimedia advert addressed to prospective employers or clients. My self is the brand or product that is on sale, and the objective is to create a "profile" that will be noticed.

- **a stage or blank canvas for self-expression,** with the main aim being to recruit friends and followers and broadcast my opinions. In this aspect, the internet is like some mad television show in which there is space for every would-be performer who wants to join in, in any capacity he wants. All

the characters and the audience in this chaotic spectacle are in the studio at the same time, and they all talk at once, mostly off the cuff. There are no auditions and little editing of scripts; it is all live and impulsive. Celebrity has become oxymoronically democratic.

The other way we play with our identities online is by concealing them. The internet encourages the taking and using of pseudonyms as a rough form of egalitarianism. This grants temporary freedom to the individual—and with it, freedom from responsibility. Pseudonymity undoubtedly has its virtues. If my life is threatened by giving my real name, I would have good reason to withhold it. If, on the other hand, I merely leave a comment on a website or write a book review or deliver trenchant insults about a celebrity I don't know—these don't seem like much of a reason for pretending I am someone else. Rather a pseudonym can have the effect of curbing or dissipating identity: if no one identifiable makes the remark, in effect no one is making it.

Whether we flaunt ourselves or conceal ourselves, the internet is a playground where we can experiment with being more or less than we really are. We accept it as it is largely without question, instead of debating how we would like it to be. In putting on and taking off our virtual identities, we would do well to at least be aware of certain underlying principles of life online:

- **The internet is owned not anarchic**. It may once have had a free and easy ethos, but it is no longer a blank page without restrictions. Some of the most popular parts of it are owned and controlled by large companies, and they steer our actions on it with the aim of maximizing their profits. There is, therefore, a correlation between how we are online and the promotion of goods and services. My online identity might be personal to me, but it is merely a commodity to anyone doing online business.

- **We serve machines.** Online, we do things in the way that suits the software designer, his code, and the machine that runs it. We are, to some extent, dictated to by the requirements of the circuitry, not by what is best for us. The server remembers I have a created an identity on it, even if I forget.

- **Disclosure is desirable, even obligatory**. When I press the return key, my personal information becomes public property. I may intend it to go to one other person, but as soon as it is digitalized it can be copied and shared ad infinitum. This inevitability leads to the common philosophy on the internet, which holds that if we can't stop data spreading, we shouldn't try. If data does spread, we *should* share it, all of it. In this view, information is meant to be freely available, and all internet users have a right to know anything and everything, including about all other people, whether online or not. If, like some celebrities, they choose to protect themselves, this is seen as reason to find out what they want to conceal. Privacy is seen by the show-all, tell-all generation as old-fashioned, and identity is public property. It is as if we are happy to carry out surveillance on each other.

- **The trivial and the significant are honoured equally.** All information, even my most intimate details, is treated as neutral. Its import and interest is relative, depending on who is delivering it and who is receiving it. Selectivity is arrogance. Facts and thoughts that a generation ago would have been routinely discarded are now supplied to everyone online, along with information of genuine interest. Each person is served the entire restaurant menu and expected to pick out what they feel like eating.

- **All things in exaggeration are good.** The aim online is to attract attention. This requires a spectacle, a degree of showing off that we can't manage in daily life. What is the point of stating facts about yourself plainly if no one sees or hears them?

- **The internet doesn't easily discern the truth.** If everyone is theoretically equal and everything relative, then so is the truth. No one is automatically right or wrong. This allows and almost encourages insincerity: you can pretend to be what you want, because it is all a game. Rumour is as good as fact. It can spread across the internet with incendiary speed and acquire credibility through repetition, casually destroying a reputation without any one individual being aware of his involvement in it. No one seems concerned about exploring the problematic frontier between insincerity and creativity.

- **Everyone has the right and duty to answer back.** On the internet, it is assumed that communication is never one way. A response is invited and expected. Feedback is a reflex. The internet specialises in remoteness, lack of eye contact, stilted dialogue (it isn't easy to reason online with your detractors), and emotional disconnection. All this has a great impact on how we dare to be and how other people, strangers mostly, will let us be.

- **We are affirmed in our identities by each other.** Through feedback, we are judged. The comments at the foot of the page will tell you whether I (or what I have done) am valid and worthwhile. I will get a star-rating or percentage score of approval. Like some crazy classroom, everyone marks each other's work whether they have a qualification to do so or not—and whether of not they have thought before typing.

- **If everyone else is doing it, it's okay.** One of the big ideas behind the internet is that our minds can be harnessed together as an intelligent "crowd source," or "hive" (a community working together for the common good), and taken together and averaged out, these ideas will put us in a position to make sensible and informed decisions. It's mathematically possible, I suppose, that a kind of wisdom is sometimes distilled from this mass of ideas, but not always. Hives do not make complex moral choices. Another way of looking at us is as a herd. Looking around us, we can be convinced that it is desirable and essential for us to do what everyone else is doing. We assume there is safety in being surrounded by people doing the same thing: if anything goes wrong, I have a good chance of not being eaten or stampeded under foot.

Out of all these factors, our virtual identities emerge. It seems like harmless fun—a way to extend ourselves—but two things about it should cause us to stand back and ask questions before committing ourselves so blindly.

The internet is young and is growing up. And as we so often do when faced with a precocious teenager, full of himself and convinced he has some special powers that the rest of us lack, we may give the Web credit for being more mature than it actually is because, actually, we are a little scared of it. We are still enjoying the sensation of having just taken it out of the box, and we want to play a little more before we consider the serious implications that come with it. It is hard to know where to begin to ask questions about it, because it is such a singular phenomenon there is nothing we can compare it to.

This creepy-charming teenager is not in the same earthly dimension as us. Everything on the internet is unreal, in the sense that it cannot be verified by our five senses. You can't shake hands on it or smell perfume. It may come out of the real world and interact with the real world, but it is not the real world.

It is like a magic trick on autopilot. Everything that appears on the screen is a two-dimensional representation, an echo, a teletransported shadow of the real 3D thing. It is an exchange or energy, a ripple of electrons.

It takes its vocabulary from life to draw us into the illusion, such as the slick redefining of the word "friend." Or rather, we don't know how much reality there is behind what we are seeing. It might be entirely trustworthy, or it might be entirely untrustworthy; it is impossible to say.

None of our human checking mechanisms work through the computer screen. We don't know who is dealing with our data, or even if there are human beings involved in it at all.

We should therefore be wary of this dazzlingly gifted, tentacular hyper-monster in our midst. In particular, there are two reasons for at least a little disquiet and reticence in the way we behave online. If we give ourselves to it freely, our future selves may be at stake.

The first of these causes of disquiet grows out of the nature of the medium. Online, anyone can be anyone; we have no way of knowing who is who. This is part of the mystique of the internet, but it also allows web developers the opportunity to sneak nonpeople into our lives. To call them "robots" (bots for short) is to give them a misleading persona. They are pieces of code that simulate human beings. As we are communicating remotely through our screens, it can be hard to know if there is anyone living out there at all. We are thus seduced into accepting artificial intelligences as a harmless improvement to our lives: if it is cheaper for companies to employ avatars, and we can't tell the difference, where is the problem?

Some proponents for the internet regard the whole thing as an experiment in artificial intelligence and look forward to it escaping from human constraints. If we keep feeding this thing data, they hope, out of complexity something new, surprising, and by implication better will grow itself. I think this is another case of "Just because we can doesn't mean we should." The desirability of creating artificial intelligence, the ownership of it, and the ethics surrounding it are far from decided.

The other reason why we should think carefully about our online behaviour is that the internet, like an elephant, never forgets. It may churn over new ideas and be on to the next thing before we have got used to the last one, but it has an ability we don't often think about: storage. We volunteer our sensitive personal information by the bucket load, and it voraciously sucks all this up, as if space to put it were not a problem. Computing's fabled ability to increase its power year on year means that the internet can effectively save everything we can generate. It is really a vast warehouse—endless as far as we are concerned—and the biggest junk shop in the universe: there is always room for more, and nothing is sold or thrown away.

Everyone who lives for the moment online, in the eternal present, is contributing to his identity in the future. We use the internet's capacity as an overspill for our own brains, making the machine custodian of our identity, and it dutifully backs up everything just in case. Everything.

Much that it remembers about us is unintentional. As we wander around the internet we leave behind us a trail of our presence. Each clip we watch; each glance we take; each act of bored curiosity; each banal comment we feel compelled to leave sets off a tripwire, and a robotic FBI man meticulously records the event for posterity. Some proponents of the internet talk about this backing up operation as if it were almost a sacred duty. Just as we regret our ancestors throwing so much away that would be interesting to us now, so we are determined not to delete even one detail.

This means that the identities we create today might be around forever, long after we think we have eradicated them. Youth might no longer be a time of experiment and indiscretion best forgotten; we may have to relive it for eternity, pain and all. We are all, if we don't choose otherwise, going to be on television for all time.

Any doubts raised here could be put down to vanity, sentimentality, and nostalgia. Anyone who doesn't fully embrace the internet and all it can do is showing an irrational mistrust of progress. The internet is a gift to us from science, tangible proof that science will come up everything we are ever going to need. And that includes all the answers to the question, "Who on earth am I?"

The Material Me

· · · · ·

CODED MESSAGES

The question "*Who* am I?" is meaningless to a scientist, who might rightly ask what a "who" is before wanting to know anything more. "*What* am I?," however, is a question with a more straightforward set of answers.

To address it, science must set aside anything I have to say. I am a subjective contaminant in the experiment, with an emotional attachment to a particular outcome. It must ignore all the cultural, pseudo-anthropological pontificating I have come up with so far. Good science cannot afford to get personal. It always proceeds objectively, through direct observation of reality, using information that can be verified. Only in this way can sound conclusions be reached.

A lot depends on which level you want to look at me—and what sense you hope to make. With caution and judicious use of the evidence, I can be scientifically defined in five different ways: as an animal, an organism, a formula, a flowering-cum-conveyor belt of DNA, and as a self-conscious brain and/or mind.

I am a beast

The first way I may be asked to view my scientific identity is to see myself for what I really am: a beast.

If I undress in a laboratory and keep my mouth shut, the first clear fact about me is that I am an animal, and as such I must belong to a genus and species and have an evolutionary history. I am an example of *Homo sapiens*; I have a shared identity with my own kind. It is possible that I have an inner sense of my individuality, but from the outside this is not obvious.

There is much argument about whether human beings are categorically different from other animals, or whether we merely differ from them by degree. A long list of qualities, abilities, and habits distinguishes us from our relatives, the other apes; chief among them is that we put apes in cages and try to teach them to "talk" our language, while they do not do the same to us. However, a true biological determinist would warn us not to make too much of this. We are still only animals, and we must be studied on the same level as any other creature.

The obvious way to define my individual identity, therefore, is to describe the generalities of my species and then observe my particular behaviour, how it varies from the norm, and my relationships.

Were an anthropologist (or better still, an intergalactic zoologist of some non-human species) to train his binoculars on my house he would gradually learn about my rank in my troupe and pick out my idiosyncrasies. He would see how well or badly I interact with others of my kind, whether I hunt well, give orders or take them, my instincts of fight or flight, and whether I growl or whimper in response to a threat. He would notice my attitude to territory, especially my determination to fight for it—an ancestral urge that comes out today in aggression and war. He would also be interested in how well fed I am: whether I get the first choice of food, or even decide how food is shared with my fellows. He would look at my success or failure at mating, how well I flaunt my attractions and fight off rivals. I don't know what he would make of my sedentary life generating words on a screen.

Under close scrutiny and after extended study, our anthropologist would get to know me, and he would be able to see the ways I differ from other individuals who resemble me. I may have scars and fractures in particular places, perhaps deformations or congenital weaknesses—certainly, conditions that cause the visible parts of my body to take on idiosyncratic forms.

Having seen all this, he may well give me a name based on something that sets me apart: the way I walk, my favourite food, my kinship ties, or an involuntary gesture.

I am an organism

If this scientist were to isolate me from my herd and observe me closer up, they would see me in another way: as a biological device for living. As any curious child knows, a good way to understand something is to take it apart and see what is inside. I am, if we are being wholly unsentimental, no more than an object. I am an organism packaged in skin. I consist of a composite system of organs and other body parts, similar in many aspects to other human beings but never quite identical. If we strip this down to its basics, we find that I am a colony or commune of around 100 trillion interdependent specialized cells, with each knowing what to do in the cause of me-ing. I am an assembly of bone and soft tissue—a sort of jellyfish with a brain, backbone, and vocal chords.

Actually—and this takes some admitting—I am outnumbered here in this body. I am less *me* than I am *them*. If we are going to be democratic about this, I am the minority inhabitant of my body. For every one cell of my own, I have ten microbes (bacteria, fungi, viruses, and protozoa) formed into ghettoes of immigrant subcommunities living in me or off me, mostly symbiotically. I depend on them for my economy to work. I should talk of myself not as "I" but "we."

I am a chemical formula

So much for life, that mysterious force that eludes definition. I can also be identified by my elemental composition. Boil me up and precipitate me, make piles out of the residue, analyze and weigh them, and this is what you will get:

- oxygen – 65 percent
- carbon – 18 percent
- hydrogen – 10 percent
- nitrogen – 3 percent

Miniscule amounts of calcium, phosphorus, potassium, sulphur, chlorine, sodium, magnesium, and iron

A seasoning of cobalt, copper, zinc, iodine, selenium, fluorine, manganese, molybdenum nickel, chromium, and several other elements

If the birth recipe for each of us is the same, what differentiates the desiccated me from you will be the trace contaminants I have picked up in my life. I am, in the most extremely deconstructed definition, in my most pure form, my impurities. You and I are nothing more than one arrangement of chemicals communicating with another one.

All the materials, of course, are on loan from the material world and only borrowed, since I am compost in the making. They are not mine, so it is hard to think of them as me. Science, quite literally, confirms that we are dust to dust.

If you want to keep closing in on me, you will find that I really consist of uncountable busy little atoms charged with energy and in constant motion.

However, there is an obvious problem with the extreme scrutiny of matter as a way of identifying me. It is difficult to appreciate the whole and the component parts at the same time. There is still a me who thinks he is a me to account for, and this is easily lost in dividing me up. A reductionist scientist would argue, however, that this is not really a problem but mere vanity on my part.

I am a sequence of code

All that gives a fairly comprehensive description of me, but it fails to address the implied questions of why?—why am I like I am, and why am I here at all?

If we allow that I am more than a neat heap of minerals, and that what holds these particles together is something called life, then we have to ask what that is and why I have it. Life has been defined as information with the capacity to pass itself on, and I could be defined as a particular configuration of such information that is encoded in DNA. Here surely is something uniquely mine. Am I not my genome, a unique set of sequences of DNA, switches that dictate everything about me?

To the evolutionary biologist we are all transporters of genes. Each of us is a mere breath on the continuum of life, a step in the chain reaction, from the chance fusion of chemicals in the year dot of life to the extinction of life sometime before the heat death of the universe. The process is blind and meaningless. I inherit a union of DNA from my parents and bequeath a portion to my children.

My identity is that of carrier, temporary proprietor, and mobile laboratory of my genes. All else I can say about myself is invention to stop myself seeing the awful truth.

Not long ago, a lot was expected from genetics. It was making such rapid advances that we were assured it would explain everything about us. It would turn out to be the key to how and who we are. Gene analysis was meant to be our definitive pin through the butterfly, fixing human nature for all time. Instead, we have proved elusive.

A great amount has been learnt about human genetics, but not all of it has proved useful. Genetics is far from the exact science it was hoped it would be. While we have a clear genetic "blueprint," its translation into meaning is not yet clear. You can have your genome typed out at a cost, but you might not find anything in it worth the effort. If you are looking for a "me sequence" of code, you are likely to be disappointed.

No one these days talks about "nature" and "nurture" as separate, rival forces. It is clear that they interact, and any genetic identification parade has to take this into account. We are both. We are launched into form by our genes, and they continue to influence us, but we are also shaped by the lives we live—and possibly, although this is contentious, by the thoughts and emotions we have.

I am, in short, my DNA and how it impacts on the world, plus my personal experience. Research continues into exactly what this might mean.

I am a brain

What about the sense that I am someone? Science cannot ignore this altogether in favour of materialistic theories. It might have sight-stepped the question, "Who am I?" and half answered the simpler question, "What I am?" but there is a third, and very valid question, which it would also like to answer: "Where am I?"

I have a sensation of being, of consciousness. Most people in the western world locate this behind their eyes, and this seems to be the logical place to go looking for our identities through scans of living brains and dissections of dead ones.

The search for the location and nature of "I" is known as the mind-body problem, although the word "mind" itself is problematic, because it suggests that I am a thinking entity independent of the physical brain.

Mainstream neuroscience works on the principle that if I exist, I must be incarnate. I must be in my brain, mustn't I? Where else could I be? My sensation of "somebodyness" must come down to a pattern of fiendishly complicated electrical impulses. Neuroscientists believe that one day they will be able to point to a part of my brain that lights up on a scanner screen and say, with a completely straight face, "There you are!" I don't believe it, but then that might be because I don't want to. Imagine if it turned out to be nothing more than a series of miniature electric shocks.

Fortunately, other scientists are sceptical. Consciousness, they say, will not be reduced to physical phenomenon. No one is ever going to find where I am hiding. Instead, they suggest, we might be better off looking for it by two concurrent routes: objective and subjective. We can continue to use instruments to examine brains, but we should also look inside our own heads and try to work through the problem that way.

Which brings us to the nub of all this identity business. How can one brain-being (who might or might not be mindless) examine another brain-being and say anything meaningful? If we have to explore inside ourselves, how exactly would we go about it?

PART C

Inside Out

23

The Interpreted Self

· · · · ·

MISSING A LINK

So much for the label on the packaging. My outer identity is the relatively easy bit of me to talk about. It consists of substance: facts that we can demonstrate to one another, evidence we disagree about.

Interesting though it may be, however, that has nothing to do with me. The important elements of my identity are inside, out of reach. Not even I can see them or touch them. I cannot even prove they are there at all, let alone tell you how they work.

It would be reasonable of you to doubt the existence of this inner self that I allege, because it is insubstantial. The only motivation to keep reading might be that you have the same peculiar sensation of selfness as I do, an acutely personal part of you that you want to know more about.

Be warned, from here on there are no definites. It is my word against yours. We may not even agree on the way in.

There is a game played as an icebreaker in some self-help workshops. You choose a partner, someone you have never met and know nothing about, and you take it in turns to look at each other and make three pronouncements. The first begins with "I see ...," and you say what you see looking at the face of the other person. The second sentence begins with "I perceive ...," and you end it with what you think you see, by looking a little harder, beyond the blatant information of the face. The third sentence begins with "I wonder ..." and is an invitation to free speculation; ideally you use it try to make intelligent guesses about the person beneath the skin. When you have said what you have to say, your partner tells you how accurate your report has been. Most people do reasonably well on the first level of straight observation. We are good at the outside, appearance stuff—how can we not see if we are looking? This information is verifiable and usually beyond discussion, although it might occasion some debate about exact eye colour, for instance, and stray into judgement ("You have a beautiful nose").

The second two levels of the game invariably produce poor results. Perception is harder than seeing. It demands more effort and has an element of seeking. So much can get in the way to distort our judgement. We can read an expression, an emotion—perhaps pick up tiredness and suffering.

But seeing behind the eyes of another is not a precise art. We get some things right and others wrong through concentration but also guesswork and luck. When we wonder about the other—which is what we do most of the time—we usually confess more about our own internal processes than we stumble upon theirs. Of course, we are never going to know how right we were because the other person might be self-deluded or dishonest.

The game usually reveals how we fool ourselves about the state of mind of each other. We are not generally good at seeing beyond appearance and producing fact. We think we are good at making perceptive and intuitive judgements about other people, but the truth is we don't know much about what goes on in their heads. Mostly our reading of them is clouded by our assumptions, our judgements, our desires, our likes and dislikes, who they remind us of, and so on. We project information from our own minds onto their faces, and it does not result in accurate interpretation.

There are two ways to get to know the self sealed inside:

- **From within**. Only I can do this and I go about it through thought, reflection, meditation, and creativity. You cannot participate or even help. This is a very direct approach but also necessarily a self-conscious and subjective one. It is not methodological or scientific; it is not repeatable, least of all under control conditions. There is no one to guide me or review my work, and I may go about it in a chaotic fashion. One risk of it is that I may waste my time: I may find myself asking lots of incoherent questions but getting only perplexing puzzles for answers. Another risk is that I get snagged on booby traps that I set myself—that I kid myself or do not allow myself to see how things really are. I may also sabotage my search by referencing pre-existing beliefs or by believing what has been written about other people engaged in this exercise. At the end of my quest, I may know myself well but I will only know myself: I will not be able to share the information I have acquired and I will have no idea whether anything I have learnt applies to other people. (None of these shortcomings seems to be a cause for reflection for the many self-appointed gurus who peddle their own personal insights as universal principles, however.)

- **Through interpretation**. This is how you look into me if you are not me. To understand how another person operates inside, or even how all people operate, you have no option but to find an indirect route, a theory or investigative technique, and hope you get to the same—or a better—place as your subject . . . in this case me.

We haven't yet given up on the idea of reading the inner person through the outside of his head. It seems such a self-evident idea. People must give themselves away through their faces, surely, even if it is in some coded way that we have to learn to decipher. Crack the code and you drag me out from my solitary cell. Why else is my face so potentially expressive if it doesn't give more away than my basic emotional state?

From the ancient world to the pre-modern era, physiognomy, the art of reading character through the face, was trusted but never produced guaranteed results. One insurmountable problem of face reading is that there is no way to know when you have got it right. The same goes for its successor, phrenology, in which the character of the brain is understood through feeling the shape and size of the skull. Science relegated both methods to pseudoscience in the 19th century, but the desire to see through people from the outside has never faded and has recently returned in the shape of Facial Recognition Technology (FRT). Forget the fallible human scrutinizer and his quaint numbered diagrams; this has nothing to do with physiognomy of old. The idea now is to feed a digital photograph into a computer and let it work out what the expression on the face says about the thoughts and feelings of the person.

Another means of interpretation is to get us talking and simultaneously study us. Then you develop a theory to explain what you hear and see. This is the methodology of the "psy" family of sciences: psychology and psychiatry and their derivatives. The prefix comes from "psyche," an ancient Greek word that is normally translated as "spirit," or "soul." This is anathema to modern science, but "psy" still stands as placeholder for the lingeringly ethereal being that is me.

The psycho-sciences have carried out no end of interesting experiments and provided us with thought-provoking observations, but they have not come up with any laws about human nature. Which means they have much to say about me, in the universal sense, as part of the human race, and they would have more to say about me in a particular sense if I were to consult a practitioner.

None of it is beyond dispute. Everything rests on certain assumptions, including:

- Being of the same species we are essentially all the same, with variations. We are, biologically speaking, animated meat. If we have "minds," they must be squarely rooted in our brains and the mind is entirely inconceivable outside its housing.

- There is a normal, healthy mind and abnormal and unhealthy minds.

- A trained practitioner can distinguish between the two, that is, he can diagnose mental illness.

- Once diagnosed, conditions can be cured using scientific means including drugs, surgery, and techniques of behaviour modification.

Many of us eschew the rigours of science for the parallel world of character portrayal and fortune telling.

In general, systems of divination—astrology being the most well known—do not claim to be true in a scientific sense (that is, provable) but nonetheless accurate in a personal sense. They do not concern themselves with universal pronouncements about human nature that apply to all of us equally; rather they place the individual at the centre of his own reality and treat everyone as unique.

Each of us has a different identity in whichever system we choose to follow: a sign of the astrological zodiac, a Chinese horoscope animal, and so on. It is easy to see all this as so much superstitious nonsense—easy to ridicule it; however, divination can be used constructively. From my little experience of astrology, I know that it is best used not as a prescriptive tool (telling me what is going to come to pass) but a suggestive tool whereby I follow the symbols that come up as a means of exploring myself. Even if I don't believe in its root principle—that my character was fixed at birth and a precise reading of my birth chart will tell me much about who I am—I can still use it as a way of asking myself questions.

Systems of alternative healing also take an interest in who I am inside in their search to precisely target remedies, especially the ones that see the illnesses of the body as reflecting the person within. My physical condition becomes a direct language of how I am.

All these systems of self-knowledge, whether science based or shunned by science, have the potential to show me something about my identity, as long as I remain aware of their methodology and its limitations.

Every interpretive system has all or at least most of the following characteristics:

- **It promises to tell me something I can't find out by myself** (unless, that is, I study the subject in depth).

- **It depends on a human expert to interpret the evidence.** It is assumed this person knows more about me than I do, within his field of expertise, even if he or she acts as a facilitator and a guide.

- **It is based on a model of my inner world.** This model, like any model, is inevitably imperfect.

- **To fit into the model I must be placed in one or more invented categories.**

- **There is always a risk that the practitioner finds what he wants to find, what he is looking for.**

- **The diagnosis about me is conveyed in words,** usually its own jargon.

- **It may make bold—but always dubious—statements of cause and effect.** Two phenomena may seem to be connected but may have nothing to do with each other.

- **Success (an accurate depiction of me) might be down to the skill of the practitioner, or some unknown variable, not the system.**

There is one other interpretative system that must be mentioned. It is not personalized but it does give us valuable insights into our identity. Literature very often concerns itself with questions of who we are, and even if a book or play or poem is not about me, it may touch on some poignant aspect of the human condition that I respond to. A protagonist may not be in any way like me, and I might not even like him, but in some way I may still learn about myself through his predicaments and choices. A novelist or playwright can enter into the thoughts and motivations of a character to see what understanding can be had. An autobiography or diary also gives vicarious access into the inner sanctum of another person into which we cannot normally go.

Every technique I have discussed here offers an indirect approach to the subject under examination, me. A simpler way to understand myself is to look directly and see what's there.

24

The Indefinable Me

· · · · ·

I DO MIND

Forget the outside world and all that it has to say about me, as detailed previously. Forget all that I have told you about myself, the routine practical stuff I trot out in answer to enquiries. Forget the bumbling attempts of psycho-interpreters to construct their models of me. The truth about me is straightforward. I am this sensation in here. That's all I am.

There are two blatant problems to confront if I am to say more than this. One is that there is an unbridgeable gap between my intimate self and the rest of the world. You can't see me, and I can't show you.

There is a connection between us but it is indirect. I talk or write and you listen or read, and you make what sense you want of what I have to say. If, as I suspect from many conversations I have had with other people, you have a similar experience of selfhood to mine, we will be able to compare notes as to how we differ. To get to that, you have a choice to make. Do you believe what I have to say? Does it sound plausible and fit in with your experience? Or do you think I am my hallucinations?

Even if you are willing to hear me out, we have to be extremely cautious because we have to agree on a lingua franca.

This invisible, insubstantial, intangible, indefinable sensation of being me is impossible to put into words. Inside, I am a shapeless realm with no straight edges. There is nothing concrete to pin a name to and it would be more accurate to talk of "non-things" or "insubstances" to remind ourselves not to be too literal. Almost the less we say the better, because every time we use language we lose precision and introduce ambiguity.

This can cause a lot of misunderstanding, and yet what else can we do? It is the human predicament to cryptically and suggestively to one another in poetry, myth, metaphor, symbols, or arcane jargon. All these ways of communicating work fine for me, but I prefer plain speech if possible. All I can ask is that you put aside any preconceptions for the moment and accept that we will be dealing with abstract nouns that must not be given too-precise definitions. I know this won't make a scientist or lexicographer happy, but I can't see how it can be helped. We must also be wary in case we run up against cultural connotations, and perhaps emotions, too.

Here, I must declare my ignorance. I don't know how much my exploration of things inner is affected by what goes on outside me. How different would things be if I were illiterate? What if I had never read a book? If I did not have time free from physical labour? If I lived in an oppressive society that forced me to think in a particular way on pain of death? If I lived entirely alone or in a silent monastery? Do you need to have had the same broad experience of the world as I have to resonate with what I have to say? I don't know. Perhaps it wouldn't make any difference and the core of me would still be the same.

Before I explain who I am inside, I should say how I come to know it. I have almost permanent access to this self of mine, and I can stop typing at any moment, sit back, and think about it. That's one way I find out what is going on. There are better ways, but my overactive brain quickly gets distracted by other matters and starts asking clever questions such as "Who is observing whom?" Losing myself in contemplation works well, as does meditation, listening to music, and dreaming. Extreme circumstances of life and altered states I get into can be particularly rich in information, because in them I am often taken by surprise while my normal psychic defences are down.

Returning from these various routes of exploration, I have learned that being me is a rich, complicated thing. I can, and do, often divide the experience into different facets, but in reality they are all mixed up as a compact and indivisible self.

However, if I had to lay the pieces of my identity on the table, I would organize them as follows:

- **My Solitude and Autonomy.** I am alone. I can only get so close to other people and can only ask them to share my responsibilities for my inner self, never expect them to take charge. Other people cannot hear or see "me."

- **The Hub of My Senses and Instincts.** This is probably just my mechanistic brain doing what it has to do, but I am the receptor of sight, sound, touch, taste, and smell. I experience these incoming signals, and sometimes I react in a purely animal, instinctive way: I grab for food or run away from a threat, and so on.

- **Mind.** Mostly when I speak of myself I mean this, the part of me that makes sense of the world. This may be a function of my brain. I am not really bothered what it is or where it is. All I know is that the way in which it operates makes me the individual I am. It carries out several tasks worth listing as separate items.

- **Self-Consciousness.** I am aware of myself and this can lead to a sense of responsibility and the conviction that I have free will. It is possible, however, that I use this capacity not to be honest with myself but to fool myself. Consciousness, of course, has two meanings: to be awake and to be aware.

- **The Person Behind the Personality.** My character seems to be part of the outside world, but it is certainly connected to my self, which is aware of it. Sometimes I feel I have control over my personality, but not always. Arguably, happiness consists in widening my field of choices and aligning my decisions with the sensation inside.

- **Self-instruction.** I have a sporadic mental chatter going on, sometimes a monologue, sometimes more of a dialogue. It is forever looking for correlations and chains of cause and effect. Sometimes this enables me to play a sport or perform another skill, but sometimes it gets in the way, as if my body and my unconscious can do a much better job than my brain can.

- **Purposeful Thinking.** If I make an effort I can apply my brain-mind to problems. My brain spends a great deal of its time monitoring situations and deciding whether or not it should instruct the body to take action.

- **Imagination.** This facility allows me to reflect on what is not in front of me, to go backwards and forwards in time, to travel without moving, and to create things that have not previously existed. I can imagine dinosaurs and aliens, and I can imagine myself as if I were outside my own body. I can imagine what you think of me. I can contemplate mysteries and impossibilities. The use to which I put my imagination can distinguish me from other people. My imagination uses my senses as its language, and I can see pictures and hear sounds, particularly voices, in my head.

- **Empathy.** I am aware that I am not alone on the planet and that my life is interrelated with others. I can use my imagination to make assumptions about what goes on inside other people.

- **Emotions.** These are very strange phenomena. I feel them at once mentally and physically. Sometimes I have control over them; at other times they slip out of my grasp. They can be painful or pleasant, or a mixture of both. They are seldom predictable. They can be transient or long lasting; I even believe some of them get stuck in various parts of my body. They can manifest as illness. I certainly have an emotional identity.

- **Reservoir of Knowledge.** I know all the answers to the questions that this person with this face and name can be asked, both trivial and transcendental. No one else does. I don't even have to think about most of them: I can respond immediately. This aspect of me knows how to decipher the questions in the first place, divine the intentions behind them, and determine what is appropriate. This is an important daily job undertaken by the self, to hold the whole of me together in a fashion that appears coherent to the outside world: to speak up for myself, to make demands, correct injustices, and so on.

- **Intuition.** This is an entirely different kind of knowledge that I have access to. I sometimes know without knowing how I know, and without being sure in a conventional sense. Other people may doubt me in this. They may warn me to keep to the known facts and to act with caution and common sense; but this other knowledge, which is mine alone and goes beyond animal instinct, is infallible. I may misread it—follow my desire, for example, and pretend it is intuition—and I often mistrust it, when I don't want to accept the consequences of what it is telling me. But how I use it or do not use it makes it clear who I am.

All these inner operations, taken together, define the indefinable me, but they cannot be extracted and presented as an unmistakable identity without taking one other phenomenon into account. I may be invisible and indefinable, but I am still a creature of time.

25

The Remembering Me

· · · · ·

LOOK BACK, CARRY FORWARD

For my identity to work, both of us have to remember who I am. I can only be what you recall and I confirm, or vice versa. It is the only continuity I have.

Without this the actual "I" cannot exist. I can't hope to live entirely in the eternal present, however good an idea it sounds, without memory to sustain me. What would I do without it? Reinvent myself every second, giving myself a new name each time? This would be merely pretending to be a different person, and I would be insubstantial.

My past is not some weight that I should seek to be free of, a burden that skews my judgement. Time is not the enemy of healthy living. It is our environment. We live in it as fish live in the sea. My history is as real, in some ways, as the present. It made me who I am, and it is a resource that I cannot and should not deny. I do not have to live in one long now to be whole; I can learn to be time-dynamic.

My identity, then, depends on my memory, and my memory makes me who I am. It links all of the shades of me at different ages of my life, feeding them into a common stream. Herein lies the answer to the question that people argue over: "Am I—do I have to be—the same person as I was 20, 30, 40 years ago?" How can I help but still be that person, even if I feel utterly different to him inside.

Memory is the backbone of my life, but it is a strange, even unfathomable phenomenon. It is simply defined as the laying down of events and feelings about them and the retrieval of them at a later date—a psychobiological version of a filing system.

This is to say everything about it, and nothing at all. Mostly, all we can do is wonder. Is it matter or energy? How can a memory of some trivial childhood event be so vividly recalled decades later, as if it were a professionally produced film stored in solid state? More than that, this is a film that comes with texture and smell incorporated.

Memory is an idiosyncratic thing. Some memories I am in semi-control of. I can deliberately recall them and even edit the action as I go along. Others suddenly overwhelm me. And a few stay tantalizingly half-formed, out of my grasp, as I struggle to fit details into the sequence.

Scientists are doing their best to understand memory, but they haven't yet got it pinned down. They do not know exactly in what manner memory is recorded or retrieved, although experiments on brains have yielded a few clues. They know that they can stimulate parts of the brain and produce particular memories, but it is far from clear where memories are located precisely or the biology of their functioning.

Many questions are yet to be answered. Do we keep a complete or partial record of what happens to us? Is everything we live through, feel, and witness laid down with unfailing accuracy somewhere? Or do we remake memory as it is remembered, rearchiving it in a different form, interpreted by the present? Or a combination of both?

What we do know is that memories don't come as one solid lump. There are various ways of distinguishing between kinds of memory.

A first, simple division is between short-term and long-term memory. Some memories are attached to fleeting sensation—a finger punctured by the thorn of a rose, say; others are generated internally, such as the desperation of undeclared love. Then there are conscious and unconscious memories: those that I know I have and those that I recorded without knowing or had forgotten about until they return to me unexpectedly. Some memories are efforts of the mind (remembering a poem) while others feel they have more to do with the body (how to balance on a bike or place my fingers on the frets of a guitar). There are memories that are clear and memories that are vague; memories that are captured and played back visually, and memories that are aural or olfactory. I have many specific memories (of a particular object or person, for example), but others are generalizable and enable me to make statements about reality. For instance, I may guess at the author of a piece of art or a musical composition on the basis of similar works experienced in the past.

Every one of us also has acute, intense memories of an exceptional moment in life—such as the births of our children, in which a lot is lived in a few hours—contrasting with diffused memories of, say, a hot and happy summer in which all the days over three months are squashed together and the intervening bits (bouts of bad weather, periods of passing misery) are not included in the scenario.

Some of my memories are charged with emotion (even decades after the event) and others are emotion free. A few mix the two. I may, for example, remember the nerves I felt before an exam and the jubilation afterwards as emotional, but think of the doing of the exam in a more rational way.

Memories may lack feeling, but they are rarely neutral. I keep them for a reason, because they meant or mean something to me. They have judgements attached— an incident that I think worked out well for me, a decision that paid off, a moral issue that was not in doubt at the time. I may later reassess these judgements. A few choice memories I may not interpret: they remain as puzzles that I don't need to resolve.

In addition to these, we also hold memories outside ourselves in physical, real-world ways: as souvenirs and old photographs; in drawers of old clothes; in sentimental possessions; in diaries and other writing; on computer drives; and, shared with others, as traditions that are kept alive by groups of people repeating the same ritual periodically.

Some memories are a combination of all ways and forms of storage. We each have a different formula or cocktail for remembering. Science may turn out to be on the wrong track if it thinks that one day it will be able to categorically map the areas of the brain we use. I doubt if it will ever be able to tell me exactly how I do my remembering. I do it in my way, idiosyncratically, using interior and exterior resources.

Memory is clumsy and cumulative rather than methodical and discrete: each new memory is piled on to the old ones, sometimes causing the old ones to fade. It is certain that we remember more than we think. We can recover memories that were buried or lost.

It is almost the wrong question to ask whether memory is reliable. If it is sense we are after, accuracy of facts comes second in importance. To some extent, undoubtedly, I select what to remember and what to recall to suit the story I want to tell myself. In some aspects, I trust my memory—what choice have I got? How could I live and make judgements if everything was debatable? I may take some convincing that I have got it wrong and that a friend remembers better than me. More likely, we will each bring something complementary to the story. It is almost like assembling hallucinations and expecting to get a reality. Certainly, too, the moment of recall counts, the conditions of the present when I do the retelling. A happy occasion can become sad and nostalgic, depending on circumstances. The emotional charge of a memory can change, as it does, for example, after someone has died.

The death of someone is also the death of some of my memories. We may both remember the same events, but the person who has died remembered them in his way. He could confirm my memories and complement them.

I am an accretion of my personal memories, a box of souvenirs I lug around with me. Other people know the verifiable facts about me, but the really important stuff only I know. I am the sum of my past, as lived within, of everything that has brought me here today.

I wouldn't claim that I have a particularly good memory. Like everyone, I remember some things well and some things not at all. Some people, I know, have excellent memories, and I wonder if that somehow gives them more identity that the rest of us.

The recording equipment and techniques of memory are only the raw material we are provided with; it is what we do with them that is important. Memories are nothing unless we give them meaning. The kind of memory I am interested in here is autobiographical memory, which is a mixture of facts about me as perceived exclusively by me but given shape by the narrative I impose on them.

My memories transfused to you would look like a strip of charmingly amateur film of people you don't know doing odd things. Without the context and emotions I give them, they would just be entertainment.

Memory is not just a form of storage and recall; it is also a process of fitting bits of information together and making sense of them. It enables comparisons to be made, responsibility to be taken. It is connected to guilt and shame and remorse and forgiveness. To suggest that the me who did some terrible thing long ago wasn't me, was some other person, is a dodgy road to take. Far better to accept and assimilate a memory, however uncomfortable it is, tempering it with other people's interpretations if necessary, if it helps.

And what of intelligence and wisdom? What role does memory have to play in them? For me, intelligence consists of relating current information to memory, making sense out of what you see before you and what you remember. I imagine a person can be intelligent but chronically forgetful, but I doubt that it is possible to have wisdom without memory. Certainly self-knowledge depends upon it.

Intelligence is also a process of selecting and editing. It is knowing what can be discarded and ignored. I cannot speculate on my memorized identity unless I also think about its opposite. Even if I could remember everything, I doubt if it would be desirable. Forgetting is an important part of me, and can be used to define me. In a curious way, I am not only as I am (the way I remember to be) but also what I am not (what I have forgotten).

A little forgetfulness is to be accepted as part of my personality—a lot can be alarming. Senility could render me into a state of living in the permanent present without knowing it and against my will.

I have seen what it can do to someone close and loved by me. It is disconcerting to see someone you have known all your life lose her memory. It is more than memories that are lost; it is the meaning of life. Memory is a fragile but reassuring link across the space between two people. If one loses her memory, both undergo a forced separation. Gradually, we lost our shared habits—our mutual vocabulary, even. As I watched this happening, I realized how much common daily recognitions count—how important it is to be able to give the same name to an object or a person, and to know at least one thing about it that makes sense to both our brains. Who was she inside now, I wondered, when outwardly, to me she seemed to be the same person?

How must it be, I wondered, to lose the memory of memory: not only not to remember but to forget that you ever remembered at all? Whose tragedy is it if the person whose mind has gone doesn't know? If there comes a moment when I no longer know who I am, will I be blessed in one sense at least, that I am no longer aware of my own suffering?

The Suffering Me

. . . . .

WHERE DOES IT HURT?

There is a process going on inside me all the time that I don't like to talk about, but which must be mentioned for the sake of completion. This is my identity of pain: the pattern of suffering that marks me out from everyone else as definitively as my fingerprints.

Suffering is part of life. It is the price we pay for being here. This world cannot be paradise. How would we know joy if we didn't know its opposite? And how would we learn and make decisions were we not guided by pain away from harm and sorrow towards better states of being?

How much I get to suffer is partly a lottery and partly up to me. My suffering is mine alone; I do it in my own way, and it cannot be compared to anyone else's suffering. Tortured by the same demon, you and I will not necessarily feel the pain in the same manner, although neither of us will ever be sure of this.

I believe you cannot understand what I go through. This is one reason why I don't talk about suffering much unless a particular person can do something to ease my burden. What would be the point? I fear I will lose friends if I complain too much, and that people who don't care about me will judge me, as if my misery were all my fault.

Most suffering is invisible, and I am loathe to think of it as comprising an identity, but it does. So, how do I explain to you my suffering?

Some suffering we can all probably agree on. The cause is clear, and we can identify with the effect it has on a human being. This kind of suffering is mostly physical, and includes illness and deformity. Everybody has sources of at least minor irritation no one else notices or feels. Each of us to lesser extent is a map and a history of flaws and peculiar sensations, of itches or aches, that come and go or linger. We all have our vulnerabilities, although, of course, some suffer more than others. Serious illness, especially terminal illness, can overwhelm all other aspects of an identity, conditioning how the sufferer is seen and how he sees the world.

Also understandable is suffering as the result of natural disaster, accident, violence, and financial ruin. (Leaving aside, that is, any action that I may have taken to get into the unfortunate situation.)

Beyond all this, most of us manage to also suffer for inconspicuous reasons—at least I do—and I have an entire recipe book of imperceptible mental/emotional hardships that have no apparent cause. These troubles of mine divide neatly into bad times that I have on my own and those that require the input of other people.

I have a range of mechanisms for self-torture, conscious and unconscious, voluntary and involuntary, with which I can afflict myself whether other people are present or not. They are not dependent on company.

Everything is all mixed up, as I frequently am, but my solo sufferings could be broken down as follows:

- **Self-criticism.** In my head, I am engaged in more or less continuous running monologue. Sometimes it takes the form of a dialogue between two parts of myself. Whatever it is I am doing, I know how to do better but I can't always put the technique into practice. I, therefore, keep up a more or less continuous tirade of instructions, imperatives, prohibitions, conditional warnings, chastisements, admonishments, reminders of duties and obligations, corrections, criticisms, questions (rhetorical, naturally, because there is only me there to answer them), exclamations, promises, and other good advice. This monologue is wearying to deliver and wearing to listen to. It is a good thing no one else can hear me. Only occasionally do I allow myself to do what I am doing uninterrupted by my know-all alter ego.

- **Failure.** This hurts. It is usually me who sets the standards I am trying to achieve, and it is always me who acts as judge. Failure can be large or small, but small failures can accumulate into large ones. I also sometimes judge myself prematurely—think I have failed when I haven't, and precipitate failure almost as if it were desirable. Failure has many subheadings: not earning enough money, not being recognized for my achievements, not getting the sexual satisfaction I want, and so on.

- **Inadequacy.** If I accumulate enough failures, and if I estimate that there is more wrong with me than right, I can consider myself not good enough for the task in hand. This may mean something minor, such as playing tennis, or something enormous, like being a decent human being. Self-doubt can lead to self-sabotage and, if I am not careful, I can get into a destructive spiral.

- **Anxiety, Hesitancy, and Procrastination.** These usually involve decisions I have to take. Often hindsight says there was only one course of action and I took it, but I still managed to suffer in the leadup to it.

- **Guilt and Shame.** If only there were a way to know how much guilt and shame I should suffer so that I could feel I had paid my dues.

- **Regrets.** This pertains to what's past. I know I can't change what is done, but I would still like to.

- **Dissatisfaction.** This pertains to the present.

- **Disquiet.** This pertains to the future. I am quite capable of anticipating suffering that never comes.

- **Fears, Real and Imagined.** These are mostly to do with change and unpredictability, rather than fighting off wild bears. Things may be smooth now, but what if the worst happens? I consider myself an optimist, but I admit that I have a streak of foreboding running through my character.

- **Vices, Obsessions, and Addictions.** In my case, these are mostly (I hope) mild and relatively harmless and often result in pleasure. But too much of a good thing can lead to a fall—or a hangover.

- **Existential Panic.** The grand questions of life force themselves on me periodically and then I dwell on my insignificance and the futility of it all—supposing everything I have done with my life is a mistake, and so on.

- **Loneliness.** This is sometimes an overwhelming feeling that can cause me sadness and despair beyond any description. There have been times in my life when I have been willing to do almost anything to escape from being me by myself, isolated, unreachable, inconsolable, and beyond all help. My dependency on other people introduces another list.

I am fairly certain that most people don't mean any harm in their interactions with me, but I associate them with another range of sufferings. Because suffering is interactive, the effect is often mutual and then I suffer a little more for having caused reciprocal suffering.

I have different ways of having a hard time, depending on the people I am dealing with. Much surrounds the people I feel I am stuck with, whom I am supposed to love—that is, my family. I don't like it when they don't do what I want them to do, or do want I don't want them to do. I can't understand why they won't change to be more like I want them to be. Love is a complicated thing: it can easily flip over into loathing and resentment on either side.

People I like, and who I want to like me, can also trigger suffering if they don't respond in the way I hope. It can be very difficult when people don't seem to like me just as I am, because then I have to decide whether or not to try and change myself to suit them. If I do that, I might not like myself for doing it, and they may still not like me for being the person I thought they wanted me to be.

A third and more obvious group are the bullies and other obnoxious people I can't avoid and must endure. This includes anyone who ever triggers any disagreeable emotion in me, including jealousy because they are more successful than I am.

There's a lot more to my suffering than this sketch, but at least it gives the basic blueprint. It shows just how I operate inside and explains, to some extent, the dramas that are staged outside me.

I must quickly add that this isn't a complete picture of life. My suffering is only one aspect of me and is diluted by other experiences. It is important to add a note of balance, remind myself of the counterweights, lest I plunge into self-harm or even self-destruction.

Suffering itself does not have to be "bad." It can be—but is not always, I know—a positive thing to learn from and with which to create. Some of life's most intense experiences are during times of great suffering, such as grief, and bizarrely it is sometimes in the hardest moments (ones that I do not wish for) that I feel most alive.

I could make a chart of my pleasantnesses and happinesses here, but they have largely been covered in the book already. These are also more manifest in the world, and I do try to share them with other people.

My suffering, then, is one good way of getting to know me well, but it is not yet concluded. There is one event that colours the whole procedure of living and raises an entirely different set of questions about identity. Who on earth am I going to be when I die?

The Immortal Me

· · · · ·

HAPPY UNENDING?

I have been dreading writing this chapter for two reasons. Firstly, because the subject forces me to think about a subject I would rather not think about too often, and secondly, because I am not sure what there is to say. I don't want to lapse into platitudes and false hope.

My purpose here is to consider who I will be at and after my death. I have to decide what happens to the protagonist of this book: do I kill him off or not? Do I have any option? Isn't death the end of my life, my identity, my everything? That is the point at which I will stop being on Earth, and my question will become redundant.

Can anything be said to reopen the investigation? Isn't this a subject that generates questions out of desperation but which reduces to one bald fact we would all rather avoid facing?

Isn't it only people with supernatural beliefs and preposterous metaphysical opinions who object to the consensus we currently live under: that you only get one life; it is chance that you are who you are; and when you die, that's it? Isn't it even a kind of cowardice, a way of not facing the truth, to suggest even tentatively that I may be something other than a meaningless arrangement of atoms with a sell-by date, a soon-to-be obsolete organism?

Intellectually, it would be easier to assume that I end at death, but something tells me this is too rushed an answer.

At the beginning of the book I said we are engaged in a battle for our souls, and I believe this to be true in a literal sense. The word "soul," of course, has religious overtones, but that's not how I use it. I regard it as a useful way of talking about a concept that we have no other name for. It symbolizes the issue here. The modern world has become a tussle over our dead: are we lumps of meat, their purpose served when the life goes out of them, or is that life a clue to something else?

Superficially, there is little to say about mortality, but in reality there's a great deal. As mystery stories go, it can't be bettered. How are we ever going to know for sure? I'm not sure, deep down, we would want to know, even if we could, because it would change the experience of living. Notwithstanding, I do think we can make some interesting conjectures and come close to comprehension.

To this end, I would like to set aside both religion and science, because the former generally leans on dogma (and is vague and possibly reliant on the imagination of Renaissance painters) and the second demands evidence (and risks being too focused, too literal, and not able to ask pertinent questions about things that are hard to classify), which in this area is impossible to provide.

The question of who I will be when I die depends on knowing two things:

1. the exact nature and, hence, degree of durability of this inner me; and
2. what happens as and when we die and after we have died.

They can be discussed in either order, but as I have given some preliminary thoughts to the first two chapters ago, I want first to think about dying.

My death scene will be experienced by the participants in two different ways, depending on the role played in it. Anyone watching or assisting will have one experience, while I will have another. The first experience, which could be called "hard, external" death is well documented. It is clear what will happen to my body when the time comes.

The more interesting question is what will go on inside me, what we might call soft or inner death. There are only a certain number of ways it can be: instant extinction (one moment alive, the next dead), gradual fade or some sort of transition from one state to another. Perhaps it is different for each of us, in which case I would be presumptuous to suggest a general rule.

It is certain that all exterior trappings of identity will lapse. They belong to this world, this lifetime. Everything I have learned, my appetites, the personality I developed to be approved of and mated with, my name, all elements of my terrestrial being will be uncoupled from my body. They never were firmly attached, anyway.

After I die I will have at least one identity. Those who care about me will remember me: I will have been a person, and there will be a lingering notion of me having been on Earth.

That part is sure. But what about me? Will I have my own identity, separate to that of my memorial? Will I undergo some kind of transformation at death? Will I go to paradise? That sounds too much like the idyll of a keen gardener or a colonial explorer. It is altogether too geographical: I doubt if there will be locations in the afterlife. What about those tunnels ending in bright white light? It's a strikingly visual image, but I won't be taking my eyes with me.

Will I instead reincarnate or become a ghost (a reincarnatee who missed)? The evidence for this would have to be here with us, but all accounts are more or less dubious. Besides, having "survived" death, why would I want to go through the process again? I suppose you could argue that I do a little incremental improving of my soul each time, but it still sounds like returning to a funfair to go on the best ride over and over again? I don't rule out any of these possibilities, but these ideas seem like human fantasies, products of a brain inspired by too much television.

The "when you're dead you're dead" school of thought seems as unsatisfactory to me as heaven, lights, and many happy returns. This may because I just don't want to accept it, a vain wish for my life to mean something, but it think my doubts indicate more than that.

Isn't there always a loose end in every satisfactory explanation? Something that doesn't tie up, that troubles the detective mind. A fact that has been precipitously jumped over and yet turns out to be vital to the solution?

We must be wary of being taken in by appearances and assumptions. Both may be right, but they are away open to question. From the outside, death is pretty convincing. Life vanishes, personhood vanishes, and that individual is never seen again on Earth. It seems safe to conclude that it is a terminus, that any other suggestion is absurd.

If, at this point, we turn and walk away with that thought in mind we are forgetting one thing, an ontological loose end. What about the free-floating, unlocatable entity inside me that is, at the moment, my self? We never did succeed in pinning the indefinable me to the body, and we can't rule out the possibility that it has a life independent of the body, independent of biological breathing. Materialists rule such ideas irrelevant. They put them aside for later consideration, knowing that one day they will be able to account for consciousness scientifically. That is a neat copout, because they may never explain consciousness, and they can't face up to the reality of death without some firm notion of what it is.

The brain may be akin to a computer that is either plugged into a power source or it isn't, but if we take into consideration the larger definitions of mind and spirit, this analogy becomes altogether simplistic. To accept it, we have to find a mechanistic explanation of dreams and the myriad other altered states human beings experience. It would also help if we could define life and animation, why we come into being, and how we are able to discuss these enigmas.

So who and what am I really? What do I know about this most intimate self of mine after all my enquiries.

I know that it has an extraordinary range, and perhaps I should think of it as a continuum. At one end of me is my body walking in the world and typing out books; at the other end I touch everything else in existence, to which I belong and from which I am inseparable. I seep into you, and you seep into me. I don't mean this in a material sense. It doesn't help to think of this idea visually, or we will start looking for the join and start arguing about evidence or the lack of it. I mean this as an idea for your imagination to entertain, an idea to entertain your imagination.

This would mean that my identity is a seamless gamut whichever direction you look in—from the entire universe to my meanest, most selfish, most corporeal action. Neither one extreme nor the other would be the only me.

In this book, I have been slicing up this continuum and rearranging the principal parts of it for effect. In life, I tighten or release my grip on the various dimensions of my identity according to whim and circumstance.

This self of mine is connected to everything but cannot afford to remember and know this. It needs to feel separate in order to get its living done. We are necessarily discrete beings. If the universe were all squashed together in a dense ball of dough, with no me or you poking out of it, what would be the point? Nothing would get done. No one would go anywhere. There would no one to have children and no one to have thoughts. Everything and everyone needs to be spaced—in a literal sense, but I can see why drug experiences used to be talked of in this way.

I am someone—some force, if you will—that coalesced out of this everything, via my mother and father, that took on separate form and became identifiable in human terms. At death, I will lose that form but remain a part of what I have never been separated from. I will still be me, but I will no longer be a human "I."

You can believe that my atoms disperse at random when I die, if you want, but you are always going to have that niggling doubt: how did that late arrangement of atoms come to know that it was human? How did it manage to ask questions of who it was on Earth? If it happened once, could it happen again? Could it happen an infinite number of times?

Does this mean that I am a crystallization out of universal chaos—a temporary and unstable arrangement, pattern, or piece of order; a neutron-electron dance; an assembly of parts, both material and immaterial? Why not? I don't mind thinking of myself like that, amongst all the other ways that I can think of myself. That is as good as any way to know my true nature. Right now, if you will excuse me, I still have business being me on Earth.

The Future Me

· · · · ·

**NOW YOU SEE ME,
NOW YOU DON'T**

A field guide has done only half its job if it sticks to what can be seen right now; to be complete it has to anticipate the future. What will you and I—and our descendants—become over the next decades or centuries? Is the answer to this question self-evident? Or will we be radically different from how we are now?

All that follows from this thought is conjecture, but it is more than a venture into fantasy or science fiction. Speculation about the future makes for a useful thought experiment, one that offers insight into who we are now and could give us the power of choice over our destiny.

Prediction is not, of course, an exact science and when we look at the history of foresight (the past of the future, as it were), it is clear that we should not believe everything we are promised or warned about.

We tend to think of the world ahead as either utopia or dystopia, spectacular disaster or the further fulfilment of human ingenuity. We don't like to hear about mediocre, half-baked variants of the future, in which we live through more of the same—staring at screens and using technology merely to satisfy human whims or to relieve boredom.

Life in the years ahead won't be quite the same as the life we leave behind. It will almost certainly be interspersed with "ordinary" unexpected events—natural disasters, wars, financial crashes—but there will be no fundamental changes to what it means to be human. According to this version of historical futurology, there will be great waves of dramatic change to come but everything will stay the same because we will stay the same. We will be stuck being who we are, no matter what happens around us.

We can see the truth of this, looking back. Everyone alive today is used to fast and accelerating technological progress. The world has been transformed around us, yet we have not been transformed ourselves. Even though we have modified our behaviour in accordance with new possibilities presented to us, in most respects (allowing for the superficial gloss of culture) we're still recognizably the same creatures who lived a hundred, a thousand, or even a hundred thousand years ago.

We are still, as I write this, bound by the perennial biological terms of our parole on Earth. It's possible that we will be shaken out of our complacency by some great *unexpectable* unexpected event, such as the discovery of alien life, which will force us to question who we are in an acute way.

There is, however, another way in which the future could be radically different to any future that comes before it. In this scenario, we give up waiting for extraterrestrials to come and show us what an advanced, post-Darwinian race looks like and, instead, get to work sculpting ourselves according to our dream of how we would like to be. There are two main ways we could do this—which could be dubbed, "natural" and "unnatural"—and either would mean a profound reevaluation of what it means to be human.

The first of these, the "natural" approach, is to extend and eventually, perhaps, break the limit of our life span. Thanks to hygiene, medicine, and prosperity (creating better standards of living), average life expectancy has been steadily increasing across the globe, in general, but specifically in developed countries. This in itself is steadily changing who we are, as we outlive the ages of procreation, work, and childcare.

What, though, if we could live longer still? Much longer? If the key killer diseases can be controlled or even eradicated, and if we can replace cells as needed and make the replacement of worn-out body parts routine, we will be on our way to enhanced longevity. An advanced understanding of the reason why our bodies age will further help to slow down our decline, or even halt it altogether. Decades of perfect health may become not a matter of luck or sound living but a human right.

Given that part of identity is expecting to grow old and die, this prospect will force us to rethink things. If a young person knows that he is going to live longer than his father, he will plan his life differently. There won't be so much hurry, and the risks of mistakes will be reduced. He might decide to have several careers— why choose one, when he can retrain for another after what was retirement age for the previous generation? And he might want several long, committed relationships—perhaps an amicable divorce after the golden wedding anniversary, so that each can try again with a new partner.

The adjective "long" (with respect to time) would take on a different connotation, being judged according to the length of a human life. Regret for time wasted, meanwhile, may become an incomprehensible concept. As a society we would have to invent new categories for the ages of people. Middle age wouldn't be the middle of life any more and might have to describe someone as being in youthful old age, that is, at the start of something rather than near the end.

The possibility of a much longer lifespan, however, would raise questions that we have not yet had to consider: would everyone have the same right to longevity? Or would this, say, exacerbate the divide between the rich and the poor, the powerful and the powerless?

Could we carry on having children (all of them with extended life spans)? If we did, Earth would become quickly overpopulated.

Would our memories cope? Or would they be reduced to dreams—hopeless combinations of accuracy and fallacy? It would be hard enough to remember our own biographies, but other people's would overload us. Would the faces of our mothers, fathers, sisters, and brothers fade into vagueness?

Would we still consider ourselves responsible for our distant pasts? Would I feel like the same person at 150 as at 15?

How would we finance our extended lives? Would we really want to work for decades longer than we do at present?

How would our relations with other people change?

Would some people, such as those with psychological problems or insecure employment, choose to die rather than to live on? How would that affect the survivors, ethically and emotionally?

The longer we manage to live, the more implications such questions—and ones that will occur to us in the face of reality—will have for us.

Contentious issues would also derive from the way that super-longevity is achieved. If we are able to take control of aging, would that not mean we would assume the choice of what age we wish to remain? And for how long? Wouldn't most people want to stay at their favourite age for as long as possible?

This might be a harder decision to make than it appears. Isn't your best age the one you look *back* on fondly, that is associated with other people and specific conditions of life? It might not be possible to live a whole sample lifetime and then decide; and it certainly wouldn't be possible to rearrange everyone else's lives so that you can stay in a golden moment. Nevertheless, we'd run the risk of a future entirely populated by 16-year-olds who don't want to finish school, a future in which people would have to be refused permission to remain adolescent for more than an allotted time, for the good of society. Perhaps, we will be able to jump around from age to age, backwards and forwards in time. Think how that would play havoc with our notion of generations.

Implicit in all this is the notion that we will be able to perfect medical techniques that include replacing bits of us as they wear out. This prompts the existential doubt: how many bits of me can be replaced without me losing my sense of me? That is, would I still be me if all my limbs and organs (including my brain) are made with refurbished parts?

One alternative to being shaped as we live and age may be that we will develop the ability to design more perfect beings before birth (old-fashioned pregnancy and birth having been superseded by a risk-free, super-sterilized, and painless process using an artificial womb) and cloning and editing individuals, as required. For example, a copy of an individual's genes might be made, then pruned and rewritten to remove undesirable physical traits and weaknesses to disease. What will happen to my consciousness and individuality if there are (against logic) two of me?

All such techniques would take us a long way from what we think of today as being human, but the "natural" procedure for producing a new me is not quite finished. If aging can be defeated and life extended, why should it have to come to an end? Couldn't it be prolonged indefinitely? We could become, in effect (barring accident), immortal? We are born, we hang around, and we don't leave—meaning that all the problems of extended lifestyles mentioned above become perpetual.

The dream of endless longevity is likely to overtake the old idea of cryonics, or freezing a body at death so that it can be revived one day in the future. This semi-scientific notion of resurrection—the freezing part is scientific but not yet the revival—raises many of its own questions about identity. Who would I be if I went through the rituals of death a few centuries ago and woke up (an old man?) in a world in which I had no friends, family, or sense of orientation? At the very least, I would have a huge, unbridgeable gap in my memory, during which my descendants lived and died.

Living forever poses commensurately large puzzles. All the problems of longevity are multiplied by infinity. Imagine being on your 120th marriage and not being able to remember the voice of your mother who lived in the equivalent of our 16th century.

Then, who will I be if I do not die—if I have no fear of death? Isn't the destination part of the definition of me: I am mortal and that, in a large part, is what makes me, me? Do I really not want to die, once I have got past the fantasy of it? Isn't it born of the fear or a rite of passage rather than a positive schedule of things to do? Would we become a race divided between those who choose to die (or have to, for lack of necessary funds) and those who know they will live forever?

A dream of survival would become an identity crisis to look forward to. Isn't it, in many ways, better to accept death as a part of life rather than to resist? Wouldn't I only be postponing the inevitable? Eventually the sun will cool down and the universe freeze over. All that separates me from that outcome would be a few billion years of extra, avoidable boredom. Will I really be able to put up with myself for that long, even if I manage to fit in every experience it is possible for a human being to have?

The other option for immortality is to go down the route recommended by those technophiles who believe that messing about with human bodies is akin to tinkering with old cars: okay for enthusiasts with time on their hands but not as efficient as buying a new model just to get around.

According to the materialist definition, we are, like everything else in the universe, merely information. I may feel complex and unique, but I am still only a permutation of data—even my mental processes and emotions. Know enough about me, and you know everything there is to know about me; you can digitalize me, and I can live without my analogue body. "I" will be uploadable to a hard disk (or whatever technology takes its place) for storage and onward transfer. As sequences of code, I can then be downloaded to another modified body, or even to a robotic self. I will be able to choose my next model, according to my means; pay more, and I can have more power and an improved brain. Abdication of our humanity in favour of the machine will become standard practice and individuality—one self, one perishable body—will be relegated to an anachronism.

Meanwhile, whatever physical state I am or am not in, I will be able to park my memory permanently with an internet company to whom I pay a subscription for security, maintenance and the occasional spring clean.

Simultaneously, we face another prospect in the advance of invented life. We already depend on machines to carry out many routines functions, and the future will be increasingly populated with them. What happens, though, if we perfect them in our image? If we teach them to learn for themselves and let them have ever greater autonomy? If we delegate ourselves to them?

If man not only turns into machine (transferring his consciousness as desired) but also machine turns into man in the form of androids, our sense of identity will be thrown completely awry. Will we one day have to look closely at each other and ask ourselves whether we are dealing with a real or a fake human being? How will we do it?

Seriously. How do you know that the person sitting next to you is not an android? We are already used to dealing with robot personalities on the internet. Perhaps this book has been generated by one of them and you are the first person to read it. A more challenging question, perhaps, is whether it will matter if you are dealing with an android or not. If an android can be taught to cluck sympathetically and make caring gestures more convincingly than any human being, will we care whether or not he has a fragile, screwed-up, psychological, meaning-seeking self inside?

It could matter. Maybe these artificial creatures will carry out "being human" better than we ever can and will have no future need of us, the real thing. Once they realize that life can be conducted without appetites, vices, neuroses, dramas, grudges, and crazed, destructive feelings, will they get on with building the model world that we tried and failed to build?

If any of these proposals alarm us, claim those who promote a dash towards the future, we should be reassured. Every new technology introduced in the past, they remind us, has been greeted initially by a measure of resistance and panic, but over time we learn to live with the modifications it makes to life. We fear social disaster and moral breakdown and then it becomes part of the background. At least, this is true—with exceptions—of *things*. The question is, will it hold true for people, too? What if there is a threshold of radicalism we are unaware of: go beyond it, and we find ourselves in a new kind of world with no possibility of return? It may be that there are limits to how we should use our clever brains. Maybe we should make the best of being human in the conventional way, while we still can.

Afterword

· · · · ·

HAVE YOU SEEN THIS MAN?

As you have now read this book (assuming you haven't skipped straight to the last page) you know a little of who I am. Or rather was. Because, of course, I wrote this book in your past tense (which is, at the moment, my present).

Now I could be anyone. And I am. That is, I could be either a somebody or a nobody to you. I could be the person sitting next to you, as you read this. Or the person who served you in a shop earlier on. I could be the person at the front of the queue in the bank making a fuss about proving his identity, who made you late for work by asking his idiot questions. I could be the person on the other end of the phone line, wanting something from you. I could be the person you had an argument with at a traffic light. I could be the person you caught out of the corner of your eye, walking along a street, or who you didn't even see, and who you weren't curious to know any more about. Just another person among the many, many you will or will not come into contact with today.

And vice versa. Maybe I have seen you today without realizing it. Maybe I have dismissed you as not very interesting-looking. Maybe I brushed past you in a crowd, and we avoided each other's glance, as if the other didn't exist, wasn't significant, and didn't have a matching, palpating consciousness within.

Who knows whether we will meet or not meet in the next second after this one? Or whether we did or didn't meet in the past, or whether we will encounter each other sometime in the future, in another life or another existence? It is all the same. Present, past, and future. Before and after our meeting we will be unchanged: just two intensely self-absorbed somebodies going about being who they are.

Appendix

· · · · ·

A FEW POINTERS FOR
THE IDENTITY POLICE

I now know more about who I am, but that doesn't help my bank to identify me. It is left with the same problem—a problem that is of daily and universal relevance to us all: how can we be sure who each other is? Much money and brainpower is dedicated to asking this simple question. What advice might a self-appointed expert on himself give to the growing legions of identity checkers who stalk the modern world. How can they check up on us efficiently and securely with the minimum of cost, inconvenience, and curtailment of rights?

We have a choice of three basic ways of identifying another person. The first of these is almost too obvious to describe, but it needs setting out for anyone who doesn't remember the pre-internet, pre-smartphone, pre-call centre, pre-money laundering, even pre-credit card age. Then, we knew each other in simpler low-tech or no-tech ways. There were still con artists and fraudsters about, but they were exceptions to be exposed, unlike now, when we are all branded liars until we prove otherwise.

Because there was less mobility and less communications technology, we knew the people we knew. Most people stayed put, near where they were born, and worked for the same employer for decades. Banks and government agencies maintained local branches, where business was done face to face. We could triangulate almost all the people we met according to family or school, and if we had to deal with someone distant it was by handwritten, signed letter not cut-and-paste messages from some dodgy-sounding email account.

This is how humanity has operated throughout history, regardless of culture—through familiarity, common sense, prudence, and intuition. It seems almost quaint now, but there it is.

A second historical system was operated by bureaucracies, large and small, public or private. People were classified by the paperwork relating to them contained in the files named after them. The more paperwork there was, the more a bureaucrat could be sure of who he was dealing with. Bureaucracy is far from ideal, but it has a certain fairness and substance: you can't usually argue with a piece of paper that you are holding in your hand.

Nowadays, we prefer a third system, one that is held to be much better than anything that has gone before it. Science and technology, we are told, can override our error-prone human faculties and identify us more accurately than we can identify ourselves. Their efficacy makes them worth any inconvenience, complication, or expense.

Behind our obsession with technology, however, are motivations that go beyond rational choice.

We like to apply technology, simply because we can. Why keep it in the box, when we can try it out and see what it can do? We assume that because so much work has gone into it, it must be intrinsically good. We seldom ask who is encouraging us in these ideas—too often, those who stand to gain from the acceptance of technology. New machines at premium prices make profits for the companies that supply them. The individuals involved in the biometric industry build their careers on our technophilia. Who knows how far technology is deployed because it is needed, or because it fulfils the needs of the deployers? Whether identities are questioned merely as a means of paying the bills of the families of the questioners of identities? How will we know if our surveillance industry is mostly self-serving? Which of us has the skill to judge? The modern identity business thrives on an arcane knowledge and a coded warning: now that we are here and everywhere, try to live without us and see what perils you encounter. Safer, we think, in a complex world, to trust the machine and its minders.

We have thus worked ourselves into a strange situation—it's almost as if we are trying to get out of the need to be human. The way in which we have delegated our identities to technicians is worrying. The process of identification is a wholly human affair, a ceremony involving two or more people. To be blunt, we are gradually handing over the mediation of human relationships to machinery.

To check up on someone is to enter into a relationship with them. However many people are involved in an operation, it always comes down to two: the person who wants to know and the person under suspicion. The company or state that monitors me does not want to relate to me on equal terms, however. It wants its operators to know me, but for me to not know them. Such an unbalanced relationship is incompatible with a free and open society. It could be said that the greater the lack of trust shown by an organization (or someone within it) towards others, the greater it demonstrates its own untrustworthiness.

The nameless identity checker with his biometric equipment seeks to know who I am but doesn't *really* want to know who I am. He wants to know certain things about me, just enough to positively separate me from everyone else. In this he confronts a paradox. He can only determine so much of me by a study of the outside. To find out what makes me unique—to access the part of me that knows all the answers—he has to ask me the right questions. To do that he either has to force me to confess my secrets or encourage me to trust him. The latter option requires that he cares enough about me to take time to listen to what I have to say, in the way I wish to say it.

Cold-blooded identity checking stops far short of intimate relationship, and this leaves an element of doubt. The identity-checker learns to be realistic about what he can hope to find out. In even the best system there is a margin of error, but too often this is played down rather than admitted.

Given this weakness, we have to ask how efficient all this technological identity checking really is. It is easy enough to identify someone who has nothing to hide: get him talking at his ease, and he'll tell you all you want to know. In other words, the sophisticated gadgetry can prove very good at identifying the people who don't need identifying and useless at catching those who need catching. Ruthless identity invaders have access to the same training manuals as the checkers and simply learn to play the system.

Counterintuitively, when the mania for identity checking pervades a society it can lead people to feel less safe, not more so. Treating us all as suspicious unless we can prove otherwise generates fear all round. We learn to doubt each other. Old-fashioned virtues, such as honesty and loyalty, come to look naïve, and amorality takes their place. We also become more careless. When officialdom insists that it is its prerogative to do the checking, the rest of us give up the informal procedures we have always used to identify one another and cease to care about each other. Also, the risk of confidential data going astray is greatly enhanced when it is concentrated as bytes stored on a portable computer drive.

Before we hand ourselves over entirely to the rule-ordained, automated identity-checking industry, we would do well to ask ourselves a few pertinent questions. Meanwhile, anyone who sets himself up as an identity policeman might like to think about the following seven recommendations:

1. **Keep it simple, keep it human.** Identity checks need to be carried out at the lowest level possible, based on common sense and humanity. Everything else—documents, biometrics machinery—gets in the way of what matters: whether one person believes what another person says.

Although we're not infallible, most of us manage to spot fraudsters most of the time. We know—although we may not be able to put into words how we know—that some elements of personality and ways of behaving ring true while others don't. A human expression, a laugh, a quirk, or a tone of voice can tell us more than any formula or computer simulation.

Successful identity checking involves the application of human intelligence—the posing of pertinent questions and the deciphering of the answers. If you really want to know who I am—whether I am telling the truth to you—look me in the eye and decide for yourself.

2. **Only ask for what you need**. It's possible to ask too many questions. You want to know just enough for your immediate purposes. To ask for more information than you need is to intrude unnecessarily and unjustifiably.

3. **Don't be a slave to rules.** A set of rules sounds like a great idea. Someone has worked them out for the good of all, and they can then be applied uniformly. Everyone can refer to them to make sure things have been done correctly. Rules, however, have their problems:
   - Every set of rules is a rigid, outmoded code.
   - All rules are theories that have to be interpreted and applied to actual conditions. Reality may not look like the rules say it should.
   - No set of rules can ever cover all eventualities. Rules can lay down general principles and give advice, but they can't stipulate the requirements of each situation. Every situation is an exception in some way.
   - There is a risk that exceptions will be scooped up and made into new, more intricate rules that are still incomplete.
   - The longer the rules get, the less useful they are. The more rules, the more time spent in understanding them, and the more difficult it is to apply them all.
   - Rules encourage successful, obedient rule-keeping but do not necessarily encourage efficient action towards the required outcome. The existence of rules can make people think they don't have to think; it can give managers and staff a reason not to use their own common sense.
   - Identity thieves can learn the rules, too, and figure out what it takes to circumvent them.

4. **Know what you already know.** Each organization within an industry, and each department within each organization, likes to go about things in its own way, collecting its own information and carrying out its own checks. This is extremely wasteful and wearisome to the individual who has to feed the same information into an infinite number of mouths. It is foolish to amass data for the sake of it, and obstinate not to check against official or other respectable sources. If one institution has already checked up on me, it may not be necessary to go through the procedure again. Given that you are going to have to trust some person or body sometime, why drag the process out?

5. **Don't trust science and technology entirely**. Make use of science and technology, but don't rely on them entirely. Machines are fallible, and they are only ever an indirect medium between two people. Biometric techniques sound as if they must lead to scientifically unassailable conclusions, but that is to ask too much of them. The dream that we can be clinically certain of someone's identity is only a dream.

6. **Give yourself away.** In a free society, identity checking must always be two-way. A job title or the name of an organization is not enough to describe an individual who wants to know who another individual is. When spies are allowed to operate covertly, anonymously, they mock justice. We'd automatically live in a better world if everyone who wears a uniform would willing identify himself.

7. **Have an answer ready for the question, "Who checks the checkers?"** Any surveillance organization is only as good as the quality, competence, and honesty of its staff. If one of them slips up or is corrupt, no amount of rules or high-powered machinery will be of any use. Someone has to be entirely responsible for what is done. In a democratic state, the only half-good answer to this question is to ensure the maximum amount of transparency and accountability.

Notes on Sources

Where, I wondered, should I begin to research who you and I are, and what we are doing on the planet? I should read the whole of Western philosophy for a start, then move on to Eastern philosophy, which would bring me to the great world religions.

I'd need to balance metaphysics with physics by reading as much as I can about contemporary scientific knowledge (particularly biology, psychology, and anthropology). By definition, the social sciences would also be essential to know about.

It would be useful to go through the literature of the world—novels, plays, poems—in search of insights that other writers have had into the human condition. Then there is biography and autobiography: an endless parade of case studies into how to live a life.

Popular culture shouldn't be ignored, either. I could spend a lifetime at the theatre, in the cinema, listening to the radio, and watching television. Almost every drama concerns itself with what drives us and what we are capable of. It was clear I was going to need a reading list like no other and a few centuries of free time to get through it.

I seriously gave it a go. I set out with the intention to watch and read as much of relevance as possible but I quickly realized the immensity of the task. Besides, would that really be the best use of my time? I needed facts, naturally, but much of what we have to say about ourselves is commentary rather than certainty. I didn't want to write a book relaying secondhand opinions. I wanted to have my own thoughts. A few prompts would do, not a complete script.

I, therefore, took an eclectic approach. Sometimes, I went looking for answers; otherwise I let them come to me.

The result is a serendipitous collection of sources. Those on a specific subject are mentioned in the relevant section of notes. Books of more general interest and listed in the bibliography.

Four of these stand out. There may be no direct influence traceable from them to my own text, but they certainly helped form the mind that communicates in my words.

The first of these is *The Lazy Man's Guide to Enlightenment* (Seed Center, 1971) by Thaddeus Golas. Somewhat dated in its language, it is still ludicrously simple and cunningly wise. It makes me smile to think that this short book, self-published in San Francisco in 1971, now has a connection to the Money Laundering Regulations passed by the UK parliament in 2007, which caused me to start thinking about identity. If two such forces not even remotely connected in time, space, or purpose can come together to produce ideas in my head, what other strange marriages are possible?

Another foundational source is a cassette tape given to me by a late friend. It is a recording of a talk given in Bristol in 1987 by the American Harvard psychiatrist turned spiritual teacher Ram Dass, and I never tire of listening to it. I've never had much time for gurus, and I know barely anything about Ram Dass, but I like this tape of him because he speaks with humour and humility. Once he has got beyond the folly of trying to tell anyone anything, his message condenses into two pieces of advice. One is that we humans cannot be entirely holy, and we cannot be entirely earthly. The only solution for us is to continually hop between the two states, losing touch neither with our humanity nor our divinity. Wherever we are in this impossible balancing act, the best we can do for other people is be ourselves and let them be who they are.

If I had to name the writer who most shaped my thinking it would have to be Alan Watts, my third major source. In particular, *The Book: The Taboo Against Knowing Who You Are* (Pantheon, 1966) convinced me that I had my own book to write. Every time I start reading it, it triggers thoughts of my own. Watts was a great interpreter of Eastern mysticism for the Western mind and was himself a lucid thinker who was able to make ancient wisdoms relevant to the modern world. I'd recommend any of his works.

Very different is my fourth source: Michel de Montaigne, inventor of the confessional autobiography. I have nothing in common with a classically educated, mildly Catholic, 17th-century French nobleman, yet his book is irresistible. His subject is himself. He writes what he wants to write about. His essays are intensely personal, often digressive, and mix first-hand knowledge with counterfactual hearsay in the most entertaining way. By concentrating on the familiar and specific, he identifies the perennial and universal.

Chapter Notes

Chapter 9: The Nominated Me

Names—forenames, surnames, and the way they are arranged—vary from culture to culture, and herein lies one of the main challenges of this book: to compress humanity into a single narrative, without leaving anyone out and, at the same time, pick out what we have in common while respecting our extraordinary diversity. Each culture has its own way of naming its children. Ideally, the aim is to make sure that two individuals do not have the same name, but this does happen. For a humorous look at namesakes, see *Are You Dave Gorman?* by Danny Wallace and Dave Gorman (Ebury Press, 2001). A far more serious and thought-provoking approach is that of Brian Cathcart in *The Lives of Brian* (Granta 85, Spring 2004).

A final thought on names: it is curious how we occasionally transfer them as we think appropriate. In Mary Shelley's horror book, *Frankenstein* (Wordsworth Editions, 1992), it is the creator not the creation who is thus named; but in the retelling of the tale, we have collectively decided that it is the monster who is more in a need of a name.

Chapter 12: The Stinking Me

We may try to play down its importance, but some repressive regimes take an interest in what we smell like. The Stasi Museum (www.stasimuseum.de) in Berlin has a collection of jars containing specimens of clothing taken from enemies of the East German state in case of escape so that blood hounds could be set on their trail.

Chapter 13: The Recognizable Me

Some unfortunate people suffer from a condition known as prosopagnosia or face blindness, that prevents them from recognizing their own spouses or children. This can be caused by brain damage or can be genetic. The condition is still little understood (see www.faceblind.org).

All of us, perhaps, have difficulty in distinguishing between identical twins or unconnected strangers who look strikingly similar, and this is a much played-upon theme in literature and cinema. Charles Dickens's *A Tale of Two Cities* (CreateSpace, 2013) is about two men who look alike. In Daphne du Maurier's *The Scapegoat* (Virago, 2004), a French aristocrat hands over his life to an Englishman who resembles him. The film comedy *Dave* (1993) is built around the similarity between a manager of a temp agency and the President of the United States.

Chapter 14: The Imagined Me

I owe at least a subliminal debt here to John Berger's *Ways of Seeing* (BBC/Penguin, 1972), especially chapter 3. Berger's book urges us to look carefully at images—both historical and those we are bombarded with daily—and ask who made them, how, and why.

Looking into the history of portrait, re, it is noticeable how recent an obsession this is. When and why did we become gripped with the urge to look at ourselves in so many poses and to pass our images around? Is it merely because we can do it that we do it—because we have the technology and the cost has steadily fallen until it is now negligible? Did prehistoric cave artists, who were so good at observing animals, never have the same urge to paint themselves? Perhaps they did, but on perishable supports such as bark and wood, disposable documents that have not survived. Or did they think that they weren't important enough?

Chapter 15. The Documented Me

The ultimate answer to the problem for identity checkers of having documentation detachable from the person has to be to implant a microchip under our skin, as we do with our pets. This way, there can be no confusion. Just scan a person's arm and you get a digital readout that connects to his file. Proponents of chipping say that it only requires light surgery and could be beneficial to the tagged individual. For example, he could sit in a bar and order drinks without having to hand over cash, just have his arm swiped for each round. Hospitals could find it useful, and it could be a useful way to implement gun control, as a gun could be linked to the chip so that it would only fire in the hands of its rightful owner. The rest of us worry about issues of freedom and ethics. There is also a danger that a person could be hacked into.

Chapter 17: The Categorical Me

I run the risk here of making the procedure of categorization simpler than it is, but only because that is how bureaucrats think. In reality, many of us straddle divisions. I'd like to spare a thought for children born of parents of different races or nationalities. While they can have the best of both sides they can also have a hard time, feeling they are neither one thing or the other. Genetic and cultural hybridization, however, is a source of richness and diversity in the population and to be welcomed. Only bigots disagree.

Chapter 19: The Inherited Me

Family identity matters most to usurpers, pretenders who abort a bloodline in order to set themselves up in the position occupied by the deposed. Shakespeare's plays turn a great deal on this subject. Richard II is forcibly replaced by Henry IV; Macbeth and Richard III both tempt fate in taking the crown by force; Hamlet is a tragic son deprived of his inheritance by villainy; and King Lear is effectively a king who excommunicates himself through faulty parenting. The theme running throughout, and still of concern to supporters of monarchies and elites today, is what to do about an heir who is not considered fit for the job.

Chapter 20: The Reported Me

In contrast to our wanting to be sure of who each of us is, there is nothing we like more than a good tale about a mysterious identity: is he who he says he is? Fiction is full of them, but there are also famous true stories that tug at our credulity, such as those of Anastasia, Martin Guerre, Kasper Hauser, the Man in the Iron Mask, Fulcanelli, and Saint-Germain. For more see *The Encyclopaedia of Unsolved Mysteries* by Colin Wilson (McGraw Hill Contemporary,1988) and *Rogues, Villains, and Eccentrics: An A to Z of Roguish Britons Through the Ages* by William Donaldson (Weidenfeld & Nicholson, 2002), which excels in portraits of picaresque conmen. Probably the best novel about an identity thief is *The Talented Mr. Ripley* by Patricia Highsmith (Vintage, 1999).

Chapter 21: The Virtual Me

We tend to get whisked away by technology and forget that solutions can always throw up new problems of their own. The internet is always a double-edged sword: while it gives us a spurious freedom, it also acts as one big surveillance machine by which we can keep watch on each other. We are currently passing from the age of online loquaciousness into the age of "identity management and repair," whereby you pay a company to push positive news about you up the search result order so that you clean up your reputation before posterity gets a hold of it.

Meanwhile, the arrival of artificial intelligence is treated as if it were inevitable and a wholly good thing. We should be very wary of this notion as it will raise questions about both the identity of the machine and of us. It may not be too far-fetched to start thinking about how we will behave towards androids; if we decide to create them one day, we should ask who they are going to be and will they escape from any bounds set for them. We always have a choice about our future that we shouldn't forget to exercise. For more on the forward march of the internet, see

Out of Control: The New Biology of Machines, Social Systems, and the Economic World by Kevin Kelly (Addison Wesley, 1994), Ben Agger's *Oversharing: Presentations of Self in the Internet Age* (Routledge, 2012), and *Who Owns The Future?* by Jaron Lanier (Simon & Schuster, 2013).

Chapter 22: The Material Me

Since this chapter spans several scientific disciplines, it draws on a variety of sources. Four points need to be made before you go in search of good reading:

1. Science often presents itself as more certain and consensual than it is, whereas its working conclusions are often based on statistical probabilities and judgements. Knowledge is always in evolution. Today's solid conclusion may seem like an antiquated theory in a few years time.
2. Despite the boasts of radical materialists, it is debatable whether science will *ever* solve some of the problems addresses.
3. Some scientists would like to bring their methodology to bear on nonscientific subjects, such as ethics. Arguably, a complete explanation of human nature is as unlikely as a theory that tells us what is good and bad.
4. The website *Edge* (www.edge.org) is a good place to start finding out about the contemporary state of scientific knowledge. Michael Brooks's *13 Things That Don't Make Sense: The Most Baffling Scientific Mysteries of Our Time* (Vintage, 2009) is a readable introduction to remaining mysteries. Chapter 5, on life, is particularly relevant here.

Chapter 23: The Interpreted Me

A new edition of the American Pyschiatric Association's Diagnostic and Statistical Manual of Mental Disorders, published since 1952, always causes controversy by its descriptions of new adverse syndromes that eat into the definition of normality. As one sceptic pointed out, the APA comes dangerously close to classifying 48 Americans as being mentally ill. Its defenders say it is just a useful tool to be interpreted with intelligence by practitioners. See www.psychiatry.org/practice/dsm.

Chapter 24: The Indefinable Me

We'd settle a lot of arguments, particular across the science-religion divide, if we could agree on one matter: are we one or two? Are there two kinds of stuff that make us (body and mind) or just the one (a body with a brain but no mind)? The two-speed explanation is called dualism and Descartes was its most famous exponent. Interestingly, to be "nondualist" has come to imply two diametrically opposed views: it can mean a scientist who believes that there is nothing but matter, or it can mean someone who subscribes to a spiritual philosophy that states that we are not separate beings but part of the same thing, the universe.

Chapter 26: The Suffering Me

Two good books to continue reading on this subject are *The Problem of Pain* by C.S. Lewis (Collins, 2012) and Paul Watzlawick's *The Situation is Hopeless But Not Serious: the Pursuit of Unhappiness* (Norton, 1993). A whole branch of alternative medicine interprets all physical illnesses as helpful messages from the body to the conscious brain. See *You Can heal Your Life* by Louise Hay (Hay House,1984) and *Metamédicine* by Claudia Rainville (FRJ Editions, 1995, French).

Chapter 27: The Immortal Me

Death, if you will pardon the understatement, is a big subject and there is plenty written about it, both from the medical and the possibly metaphysical aspects. The principal texts of all the world religions have something to say about it, for example, the famous *Tibetan Book of the Dead: The Great Book of Natural Liberation Through Understanding the In Between* (Bantam, 1993). The book that I most enjoyed reading, because of the clarity and brevity of its argument, is Alan Watts's *Death* (Celestial Arts, 1975), Book 4 in the Essence of Alan Watts series.

Chapter 28: The Future Me

For more on immortality through longevity, see *The Living End: The Future of Death, Ageing and Immortality* by Guy Brown (Palgrave Macmillan, 2007) or Brian Appleyard's *How to Live Forever or Die Trying: On the New Immortality* (Pocket Books, 2008).

Bibliography

NONFICTION

Agger, Ben. *Oversharing: Presentations of Self in the Internet Age.* New York: Routledge, 2012.

Appleyard, Brian. *How to Live Forever or Die Trying: On the New Immortality.* London: Pocket Books, 2008.

Ardrey, Robert. *The Social Contract.* New York: Atheneum, 1970, pp.171–3.

Baggini, Julian. *The Ego Trick: What Does it Mean to Be You?* London: Granta, 2012.

Berger, John. *Ways of Seeing.* London/Harmondsworth: BBC/Penguin, 1972.

Bly, Robert. *Iron John: A Book About Men.* Oxford, UK: Addison-Wesley/Pearson, 1990.

Brooks, Michael. *13 Things That Don't Make Sense: The Most Baffling Scientific Mysteries of Our Time.* New York: Vintage, 2009.

Brown, Guy. *The Living End: The Future of Death, Ageing and Immortality.* Basingstoke, Hants, UK: Palgrave Macmillan, 2007.

Bullock, Alan and Stephen Trombley. *The New Fontana Dictionary of Modern Thought.* London: HarperCollins, 1999, pp.412–414, pp.780–781, and p.159.

Donaldson, William. *Rogues, Villains, and Eccentrics: An A to Z of Roguish Britons Through the Ages.* London: Weidenfeld & Nicholson, 2002.

Eiseley, Loren. *The Unexpected Universe.* New York: Mariner Books/Houghton Mifflin Harcourt, 1972.

Ferguson, Marilyn. *The Aquarian Conspiracy.* Los Angeles, CA: Jeremy Tarcher, 1980. Chapter 4.

Garreau, Joel. *Radical Evolution: The Promise and Peril of Enhancing Our Minds, Our Bodies—and What It Means to Be Human.* New York: Doubleday, 2006.

Golas, Thaddeus. *The Lazy Man's Guide to Enlightenment*. Palo Alto, CA: Seed Center, 1971.

Gray, John. *Men are from Mars, Women are From Venus*. New York: HarperCollins, 1993.

Greenfield, Susan. *ID: The Quest for Meaning in the 21st Century*. London: Sceptre, 2008.

Greer, Germaine: *The Female Eunuch*. London: MacGibbon & Kee, 1970

———. *The Whole Woman*. London: Doubleday, 1999.

Grof, Stanislav and Christina Grof: *The Stormy Search for the Self: A Guide to Personal Growth through Transformational Crisis*. Los Angeles, CA: Jeremy Tarcher, 1990.

Harris, Marvin. *Our Kind*. New York: HarperCollins, 1989.

Hay, Louise. *You Can Heal Your Life*. Carlsbad, CA: Hay House, 1984.

Hood, Bruce. *The Self Illusion: Why There is No 'You' Inside Your Head*. London: Constable, 2012.

Inayat Khan, Hazrat: *Spiritual Dimensions of Psychology*. New Lebanon, NY: Omega Publications (Sufi Order International), 1981.

Keller, Helen. *The Story of My Life*. New York: Doubleday, 1903.

Kelly Kevin: *Out of Control*. Oxford, UK: Addison-Wesley/Pearson, 1994.

Koestler, Arthur: *The Ghost in the Machine*. London: Hutchinson, 1967.

Lanier, Jaron. *Who Owns the Future?* New York: Simon & Schuster, 2013.

Levi, Primo. *If This is a Man*. Translated by Stuart Woolf. London: Orion, 1969. (First published in Italian by Giulio Einaudi in 1958).

Lewis, C. S. *The Problem of Pain*. London: Collins, 2012. (First published in 1940.)

Montaigne, Michel de. *The Complete Essays*. Translated by M. A. Screech. London: Penguin Classics, 1993, (Originally published in French, 1580–1592.)

Morris, Desmond. *The Naked Ape*. London: Jonathan Cape, 1967.

Rainville, Claudia. *Metamedicine*. France: FRJ Editions, Inc., 1995.

Sardar, Ziauddin. *The A to Z of Postmodern Life*. London: Vision, 2002, particularly the chapter "Identity," p.93.

Sheldrake, Rupert. *A New Science of Life*. London: Blond & Briggs, 1981. Chapter 12.3.

Tallis, Raymond. *I Am: A Philosophical Inquiry into First-person Being.* Scotland: Edinburgh University Press, 2004.

The Tibetan Book of the Dead: The Great Book of Natural Liberation Through Understanding in the Between. Padma Sambhava (Compiler), *Robert Thurman* (Translator), *The Dalai Lama* (Foreword), *Karma Lingpa* (Collaborator). New York: Bantam, 1993.

Toffler, Alvin. *Future Shock.* New York: Random House, 1970.

———. *The Third Wave.* New York: Bantam Books, 1984. (Particularly chapters 1, 13, 14, and chapter 25).

Turkle, Sherry. *Alone Together: Why We Expect More from Technology and Less from Each Other.* New York: Basic Books, 2012.

Wallace, Danny and Dave Gorman. *Are You Dave Gorman?* UK: Ebury Press, 2002.

Watson, Lyall: *The Nature of Things.* London: Hodder & Stoughton, 1990.

Watson, Peter. *Ideas : A History from Fire to Freud.* London: Weidenfeld and Nicolson, 2005.

Watts, Alan. *The Book: On the Taboo Against Knowing Who You Are.* New York: Pantheon, 1966.

———. *Death.* Essence of Allan Watts series, Book 4. Berkeley, CA: Celestial Arts, 1975.

Watzlawick, Paul. *The Situation is Hopeless But Not Serious: The Pursuit of Unhappiness.* New York: W.W. Norton, 1993.

Whitman, Walt. "Song of Myself," from the poetry collection *Leaves of Grass: The Original 1855 Edition.* CreateSpace Independent Publishing Platform, 2013.

Wilde, Oscar. *De Profundis.* New York: Dover Publications, 2011. (First published in 1897.)

———. "The Ballad of Reading Gaol," in *The Complete Works of Oscar Wilde,* J. N. Foreman, ed. London: Collins, 1948. (First published in 1898.)

Wilson, Colin. *The Outsider.* London: Victor Gollanz, 1956.

———. *The Encyclopedia of Unsolved Mysteries.* London: McGraw Hill Contemporary, 1988.

FICTION

Dickens, Charles. *A Tale of Two Cities*. CreateSpace Independent Publishing Platform, 2013.

Du Maurier, Daphne. *The Scapegoat*. London: Virago, 2004.

Haig, Matt. *The Humans*. Edinburgh: Canongate, 2013.

Highsmith, Patricia. The Talented Mr. Ripley. London: Vintage, 1999. (First published in 1955).

Huxley, Aldous. *Brave New World*. London: Chatto & Windus, 1932.

Lessing, Doris. *Shikasta*. London: Jonathan Cape, 1979.

Orwell, George. *1984*. London: Secker and Warburg, 1949.

Shelley, Mary Wollstonecraft. *Frankenstein*. London: Wordsworth Editions, 1992.

PERIODICALS

Carr, Geoffrey. "Who Do you Think You Are?" *The Economist*, 19 December, 2006 .

Cathcart, Brian. "The Lives of Brian." *Granta, Vol. 85*, Spring 2004, p.51–68.

RECORDINGS

Ram Dass. Talk given in St. Georges Church, Bristol, 28 April, 1987.

About the Author

Nick Inman was born in Yorkshire and graduated from the University of Bristol with a degree in politics. After having travelled widely, he worked as a teacher and ran an alternative arts festival before spending nine months with the Findhorn Foundation in Scotland. He settled in Spain and became a writer. Subsequently, he moved to London, where he worked as a book editor. He now lives in France with his wife and two children. He is the author of a number of travel guidebooks. His other works include *Politipedia* and *The Optimist's Handbook*. For more information see www.nickinman.com.

FINDHORN PRESS

Life-Changing Books

For a complete catalogue,
please contact:

Findhorn Press Ltd
117-121 High Street,
Forres IV36 1AB,
Scotland, UK

t +44 (0)1309 690582
f +44 (0)131 777 2711
e info@findhornpress.com

or consult our catalogue online
(with secure order facility) on
www.findhornpress.com

For information on the Findhorn Foundation:
www.findhorn.org